S0-BJQ-200

The Challenge of Political Islam

D'Youville College Library

JAN 0 4 2011

The Challenge of Political Islam

NON-MUSLIMS AND THE EGYPTIAN STATE

Rachel M. Scott

Stanford University Press
Stanford, California

Stanford University Press
Stanford, California

© 2010 by the Board of Trustees of the Leland Stanford Junior University.
All rights reserved.

No part of this book may be reproduced or transmitted in any form or by any means,
electronic or mechanical, including photocopying and recording, or in any information
storage or retrieval system without the prior written permission of Stanford University
Press.

Printed in the United States of America on acid-free, archival-quality paper

Library of Congress Cataloging-in-Publication Data

Scott, Rachel M.

The challenge of political Islam : non-Muslims and the Egyptian state / Rachel M. Scott.

p. cm.

Includes bibliographical references and index.

ISBN 978-0-8047-6905-1 (cloth : alk. paper) -- ISBN 978-0-8047-6906-8 (pbk. : alk. paper)

1. Islam--Relations--Coptic Church. 2. Coptic Church--Relations--Islam. 3. Islam and
state--Egypt. 4. Religion and state--Egypt. 5. Copts--Politics and government.
6. Religious minorities--Egypt. I. Title. BP172.5.C6S36 2010

297.2'83--dc22

2009052983

Typeset by Bruce Lundquist in 10/14 Minion Pro

BP
172.5
.C6
S36
2010

For Roma

CONTENTS

ACKNOWLEDGMENTS

The completion of this book has given me the opportunity to reflect upon everyone who has helped me—either directly or indirectly—to get to this point. This book is the cumulative result of all of my studies since I began as an undergraduate at the University of Oxford. I would like to thank all of those who mentored me there while I completed a B.A. in Arabic and Islamic Studies and an M.Phil. in Modern Middle Eastern Studies. While I would particularly like to mention Alan Jones and Eugene Rogan, the person whom I would most like to thank is Ron Nettler. He has been my constant intellectual mentor and friend from the time—many years ago—when I sat in his office and wrestled with texts by Sayyid Qutb and Muhammad al-Tālbī. He encouraged my interest in modern Islamic thought, and it is to him that I am most in debt.

I would like to thank my Ph.D. supervisor, Kate Zebiri, at the School of Oriental and African Studies (SOAS), University of London, for all the support and encouragement she has given me both intellectually and personally: she has always responded to my drafts most helpfully and constructively. I would also like to thank Gerald Hawting, James Piscatori, Charles Tripp, and Sami Zubaida for their constructive comments. Many thanks go to the Arts and Humanities Research Board in the UK, whose financial support enabled me to undertake fieldwork in Egypt.

Much of this research was done in Egypt in 2003 and 2007, and I would like to thank all—friends, colleagues, and people with whom I had chance encounters—who contributed to my time there, from which I learnt so much. I would particularly like to thank all the people whom I interviewed. If they had not given of their time, this book would not be what it is today. While I am sincerely grateful to all of them, I would particularly like to thank Samīr Murqus, Vivian Fu'ād, and Rafīq Habīb. My hope is that this book does some justice to the complexity of Muslim-Christian relations in Egypt.

Special thanks go to Sāmir al-Qaranshāwī. I miss our chats over coffee, when I would discuss all that I had learnt. I would also like to thank Joshua Stacher, Khālid ʿAbd al-Rusūl, Lūʾay al-Sharwārbī, and Hadīr al-Mahdāwī. My particular thanks go to Cornelis Hulsman and all the staff at the *Arab-West Report*, who must be congratulated for their tireless efforts in bringing many of the topics discussed here to a Western audience. It is a tremendous resource, and I am so grateful to have had access to it.

I would also like to thank those who have helped me by making comments at conferences and meetings of the American Academy of Religion, the Middle East Studies Association, the Center for the Study of Islam and Democracy, University of Oxford, and ASPECT (Alliance for Social, Political, Ethical, and Cultural Thought) seminars at Virginia Tech. The responses I received there helped the book in important ways. In particular, I would like to thank all those who have read and commented on the manuscript, including the anonymous reviewers of Stanford University Press, Emran Qureshi, and others.

I would also like to thank my colleagues at Virginia Tech. I have truly valued the time and space that the College of Liberal Arts and Human Sciences has given me to undertake significant revisions. I would especially like to thank Elizabeth Struthers Malbon and William Ochsenwald for all the wonderful advice both of them have given me about the complexities of publication and Brian Britt and Ananda Abeysekara for their thought-provoking comments. I would also like to thank the Humanities Summer Stipend and the Institute for Society, Culture, and the Environment for providing me with the financial support to continue my research in Egypt.

I would like to thank the journal *Islam and Christian-Muslim Relations* for allowing me to reprint parts of the article "Contextual Citizenship in Modern Islamic Thought," from *Islam and Christian-Muslim Relations* 17, no. 4 (October 2006): 1–18.

Much gratitude goes to the excellent editorial skills of Kate Wahl, Joa Suorez, and Emily Smith at Stanford University Press. They have all been a pleasure to work with. In particular I would like to thank my copy editor, Jan McInroy, who did such an excellent and thorough job of smoothing the rough edges.

Last but not least, I would like to thank my family, particularly my mother, Roma Diviani, and my husband, Michael Horton, for their moral support. Without my mother I could not have started this project, and without my husband I could not have finished it.

NOTES ON TRANSLITERATION

I have used the IJMES system of transliteration (based on the modified Encyclopedia of Islam system of transliteration), although with a few modifications. While I have included macrons, ʿayns, and hamzas, I have not included dots. I have applied this transliteration not only to technical terms but also to names of political parties, titles of books, and personal names and place names when the English names are not well known. I have used the English version for names and places that are well known in English, such as Nasser, Sadat, and Shenouda. The only concession I make to Egyptian pronunciation of these names is the use of the "g" instead of "j."

I have cited the source in the language in which I consulted that source, which means that I have cited Arabic sources in transliterated Arabic and I have cited translated sources that I consulted in English.

Readers might notice inconsistency in the transliteration of names in the footnotes. I consult a range of Arabic and English texts. In the footnotes, I have used the spelling of the name as it is found in the original source. In the case of Arabic texts, I have transliterated the name according to the system stated above. In the case of English texts, I have kept the transliteration that was used by the translator of the document.

The Challenge of Political Islam

INTRODUCTION

IN DECEMBER 2004, sectarian tension broke out between Muslims and Christians in Egypt over the alleged conversion of Wafāʾ Qustantīn, a Coptic Christian, to Islam. Qustantīn was the wife of a Coptic priest and had allegedly converted to Islam to escape marital problems, having previously and unsuccessfully sought a divorce (Islamic law forbids a Muslim woman from being married to a non-Muslim man, so on Qustantīn's conversion, her marriage would be annulled). Due to social and economic pressures, the conversion to Islam by Egyptian Christians is a relatively common occurrence in Egypt. However, in a society that is based on the religious family, such conversions are also a source of considerable shame.[1] The conversion of a priest's wife was viewed as particularly egregious and was vehemently resisted by many Copts.

The Coptic Church claimed that Wafāʾ Qustantīn had converted under duress.[2] The U.S. Copts Association (USCA), which lobbies on behalf of Copts in Egypt, claimed that Qustantīn had been forced to convert and petitioned President George W. Bush to intervene.[3] Western media seized upon this allegation and did not report the Muslim perspective. In Egypt, many Copts, having been mobilized by the Coptic Church, demonstrated. Pope Shenouda III, the current Coptic patriarch, demanded that Qustantīn be returned to the church. She was subsequently handed over by security forces, symbolizing, according to one commentator, that the church had "twisted the arm of the state."[4] Qustantīn was then detained in a monastery in Wadi al-Natrūn, north of Cairo, for closed-door church advisory sessions. There are indications that she is still being held in a monastery, possibly in a monastery for Coptic Orthodox nuns. The church has stated that Qustantīn still embraces her Christian faith and that she has not been forced to convert back to Christianity. However, according to the London newspaper *al-Sharq al-Awsat*, in a telephone interview Qustantīn affirmed that she had converted to Islam.[5]

The incident sparked debate within Egypt over the relationship between the Coptic Church and the Egyptian state. Some criticized the state for failing to protect Qustantīn from the church's illegal and unconstitutional detention, while others argued that the political role of the church was an "unchristian" aberration and called upon Copts to become fully involved with Muslims in Egypt's state institutions.[6] Such a critique of the political role of the church poses interesting questions in contemporary Egypt when such Islamists seek to Islamize both the state and the political process. How can Copts, it might be asked, be expected to become more politically involved in the institutions of the state when the state itself has been Islamized?

The Wafā' Qustantīn incident illustrates the challenge facing contemporary Egypt concerning the relationship between religion and state and the role of non-Muslims. It raises the question of what kind of role and status non-Muslims have in contemporary Egypt. When Islamists call for the implementation of *sharī'a* (Islamic law) and for the fulfillment of what they see as Egypt's constitutional commitment to an Islamic state, what implications does this have for non-Muslims, both as individuals and as members of religious communities? How do both Muslims and non-Muslims understand issues such as religious freedom, conversion, and individual autonomy? What does citizenship mean in this context and what is its relationship with religious identity?

This book addresses these questions by examining Egyptian Islamist attitudes toward non-Muslims—the vast majority of whom are Coptic Christians—focusing on the rights, role, and status of non-Muslims. It also examines non-Muslim responses to these attitudes. It explores the ways in which the concepts of religious tolerance, pluralism, and citizenship, and the relationship between religion and state are articulated and understood within the Egyptian Islamist framework. While literature in this field has given much attention to Islamist attitudes toward the West and Westerners and has provided important insights into Muslim historical and doctrinal positions on Christianity, little work has focused specifically on how modern, politically oriented Egyptian Islamists perceive Christians in an Islamic state.[7]

ISLAM, CITIZENSHIP, AND PLURALISM

The rights and role of non-Muslims within an Islamic state is an important issue in the current context. The rise of political Islam and calls for the application of *sharīʿa* have provoked considerable debate about the compatibility of democracy, tolerance, and pluralism with the Islamist position. Central to this debate is how *sharīʿa* will be applied and by whom. An analysis of Islamist views on how the application of *sharīʿa* will affect non-Muslims provides important insight into these questions.

The question of the rights and role of non-Muslims is a politically charged topic. From a historical perspective, the role of non-Muslims in Islamic societies has been used by Islamophobes as evidence of Islam's intolerance. This is still true today. Coptic activists, particularly Coptic expatriates, have exploited these assumptions, and Michael Munīr, who heads the Washington-based U.S. Copts Association (USCA), repeatedly appeals to the U.S. Congress to penalize Egypt for alleged persecution of Copts. In 1998 the U.S. Congress passed the Freedom from Religious Persecution Act, largely as a result of Coptic lobbying. The law imposes automatic sanctions on those countries seen to engage in ongoing persecution of persons on account of their religious beliefs.

Claims that the application of *sharīʿa* in Egypt will inevitably lead to the persecution of non-Muslims are central to the popular assumption that Islamic civilization is somehow antithetical to a reified and idealized Western civilization that is based on democracy, citizenship, and human rights. The view that Islam is unable to evolve these values is linked to the notion that Islam is a political religion in which religion and politics are unified, a relationship that is held as problematic. The assumption is that democracy and tolerance are conditional upon the separation of religion and state and of civil and religious law. Hence, from this perspective, Islam poses a problem because it is assumed that it does not accept such distinctions.

Academic literature has challenged the assumption that toleration is contingent upon the separation of religion and politics. Talal Asad has questioned secular modernity's monopoly on tolerance, human rights, and democracy.[8] Asad argues that one should question the notion that secularism is the modern formula for toleration, pointing out that "there are intolerant secular societies and tolerant religious ones."[9] This position has coincided with an important shift in our understanding of Islamism. Literature on liberal Islam has emphasized that Islam is not a monolithic entity and is currently represented by divergent views.[10] It holds that liberal principles can be found in an Islamic framework.

However, arguments that Islam can be and is tolerant may fall into the trap of essentialism. The tendency has been to use the freedom of religion that non-Muslims historically had under Islamic law as an indication of Islam's tolerance. Such approaches are sometimes accompanied by assertions about the intrinsic nature of Islam and assume that intolerant acts toward non-Muslims are an "un-Islamic" aberration and a "misinterpretation" of its foundational texts. It is asserted that Islamism is a political ideology that is somehow distinct from Islam itself. This approach assumes that there is a fixed Islam from which it is possible to depart. While such a reification is a problem with many discussions about religion, Islam, particularly in the current context, is especially prone to being defined and reified.

The danger is that this view descends into a dichotomized debate that is represented either by claims that Islam is, in essence, antithetical to human rights and democracy or by claims that it is the opposite. In fact, the question of whether Islam as a religion is or is not democratic is of limited use. Asef Bayat argues that a more appropriate question is "under what conditions Muslims can *make* them compatible."[11]

This book does not attempt to address the question of the "essential" nature of Islam. Rather, it focuses on Islamist thought as articulated by Islamist thinkers and actors and looks at how Islamists are framing discussions of democracy and citizenship. Rather than asking the question of whether Islam is compatible with tolerance, pluralism, and citizenship, it asks how contemporary Egyptian Islamists are articulating, responding to, and interpreting the concepts of tolerance, pluralism, and citizenship. This is done by exploring the specific implications and underlying assumptions behind these ideas.

CITIZENSHIP AND PLURALISM IN EGYPT

This book analyses Islamist discussions of citizenship and pluralism within Egyptian Islamist thought. Egypt is the intellectual center of the Middle East. It is where political Islam was established with the foundation of the Muslim Brotherhood in 1928. Egypt's experience of Islamic thought and activism has considerable influence throughout the Middle East and the Islamic world. The direction in which Egypt goes in terms of the development of political Islam will reverberate throughout the region. Egypt also has the largest Christian community in the Middle East, which is why the issue of the role of non-Muslims features so prominently in Islamic thought.

The current prominence of the issue of religious minorities is also related to the fact that it connects with broader issues such as the place of pluralism, democracy, and Egyptian identity in contemporary Egyptian society. These issues are caught up in the conflict between the current ruling regime, secularists, and Islamist opposition groups. When Egyptian Islamists write about citizenship and pluralism within an Islamic framework, they are both responding to the reality on the ground and, in turn, contributing to the Egyptian political debate. Thus any analysis of Islamist discourse on citizenship must consider its contextual constraints.

At the same time, this is not to say that Islam has no role. Many aspects of Islamist thought are influenced by what Asad has defined as the Islamic "discursive tradition" or "a tradition of Muslim discourse that addresses itself to conceptions of the Islamic past and future, with reference to a particular Islamic practice in the present."[12] Islam's foundational texts—the Qur'an, the Hadith (written records of the sayings and doings of the Prophet Muhammad), and Islamic jurisprudence—make up this tradition. Islamists engage with these texts and use them to legitimize and understand current realities. However, this does not mean that modern Islamists respond to the tradition monolithically or that these texts determine how Islam is applied and invoked today.

In fact, modern manifestations of Islam should be understood in terms of local manifestations of Islam being organized through the Islamic discursive tradition. While contemporary discourse is influenced by Islamic history and thought, it cannot be understood as a direct continuity with that thought. This engagement with tradition and context produces considerable diversity within a supposed rigid ideology.

This book is an analysis of this debate within Egypt, and the responses examined here are distinctly Egyptian ones. One can find a range of different responses within the Islamic world to the question of religious minorities. For example, in Indonesia, the Islamic discourse has given attention to the rights of non-Muslims and has drawn upon the Islamic tradition to argue for equality and citizenship.[13] On the other hand, there is Pakistani experience whereby the Blasphemy Law has been used as a tool for "exploiting and oppressing the weak and the vulnerable in the nation, such as the religious minorities and sects."[14]

The historical and contemporary context—in this case the relations between Muslims and Copts in Egypt—therefore influences the formation of thought. An analysis of Islamic views on citizenship in the Egyptian context must also analyze the Coptic response to these views. Copts themselves are not passive recipients or victims of Islamist ideas and political behavior. Recently there has been an increase in literature that goes beyond the effect of Islamism on Muslim-Christian relations and addresses the Coptic community itself.[15] Copts are in fact part of an ongoing debate within Egypt and with Islamists themselves about the relationship between religion, state, and Islamist conceptions of citizenship.[16] Coptic views on these issues illustrate the variety and complexity of the Coptic position.

ISLAMISM

While this book examines the effect of modernizing pressures on political Islam, defining the term "political Islam" is not an easy task. While I use the terms "Islamism" and "political Islam," there is no shortage of debate about when, how, and even whether we should use such labels. While Gilles Kepel argues that Islamism "is in effect nothing but a name among others," and others hold that it is not a term of self-designation, the term does have a certain function.[17]

A working definition of Islamism is the belief that Islam is an all-embracing ideology for state and society, which is one of the most fundamental concepts of the Islamic revival. It holds that Islam needs to be expressed politically: Islam is more than a system of religious belief and practice. Political Islam is a reaction to the perception that the modern Islamic world has been disconnected from the premodern Islamic order. While Islamists hold that this disconnection began to occur when Muslims drifted away from Islam in the medieval era, it was consolidated with the imposition of Western law during the second half of the nineteenth century. Political Islam calls for the reversal of such secularization and for the unity of religion and state. Islamists include a wide range of thinkers who have differing attitudes about what kind of political system would result, including whether that system would be democratic and, if so, in what way.[18] Islamism also includes a range of attitudes about whether or not the current political system in Egypt is considered Islamic.

The Islamist agenda has evolved from being a position taken by radical Islamist activists to being the status quo, in the sense that the majority of the Egyptian population supports the application of *sharī'a*.[19] This is not to say that Egyptian secular intellectuals do not exist or that there are no other ways of conceptualizing this question. However, this book is primarily a book about political Islam. In the process of becoming the status quo, the Islamist agenda has become more diverse, and there has also been a general shift away from utopian agendas to more pragmatic ones that take into account the reality of the Egyptian nation-state. At the same time, Egyptian society and, to a certain extent, the state have become increasingly Islamized, a development that has meant that the space within which Islamist opposition to the state can operate has narrowed.

Some have argued that the increasing pragmatism of Islamists is an indication that the movement has failed. Kepel has taken the position that Islamic radicalism reached its peak long ago and has failed to bring about an Islamic revolution, establish an Islamic state, or effect substantial political reform.[20] He differentiates Islamism from post-Islamism, defining the latter as a movement in which intellectuals are calling for a transition from militant Islamism to an Islamic democracy. He argues that this reinvention is effectively a "disqualification of its ideology as a global vision."[21]

While it is true to say that most Islamists have moved away from rejecting the state to working within it, the Islamists' capacity to change their approach is not necessarily an invalidation of the movement or of its aims. If Islamism is simply a movement to express Islam politically, then this is just as true of movements that call for an Islamic democracy as it is of those that reject democracy in the name of Islam.

Even in Muslim states where Islamists have failed to bring about an Islamic revolution and establish a self-proclaimed Islamic state, a considerable process of Islamization has occurred. A large number of Muslim-majority states have some sort of constitutional commitment to Islam: some states are deemed "Islamic States"; some declare Islam as the state religion; some define *sharī'a* as *a* source or *the* source of national legislation; and some maintain that any law enacted must not be contrary to Islamic tenets.[22]

In Egypt, since 1980, Article 2 of the constitution has stated that "the principles of *sharī'a* are the major source of legislation." The Supreme Constitutional Court has developed a substantive body of jurisprudence applying Article 2, which has involved upholding some laws as consistent with the principles of *sharī'a* and striking others down as inconsistent.[23] While Islamist parties are illegal and face persecution under an authoritarian regime, a process of Islamization has been under way since the early twentieth century and, in particular, since the 1970's. This Islamization has altered discourse on morality, politics, economics, dress, and the symbols that leaders use to gain legitimacy. While Egypt might not have turned into a fully Islamic state from the perspective of some Islamists, the pervading influence of the Islamist agenda is clear, so that many secularists feel that Egypt has become more Islamic despite the fact that the Islamists have not come to power.

It is perhaps the very failure of the Egyptian Islamist movement to bring about an Islamic revolution that has contributed to its endurance. The opposition status of the Islamist movement, which astutely emphasizes government corruption and provides social services that the state has failed to offer, has served to bolster their popularity. The capacity of the Islamist movement to respond to the practical demands of political organization in a modern nation-state has also contributed to its endurance.

In the 2005 Egyptian parliamentary elections, the Muslim Brotherhood, which is not a legally recognized party, gained 20 percent of the seats by fielding candidates as independents. Such electoral success raises the question of what changes the Muslim Brotherhood would make. How would the Islamists mould Egypt into an Islamic state in which Islamic law is fully applied? What would constitute national identity? What would their position be on democracy, citizenship, and the rights of non-Muslims?

In Egypt, there is a sizeable Coptic community, about 90 percent of whom are Orthodox, with the remaining 10 percent made up of Catholic and Protestant Copts. It constitutes the largest Christian minority in the Middle East. The percentage of the Egyptian population that is Coptic Christian is disputed. It is impossible to know the number, since censuses do not reveal the number of Christians in Egypt.[24] When asked why the number of Copts was not included in the 2007 census report, the head of the Central Apparatus for Public Mobilization and Statistics said, "Ask about anything but this matter which is bound to bring us a headache."[25] Radical Coptic activists have claimed that Copts constitute 25 percent of the population.[26] The Coptic Church has stated that Copts make up anywhere from 12 to 18 percent of the population, a number that is supported by the U.S. Copts Association.[27] In 1994 Saad Eddin Ibrahim argued that Copts represented 10 percent, a figure that is supported by the *CIA World Factbook*.[28] The most reasonable estimate comes from the Center for Arab-West Understanding, which closely monitors Muslim-Christian relations in Egypt and holds that Copts cannot be more than 5 or 6 percent of the total population, since the Coptic population has been steadily decreasing because of a lower birth rate, conversions, and emigration.[29] This has been confirmed by the 2009 Pew Forum on Religion and Public Life, which states that 94.6 percent of the Egyptian population is Muslim.[30] There are also other non-Muslim communities in Egypt. While it is impossible to be specific, those include a small number of Bahā'īs, estimated to be around 1,500 to 2,000, and a few hundred Jews.[31]

The reluctance to ascertain the number of Copts is a further indication of how politically charged the subject is. While discussion about the Copts has become much more open since the turn of the century, references to national unity serve to deflect attention from a frank discussion of the issue. The question of the role and status of Egypt's Copts cuts to the core of the challenges facing the Egyptian state, challenges that include the relationship between religion and state and the extent to which Egypt is in fact a secular or an Islamic state. Discussions about minority rights are viewed as threatening the status quo, which the government wishes to maintain.

MODERNIZATION

The challenges facing Islamists in modern Egypt are similar to those facing Islamist movements throughout the Islamic world. Modernization has brought with it the pressure to evolve democracy, human rights, and citizenship, concepts that are theorized and thought about under the influence of Western ideological hegemony. Contemporary Islamists face the test of how Islamic law, which was formed in the context of a victorious premodern empire, can be applied in a very different context such as that of the modern nation-state. Before Egypt's dislocation from the Ottoman Empire in 1914, it was part, albeit loosely, of a unified Islamic Empire, which, before the Ottoman *tanzimat* reforms (1839–1876), was conceived of as being based on *sharī'a* even though in practice there was considerable recourse to non-*sharī'a* elements. The application of Western law and the abolition of the caliphate in 1924 symbolized the break—although it was more symbolic than real—with the concept of a unified Islamic political order.

Marshall Hodgson has argued that while all modern societies face some kind of dislocation, in the West this process has been less traumatic because it has been slower. For the Islamic world, such dislocation is less easy to absorb because it has been more sudden and severe. In addition, the political and legal institutions that were imposed upon the Islamic world largely evolved in the West.[32]

This dislocation has been keenly felt. While it may be that the notion of a rupture has been exaggerated, on a psychological level it is integral to Islamist self-definition. In 1928, the Muslim Brotherhood called for a return to an original and pure Islam, in which religion and state would be unified. In advocating an Islamic state, Islamists are functioning in a context that is very different from that of the Ottoman and other Islamic empires. Modern Islamists face the challenge of how to apply Islamic law and premodern Islamic institutions in a new context, raising the question of what meaning the Islamic religious heritage can still have for contemporary Muslims.[33]

Answering such a question is often hampered by claims made by Muslims and by non-Muslims that the Islamic tradition is fixed, based on the assumption that the divinely revealed law cannot be changed.[34] However, that is not the case. Though Islamic historical models are invoked as important precedents, in fact, as Dale Eickelman and James Piscatori point out, "emendations and additions to a purportedly invariant and complete Islamic law (*shari'a*) have occurred throughout Islamic history, particularly since the mid-nineteenth century." They argue that the division between tradition and modernity oversimplifies the interaction between religion and tradition.[35] In fact, when Islamists invoke traditions when claiming to return to an earlier practice, they do in fact reinvent those traditions. While Eickelman and Piscatori illustrate that the invention of tradition is an ongoing process, referring to Hodgson they show that it is more likely in societies where a rapid transformation that undermines social patterns occurs.[36]

By examining Islamist articulations of pluralism and citizenship in relation to the role of non-Muslims, this book illustrates the complex ways in which Islamic tradition is modified, reinterpreted, and changed in response to the demands of modernity.

SOURCES

The book is based on writings and political tracts by Islamist and Coptic intellectuals, activists, authors, and politicians as well as a broad range of newspaper articles. The materials include popular texts by Islamist preachers and activists as well as texts by Islamist thinkers and intellectuals. I have examined the work and writings of intellectuals, preachers, and activists because in Islamist thought the boundaries between the intellectual and the political worlds are porous. The ideas of intellectuals are used and referred to by activists, and many intellectuals are aware of their political role when writing.

In as many cases as possible, I have supplemented the writings of Islamists and Copts with interviews conducted with prominent Islamist and Coptic activists, thinkers, and politicians during fieldwork in 2003 and 2007. Interviews are always influenced by the perceived relationship between interviewer and interviewee, and there is no doubt that my position as a non-Muslim (I was frequently asked whether I was a Jew or a Christian) meant that my interviewees were interested in presenting the most favorable position on non-Muslims. It is inevitable, given the history of the topic, that my position as a non-Muslim looking at the question of the role of non-Muslims in an Islamic state would provoke some defensiveness. The role of religious minorities cuts to the very core of issues that are contested in contemporary Egypt. However, I did not encounter significant differences between what was said in interviews and what is written in texts. The subject is a politically charged one, so the preponderance of rhetoric and politicized statements is evident in both texts and interviews.

Nevertheless, this defensiveness should not be used to discredit the integrity of the statements. Islamists are particularly prone to accusations of duplicity, and are frequently accused of presenting one picture to the public—and to a person such as myself in particular—and hiding an alternative, more "Islamic" agenda. Islamists are like any other political group, and their positions shift and change. Their organizations are made up of members with different views and agendas, and policy statements can often be the result of one group gaining the upper hand. Neither is the problem of the relationship between interviewer and interviewee or text and audience particular to Islamism. It is inevitable that my presence as an interviewer would have an effect on the information given by Copts. In this case, there might be a tendency for Copts to impart more antipathy about Muslims and Islam than they would otherwise admit to, in the hope that a supposed coreligionist would have more sympathy for their views.

1 NON-MUSLIMS IN CLASSICAL ISLAM

ONE OF THE PRINCIPAL FEATURES of the Islamist movement is the insistence upon the application of *sharīʿa* as the foundation of a proposed Islamic state. Islamist slogans have included "Islam is the solution," "the Qurʾan is our constitution," and "Islam is a system." Such statements imply that there is some kind of certainty about what constitutes Islam and what constitutes an "Islamic state." It is often assumed that Islamists are seeking to reinstall a type of religious state—in which religion and state are unified—that existed at some idealized point in Islamic history. Implicit in this view is the assumption that Islam has a specific theory on politics and the state, which the Islamic revivalists are attempting to implement anew.[1] The reality is, in fact, far more complex. *Sharīʿa* is not a codified body of law that can simply be applied. Islamic political theory—which was more diffuse and varied than the term itself allows for—often responded to the status quo and legitimized that status quo.[2] In addition, both the interpretation and the practical application of *sharīʿa* were subject to change over time. They also varied from one geographical entity to another. An analysis of Islamic history illustrates the divergent interpretations of the law and the flexible and selective ways in which it was applied. The way in which it was interpreted—or selectively ignored—was contingent upon local political, cultural, and social conditions and the pragmatic needs and choices of rulers and elites.

The challenge for contemporary Islamic thinkers therefore lies in differentiating *sharīʿa*, or Islamic principles, from the various historical contexts in which *sharīʿa* was applied. Regarding the role of non-Muslims, contemporary Islamists face the challenge of identifying what the role and status of non-

Muslims in different historical contexts was, and the extent to which that role was—from their perspective—a true reflection of their perception of an essential and immutable Islam. These questions have been addressed by only some Islamists, the majority of whom tend to refer to an immutable transhistorical *shari'a*. However, an analysis of the Islamist position on the proposed role of non-Muslims within an idealized future Islamic state cannot proceed without a consideration of these issues.

RELIGION AND STATE

Hasan al-Bannā (1906–1949), the founder of the Muslim Brotherhood, argued that "Islam is a complete system which deals with all areas of life. It is a state, a nation, a government, and a community."[3] Al-Bannā assumed that the concept of Islam as a system was embodied in the past, though he was not clear as to the specific historical period that this ideal Islamic state related to.

The discourse of an "Islamic state" or Islam as "religion and state" is a modern ideological construction and is not supported by either a historical analysis or an analysis of Islamic political theory. Indeed, the whole concept of "religion" and "state" reflects deeply secular assumptions about the concept of religion. The concept of "state" is also ahistorical. While the idea of a fixed corpus of Islamic political thought is problematic, "Islamic political thought mostly concentrates on non-state unit analysis such as the community (*umma* or *jama'a*), justice ('*adl* or *shari'a*), and leadership (*khilafa*, *imama*, and *sultan*)."[4] It also tends retroactively to justify the status quo.

Contrary to the Islamist notion that Islam is a system, the legislative details of which are clearly laid out in the Qur'an and the Sunna (sayings and actions of the Prophet recorded in the Hadith), the Qur'an provided only general guidelines for legislation. Qur'anic legislation is predominantly ethical. Legal verses tend to be very detailed on some subjects, such as inheritance, and sparse on others, such as decision-making processes. The Sunna are more legalistic but tend to respond to specific incidents and do not lay down general guidelines. In the case of guidelines for the rights and role of non-Muslims, verses in the Qur'an about non-Muslims are often unclear and inconsistent. The Sunna are relatively sparse concerning concrete stipulations for the treatment of Christians.[5]

Historical analysis shows there was no single relationship pattern between religion and state. Indeed, that relationship is contested terrain, and modernists, secularists, and Islamist revivalists read and interpret history to support their own narrative. Many contemporary Islamists argue that religion and state were unified only under the small polity established by the Prophet that continued in the early decades of the Islamic caliphate. Muhammad reportedly had religious and political authority by virtue of his role as the Prophet of God and leader of the early Muslim community. However, Asma Afsaruddin argues that the idea that an Islamic state was fully conceived of during the prophetic period is ahistorical and that "there is no evidence at all in the early sources that the Companions invoked a supposedly divinely mandated blueprint for an 'Islamic Government' or an 'Islamic State.'" Rather, she says—in line with a modernist position—that "the *shari'a* is largely apolitical" and that in "the formative period . . . there was no universal consensus regarding a *religious* mandate . . . to elect or appoint a ruler for the polity."[6]

Regardless of the competing claims that have been made about the relationship between religion and state—and these terms are used tentatively and heuristically—in the early formative period, by the middle of the ninth century religious groups had emerged independently and in opposition to the caliph. It is this relationship of distance between the religious groups and the caliph that came to characterize normative classical Sunni Islam. These religious groups were represented by the *'ulamā'* (religious scholars), who evolved into the recognized carriers of religious knowledge on account of their expertise in the Qur'an and the Hadith. Their religious authority was, in theory, limited to interpreting God's divine law. Ahmad Ibn Hanbal (780–855) argued that religious obligations stemmed not from caliphal declarations but from the Qur'an and the Sunna as interpreted by the *'ulamā.'*[7] The *'ulamā'*, fearing proximity to power, were keen to remain at a distance from the caliph. In fact, the *'ulamā'* were reluctant to attach *sharī'a* to the authority of a specific ruler and to codify the *sharī'a*, as this would invalidate the *sharī'a* as God-given law. This separation between the *sharī'a* and the ruler was compounded by the fact that by the time the law had developed in its classical form—the early tenth century—"there was no unified state left in the Islamic world."[8] In Egypt, the center of power of the *'ulamā'* was the mosque and university of al-Azhar, founded in 969 CE, from which the *'ulamā'*, possessing much independence from the state, operated as leaders of the community.[9]

According to the normative classical Sunni position, the caliph possessed neither God's power to make law nor the Prophet's function of proclaiming it. The caliph inherited only judicial and executive power.[10] The role of the *'ulamā'* was a theoretical limitation on the caliph's power, since the caliph was subject to the law and the state was created to enforce the law.[11] According to Ibn Khaldūn, the North African historian and scholar of the fourteenth century (1332–1406), the caliph was head of the Islamic state, and he was representative of the *umma* (Muslim community), which was based on the shared acceptance of Islam. The caliph was obliged to protect Islam and create the circumstances under which *sharī'a* could be implemented and followed. Other religious duties included waging holy war, administering public interest, and venerating learning and religious scholars, which included the appointment of the *muftī*, the religious scholar who issued legal judgments.[12]

At the same time, however, the caliph was subject to the limitations of the law only in a general ethical sense.[13] The scope of religious law, which was developed by incorporating elements of the law prevailing in the areas conquered by the Muslims, was limited. From early on, governments had appropriated the administration of criminal justice from the *sharī'a* courts, and practice and custom increasingly influenced the law of contracts and obligations. Some have argued that a gulf evolved between the ideal doctrine of *sharī'a*, which defined the state, and historical reality.[14] This view holds that "practice almost always involved breaches with the doctrine; and that such breaches were due to the idealistic, impractical, and exacting nature of a doctrine that had not changed since the tenth century."[15]

However, such a rigid disjuncture between law and practice is problematic, since in reality the law itself was not isolated; rather, both the interpretation and the application of the law changed over time. During the Umayyad period (661–750), Islamic law developed on an ad hoc basis and included much customary practice. As the ascendant Abbasid Empire (750–1258) encountered new situations, the elaboration of Islamic law accelerated. Claiming the Qur'an and Sunna as sources, Muslim jurists began to develop a body of law known as Islamic jurisprudence (*fiqh*). The jurist would undertake *ijtihād*, the process of employing intellectual reasoning to read the sources of *sharī'a* in order to arrive at a legal judgment. In theory, there is a distinction between *sharī'a*, the transcendental idea of law, and Islamic jurisprudence, the interpretation of that law by religious scholars. In practice, however, this distinction has often not been maintained and Islamic jurisprudence was conflated with *sharī'a* so that Islamic jurisprudence itself acquired an unquestionable status. Some have claimed that the door to *ijtihād* closed in the eleventh century. Certainly the books of the early jurists of Islam were granted "a special and indisputable status."[16] Both Islamists and Muslim modernists have claimed that Islamic jurisprudence became ossified in some way, although historically the idea that the door to *ijtihād* closed is questionable.

Most of what emerged in Islamic political thought, at least within the Sunni tradition, reflected historical reality.[17] Thus Islamic jurisprudence sanctioned the status quo, and as a result there was no need for Islamic political thought to theorize on the dynamics of the state in the abstract.[18] This was true in the case of non-Muslims. The classical legal position concerning non-Muslims evolved from the complex interaction between Qur'anic verses, prophetic models, and the political development of the Umayyad and Abbasid empires.

Even once the classical position had evolved, a number of factors combined to create considerable fluidity in how it was applied. First, relations were more harmonious in the early centuries of Islamic rule, at least as far as Jews and Christians were concerned. While there was a great deal of interaction between Muslims, Jews, and Christians early on, that receded and, as Albert Hourani points out, "as Islam changed from being the religion of a ruling elite to being the dominant faith of the urban population, it developed its own social institutions, within which Muslims could live without interacting with non-Muslims."[19] This lack of interaction resulted in the further restriction of the rights of Jews and Christians.[20] In the case of attitudes toward Zoroastrians and polytheists, however, an evolution toward greater leniency took place.[21] Other factors that inhibit a firm definition of the classical normative position include regional differences and changes from ruler to ruler. While rulers were formally obliged to recognize the authority of the *sharī'a*, there was considerable latitude. Some rulers were particularly harsh on the subject and others were particularly lenient. There were also differences of interpretation between legal schools.

THE *DHIMMA*

Despite temporal and geographical variations, Islamic jurisprudence did evolve a general framework for determining the relationship between the Islamic state and non-Muslims, notwithstanding the fact that there was considerable variation in how it was interpreted and applied. The framework was based on the concept of the *dhimma*, a contract of protection, and was used to designate a sort of indefinitely renewed contract through which the Muslim community accorded hospitality and protection to Jews, Christians, Zoroastrians (known collectively as People of the Book), and in some cases other non-Muslims, on condition that they paid the *jizya* (a poll tax) and acknowledged the domination of Islam.[22]

The contract of the *dhimma* was linked to *jihād* theory, which emphasized that the Islamic Empire's ruling authority would wage *jihād* against non-Muslim territories.[23] According to Ibn Khaldūn, this idea arose from the obligation to convert everybody to Islam either by persuasion or by force.[24] However, extending the Islamic territories did not mean the annihilation of all non-Muslims. All jurists agreed that for non-Arab People of the Book, *jihād* would cease as soon as they converted to Islam, or submitted and paid the *jizya*.[25]

The Qur'anic basis for the *dhimma* is not extensive. There are only two references to the word *dhimma* (Qur'an 9:8 and 9:10), in which the polytheists are accused of violating their covenant with Muhammad.[26] It is in the same chapter that the main Qur'anic precedent for the *dhimma* appears:

> Fight those who believe not in Allah nor the Last Day nor hold that forbidden which hath been forbidden by Allah and His Messenger, nor acknowledge the Religion of Truth from among the People of the Book until they pay the *Jizyah* with willing submission and feel themselves subdued (Qur'an 9:29).

The *dhimma* was also based on Muhammad's dealings with non-Muslims, the most important of them being the so-called Constitution of Medina. While some revisionist historians doubt its authenticity, according to traditional knowledge a document preserved in the biography of the Prophet that later came to be known as the Constitution of Medina reflects the political compromise that was made with Jewish tribes, probably shortly after the *hijra* (call for flight) in 622.[27] The constitution establishes the terms for an alliance between Muhammad, his religious community, and the eight tribes of Medina. In it the contracting parties agreed to recognize Muhammad as their leader.

The constitution was an agreement between Muhammad and the Jews, who, as monotheists, were distinguished from other nonbelievers at the time, the Arab polytheists. The constitution stated that "to the Jew who follows us belong help and equality. He shall not be wronged nor shall his enemies be aided." The Jews are even described in the constitution as "one community with the believers" while allowing "the Jews [to] have their religion and the Muslims [to] have theirs," although elsewhere the Muslims "are one community (*umma*) to the exclusion of all men." Ambiguity regarding the precise meaning of *umma* was natural at such a time of flux. Jews received the protection of the state and were allowed to follow their own religion and to own property. Jews were also able to fight with Muslims.[28] Muhammad did employ non-Muslims in his fighting forces, although this practice was subsequently ended by 'Umar Ibn al-Khattāb (caliph 634–644).[29] While the terms of the document represented political compromise and a form of toleration toward non-Muslims, it also rendered Jews subordinate on some level, as illustrated by such statements as "a believer shall not slay a believer for the sake of an unbeliever, nor shall he aid an unbeliever against a believer" and "believers are friends one to the other to the exclusion of outsiders."[30]

While there was a clear distinction between Jews and other non-Muslims, there was some ambiguity about whether the *dhimma* contract could be made with other non-Muslims. Muhammad's treaties with the outlying tribes of Arabia mention both "the *dhimma* of God" and a lesser "*dhimma* of Muhammad." According to C. E. Bosworth, it was possible that the cases in which only the *dhimma* of Muhammad was given refer to situations in which the Prophet made an alliance with pagan tribes and was hesitant to extend God's *dhimma* to them. However, Muhammad seems later to have extended the *dhimma* of God to all tribes and individuals.[31] This was an extension of a pre-Islamic Arab custom of giving protection to strangers, a custom that continued in Islamic times, as illustrated by Qur'an 9:6, which encourages Muslims to provide protection to polytheists.[32]

Other examples of Muhammad's dealings with non-Muslims are equally complex. The first concerns the contract of al-Hudaybiyya, a settlement north of Mecca. In the year 628 Muhammad decided to make the pilgrimage from Medina to Mecca to perform the lesser pilgrimage at Mecca. Muhammad made a treaty with the pagan Meccans, in which he agreed to withdraw from Mecca. The treaty was to last for ten years. It was also agreed that there would be no raiding between Muhammad and his followers and the Meccans, and that each year Mecca would be emptied for three days to allow Muhammad and his followers to perform the pilgrimage. The treaty held for only two years, after which quarrels between allies of the contracting parties broke the treaty and Muhammad made a victorious entry into Mecca.[33]

A less liberal example of Muhammad's dealings with non-Muslims occurred about six weeks after the agreement at al-Hudaybiyya in 628–629. According to the historian al-Tabarī (839–923), Muhammad attacked the Jewish tribes at Khaybar, southwest of Mecca; after about a month and a half they surrendered, agreeing to give up all their land to Muslims and to pay the *jizya*. Muhammad agreed to employ them on the property and allow them a half share of the produce, provided that "if we want to make you leave, we may."

The first caliph, Abū Bakr (caliph 632–634), subsequently confirmed these terms, but the second caliph, ʿUmar, having been informed that the Messenger of God had said during his final illness that "two religions cannot coexist in the Arabian Peninsula," expelled those Jews who did not have a treaty with Muhammad.[34]

A more liberal precedent was established with the Christians of Najran (southwest of Mecca). The traditions connected with Najran are unclear and they disagree. They generally relate that a delegation was sent in 630–631 to Najran. The area was conquered and a large number of its inhabitants converted. Inhabitants who remained Christian were not forced to convert, although each adult, both man and woman, had to pay a tribute. Some versions, including al-Tabarī's, say that the Najranis received the protection of God and the *dhimma* of the Prophet.[35]

The above formed the Qur'anic and Prophetic precedents for the development of a contract that promised protection, *dhimma*, in return for the acknowledgment of Islam's dominance.[36] However, the actual implications of the *dhimma* in terms of the specific rights and duties implied therein were not firmly laid out in the Islamic sources. Islamic law and the *dhimma* in particular gained meaning in the context of the growth and consolidation of the established Umayyad and Abbasid empires, but even then the application of this law varied from place to place and time to time. Many of the ways in which *dhimmīs* were treated—which included a level of respect with an emphasis upon their inferiority—were foreshadowed by the treatment of religious minorities under the Zoroastrian and Byzantine empires.[37]

One of the underlying assumptions of the *dhimma* as it came to be known in classical Islam was a firm distinction between Muslims and non-Muslims. Such a distinction had not always been so rigidly defined, however. There are indications that the Prophet saw Christians and, in particular, Jews as part of the early Muslim community.[38] The *dhimma* was initially applied only to non-Arabs. The early Islamic rulers exempted Christian Arab tribes, which joined in the conquest and fought for the *umma*, from paying the *jizya*.[39] They were recognized first of all as Arabs and were not classified with the conquered *dhimmī* Christians.[40] Muslim jurists agreed that it was not permissible to take the *jizya* from a Jew or a Christian who was a member of the Quraysh (Muhammad's tribe), and in some cases an exception was made for Arab Christians in general.[41] Early Muslims saw themselves as both Arab and Islamic: conversion was not encouraged until about the eighth century. It was not until the early part of the Abbasid period (750–1258) that a firm sense of a "supra-national Islamic community" developed.[42] The religious connotation of the term *umma* is therefore a relatively late development and was a response to divisions within the Islamic state, which were "compensated for by over-emphasizing the spiritual unity and one-ness of the community."[43] Subsequently, the distinction between Muslims and non-Muslims became more clearly defined in Islamic law. By the eleventh century, the Shāfiʿī jurist Abū al-Hasan al-Māwardī (974–1058) is clear that the *jizya* should be taken from Arabs as well as from other peoples.[44]

While the distinction between Muslims and non-Muslims became firmly established in Islamic law, there was debate among jurists about whether the *jizya* could be taken from non-Muslims who were not Jews and Christians. Most jurists agreed that it could be taken from Zoroastrians on the strength of the Prophet's statement "treat them like the People of the Book," although there are indications that this was a later development: ʿUmar did not take *jizya* from Zoroastrians, and early jurists equated Zoroastrianism with idolatry. It was only after the establishment of Muslim rule in Iran that this position softened.[45] The Mālikī and the Hanafī schools argued that the *jizya* could be collected from any polytheist, although the Hanafī school made an exception for polytheist Arabs.[46] The Shāfiʿī and the Hanbalī schools argued that *jizya* could be accepted only from People of the Book and Zoroastrians.[47]

This distinction between People of the Book, who have their own revealed scripture, and other non-Muslims, who were generally defined as polytheists, was seen to be based on the Qurʾan. In the Qurʾan, the People of the Book are differentiated from polytheists (Qurʾan 98:1, 98:6). They are also, at times, classified as believers (Qurʾan 3:199). This distinction can also be found in the Hadith.

Richard Bulliet points out that the question of what to do with polytheists was not a pressing one until the year 1000. Before then, the conquered areas were largely populated by monotheists.[48] From the eleventh century on, however, Muslims expanded into India and sub-Saharan Africa, which were predominantly polytheist. Bulliet says that Muslim rulers responded "with a fluctuating mix of military action, persecution, commercial exploitation, and religious preaching."[49] Sufism was a very successful vehicle for conversion in these outlying areas of the empire, since it more readily embraced unorthodox rituals and practices. In many cases, political pragmatism overtook Islamic theory, and polytheists were not forced to convert.

This distinction between People of the Book and other non-Muslims also became blurred by theological polemic. Later classical jurists, including Ibn Taymiyya (1263–1328) and Ibn Kathīr (1301–1373), became increasingly condemnatory of Christians and accused them of being polytheists or unbelievers.[50] Numerous Hadith refer to Christians as polytheists on account of the doctrines of the Trinity and the divinity of Christ. It was argued that the Trinity was irreconcilable with the unity of God and that the incarnation was a blasphemous offense against God's transcendence. The notion of distortion was also stressed, with Jews and Christians being accused of having deliberately falsified their scriptures.[51] In addition, for some classical exegetes, the Qur'anic verses that praised Christians or promised them salvation or reward were regarded as applicable to only a small minority of Christians: those who either accepted Muhammad or would have accepted him if they had heard about him.[52]

Jurists also differed over the precise meaning of the *jizya*. Some modernist scholars argue that the *jizya* was a payment in lieu of the *dhimmī*'s service in the military, although *dhimmīs* did not, after the time of 'Umar Ibn al-Khaṭṭāb, have the right to serve in the Muslim army. While such an interpretation features heavily in modernist discourse, it does not figure greatly in premodern legal discussions. It is, however, mentioned by Hanafī scholars, who say that the *jizya* is a substitute for military service from which the *dhimmīs* are exempt. There is also a tradition which relates that a companion of the Prophet, Abū 'Ubayda (d. 639), returned the *jizya* to the people of Syria after he was informed that Byzantines were raising troops against him and that the Muslims were no longer able to protect their non-Muslim subjects.[53] However, this exemption from the *jizya* was not perceived as some kind of privilege, as modernists have argued, but because non-Muslim subjects were suspected of having sympathy for their coreligionists from non-Muslim territories.[54] In the 1830's, the Copts were envied for their immunity from military service, although the reason for their exemption was that "no Muslim prince would honour a Christian by employing him to fight against a Muslim enemy."[55]

The *jizya* had a multiplicity of meanings. One was as a substitute for converting to Islam and for receiving protection from attacks by Muslims or others.[56] It also meant remuneration that unbelievers paid for a safe life, the right to stay in Islamic lands, the right to remain in their infidelity, and the right to the protection of the state. Another meaning was that it was a rent on the lands of unbelievers in lieu of not having been expelled from their lands. While this is not usually mentioned as one of the imam's options, 'Umar is famous for having expelled all non-Muslims from all of Arabia except Yemen.[57] More austere interpretations held that the *jizya* was a payment for unbelief, a punishment for infidelity, and an instrument of humiliation by which the unbeliever was vilified and brought low.[58]

RIGHTS AND DUTIES

The *dhimma* contract was based on the concept of religious tolerance, although it was tolerance in the hierarchical sense of the word. While coercion was condemned and faith as a voluntary act was emphasized, the premise behind it was that while the political supremacy and dominance of Islam were necessary, uniformity of religion was not.

Despite this religious tolerance, Islamic jurisprudence made no presumption of equality. The main values of the premodern Islamic order were not necessarily freedom or equality but justice, which was "a vague and apportionate concept close enough to the elusive English concept of 'fairness'" or giving to each his due.[59] Notions of justice were not linked to any conception of natural rights. This is not to say that there was no concept of rights as such: rights and duties in Islamic law were seen as originating in the Qur'an and the Sunna, and Islamic law placed a greater emphasis on obligations than on rights.[60] The *sharī'a* gave *dhimmīs* civil or human claims, whereby their lives, property, personal freedom, family relations, and commercial transactions were protected.[61] However, the rights of the *dhimmī* were due to him not because he was an individual but because he was a member of a protected community, and those rights were contingent upon his membership in that community.[62] The conception that rights were not due to an individual as a human being applied to Muslims as well, whose rights were created by the law and were due to them as Muslims.[63]

The rights and duties entailed in the *dhimma* formed slowly and informally. As a general rule, as the Abbasid Empire was reinforced numerically and was organized institutionally, the rights of *dhimmīs* tended to be more restricted. The *dhimma* contract offered non-Muslims security of life and property, defense against the enemy, communal self-government, and freedom of religious practice. The payment of the *jizya* gave *dhimmīs* the right to the cessation of hostilities against them and positive protection.[64] *Dhimmīs* were allowed to retain their own religious organizations and places of worship. They were also entitled to their own personal status codes with access to their own personal courts and religious trusts. They had a right to enforce their own marriage laws. *Dhimmīs* were not subject to the prohibition of wine and pork and could therefore trade in those items. However, they were not exempt from the Islamic penal code. Property rights were generally respected by all schools of law except the Mālikī school.

Despite the claims that were given to *dhimmīs*, there was no presumption of equality. This was reflected in the theoretical legal differentiation between Muslims and *dhimmīs*. For example, it was often assumed that *dhimmīs* should not be allowed to give evidence against Muslims in court.[65] Most schools of law held that blood money was not required when a *dhimmī* was murdered by a Muslim, although the Hanafī school held that both *dhimmīs* and Muslims should suffer the same penalty for similar crimes.[66]

Inequality also applied in the area of personal status and the family. For example, Islamic jurisprudence held that a Muslim man could marry a Jewish or Christian woman (Qur'an 5:5) but not vice versa, on the understanding that this would put a believing woman into the power of an unbeliever. For the same reason, a Muslim could own a *dhimmī* slave, but a *dhimmī* could not own a Muslim one. While a female Jew or Christian was allowed to marry a Muslim man, she could not inherit from her Muslim husband unless she converted.[67] She was also not allowed to be buried with her husband.

While the *dhimma* was based on the concept of no compulsion in religion, this was not absolute. There are indications that in the early Islamic community conversion was not encouraged, but that did not remain the case. Social and economic pressures to convert were plentiful. It was frequently the case that in order for a *dhimmī* to secure or retain a high post he would have to convert.[68] Marriage laws effectively exerted indirect pressure to convert. However, cases of forced conversion were rare. The Fatimid caliph al-Hākim (985–1021) persecuted *dhimmīs* and forced them to convert. The Mamluk period was a particularly difficult time. Under the Bahrī Mamluks (1293–1354), excluding the period of the Crusades from consideration, Egyptian Copts were reduced to a small minority, and by the end of the fourteenth century they were barely one-tenth of the population. The Mamluk government and the Muslim populace of Cairo and other cities pressured non-Muslims by burning churches and appropriating endowments.[69]

Freedom of religion did not extend to Muslims who wished to convert from Islam. On the basis of a Hadith that supposedly stipulates the death penalty for apostasy, the majority of the four schools of law agreed that the death penalty should be imposed on any man or woman who does not repent from such apostasy. However, the Ḥanafī school held that female apostates should only be incarcerated.[70] Most jurists argued that the apostate should be given the opportunity to repent and that capital punishment was to be pursued only in the case of the apostate's refusal.[71] There are, however, indications that punishments for apostasy were inconsistently applied.[72] Some jurists argued that the wealth of the apostate should be suspended in the hope that he would return to Islam.[73] The caliph al-Zāhir (1020–1035) issued an edict allowing Jews and Christians who had converted under pressure during the reign of the Fatimid caliph al-Ḥākim to return to their religion. This was authorized by the Shi'i, Mālikī, and Ḥanafī schools of law.[74]

Other punishments for apostasy included the confiscation of goods and the annulment of marriage.[75] Change of religion was also a bar to inheritance: when a *dhimmī* became a Muslim, he surrendered his property.[76] The majority of jurists argued that the Muslim does not inherit from a *dhimmī* or vice versa, although the Ḥanafī school allows a Muslim to inherit from an apostate.[77]

The *dhimmī* was also subject to restrictions on activity in the political sphere. It was generally believed that *dhimmīs* should not hold positions of authority over Muslims, which was based on the Qur'anic verses 4:141 and 4:144.[78] The medieval thinker Abū Ḥāmid al-Ghazālī (1058–1111), argued that one of the qualifications for undertaking the commanding of good and the forbidding of evil was belief.[79] *Dhimmīs* with considerable power were viewed as disruptive to the social balance and perceived social order,[80] which was regarded as a violation of the concept of justice, i.e., giving each his due. Muslim jurists and preachers decried the practice of *dhimmīs* holding any position of authority over Muslims, and pious edicts by rulers, such as the decree of the Abbasid caliph al-Mutawakkil (821–861), occasionally purged non-Muslim officials.[81]

However, such restrictions were frequently violated, as indicated by the fact that the dismissal of *dhimmīs* was often called for.[82] From the earliest days of the Islamic conquests, *dhimmīs* were employed in government service because of their administrative expertise. In the eastern provinces, Nestorian Christians and Zoroastrians were particularly prominent in government offices; in Egypt, the same was true for the Copts—especially in the Fatimid period (909–1171). In North Africa and Spain, Jews were prominent in government administration.[83] The only position not normally open to a *dhimmī* was that of vizier (the chief minister or representative to the caliph). Conversion to Islam, however, easily removed this obstacle to advancement.

The prohibition against the employment of a *dhimmī* vizier was eventually solved by al-Māwardī's (974–1058) theory of the caliphate. Effectively sanctioning the status quo, he argued that a *dhimmī* could not be a vizier if he was of the delegated type, since such a vizier may implement his own policies. However, he could become a vizier if he was of the executive type, since that simply involved enforcing the sovereign's policies. For this post, al-Māwardī argued, neither freedom "nor learning is considered a necessary qualification for it, for the minister has no separate jurisdiction or power of appointment for which freedom is requisite, nor may he pass judgment, for which learning is essential." While no woman was allowed to undertake this task, there was "nothing to keep the religious minorities from holding this office, except possibly arrogance, for they have no right to be overbearing in manner." This distinction between executive and delegated authority applied to other posts also, including the post of collecting the spoils of war and the post of alms officer.[84] A number of Fatimid caliphs had Christian viziers, not only in Egypt but also elsewhere in the medieval Muslim world. For example, the Buyid ruler 'Adud al-Dawla (936–983) in Iraq had a Christian vizier.[85]

Such a concern with religious hierarchy also extended to the social sphere, although there it was again inconsistently applied. The so-called Covenant of 'Umar, which had by the ninth century become an integral part of the Muslim legal tradition, set out the theoretical obligations and the rights of *dhimmīs* and formed an important part of the classical normative position on *dhimmīs*. The covenant has been recognized as the source of many of the discriminatory policies later applied to *dhimmīs*. There are disputes about the origin and authenticity of the text, since the original has not survived. A number of versions indicate that it was modified over time to reflect changing circumstances and that its provisions were often violated.[86]

Ibn Kathīr relates the details of the covenant in an exegesis of Qur'an 9:29. One of its stipulations was that the *dhimmīs* agreed not to build new churches or synagogues or to repair ruinous ones (unless they dated from before the conquest and had since fallen into ruin), and they were not allowed to enlarge churches or synagogues or to erect new non-Muslim houses of worship where none had stood before. They were also unable to build houses that overlooked those of Muslims. The covenant stipulated that *dhimmīs* were obliged to comport themselves in a self-effacing and inoffensive manner and to show respect to Muslims. They agreed to give up their seats to Muslims. They had to rise in the presence of Muslims and ride mules rather than horses. They could not carry arms or imitate the clothing of Muslims. They also agreed to have the front of their hair cut and to wear the distinctive belt.[87] The practice of Muslims distinguishing themselves from *dhimmīs* was based on various Hadiths.[88] There were also calls for Muslims not to mix with Jews and Christians, for example, "during their festivals, for wrath descends upon them at that time."[89] The fourteenth-century scholar Ibn al-Hajj deplored Muslim women bathing with Jewish and Christian women.[90] It was also accepted that the salutation of peace should be used only between Muslims and that to address *dhimmīs* other forms of greeting should be adopted, based on the Hadith of Bukhārī: "If the people of the Scripture greet you, then you should say (in reply), 'Wa 'alaykum (and on you)."[91] Ibn Kathīr interpreted Qur'an 5:51, "Oh ye who believe! Take not the Jews and the Christians for your friends and protectors; they are but friends and protectors to each other" as prohibiting making friends with Jews and Christians, "because they are the enemies of Islam and its people."[92]

The covenant also forbade public forms of religious expression, such as the celebration of weddings, funerals, feasts, and church ceremonies. Christians could not parade the cross in Muslim quarters, chant loudly, or carry the cross or sacred books in processions. *Dhimmīs* agreed not to "publicize practices of *shirk* (associating something with God), invite anyone to *shirk* or prevent any of our fellows from embracing Islam." They were not allowed to bury their dead in the same cemeteries as Muslims.[93]

According to Ibn Kathīr, Christians would agree to observe the conditions laid out in the covenant in return for safety and protection. If they broke any of these conditions, the *dhimma* would be revoked.[94] Al-Māwardī's conditions, much less onerous, included not defaming the Qur'an, the Prophet, or the Islamic faith, not committing adultery or entering into an unauthorized marriage with a Muslim female, not enticing a Muslim away from the faith, and not assisting the enemies of Islam.[95]

While the covenant was a *sharī'a* norm that was often cited, it was also often disregarded in practice. For example, Norman Stillman points out that many of the new cities founded by Arab conquerors evolved to have *dhimmī* inhabitants with churches and synagogues.[96] The fact that there were frequent calls for Muslims to distinguish themselves from non-Muslims in dress, which Stillman argues was "probably originally a security measure after the Islamic conquests" indicates that there was "a lack of consistent enforcement."[97] Evidence from Ottoman Damascus (1775–1860) illustrates that the law "was blind to religious affiliation and treated the Christian and Jewish men and women who sought it in ways identical to the ways in which it treated Muslims." This included matrimonial and inheritance arrangements and also weighing evidence and accepting testimony.[98]

While the Covenant of 'Umar was frequently violated, it points to the fact that the normative Islamic position toward *dhimmīs* hardened over time. This hardening of attitudes was reflected in Islamic jurisprudence. The judges and the jurists increasingly interpreted regulations concerning the *dhimma* in a restrictive way, although practice often fell short of the restrictions.[99] Nazih Ayubi argues that the Muslim needed "to be assured of his 'ideological' superiority over the *dhimmi*, to be provided with the ritualistic means that 'enable him to celebrate his historical victory and allow the community to re-inforce its unity by renewing its agreement over a common victim.'"[100] In addition, as Islam changed from being the religion of a ruling elite to being the dominant faith of the urban population, the necessity for Muslims to interact with non-Muslims receded.[101] Stillman argues that the "secular and humanistic atmosphere of the Hellenistic renaissance of the ninth through twelfth centuries also waned."[102]

This increasingly restrictive approach did not, in general, result in the exile of *dhimmīs*, which Islamic jurists did not consider acceptable. One exception, however, was in Arabia, where permanent residence by *dhimmīs* was forbidden after the second caliph 'Umar in 640 expelled the Jews from the Hijaz (the whole area of southwestern Arabia) and the Christians from Najran because it was reported that on his deathbed the Prophet ordered the polytheists to be expelled from the Arabian Peninsula.

However, a few jurists took the interpretation of this Hadith further. Al-Tabarī understood the Hadith "expel the Jews and Christians from the Arabian Peninsula" to mean all Arabian lands. While such a view held little currency before Mamluk times, it was taken up by Ibn Taymiyya and Ibn Qayyim al-Jawziyya (1292–1350), his student. Both advocated the revocability and temporality of the *dhimma* pacts.[103] Ibn Taymiyya sought to eliminate *dhimmīs* from political and military life. He wanted to reduce the number of Christians and eventually expel them.[104] *Dhimmī* residence could be tolerated, temporarily, if the Muslim community needed them; otherwise expulsion was necessary.[105] It could be argued that this position was based on the terms Muhammad gave the Jews at al-Khaybar in 628/627, when Muhammad reserved the right to break off his agreement with them and expel them.

Ibn Taymiyya's antipathy toward Eastern Christians and other non-Muslims can be partly attributed to the threat of the Crusades and the Mongol invasions. It is arguable that increased suspicion of Eastern Christians during this time was largely unjustified. The Crusaders considered the Copts to be heretics, and some Copts took part in some of the battles against the Crusaders.[106] For example, in the 1218 Crusade of Domyat in northern Egypt, Copts participated in the defense of the city. A few Copts did cooperate with the Crusaders, with the aim of establishing Christian independence in Egypt. While this number was very small, Robert Betts argues that all Christians "suffered from the taint of collaboration."[107]

THE *MILLET* SYSTEM

The *dhimma* contract formed the foundation for the communal structure of the Ottoman Empire, which was based on religious identity. Under the Ottoman Empire, the *dhimma* evolved into a collective pact between the sultan and the religious communities that became formalized in the *millet* system.[108] The term *millet* derives from the term *milla* in the Qur'an, meaning "a group of people who accept a particular word or revealed book." According to Bernard Lewis, it referred to both the Muslim community of Islam and other non-Muslim religious groups. In the Ottoman Empire, the term in its Turkish form, *millet*, was used to describe "the organized, recognized, religio-political communities enjoying certain rights of autonomy under their own chiefs."[109] Each of these religio-political communities was under the supervision of a leader, most often a religious patriarch or rabbi, who reported directly to the Ottoman sultan. This leader represented his community before the state and the state to his community.[110] The *millet* system, initially established during the reign of Sultan Muhammad II (1451–1481), lasted more than four hundred years. The first major *millet* established was the Orthodox Christian *millet* in 1454. This was the first time that Christians were brought under the single religious authority of the patriarch.

Benjamin Braude argues that it is important not to overestimate the level of organization of the *millet*. Before the nineteenth century there was no general administrative term or structure that defined the Ottoman government's policy toward non-Muslims. The so-called *millet* system was therefore not "a uniformly adopted system" but "a series of *ad hoc* arrangements" that gave each of the major religious communities some legal autonomy and authority.[111]

Leaders of the religious communities were responsible for their community's education, social affairs, worship, and judicial system. They had powers to maintain their own religious institutions and carry out functions that were not carried out by the Ottoman government. The *millets* could make their own laws and collect and distribute their own taxes. The *millets* were also allowed to run their own courts, which were called *milli* courts. The system granted non-Muslims a great deal of autonomy, and in some areas, such as Anatolia, Christian and Jewish communities grew.[112]

As a result, these "religio-political communities" enjoyed a certain amount of independence.[113] Such autonomy, however, has often been used to perpetuate the assumption that the status of *dhimmīs* was defined by separation and communal insularity, although Najwa al-Qattan has argued that *dhimmīs* frequently appealed to the *sharīʿa* courts of Ottoman Damascus (1775–1860) to resolve marriage and inheritance issues.[114]

In addition, while it is correct that under the *millet* system most religious communities were controlled by a religious leader or patriarch, this was not always the case. Magdi Guirguis argues that in the case of Egypt's Copts, in the Ottoman Empire, a struggle existed between the clergy and the secular elite for leadership of the Coptic community such that during the latter half of this period—from the seventeenth century onward—leadership was transferred from the Coptic Church to the Coptic notables, who then represented the "affairs of the community before the state."[115]

The Egyptian Coptic community had by this time become a minority.[116] Coptic Christians believe that Christianity was brought to Egypt by Saint Mark in the early first century and that the majority of Egypt's inhabitants were Christian by the time of ʿAmr Ibn al-ʾAsʾs invasion in 632. Arabization occurred at a faster rate than Islamization: Arabic was introduced in government offices at the beginning of the eighth century, and by the tenth century most of the inhabitants of Lower Egypt no longer spoke or understood Coptic.[117] It is impossible to link the decline of spoken Coptic to any date with certainty. There are indications that Coptic was spoken in Upper Egypt in the fifteenth century, and there are some indications that this might have continued until as late as the eighteenth century.[118] After that, the language was used for liturgical purposes only.

The speed of Islamization and conversion is contested in part because no reliable statistics exist. It is clear, however, that Islamization progressed more slowly than Arabization and was never absolute. Initially, conversion was not a priority of the conquering Arabs, who manifested a paternalistic attitude toward the church, although this began to change around 720.[119] The ninth century was a time when Christian conversion to Islam rapidly increased.[120] Due to the increased number of conversions in the Mamluk period, by 1354 Copts had become a small minority (about 10 percent).[121] Edward Lane, the British Orientalist who traveled to Egypt in the 1820's, reports that the Coptic population consisted of 150,000, which represents about 7.5 to 8 percent of his total estimated population of Egypt.[122]

Under the *millet* system, the Coptic patriarch judged cases among the Copts in the city, and lesser clergy did likewise in other areas. When a member of one *millet* committed a crime against a member of another, the law of the damaged person applied. In cases between Muslims and non-Muslims, Islamic law applied. While Copts had access to their own courts, some Copts made use of the Muslim courts. Copts who wished to intermarry with a person of another sect could be married by a Muslim judge.[123]

The *millet* system continued many of the restrictions of the *dhimma*. In the 1830's, Copts paid the *jizya*, and the traditional Islamic restrictions on the *dhimmī*, such as not riding horses or carrying weapons and wearing dull-colored turbans, were still in place, although they were much less respected in the villages than in the cities. Some restrictions were lifted by Muhammad 'Ali (1769–1849), who allowed Christians to ring their church bells for the first time, carry the cross in public, and ride horses.[124]

It has been argued that the *millet* system meant that Copts in Egypt were precluded from a significant role in government, but while they maintained their own religious identity, the Copts did form an intrinsic part of Egyptian society. They were culturally similar to Muslims with regard to birth, marriage, and death customs. Both Coptic and Jewish women were veiled in public, and Copts had similar attitudes toward apostasy and intermarriage.[125] Judgments about the relative isolation or integration of the Copts in Egypt can be only tentative. B. L. Carter argues, with particular reference to the Copts, that the *millet* system "minimised contacts between ethnic groups and was relatively successful in containing communal conflict."[126]

The Ottoman Empire was, according to Benjamin Braude and Bernard Lewis, "a classic example of the plural society."[127] While it was a pluralistic society, it was not a liberal system, for the principle of religious tolerance did not extend to an individual's freedom of conscience, since there was little opportunity for individual dissent or apostasy.[128] The society's former strength, according to some, became a weakness. Albert Hourani states that non-Muslims in Islamic society were closed communities and that they were thus margin-alized and shut off.[129] According to Kemal Karpat, the later political, social, and cultural crises that afflicted the Balkans and the Middle East can be at-tributed to the fact that the secular idea of state and the religious concept of nation rooted in the *millet* philosophy were incompatible. He argues that the concepts of nation and state, which were naturally integrated into each other in Western Europe, had no basis for success in the Ottoman Empire or its suc-cessor states, where nation was conflated with religious community.[130]

While it is true to say that there were significant tensions between the *mil-let* system and the nation-state, such a dichotomy should not be overstated. In the case of Egypt, Copts and Muslims had a long history of living together as part of a centralized geographical and cultural entity called Egypt. It is no coincidence that the scholar who was the first to introduce the concepts of fatherland (*watan*) and patriotism (*wataniyya*) into Arabic was an Egyptian called Rifā'a Rāfi' al-Tahtāwī (1801–1873).[131]

Nevertheless, the fact that the *millet* represented the autonomy of religious communities focused on the religious patriarch posed a number of impedi-ments to the shift to a centralized nation-state. As will be seen, contemporary Egyptian politics contains many echoes of the *millet*, a situation that poses important questions for what citizenship means in this context.

CONCLUSION

Islamic law, like Islam itself, is neither unchanging nor monolithic. With re-gard to the role and status of non-Muslims, the formation of a *sharī'a* norm for their treatment developed in conjunction with the context in which that law was formulated. The Qur'an did not stipulate concrete and detailed guide-lines for the treatment of non-Muslims or for the rights and duties involved in the *dhimma*. The Hadith often responded to particular circumstances and did not contain overarching guidelines for the treatment of non-Muslims. Never-theless, Islamic doctrine that claimed to supersede and correct the mistakes of Christianity and Judaism in part contributed to the assumption that *dhimmīs* were inferior to Muslims. It was this theological position that took on a politi-cal and social meaning and a political and social form in the context of the victorious Islamic Empire. The particular political form that it took was also influenced by the pre-Islamic models for dealing with religious minorities that the Umayyad and Abbasid empires inherited. While Islamic law evolved a general framework of attitudes and rules for the treatment and position of non-Muslims, these general guidelines were subject to different interpretations and to the whims and policies of different rulers and were also often subordinated to a more pragmatic approach. While the Covenant of 'Umar was a *sharīʿa* norm, it was frequently violated. The Islamic legal position on the role of non-Muslims therefore resulted from a complex interaction of both Islamic ideas and principles, based on Islamic texts, and political and social circumstances.

Anyone who undertakes narrative reporting to describe the rights and role of non-Muslims in Islamic history works within a politically charged context. Any description of Islamic law or Islamic history is often regarded as a direct judgment of Islam itself. While it is true to say that there were certain underlying assumptions that were part of the Islamic discursive tradition and that these underlying assumptions were manifested in divergent ways, the relationship between the two is complex. Accounts of the rights and role of non-Muslims have often framed Islamic law as "tolerant" or "intolerant." For example, Yohanan Friedmann argues against the "claim that medieval Islam was tolerant in the modern sense of the word."[132] However, such a judgment is shackled by modern and secular assumptions about what constitutes tolerance. Those who wish to highlight the lack of tolerance point to the social, legal, and political discrimination that non-Muslims experienced. The Covenant of 'Umar is often referred to as an example of Islam's demeaning policies toward *dhimmīs*. Certainly *dhimmīs* faced considerable restrictions, and in that respect there are grounds for arguing that the *dhimma* contract disconnects from, rather than morphs into, modern citizenship.[133]

However, according to Bosworth, the kind of life depicted by the Covenant of 'Umar, such as the restriction on the height of *dhimmī* buildings, points to a society in which Muslims and *dhimmīs* mixed. For that reason, the status of *dhimmīs* in Islam was considerably better than that of Jews in medieval Europe.[134] This is notwithstanding the fact that the covenant was frequently violated. The fact that *dhimmīs* constituted recognized communities of their own was significant for its time. A level of religious leniency was built into the Islamic polity. This was important even if that leniency was conditional upon the submission of *dhimmīs* to Islamic polity. In addition, practice was often more lenient than theory, and in reality very few actions jeopardized the protection that the *dhimmī* received.[135] Islamic law had no natural law; rights were either those given by God or those to which non-Muslims contracted themselves. Nevertheless, the *dhimmī* contract was a construct of rights that

Muslims could not violate unless *dhimmīs* renounced the contract.

Various circumstances conspired to make the classical position on *dhimmīs* the normative Islamic position. The fact that political theory often legitimized the status quo meant that it became difficult to distinguish between description and prescription within this literature and to recognize that certain concepts such as the *dhimma* developed historically. While it is important not to exaggerate the idea of the closure of *ijithād*, the body of Islamic jurisprudence was conflated with *sharīʿa* in the sense of divine law so that the jurisprudence was interpreted out of its historical context and was taken as a timeless exposition of Islamic values. This attitude toward Islamic jurisprudence has been inherited by many modern Islamists, who often overlook the fact that it was formed in a political context and performed a political function.[136]

It is a distinction that many Islamists, although by no means all, have ignored. Regardless of whether this distinction is made, the complexity of the origins of the *dhimma* and its stipulations pose challenges for all contemporary Islamists. When contemporary Islamists call for the establishment of an "Islamic state," what kind of Islamic state do they envision? Were all of the stipulations and restrictions that evolved to be associated with the *dhimma* a clear reflection—from the perspective of contemporary Islamists and modernists—of what the *dhimma* was "meant" to be? Was the *dhimma* a divine instruction or a historical response to political circumstances? How "Islamic" was the *dhimma* and its stipulations?

2 CONTINUITY, DISCONTINUITY, AND THE RISE OF ISLAMISM

THERE IS A COMMON ASSUMPTION that from the mid-nineteenth century on, the Middle East underwent some kind of break from the premodern Islamic order, adopting Western laws and institutions and then establishing nation-states in the early part of the twentieth century. From many perspectives this assessment is true, although it is important to point out that there was continuity as well as discontinuity. Regardless of the historicity of the notion of a break, it is a perception that is central to the Islamist worldview. Before 1914, Egypt had been part of a somewhat loosely unified Islamic Ottoman Empire. Its dislocation from this empire in 1914 and the subsequent abolition of the caliphate in 1924 symbolized Islam's dislocation with its past. While the notion that the Islamic world had been unified is a fallacy, it was central from a psychological perspective. As the contemporary Egyptian thinker Yūsuf al-Qaradāwī (1926–) puts it, in 1924 "the one *umma* was torn into shreds and scattered into a variety of nations."[1]

The notion of a break also came with the retreat of *sharīʿa*. Up until the mid-nineteenth century the Ottoman Empire had been—at least in theory—based on *sharīʿa*, such that when *sharīʿa* elements in the Ottoman legal system gave way to the encroaching influence of codified Western law, considerable discontinuity was created. However, the frequent recourse to non-*sharīʿa* elements enforced by the sultan, who alone had the power to enforce the implementation of the law, meant that the construct of an Ottoman Empire based on *sharīʿa* was more of an ideal. According to Knut Vikør, the colonial era was "more of a continuation of an existing situation than a dramatic break."[2]

In addition, Leonard Wood argues that "many leading Egyptian jurists in the early 20th century believed that the field of Islamic jurisprudence lacked the virtues of French law" and not until the 1930's did Egyptian intellectuals and writers begin to consider the existence of foreign law in Egypt a problem.[3] At the same time, Egypt's evolution to a secular state was partial and incomplete. Some continuity was maintained, since vestiges of the *millet* system remained in the form of personal status law for Muslims and non-Muslims.

However, Talal Asad argues that *sharī'a* law was not merely reduced in scope but radically transformed because it was at this point that important reconfigurations in law, religion, ethics, and morality occurred.[4] According to Asad, the narrowing of *sharī'a* jurisdiction and the importation of European legal codes provided for the emergence of social spaces within which "secularism" could grow.[5] *Sharī'a* law came to be equated with personal status law for regulating "the family," a modern institution built around the married couple.[6]

Regardless of the various continuities or discontinuities, Islamic revivalists reacted to a growing sense of dislocation by calling for the establishment of an "Islamic state," with the assumption that such an entity had existed at some point in Islamic history. However, Islamists have differed significantly on both the aims and the means of achieving the revival of the Islamic state. They have also differed about what kind of modern and Western values such a state can accept or reject. These challenges have created a complex Islamist landscape made up of a spectrum of ideas. Categorization of these ideas into types is fraught with difficulty, not only from the perspective of the basis of categorization itself but also because Islamists are part of the political process. Islamist ideas are constantly changing, responding to, and in turn shaping the political environment in which they are formed. While the Islamist movement in Egypt has failed to overturn the regime and establish an Islamic state, it has succeeded in Islamizing Egyptian society and, to a certain extent, the state. Islamists have also adopted an increasingly pragmatic approach, which has meant that the gulf between the Islamist vision of what an Islamic state should be and the reality of the current Egyptian state is not as wide as it once was. This development has meant that more pressure is being put on Egyptian Islamists to move away from simplistic slogans such as "Islam is the solution" and provide a firmer definition of what an Islamic state might look like.

THE END OF THE OLD ORDER

The abolition of the caliphate in 1924 and the establishment of nation-states symbolized the Islamic world's disconnection with its past, although this disconnection was more apparent than real. It is arguable that Egypt was well placed to weather the change; it had historical experience as a centralized entity dating back to Pharaonic times. An economy based upon the Nile River had fostered centralization. Muhammad 'Ali (1769–1849), who established the dynasty that ruled Egypt until 1952, laid many of the foundations of the modern Egyptian state, including the extension of the state and its administration, the establishment of a standing army, and centralized economic planning. He also built modern roads and established an education system independent of religious institutions.

The concept of the nation-state was not a developed idea in Islamic political thinking. The state, particularly when defined in individualist and secularist terms, is a Western concept, and the "Arab state is not a natural growth of its own socio-economic history or its own cultural and intellectual tradition." Islamic political tradition emphasized the concept of the community (*umma*). The Islamic theory of the state focused on government and the conduct of the ruler, not on the actual state as a concept. A concept of the state that linked community and government did not develop until the middle to late nineteenth century, and even then it was adopted only reluctantly.[7]

The establishment of the Egyptian nation-state coincided with the partial process of secularization initiated by the implementation of Western law. This secularization began under Muhammad 'Ali, who established two courts for commercial disputes, which were independent of Islamic law. He also had the criminal justice system administered by the executive authorities.[8] However, it was the process of capitulations, which were contracts between the Ottoman Empire and European powers that led to the adoption of Western law. The grandson of Muhammad 'Ali, Ismā'īl (Khedive 1863–1879), negotiated with European powers, resulting in the establishment of mixed courts to adjudicate civil and commercial matters when one or both of the parties were foreigners. A version of the French civil and commercial codes was applied in these courts. In the case of Egypt, the system enabled Britain to ensure that its citizens who were resident in Egypt were governed by British law.

The capitulations enabled Eastern Christians and Jews to improve their position by securing European nationality or protected status. They had access to Western education through missionary schools, which also enabled them to advance themselves economically. By the beginning of the nineteenth century, the average Christian was better educated and more affluent than the average Muslim,[9] which resulted in social tension between Christians and Muslims. Christian communities also became associated with Western powers. Albert Hourani reports that non-Muslims "were regarded as potential traitors, sources of weakness and instruments of European policy."[10]

Copts became more socioeconomically advanced, although they were not as connected to or associated with Western powers as other Middle Eastern Christians. Rather than eagerly adopting Western habits, as had many Jews and other Christians, the Copts tended to be more conservative in social matters.[11] Nevertheless, toward the end of the nineteenth century the Coptic elite began to assimilate modern Western culture, enabling it to acquire influence in public services and commerce.[12] Through this access to wealth and education, shortly before the First World War, Egyptian Christians claimed that they paid 16 percent of the land tax, even though they formed, at most, only 8 percent of the population.[13]

The capitulations coincided with the reform of the legal status of non-Muslims under Ottoman law. The Ottoman Hatti Humayun decree of 1856 changed the legal status of non-Muslims under Ottoman law and extended the implementation of Western law. The decree guaranteed freedom of religious practice and freedom to convert from Islam to other religions. It also stipulated that no distinction would be made on the basis of language, race, or religion. This provision applied to government service as well. Many of the restrictions that non-Muslims had been subject to under the *dhimma* were abolished so that, in effect, the former relationship between Muslims and *dhimmīs* was dismantled. The decree also established mixed tribunals, which replaced *sharī'a* courts for commercial or criminal cases involving Muslims and non-Muslims. The decree referred to non-Muslims as "non-Muslims" rather than as *dhimmīs*, which, according to Bruce Masters, was "symbolic of the radical transformation in the relationship between the state and its non-Muslim subjects."[14]

It was certainly a significant transformation, although some vestiges of the *dhimma* remained. For example, while the construction of new churches was allowed, the *millets* needed Istanbul's approval. The *jizya* was officially abolished in 1855, and it was established that non-Muslims as well as Muslims were liable to recruitment to the military. However, it was possible for non-Muslims to obtain an exemption, which was purchased through a tax, the *bedel*, which was levied on all adult non-Muslim males who chose not to serve in the military. While Christians complained that this tax was simply the *jizya* in disguise, they never asked to be drafted in place of paying the tax. In fact, in 1909, when the *bedel* was finally abolished and compulsory military service for all males regardless of religion was introduced, there was an increase in the emigration of non-Muslims.[15]

The establishment of mixed courts for commercial and criminal cases between Muslims and non-Muslims marked a significant step in the retreat of *sharī'a* law. However, it was not long before these mixed tribunals were adopted for the country at large in order to ensure uniformity.[16] By 1885 civil law, civil court procedures, criminal law, criminal court procedures, and commercial law had been adopted.

One important stipulation of the Hatti Humayun decree of 1856 was that the *millets* should be allowed to reform themselves. *Millet* reform, which was enforced by the Ottoman government, allowed laymen to elect their patriarchs and participate in the administration of the *millet*. It has been argued that such reforms strengthened the *millets*.[17] However, these reforms actually contributed to the decline of the *millet* system, because, according to Kemal Karpat, the reforms *"recognized implicitly that the government was the source of their rights and freedoms* (author's emphasis)." Prior to this reform, rights and freedoms were inherent in the *millet* and the government could not restrict those rights and freedoms. The reforms meant that the government gained control of areas that had previously been under the jurisdiction of the *millet* courts. For example, individuals were given the right to appeal to state courts in inheritance cases. The reforms also undermined the *millets* because they limited the jurisdiction of the clergy to religious duties and extended the government's authority over the other activities of the *millets*, such as education.[18] The expansion of government authority therefore undermined the autonomy of religious minorities and changed the balance between religious minorities and the state.

This process was continued by the Ottoman Nationality Law of 1869. Every person born of an Ottoman father was an Ottoman subject.[19] The Ottoman Constitution of 1876 established Jews, Christians, and Muslims as Ottoman citizens, and Ottoman citizenship was based on the notion that Ottoman subjects were equal regardless of their faith and language. In 1879, Tawfīq, the Khedive of Egypt (1852–1892), proclaimed the equality of all Egyptians, and restrictions against allowing Christians and Jews to ride horses in Egypt were lifted. In 1900 the Egyptian Nationality Law was passed.

However, Coptic Christians were slow to respond to the establishment of Ottoman citizenship. Copts were unwilling to give up control of the *millet* system. They opposed conscription by appealing, according to the *millet* model, to Pope Kyrillos IV (1854–1861).[20] In fact, legal emancipation did not lead to the cultural assimilation or to the political integration of non-Muslim communities into the Egyptian nation.[21] Non-Muslims wanted to take advantage of the new Ottoman law and at the same time preserve the privileges and autonomy of the old *millet* system. Karpat argues that secular Ottoman citizenship failed because it was established without resolving the conflict between the secular state and the idea of nationality based on religious identity. In addition, while in theory Ottoman citizenship established a direct relationship between the individual and the state, the relationship between non-Muslims and the state was impeded by the fact that the Muslim character of the Ottoman government acquired new political significance.[22]

Although the *millet* system was disrupted with the importation of Western law, parts of the system were preserved because the Hatti Humayun decree granted non-Muslims autonomy in the area of personal status law, which included marriage, divorce, capacity, guardianship, and inheritance.[23] The *shari'a* and *millet* courts were therefore retained for personal status procedures.

While some vestiges of the *millet* system remained, considerable change through the curtailment of Islamic law and the establishment of the modern nation-state, based primarily on French law, had occurred. Nadav Safran argues that this had a destabilizing effect: Egypt had inherited a system of beliefs based on Islam, which had served as the foundation of the political community. In his view, the changes were imposed from above and were not accompanied by an intellectual reawakening. The transformations therefore undermined the traditional Islamic ideological system but were not replaced by an alternative belief system. As a result, the political community became destabilized.[24]

THE SECULAR PROJECT

The Egyptian Constitution of 1923 largely embodied the values of the Ottoman *tanzimat* reforms. Article 1 of the constitution stipulated that Egypt was "a sovereign state, free and independent." While the constitution declared Islam to be the official religion of the state, it did not establish the *shari'a* as the principal or exclusive source of legislation. In fact, it made no particular reference to *shari'a* and gave the People's Assembly full power of legislation, unhampered by the *sharī'a*.[25] It established the principle of equality for all Egyptians before the law. Egyptians were to have equal enjoyment of civil and political rights (Art. 3), absolute freedom of conscience (Art. 12), and "free exercise of all religions or beliefs in conformity with established usages on condition that they are not harmful to public order and good morals" (Art. 13).[26] Article 13 was influenced by the French concept of *ordre public*, which refers to the notion of basic principles that are fundamental to any society and cannot be contradicted.

There were a number of concessions to Egypt's Islamic identity. In 1915 it was declared that the Hatti Humayun decree, which included restrictions on building churches, would be continued.[27] The original text of the 1923 Constitution stated that "freedom of religious belief is absolute." However, after pressure from Egypt's religious establishment, al-Azhar, which argued that belief and religion are two separate concepts, the word "religious" was deleted from the text. In addition, matters of personal status were to be determined by the community's religious authorities in accordance with their own religious precepts.

Despite these concessions, the constitution reflected the secular tone of prerevolutionary Egypt. Secular territorial nationalism and anticolonialism dominated the Egyptian ideological debate in the 1920's. Copts initially became caught in the anticolonialist atmosphere. Sectarian tension broke out in 1910 when the Coptic prime minister, Butrus Ghālī, was murdered by a nationalist. Public opinion had turned against the Copts because they were seen as wealthy moneylenders with political power, but overall, secular territorial nationalism appears to have had a positive effect on Coptic political involvement. By the 1919 Revolution, Copts and Muslims were celebrating national unity. This period evolved into a golden age for Copts. Coptic and Muslim secularists, such as the nationalist prime minister Sa'ad Zaghlūl (1859–1927) and the writer Ahmed Lutfī al-Sayyid (1872–1963) tried to base Egyptian identity on a shared history that emphasized the uniqueness of the Egyptian character.[28] The writer Tahā Husayn (1889–1971) promoted the idea that the existence of Egypt's distinct Mediterranean culture meant that it was part of a European civilization.[29] While this idea was less popular than Pharaonism, which emphasized the importance of Egypt's Pharaonic history, it did appeal to many liberal Muslims and Copts in particular.[30] As a result, new opportunities opened up for Copts. From 1919 to 1926, Copts occupied prominent cabinet-level and legal positions. The nationalist Wafd Party embodied this idea of territorial nationalism and secularism, and the majority of Coptic deputies were from the Wafd Party. Makram Ubayd, a leading Coptic figure of that party, declared, like Salāma Mūsā, the founder of Egypt's Socialist Party, "I am Christian by religion and Muslim by nationality."

However, secular nationalism was short-lived. It never had popular appeal and soon gave way to nationalism, which took its inspiration from Islam. In the late 1930's and 1940's, Islam was increasingly used to define Egyptian identity, and the existence of French law increasingly came to be seen as problematic.[31] During the interwar years, particularly after 1945, the tone of Arab nationalism became more and more Islamic.[32] The discrepancy between the ideal of Islamic law and the secular reality became more apparent.

The establishment of the Muslim Brotherhood in 1928 reflected the growing awareness of that discrepancy. The sense that secular law was illegitimate contributed to an emphasis upon the notion of an idealized past in which religion and state were unified. The concept of an idealized past was not necessarily new; it can be identified in calls for renewal in medieval Islamic historiography.[33] However, the sense of its political imperative was new. Hasan al-Bannā (1906–1949), the leader of the Muslim Brotherhood, called for "reform of the government until it is truly Islamic." He argued that "Islam is a complete system which deals with all areas of life. It is a state, a nation, a government, and a community."[34] While it has often been argued that the concept of *dīn wa dawla* (religion and state) represents some kind of timeless Islamic truism, it actually is a modern idea, dating to the nineteenth century at the very earliest.[35]

While a number of the Free Officers of the 1952 Revolution had sympathies with the Muslim Brotherhood, postrevolutionary Egypt was characterized by a shift toward Arab nationalism, which tended to be secular in its outlook. While the Constitution of 1956 declared Islam the state religion, the draft of Gamal Abdul Nasser's (Egypt's president from 1952 to 1970) Charter of 1962 appears to be secular, advocating freedom of religious belief and implying that all religious faiths were, in some way, equal. The charter was notable for its emphasis on Egyptian and Arab identity and for its lack of reference to Islamic identity. Although Islam was recognized as an element in the achievements of the revolution, it ranked only fifth in importance.[36]

While Arab nationalism appealed to many Arab Christians, this was not always the case with Coptic Christians. The secularism of the interwar period led to an increase in the political activity of Copts, but under Nasser, Copts increasingly withdrew from the political process.[37] A number of Nasser's policies, which were not necessarily connected with religion, isolated the Coptic community. Nasser's agrarian reforms and nationalization initiatives isolated and decimated the Coptic elite. As a result, Coptic leadership was taken up by the middle class and the Coptic Church.

Another factor in the isolation of Copts was that although Nasser's Arab nationalism was secular, it had Islamic overtones as well. Many Copts were unenthusiastic about the 1952 Revolution because of the sympathy of some of the Free Officers with the Muslim Brotherhood. The fact that the military movement did not include any Copts and that the Free Officers Movement had only one Coptic member was a source of discontent. After the revolution, in 1957, religion was made a mandatory subject in school curricula, and access to al-Azhar University was restricted to Muslim students. The use of religious symbols became a feature of political discourse, as did conspiracy theories, which often implicated Copts. In the 1950's and 1960's, a large number of Copts, lacking the "channels for self-expression," emigrated to North America.[38]

External events did little to help the Coptic situation in Egypt. When the state of Israel was created in 1948, the Copts were suspected of being affiliated with the Jews. They were also accused of working for a national home in Egypt just as the Jews were doing in Palestine. Election campaigns in interwar Egypt often featured the employment of anti-Christian rhetoric against Coptic candidates, which sometimes echoed the traditional perception that the Copts had risen above their station.[39]

The court reforms of 1955 had a significant impact on the relationship between Christians and the state. Nasser abolished Muslim *sharī'a* and Coptic *millet* courts in an attempt to unify the system. Previously, Muslim, Christian, and Jewish communities had their own personal status laws decided in their own courts. The abolition of the courts under Nasser had been preceded by attempts at reform. Salāma Mūsā (1887–1958), a Coptic socialist essayist and founder of Egypt's Socialist Party in 1920, had advocated civil marriage, believing that the government would be less arbitrary in its judicial behavior than the *millet* courts. Some Copts, including the politician Qalīnī Fahmī, supported personal status reforms because they wished to see a decrease in the power of the Lay Council, a body that acted as a liaison between the church and the government. Some areas of personal status were in fact taken away from the *millet* and *sharī'a* courts. In the first half of the twentieth century, matters such as guardianship, intestate succession, bequests, family names, family ties, and legal capacity were classified as "general" law. Most Copts were alarmed at these reforms and blocked further reform in non-Muslim personal status jurisdiction.[40]

The move to bring some areas of family law under general law was not only an attempt to weaken the Coptic Church's control over personal status issues. Many politicians, Coptic and Muslim alike, would have liked to create an entirely secular system. They wanted to reform non-Muslim and Muslim family law, but focused on non-Muslim personal status law first. The reason for the opposition to such reforms was that the minorities were unwilling to lose power over their communal affairs. Most Copts were reluctant to relinquish communal control.[41]

By 1952 the legislative autonomy of Egypt's non-Muslim communities, strictly speaking, had been confined to family law (marriage and divorce) rather than broader personal status law. The abolition of the *sharī'a* and the *millet* courts in 1955 marked the final stage in the unification process, since the activities of those courts were incorporated into the national courts. While this change opened up the possibility for personal status issues to become secularized, under the concept of public order areas of personal status law have been determined by *sharī'a* law in what have been labeled "civil courts."[42] Many Copts resent these civil courts because the application of *sharī'a* law has led to an increase in the number of Coptic divorces granted. Most judges are Muslims, and some Copts complain that those serving in the new national courts are not sufficiently acquainted with "Christian values."[43]

Egypt's military defeat in 1967 by Israel strengthened the Islamist movement and weakened secular forces. It shattered the belief that the answer to Arab backwardness, dependence, and poverty lay in unity. The writer Fouad Ajami argues that the region experienced a kind of "breakdown" or identity crisis and many Egyptians looked to Islam for the answer.[44] Islamist groups argued that the Arabs had been defeated because they had turned away from their religion.

The sense of dislocation and disconnection, previously expressed in the ideas of Hasan al-Bannā, deepened. Calls for a reversal of secularization and the application of Islamic law grew louder. Since the 1970's, however, the Islamist movement has grown and has become more diffuse. Islamists have differed significantly with regard to the aims and the means of establishing an Islamic state. The call for the revival of an Islamic state, with slogans such as "The Qur'an is our constitution," mistakenly makes the assumption that the Qur'an provides a blueprint for political organization.

The challenge of determining how an Islamic state could be established in this context has created a complex Islamist landscape, containing different types of thought. Identifying these types as radical, mainstream, or moderate is a difficult task, notwithstanding the assumptions behind such categorization. While the Islamist movement has failed in theory to establish an Islamic state, it has succeeded to a certain extent in Islamizing state and society. The gap between Islamism and the state has narrowed, and there has been an important shift toward a more moderate and conciliatory Islamist agenda that emphasizes working to change the status quo from within.

THE RETREAT OF RADICAL ISLAMISM

One of the reactions to this sense of dislocation came to be broadly defined as radical Islam because it advocated violence and delegitimized the regime and, in a few cases, Egyptian society as a whole. This strain of Islamism dates back to Nasser's regime, when many members of the Muslim Brotherhood reacted to the treatment they experienced in Nasser's prisons by arguing that the rulers who had inflicted such torture on fellow Muslims could not be real Muslims. These members found ideological tools for analyzing the new regime in the ideas of the Islamist ideologue Sayyid Qutb (1906–1966).[45] Qutb is considered the most influential theoretician of political Islam, particularly in the Arab world but also elsewhere.

Radical groups identified the regime with Qutb's concept of al-Jāhiliyya, which literally means "period of ignorance," a term used by medieval Islamic historians to refer to pre-Islamic Arabian society. However, for Qutb, it refers to the belief that the Egyptian regime and Egyptian society had turned their backs on Islam. The radical groups also adopted Qutb's modern concept of sovereignty (al-hākimiyya), the belief that the right to legislate belongs only to God. Qutb's work was interpreted in different ways, and those differences led to the fragmentation of the Muslim Brotherhood.[46] While some members of the group emphasized education to achieve their aims, others, drawing on the ideas of Qutb, proclaimed Egypt a land of disbelief and legitimized jihād against rulers of Muslim countries who abstained from applying the sharī'a. The implication was confrontation with the state and immediate action to enforce the application of sharī'a.

Confrontation with the state was first taken up in 1974 by the Military Academy Group, led by a Palestinian named Sālih Siriyya (1933–1974). Its members attempted to assassinate Sadat and bring about a coup d'état.[47] Another group, Jamā'at al-Muslimīn (Society of Muslims), was labeled by the Egyptian press as Takfīr wa al-Hijra (Charging a Person with Unbelief and Holy Flight) for its declaration of unbelief (*takfīr*) and call for flight (*hijra*). This group took Qutb's ideas to the extreme and undertook flight, withdrawal from the infidel society, to establish a community of believers. Led by Shukrī Mustafā (1942–1978), the group denounced both Egyptian society and its leadership as unbelieving, thereby legitimizing violence against them. In 1976 the group kidnapped and assassinated the head of al-Azhar, Shaykh al-Dhahabī. Mustafā and his close associates were subsequently executed, and the group was severely weakened but not eradicated.

Confrontation with the state in this way was a minority position. The reformist wing of the Muslim Brotherhood rallied around the leadership of Hasan al-Hudaybī (1891–1973), who was Hasan al-Bannā's successor and was nominated as the second supreme guide in 1951. While al-Hudaybī was initially positive about Qutb's ideas, he later refuted Qutb's work with his own book *Preachers Not Judges*, which represents, according to Barbara Zollner, "an important critique of radical thought," since it refutes the establishment of an Islamic state by armed revolution and preaches "gradual development from within."[48]

This reformist wing was led by the Brotherhood's old guard and found expression in the monthly journal *al-Daʿwa*, which was edited by the Muslim Brotherhood's third supreme guide, ʿUmar al-Tilmisānī (1904–1986, supreme guide 1973–1986), who had been one of Hasan al-Hudaybī's close associates. The editors of *al-Daʿwa* demanded participation in political life and "made themselves a legal opposition within the existing political system on which they sought to exert enough pressure to achieve peaceful evolution toward an Islamic state based on the *sharīʿa*."[49] In the pages of *al-Daʿwa*, al-Tilmisānī looked back with nostalgia to the days when the Islamic peoples were unified and mourned the current state of the Muslim world.[50] The journal focused on the four major enemies: "Jewry," "the Crusade," "communism," and "secularism."[51] This reformist wing was encouraged by President Sadat (1970–1981), who released members of the Muslim Brotherhood from jail.

More militant members of the Muslim Brotherhood movement and associates of *al-Daʿwa* were linked to the growing al-Jamāʿa al-Islāmiyya (the Islamic Organization). This group is sometimes referred to in the plural as a collection of groups known as the Islamic Student Associations. Al-Jamāʿa al-Islāmiyya was allowed to operate within the universities, where it experienced a surge in support. Central to its ideology was the idea that Islam required the unity of religion and state. It also called for the reestablishment of the caliphate and referred to secularism as the "resort of those idolatrous rulers who transgress God's limits."[52]

The rise of Islamist movements must be viewed in the context of Sadat's state-sponsored Islamization policies. In 1971 Sadat ratified a new constitution, Article 2 of which stated that "Islam is the religion of the state, Arabic is the official language, the principles of the Islamic *sharīʿa* are *a* main source of legislation." This was deliberately vague, but according to Clark Lombardi, it meant that the government wanted to negotiate with the Islamists about what role Islam should have in influencing legislation in Egypt.[53] As a result, during the 1970's, judges began to reference Islamic law in their rulings. For example, the Court of Cassation stated that the principle of public order would be used to interpret Egyptian law and that public order would be based on Islamic principles.[54] In 1980, Article 2 was amended to read, "The principles of Islamic *sharīʿa* are *the* main source of legislation." While this was a further step in favor of Islamization, the possibility of including other sources was retained for flexibility.[55]

The changes to the 1971 Constitution did not have the effect on the country's legal system that the Islamists had hoped for. This outcome aroused much discontent, which led to increasing support for Islamist groups. Sadat's peace initiative with Israel in 1978 further soured the good relationship between the regime and al-Jamāʿa al-Islāmiyya, which became increasingly radicalized.[56] In the view of al-Jamāʿa al-Islāmiyya, the peace treaty was beyond the pale. While *al-Daʿwa*'s editor, ʿUmar al-Tilmisānī, had previously been cautious in attacking the regime, he now launched vehement attacks on Sadat's peace initiative. *Al-Daʿwa* portrayed Sadat as a pharaoh, thereby implying that he was no longer a Muslim.[57]

Though the regime had been delegitimized, concrete action against it was not offered. Members of al-Jamāʿa al-Islāmiyya, frustrated by the lack of action, became attracted to an organization called al-Jihād, which advocated *jihād* involving military action to overthrow the president and establish an Islamic state based on the *sharīʿa* by means of violent agitation and popular revolution. Its ideologue was an electrical engineer called ʿAbd al-Salām Faraj (ca. 1954–1982), who wrote the renowned pamphlet *The Neglected Duty*, which delegitimized Sadat as a Muslim and sanctioned violence against him. On October 6, 1981, the Cairo branch of al-Jihād assassinated Sadat.[58]

The principal radical groups operating in Egypt during President Hosni Mubarak's regime (1981–) have been al-Jamāʿa al-Islāmiyya and al-Jihād, although there are other groups.[59] Until 1997, both groups believed in the necessity of waging military *jihād* against the Mubarak regime. Al-Jamāʻa al-Islāmiyya was based in Upper Egypt while al-Jihād was most active in Cairo. The former tried to destroy the tourism industry, while the latter tried to infiltrate the military and win the support of army officers. Al-Jihād stepped up its operations in 1987 with four assassination attempts. In April 1990 twenty-five members were killed in a clash with security forces.

During the 1980's, President Mubarak's regime continued a policy begun under Sadat in which the security apparatus gave al-Jamāʻa al-Islāmiyya free rein in areas of Middle Egypt, such as Minya, Manfalut, Fayyum, and Dirut. There it was allowed to apply its own laws, and in return it secured the area.[60] Before 1992 it was possible to walk into Cairo neighborhoods and see signs carrying the name of al-Jamāʻa al-Islāmiyya.[61]

In the 1990's al-Jamāʻa al-Islāmiyya stepped up its military attacks, including Christians, tourists, politicians, and secular thinkers among its targets. It also assassinated the secular intellectual Faraj Foda in 1991 and attempted, unsuccessfully, to assassinate Nobel Prize laureate Naguib Mahfouz in 1994 and President Mubarak in 1995. In 1997 the group massacred more than fifty tourists at Luxor. In response, Mubarak has unrelentingly pursued militant groups, facilitated by the Emergency Law of 1981. By the late 1990's, the Egyptian state security apparatus had gained the upper hand against the militants.

Before 1997 a split appeared within al-Jamāʻa al-Islāmiyya over the issue of violence. Part of the group had already been leaning toward the idea of giving up violence. The Luxor attack gave power to the anti-violence faction, and the internal leadership of al-Jamāʻa al-Islāmiyya called for a cease-fire. In 2002 the group published a number of books called the Concept Correction Series.[62] Two further books were published in 2003.[63] In these books, the group renounced violence, extremism, the denouncing of fellow Muslims as non-Muslims, and the killing of civilians.[64] They argued that they had corrected their view of *jihād* and that such a correction was allowed in Islamic law.[65] Karam Zuhdī, the leader of al-Jamāʻa al-Islāmiyya, undertook a series of interviews in the newspaper *al-Sharq al-Awsat* and stated that Sadat had died a martyr.[66] Before 2003 there was considerable debate about whether these reforms could be trusted and about how many in the organization supported such a shift in policy. Some have argued that the renunciation of violence was designed to get many of the group's members released from prison and that it was only the intellectuals within the group—and not the rank and file—who held anti-violent views.[67]

Since the release of many of its members, however, the organization has continued to take a nonviolent approach. Karam Zuhdī and one thousand other members were released at the end of 2003. Usāma Hāfiz, the jurist of al-Jamāʿa al-Islāmiyya, was released in 2004, followed by forty other members in 2007. There are indications that the group is trying to enter mainstream Egyptian political life and provide social commentary for the community.[68] In 2006 the group launched a new Web site, which demonstrates considerable change in the organization's ideological stance: the sword has gone from its logo and it has denounced al-Qāʿida.[69] The new approach raises the question of whether the group can gain legitimacy and gather support when it has moved closer to the more mainstream Muslim Brotherhood.

Al-Jihād did not commit to a similar peace initiative until recently, although the extent to which the organization is still intact is uncertain. Experts on radical Islamism claim that it is not likely that al-Jihād members have regrouped in Egypt since the organization was decimated in the late 1990's.[70] All of the underground's original leaders are now in prison, in exile, or dead, and it is difficult to find members of al-Jihād on the streets. Since 9/11, the strategy of what is left of al-Jihād has changed from that of an internal fight against the state to a fight against Israel and the West.[71] While many of al-Jihād's members in Egypt are in prison, some of those outside Egypt have joined al-Qāʿida. In 2004 there were indications that certain of the group's key members, such as ʿAbbūd al-Zumur, would also announce an initiative to renounce violence. Al-Zumur has declared his commitment to the electoral process.[72] At the end of 2007 Sayyid Imam al-Sharīf, an Egyptian member of al-Jihād and a leading figure in the global *jihād* movement, published a book in which he called for a halt to *jihād* activities against the West and against ruling regimes in Muslim countries.[73] It is reported that the majority of the leaders and members of al-Jihād in Egyptian prisons have also promised to stop armed activities. Doubts, however, are being voiced about their sincerity.[74]

This renunciation of violence is a tentative indication that radical Islam within Egypt is retreating. One journalist argues that the regime continues to exaggerate the presence of radical groups for political reasons. While radical ideas exist among a minority of individuals, she says, they do not exist in an organized way.[75] The current regime has an interest in emphasizing the continued threat of radicalism to justify the continuation of the Emergency Law of 1981.[76] Despite this, there are indications that the group Takfīr wa al-Hijra (Charging with Unbelief and Holy Flight) still exists and has rejected the peace initiative.[77] In addition, though the infrastructure of these groups has been significantly weakened since 9/11, freelance *jihādīs*, radicalized by regional developments, have begun to act spontaneously. The war in Iraq has provided fertile soil for militant ideas, and thus armed groups like al-Jihād have to some extent been reinvigorated.[78] Recent terrorist attacks in downtown Cairo and Sharm al-Shaykh were likely perpetrated by small "groups of individuals with no clear affiliation to a larger hierarchically structured jihadist organisation."[79]

The extent to which radical Islamism has waned is impossible to assess in a society in which these groups cannot operate openly. However, the fact that such groups have renounced violence indicates that there has been a shift in public attitudes. Islamist violence and radical ideas such as pronouncing unbelief on the regime no longer have the powerful appeal they once had. For example, after the assassination of Sadat, there was considerable debate in the press about whether pronouncing unbelief on fellow Muslims was legitimate, but now the concept is much less of an issue than it was.

THE MUSLIM BROTHERHOOD

The Muslim Brotherhood has evolved into the most important—or, according to one scholar, the only viable—political opposition force in Egypt.[80] The contemporary Muslim Brotherhood derived from the "reformist wing" of the organization during Sadat's regime, which included such leaders as Hasan al-Hudaybī (supreme guide 1951–1973) and 'Umar al-Tilmisānī (supreme guide 1973–1986), who were both responsible for taking a more conciliatory approach to the regime.[81]

This wing of the Muslim Brotherhood adopted a nonviolent position after its members came to believe that their fate in Nasser's prisons resulted from their failure to proselytize their cause. 'Umar al-Tilmisānī distanced himself from Qutb's ideas, writing in 1982 that "Sayyid Qutb represented himself alone and not the Muslim Brethren."[82] The group saw progress toward an Islamist state as incremental and sought participation in political life in order to exert pressure for the application of the *sharī'a*. This commitment to a nonviolent approach has remained consistent and has been reinforced by Mustafā Mashhūr (supreme guide 1996–2002), Ma'mūn al-Hudaybī, (supreme guide 2002–2004), and Muhammad Mahdī 'Ākif (supreme guide 2004–2009).[83]

The Muslim Brotherhood has proved to be adept at penetrating Egyptian society by entering its economic fabric. This strategy has been a source of strength for the organization, especially since the 1990's, when extremist violence began to alienate the population. While the Brotherhood has mobilized support through offering social services to the poor—for example, after the earthquake of 1992—it is not as well represented among the working classes as it is among white-collar workers.[84]

The Muslim Brotherhood has also proved to be politically adept. The political language and rhetoric employed by the group today is much softer and more conciliatory than that of al-Da'wa in the early 1980's. Today's Muslim Brotherhood calls for the "democratic mechanisms of the modern civil state" and argues that such a state should be founded on justice and equity without discrimination based on color, race, or religion. Confident in its own political strength, it calls for freedom of expression and the freedom to form political parties. It calls for freedom of movement and travel. Importantly, it does not delegitimize the Egyptian state and asserts its "adherence to the state system as a republican, parliamentary, and constitutional system under the umbrella of the principles of Islam."[85] The Muslim Brotherhood demands full party status. It states that the "people are the source of all power" and affirms the right to "freedom of opinion" and the right to form political parties, hold public gatherings, and undertake peaceful demonstrations.[86]

President Mubarak has sporadically tolerated the Muslim Brotherhood's involvement in the political process, but he has never accepted the group as an official party. The government has intermittently tried to make it more difficult for the Muslim Brotherhood to participate in the political process, claiming that its members are connected to militant groups. Using the Emergency Law of 1981, Mubarak has arrested and imprisoned many Muslim Brotherhood members, and those who have been convicted in military courts cannot stand in elections as candidates. This includes a number of key figures who have parliamentary experience, such as the prominent Muslim Brotherhood figures 'Abd al-Mun'im Abū al-Futūh and 'Isām al-'Aryān. One of the constitutional amendments approved on March 26, 2007, bans religion-based political activity, which means that the Brotherhood is now a constitutionally banned group.

Despite many impediments, since 1984 the Muslim Brotherhood has participated in the political process by aligning itself with authorized parties. Ma'mūn al-Hudaybī (1921–2004), son of Supreme Guide Hasan al-Hudaybī and himself the Brotherhood's sixth supreme guide (2002–2004), was a key figure in pushing the Muslim Brotherhood to become involved in parliamentary politics and syndicate activities.[87]

This effort has enabled its members to win seats in the People's Assembly. Spearheaded by the younger generation of its members, the organization has infiltrated the media and the professional syndicates. As a result, it has captured the majority of seats in the syndicates and has competed successfully in the elections of student associations and university faculty clubs.[88]

Many argue that if there were free elections, the Muslim Brotherhood would achieve a majority in the People's Assembly, even though the National Democratic Party has a strong grip on the political process.[89] The elections for the People's Assembly in 2005 testify to the organization's popularity. The Muslim Brotherhood took 88 seats out of 454 (20 percent of the total) to form the largest opposition bloc. The next biggest opposition faction was the liberal Wafd, which gained just 7 seats. The Brotherhood achieved this outcome despite the regime's efforts to hamper the electoral process, including the arrest of hundreds of Muslim Brotherhood members. The success provoked a security clampdown: thousands of members were arrested, including Khayrat al-Shātir, chief strategist of the Guidance Office of the Muslim Brotherhood. In Egypt's Shura Council elections in 2007, electoral abuses included the arrest of Muslim Brotherhood members in key areas and the stuffing of ballot boxes. The Shura Council is a consultative body and its powers are much more limited than those of the People's Assembly. The turnout was low, and of the 88 seats that were up for election, 84 were won by Mubarak's party, the National Democratic Party. The security clampdown has had a detrimental impact on the Muslim Brotherhood. The sentencing of Khayrat al-Shātir to seven years' imprisonment in 2008, along with that of millionaire Hassan Malik, has weakened the group's financial infrastructure, which has in turn affected its ability to provide social services. Khayrat al-Shātir also played an important role in mobilizing and organizing the Muslim Brotherhood youth.[90] Muhammad Habīb, former deputy supreme guide, now argues that Muslim Brotherhood candidates are unlikely to win more than 10 seats in the 2010 parliamentary elections.[91]

There is no shortage in the secular press of criticism of the Muslim Brotherhood, including the criticism that the group is becoming increasingly rural, parochial, and therefore unquestioning in its style of management. It has been argued that its failure to participate in the April 6, 2008, strike meant that it doesn't appreciate the shift toward impromptu activism. Al-Ahram Weekly argues that its "conventional, if not totalitarian, politics" is a real barrier to the new type of activism and protest movements that are emerging.[92] However, the Muslim Brotherhood played a key role in the Gaza protests of early 2009.

One of the criticisms leveled at the Brotherhood is that it has not achieved much since its success in the People's Assembly.[93] Certainly it has not rushed to pass "Islamic" legislation. It seems that the group intends to refrain from pursuing a specifically Islamic agenda. Instead, it has focused on broad reforms to open up Egypt's political system, including attempts to end Egypt's Emergency Law, which severely limits political activity in the country. The Brotherhood also takes an interest in more religiously neutral issues such as health care, building codes, and aviation safety. The group emphasizes that its priority is not to gain control of the state but to advance reform by educating the people. Its plans for action broadly focus on consolidation.[94]

The emphasis upon reforming society stems from its legacy as a missionary movement. Older members of the Muslim Brotherhood have tended to embrace the idea of maintaining a pan-Islamic missionary orientation geared toward education and social work. This approach emphasizes that it would be a mistake to assume power now and make the state responsible for educating the people and that it is "impossible to deal with such problems as interest, banking, tourism, and the sale of alcohol before citizens reach 'full belief in the implementation of Allah's law.'"[95] However, the Muslim Brotherhood pragmatists, many of whom belong to the younger generation, have focused more on political action and have pushed for the development of a party platform, a draft of which was released in August 2007. After significant controversy stemming from the platform, former Supreme Guide Muhammad Mahdī 'Ākif halted any revisions to it, indicating that the Muslim Brotherhood has suspended any movement to separate the religious movement from the political party.[96] This approach has likely been consolidated with the election of the conservative Muhammad Badi' as supreme guide in early 2010.

Despite the fact that the Muslim Brotherhood calls for democracy, a number of critics do not believe that the group is committed to the democratic process, claiming that they talk about democracy only because they think that democracy will bring them to power. The secular and liberal camp in Egypt shares this fear. Some, such as the secretary general of the liberal Wafd Party, claim that the Muslim Brotherhood still supports terrorism.[97] A militia-style march by masked members of the Brotherhood outside al-Azhar in 2006 seemed to confirm this position. Many point to the undemocratic political culture of the organization's older and more conservative members. Mustafā Mashhūr (supreme guide 1996–

2002) emphasized the traditional outlook of the Muslim Brotherhood that refers to the "enemies of Islam." He supported Hasan al-Bannā's disapproval of Muslims' breaking into "groups and parties" and called for bringing the caliphate back.[98] In 2000 Ma'mūn al-Hudaybī, Mashhūr's successor and son of Supreme Guide Hasan al-Hudaybī, responded to the question of whether democracy is just a means of getting to power by stating: "How can we speak about getting to power while the Brotherhood are still in prison camps? Besides, with whom will we share power? It is a matter of one person ruling and the rest implementing! Who will really accept the participation of others?"[99] In 2003 Tharwat al-Kharabāwī, a member of the Muslim Brotherhood, broke with the organization and argued that the supreme guide at the time, Ma'mūn al-Hudaybī, dreamt of ruling Egypt.[100] Recently, however, the organization has tried to allay fears provoked by such statements, an effort led largely by the younger generation. Khayrat al-Shāṭir wrote an article in the British newspaper *The Guardian* titled "No Need to Be Afraid of Us."[101] Saad Eddin Ibrahim argues that a number of Muslim Brotherhood members are committed to democracy.[102]

Perhaps the question of whether the organization is democratic is best addressed in light of the ideological differences within the group. There are clear divisions among the current and former members of the Guidance Office—as well as among those closely associated with it—between those best described as pragmatists, who articulate more liberal ideas and are interested in good social policy, and conservatives. The former group includes 'Iṣām al-'Aryān, who was defeated in the elections by the Shura Council to the Guidance Office in May 2008 but is one of the organization's most important spokesmen, and 'Abd al-Mun'im Abū al-Futūh, a former member of the Guidance Office. The latter group is represented by Supreme Guide Muhammad Badi' (2010–), Muhammad Mursī, and Mahmūd 'Izzat.

Thus, rather than interpreting ideological inconsistencies as duplicity on the part of the Muslim Brotherhood, one should view the group as a complex organization with competing and conflicting visions. It is "a dynamic movement. It has differences; it has different groups; it has different factions. And it is able to debate different opinions, a plurality of opinions in an open way."[103] The organization is decentralized, and the demands that are articulated at the top are the result of particular struggles within it. Currently conservatives from the provinces are the more powerful group within the Guidance Office.[104] The pragmatists suffered a setback with the arrest of Khayrat al-Shāṭir in December 2006, but according to one academic, it is more likely that the pragmatists will nevertheless win out in the long term, because of their more inclusive model for governing.[105]

There is also an important—and rising—constituency made up of younger students who have been particularly active since the end of 2006. They bring to the group their experience with university politics and the ability to spearhead Web-based initiatives (including an English-language Web site).[106] Such activities point to a generational divide within the organization. It is assumed that the old guard is considerably less democratic than the new. Though this assumption may be true, the divide should not be exaggerated, since some of the people in their forties are very conservative and only about 15 percent of the students are reformers. The other students and younger members tend to be out in the provinces and are more conservative.[107]

While the Muslim Brotherhood is the major political representative of what could be described—albeit inadequately—as mainstream Islam, mainstream Islam is also represented by a number of popular preachers, among whom a shift toward the more conciliatory and pragmatic approach in the 1990's can also be identified. In the 1980's, Emmanuel Sivan referred to these preachers as the "conservative periphery" that "shares basic beliefs with the hardcore and collaborates with it in various realms of life."[108] Representatives of this position included Shaykh Kishk (1933–1996), Muhammad al-Sha'rāwī (1911–1998), and Muhammad al-Ghazālī (1917–1996) (who, at the time, had strong tendencies toward radical Islam but no official affiliation), as well as 'Umar 'Abd al-Kāfī and the Alexandrian preacher Ahmed al-Mahallāwī.

Such preachers do not belong to organized Islamist groups, but they have considerable power and influence. Their images adorn walls, and cassette tapes of their sermons are played in shops, in taxis, and on street corners. Their popularity stems in part from their choice of medium. Charles Hirschkind argues that the cassette sermon has been a popular cultural medium that is "entertaining, politically informative, educational, and ethically nourishing," forming an integral part of the Islamic revival and providing a technology for that revival.[109] After the 1970's, the cassette tape emerged as an important "arena of popular Islamic argumentation and deliberation among ordinary Egyptian Muslims," or what Hirschkind describes as an "Islamic counterpublic."[110]

Many of the Islamic preachers have been affiliated with both official state institutions and Islamic opposition groups like the Muslim Brotherhood, reflecting the porous nature of the boundaries between "official" and "popular" Islam. One such legendary Islamic preacher was Shaykh Kishk, who employed a populist and theatrical preaching style that was distinct from Azhari sermons. His sermons, which were originally delivered to large audiences, were recorded, copied, and widely distributed. By the mid-1970's, his "taped sermons had become a ubiquitous part of the Cairene soundscape, his sharp criticisms of the Sadat regime echoing from stores, taxis, and buses, and private balconies and living rooms throughout the popular quarters." Kishk was a graduate of al-Azhar and worked for the Ministry of Religious Affairs, but he also was a staunch critic of the Egyptian government, which led to two periods of imprisonment. His popularity was illustrated by the 10,000 to 20,000 people who attended his mosque at his funeral.

Another pioneer of the use of cassette sermons in the 1970's and 1980's, who also spent time in prison, was the renowned preacher Ahmed al-Mahallāwī, whose mosque came to be identified by those who frequented it as a "counter state."[111]

Unlike Kishk, the popular preacher Muhammad al-Shaʿrāwī was an established celebrity who appeared on the state-run radio and television broadcasting recitations and Qurʾanic commentaries. Al-Shaʿrāwī was tolerated by the regime since he did not preach overthrow of the government. According to Hirschkind, "Shaykh Shaʿrawi's popularity must be understood in light of his status as a state-promoted religious figure, one deployed precisely to counter the oppositional impetus of the popular Islamic Revival *khutaba'*."[112]

Muhammad al-Ghazālī was also a popular preacher who was tolerated by the regime. One of the most important Egyptian Islamist thinkers of the twentieth century, al-Ghazālī had a long and prolific writing and preaching career that continued until his death in 1996. His popularity is in part due to the fact that being a graduate of al-Azhar and a member of the Muslim Brotherhood, he was able to straddle populist and official Islam. Al-Ghazālī was a disciple of Hasan al-Bannā in the late 1940's and 1950's. He then allied with the state against organized Islamic activism, but in the 1970's he renewed his alliance with the Muslim Brotherhood.[113] Ibrahim M. Abu-Rabiʿ argues that he is one of the few people who "stand out for having exerted lasting influence on the theoretical foundations of the thought of" the Muslim Brotherhood.[114] A similar trajectory toward a more conciliatory interpretation of Islam can be found in his work.

Another example of this ideological shift is Yūsuf al-Qaraḍāwī (1926–), who is perhaps one of the most important Islamic thinkers of current times. In 2009 he was the chairman of the International Union of Muslim Scholars

(IMUS). Like al-Ghazālī, al-Qaradāwī is powerful and popular because of his ability to relate to both sides, the populist Islamism of the Muslim Brotherhood and the "official" Islam of al-Azhar, of which he is a graduate. His contemporary ideas on non-Muslims are significantly more moderate than the ideas he expressed in the 1980's.

THE EMERGENCE OF THE ISLAMIC MODERATES

The most significant example of this shift within Islamism is the emergence of a group of intellectuals that Raymond Baker has described as the "New Islamists."[115] They are also known as the Wasatiyya intellectuals, meaning centrist or moderate, from the word *wasat* (center). The movement is also referred to as the centrist Islamic trend.[116] The term *wasatiyya* itself is relatively new. These Islamists originally saw themselves as independent Islamists—i.e., Islamists who defend the Islamic cause but do not have political associations. They are free from any associations with al-Azhar or political parties. The epithet *wasatiyya* became more popular, especially since the idea of moderation represented a refutation of radical Islam.[117]

This group includes the writers Fahmī Huwaydī (1936–), Tāriq al-Bishrī (1933–), Muhammad ʿImāra (1931–), and Muhammad Salīm al-ʿAwwā. They have produced a body of literature that advocates the establishment of Islamic law, but in a conciliatory and flexible manner. They discuss values such as pluralism, democracy, and human rights, and issues such as the rights of minorities and women. According to the Coptic intellectual Samīr Murqus, their exploration of the concept of citizenship has made an important contribution to modern Islamic thought.[118]

Many of these writers are former Stalinists or Communists who shifted to Islamism in the late 1970's and early 1980's.[119] They are writers with strong nationalist sympathies who seek to synthesize elements of nationalist ideology and Islam. They argue that the Western nationalist experiment has failed and that a combination of inclusive nationalist ideas with Islam is the answer for Egypt's political community.[120] They represent a sincere intellectual trend and a strong intellectual force, although they do not have much popular appeal. While they do not constitute a group with grassroots support, they are widely read among the intellectual elite. One of their strengths is that because they are not politically active in a direct way, they do not threaten the government and are therefore able to operate openly.

The impact of their ideas has been considerable and is growing. They have had a significant influence on the pragmatists within the Muslim Brotherhood, who refer to their ideas with respect. The organization frequently invites them to attend seminars and events. They have also had an influence on the al-Wasat Party, which was formed in the 1990's by some disillusioned younger former members of the Muslim Brotherhood and non-Muslim intellectuals from the same generation as Muslim Brotherhood members ʿAbd al-Munʿim Abū al-Futūh and Khayrat al-Shātir, representing an ideological shift toward a more moderate Islamism. The party's platform indicates willingness to deal with more concrete questions such as democracy and the rights of women and non-Muslims. The party has given up missionary activity.[121]

The formation of al-Wasat is linked to the Muslim Brotherhood's syndicate activities, which allowed members of the Muslim Brotherhood who formed al-Wasat to "gain an independent political base from the Brotherhood while allowing them to develop into Islamist politicians." These members felt that the Brotherhood was heavily centralized and that decisions were made by a small group.[122] There has been considerable tension between the Brotherhood and al-Wasat, notably between Maʾmūn al-Hudaybī, a former supreme guide, Abū al-ʿIlā Mādī, the party's leader, and ʿIsām Sultān, a lawyer and another prominent member of al-Wasat. Sultān has accused al-Hudaybī of not believing in democracy or humanity and of working to establish a dictatorship.[123]

The dispute caused a split in 1996, when a group of Muslim Brotherhood members resigned and applied for legal party status under the al-Wasat title. Most of the founding members of al-Wasat were former members of the Brotherhood, and as such they found that their application was denied; subsequently a number of them returned to the Brotherhood.[124] Al-Wasat has tried to achieve legal party status with the Political Parties Committee, but its attempts have been rejected. Nevertheless, the organization is known as Hizb al-Wasat (the al-Wasat Party). Of its 93 founding members, 24 were former Muslim Brotherhood members, including Abū al-ʿIlā Mādī, the party's leader, and prominent members ʿAbd al-Karīm and ʿIsām Sultān; 3 were Christians, including the Coptic intellectual Rafīq Habīb; and 19 were female.[125] However, the success of al-Wasat has been limited. The party faces an important dilemma in terms of how it can differentiate itself from the pragmatists within the Muslim Brotherhood. The shift of the Muslim Brotherhood to the left has considerably narrowed the sphere within which it can make an ideological impact, although the Muslim Brotherhood's recent reversal of their shift may render this less of an issue.

WHAT DO THE ISLAMISTS WANT?

It has been shown that the majority of Islamists have shifted toward accepting the legality of the Egyptian state and working within it. This change has taken place concurrently with the shift toward the Islamization of the state and society, raising the question of what contemporary Egyptian Islamists want and what they mean by an Islamic state.

The 1980 amendment to the constitution, which made *sharī'a* the principal source of legislation, resulted in some judges' ruling according to *sharī'a* rather than civil law. In 1975 the authority of al-Azhar's Islamic Research Academy was expanded to inspect all that is written about Islam. In May 1980 the National Assembly approved a law stipulating that opposing religious doctrines and inciting young people to defy religious and moral values were punishable offenses. Egyptian society became more and more outwardly and self-consciously Islamic, with religious symbols such as the veil and religious discourse referring to Islam becoming more visible. For example, Sadat declared that he was a Muslim president of a Muslim state.[126]

While Sadat encouraged the Islamization process, Mubarak has taken a more contradictory approach. Upon coming to power, Mubarak soon renounced his commitment to Islamization of the law.[127] For example, many of the parliamentary bills on alcohol proposed by the members of the Muslim Brotherhood have been rejected. Statements such as that of Prime Minister Ahmad Nazif that "Egypt is a secular state" seem to indicate Mubarak's opposition to Islamization of the law.[128]

However, the Egyptian government has always voiced its commitment to Islamic values. This position has involved giving al-Azhar dramatically increased powers of censorship,[129] and the number of banned books and other materials indicates the growing influence of Islamism,[130] resulting in a serious decline in freedom of opinion and expression. Mubarak has also used Islam as a tool of mobilization and a source of legitimacy.

The regime's approach has been contradictory and confusing. In the words of one Egyptian journalist, "The government has a kind of schizophrenic relationship vis-à-vis Islam."[131] In early 2007, during the debates over the constitutional amendments, the regime stressed that Article 2 does "not mean that Egypt is either a religious state or a secular state, but a democratic civil state that respects all its citizens and their religion, as Islam commands."[132]

Thwarted by the Mubarak regime, Islamists have resorted to the courts as an avenue to push for Islamization. However, attempts to make Egypt's

European-based civil and criminal codes comply with traditional Islamic law were blocked by the Supreme Constitutional Court, which held that constitutional change was not retroactive and that the constitutional amendment that stated that the principles of *sharī'a* are the major source of legislation was addressed solely to parliament as a guide in its legislative authority.[133] Nevertheless, in 1985 the Supreme Constitutional Court stipulated that Article 2 requires all Egyptian legislation enacted after the amendment to be consistent with the principles of Islamic *sharī'a*. As a result, the Supreme Constitutional Court has developed a body of jurisprudence relating to Article 2 and has upheld some laws as consistent with the principles of the *sharī'a* and struck other laws down as inconsistent.[134] Clark Lombardi illustrates that the Supreme Constitutional Court's interpretation of the *sharī'a* has been in line with liberal constitutionalism and the liberal rule of law. He argues that it has drawn on modernist theories of Islamic law while avoiding "taking a clear position on some of the most controversial issues of legal theory."[135] As a result, the "so-called return to the Shariah should be viewed as the invention of a new Shariah in the contemporary political, legal, and judicial setting."[136]

One of the most famous and obvious instances of the encroachment of Islamic law on Egypt's modern legal system was the case involving the secular intellectual Nasr Abū Zayd (1943–). Abū Zayd was forcibly divorced from his wife on the grounds that his views on the Qur'an as a literary work had rendered him an apostate. This was after *hisbā* (literally, "bringing to account"), a lawsuit that can be initiated by any Muslim to protect Islam, was taken out in reference to Abū Zayd. In 1982 one judge passed a ruling based on the penal provisions of the *sharī'a* for drinking, although this judgment was reversed.[137]

The existence of Article 2 means that Islamists generally accept that Egypt is a legitimate Islamic state, because Islam is the official religion of the state and the *sharī'a* is the main source of the law.[138] The Muslim Brotherhood argues that when something is against the *sharī'a*, one can appeal to the Supreme Constitutional Court.[139] 'Abd al-Mun'im Abū al-Futūh argues that while there are some aspects of the *sharī'a* that are not applied, you cannot question that Egypt is in fact an Islamic state.[140]

So what are the political and legal aims of the Muslim Brotherhood? For a long time, the organization's literature was plagued by imprecision and looked more like missionary literature than a political platform. It called for "consolidating the doctrine of monotheism," establishing an "Islamic country," and renewing calls for *jihād* and missionary activity.[141] Establishing the Islamic *sharī'a* as the basis for the affairs of state and society was and continues to be central to the agenda.[142]

There have been more and more demands, mainly from secular circles, but even from former Muslim Brotherhood members, for the Brotherhood to articulate a more specific political program.[143] To a certain extent, the organization has begun to respond. The Muslim Brotherhood's platform of 2004 was more concrete and oriented to contemporary political issues.

The platform focuses on what is wrong with the status quo more than on what an Islamic state would actually involve. It calls for making Egypt's laws conform to Article 2, with the implication that this must be retroactive and involve the cancellation of current laws that contradict the *sharī'a*. This would include, it states, the banning of usury, encouraging the spirit of being religious, preserving public manners, and respecting the nation's foundations.[144] It is to be expected, therefore, that the Muslim Brotherhood would push for the enforcement of *sharī'a* law, including, for example, the Islamic penal code, along with instituting dress codes and other laws related to public morality. In the 1990's the Muslim Brotherhood filed a series of lawsuits demanding a ban on broadcasting certain television programs, films, and advertisements. Since 1988 Muslim Brotherhood deputies have been submitting bills criminalizing alcohol and stating that offenders should be subject to the lash.

What is notable is that the changes that the Muslim Brotherhood wishes to make do not entail overturning existing institutions. Ma'mūn al-Hudaybī argues that the Muslim Brotherhood would utilize existing state institutions. He sees the Islamic principle of *shurā* (consultation) as being fulfilled in a parliamentary council with effective legislative and supervisory authority.[145] For example, the Muslim Brotherhood does not want the return of *sharī'a* courts. While Islamists want the application of *sharī'a* law, many of them are trained in the Western system and "are reluctant to follow that path as far as the restoration of *sharī'a* courts and procedures, and of jurists' law in place of state law as that would render them redundant."[146]

Since its success in 2005, the Brotherhood has not been aggressive in pushing for the implementation of Islamic law. Instead it has been working to create a commitment to Islam among the people before changing the actual law. Indeed, most of its current concerns are not specifically Islamic. While the Muslim Brotherhood aspires for an Islamic order, like any other opposition group, it is concerned with corruption and the undemocratic practices of the government. It seeks not only to facilitate a larger role for religion, but to reform Egyptian government and society.

This focus is illustrated by the organization's 2004 platform, which called for an end to the abuse of power and the illegal amassing of personal fortunes. Materialistic values, poverty, and the poor upbringing of children were mentioned as concerns.[147] The platform also called for political freedom, for the exclusion of the army from politics, and for security services to be used to preserve the security of the state and society rather than that of the government. It also called for limiting the powers of the president, canceling the Emergency Law, eliminating torture, enforcing the independence of the judiciary, and limiting the jurisdiction of military courts to military personnel.[148]

In the summer of 2007, the Muslim Brotherhood issued a draft party platform, although these revisions were halted by former Supreme Guide Muhammad Mahdī 'Ākif. The platform marked an important step toward establishing a political party, indicating that it had been spearheaded by the pragmatists. This was a significant but temporary change in the party's strategy, since the conservatives have been opposed to the establishment of a party, arguing that it goes against the legacy of Hasan al-Bannā.

The platform was divided into sections that dealt with the movement's principles, the state and the political system, education, economic policy and development, religion and society, and cultural revival. It reaffirmed Article 2 and called for reform with *shurā* (consultation) as the essence of democracy. The platform, in many respects, indicated that it was strongly influenced by the pragmatists, because of statements in its text that referred to "freedom," "humanitarian heritage," "citizens," and "civil society."[149] However, there were some controversial statements in the platform, including a statement that the principle frame of reference for *sharī'a* would be the consensus of a body of Islamic jurisprudents who would be limited to interpreting the Qur'an and the Sunna.[150] There were indications that this statement was put in by the conservatives—as a calculated move to make more reference to the *sharī'a*—without sufficient consultation with other members of the Guidance Office and beyond.[151] The pragmatists of the Brotherhood were uncomfortable with the amount of power the platform gave to the religious scholars.[152] The platform was criticized vehemently in the press, which accused the Muslim Brotherhood of seeking to establish an Iranian-style clerical state.[153] Since then the platform has been on hold, indicating a halt in the attempt to move toward establishing a political party. The issue illustrates that the Muslim

Brotherhood is evolving ideologically and that at present there is considerable fluidity regarding its political positions.

CONCLUSION

The Muslim Brotherhood platform of 2007 illustrates that the agenda of mainstream and moderate Islamists has evolved into one that largely accepts the legitimacy of the nation-state and its current institutions. It does not mention overhauling the current system but speaks of reforming and restoring the balance of power and of fully implementing the constitution. Since the 1970's, Islamism has moved away from its radical and rejecting position and toward working within the context of the current nation-state. The ideology of the contemporary Muslim Brotherhood is more pragmatic than that of Hasan al-Bannā, who called for the reestablishment of the caliphate.

A central part of the Islamist worldview established by al-Bannā aimed at reversing the sense of dislocation and disruption that was felt to have occurred in the late nineteenth and early twentieth centuries with the process of secularization. While there was more continuity than is often allowed for, Egypt had undergone considerable social and political flux, most notably with the implementation of Western law and the establishment of the modern nation-state. These changes included a reconfiguration of the relationship between non-Muslims and the state, whereby the concept of citizenship established a direct relationship between the state and non-Muslims. While this change brought some legal liberation, non-Muslim communities lost some of their autonomy.

At the same time, this discontinuity was accompanied by some continuity: separate personal status law for Muslims and non-Muslims was maintained, emphasizing that religious identity is central to Egypt's social structure. However, the establishment of the category of personal status law marked a transmutation of *sharī'a*, since *sharī'a* came to be equated with personal status law for regulating "the family," a modern institution built around the married couple.[154] Nasser's abolition of the *sharī'a* and *millet* courts and his centralization of the legal system created significant complexities in the Egyptian legal system. Vestiges of the *millet* in the context of a centralized nation-state raise questions about the relationship between citizenship and religious identity.

The sense of dislocation and disruption that occurred with the implementation of Western law—albeit perhaps somewhat retroactively—was, in part, mollified by the constitutional amendment of 1980 that the principles of Islamic *sharī'a* are the major source of legislation. On account of Article 2, most Islamists now accept that Egypt is an Islamic state and work within the context of the Egyptian nation-state. However, most Islamists also feel that the current system is not one in which Islamic law is fully applied and that there is a disconnection between the constitution and the actual implementation of the law. While Islamists agree in wishing to further Islamize state and society, they differ in their vision of an Islamic state and what the full implementation of Islamic law would entail. The question of what kind of Islamic order these Islamists want and how this relates to the current status quo—in particular, what implications this has for non-Muslims—is therefore gaining increasing relevance in the current political debate.

3 NON-MUSLIMS AND THE EGYPTIAN STATE

WHEN SHARĪʿA ELEMENTS in the Ottoman legal system gave way to the encroaching influence of codified Western law, family and personal status laws, where the *sharīʿa* traditionally had been most fully applied, were left in place. Thus the modern Egyptian legal system retained vestiges of the *millet* system in the form of what became known as personal status law. This has created a complex situation with respect to the rights and the role of non-Muslims in contemporary Egypt. Any analysis of contemporary Islamic views on the role of non-Muslims must be situated within the context of what legal position non-Muslims occupy. Islamist articulations of tolerance, pluralism, and citizenship are formed within a particular context, and they do not, on the whole, seek to radically alter that context. Thus the following questions are relevant for an analysis of this discourse: What rights do non-Muslims, particularly Coptic Christians but also other non-Muslims, including Bahāʾīs, have according to the Egyptian Constitution? What is the relationship between religious identity and Egyptian identity? How do Copts understand their role in the Egyptian state?

The rights of non-Muslims in the Egyptian Constitution and in Egyptian law are based on a mixture of secular and Islamic law. While the Egyptian state has a codified—largely Western-based—legal system, some of the rules and values of the *sharīʿa* are often taken into account, according to Article 2 of the constitution. The extent to which Egypt is understood to be either a "secular" or an "Islamic state"—or a complex mixture of both—is a deeply contested and politically charged issue, which is why the Coptic issue is central both to how the Egyptian state defines itself and to Islamist opposition to the state. An examination of a number of key incidents concerning relations among the state, the Islamists, and the Copts illustrates how the role of non-Muslims is connected to the relationship of Islamists with the state. This relationship is important in shaping the way the state defines itself vis-à-vis the presence of political Islam and the way Islamists define themselves vis-à-vis the state.

Rather than viewing Copts as victims or subjects of the Islamist agenda, as is often assumed, this chapter illustrates that the twentieth century has seen a revival in Coptic cultural nationalism centered on the political authority of the Coptic Orthodox Church. This development has important implications for the political involvement of Copts, for their identification as Egyptian citizens, and for how Islamists perceive their role in the Egyptian state.

COPTIC CULTURAL NATIONALISM

Discussing the Coptic issue as if the Copts constitute an identifiable community is fraught with difficulty. It has been argued that a community is a "social group that has in common a national or ethnic, professional, or religious origin and that has a leader or a head."[1] The question of representation reflects the complexities surrounding how the category of religion should be used. In addition, the term "Copt" is used in different ways. For some, being Coptic is more than simply a religious designation. Many articulate the terms "Coptic" and "Copt" with cultural and sometimes ethnic connotations, emphasizing that the term "Copt" derives from the Greek word *Aigyptos*, meaning "Egypt" and that the identity of Copts is intricately bound up with Egyptian identity, Egyptian history, and Egyptian culture. In reaction to the connotation of separateness that this position sometimes evokes, some Copts might identify themselves as Egyptian or Christian but not as Copt.[2]

It would also be a mistake to assume that membership in a religious community is necessarily a voluntary matter. While Magdi Guirguis argues that the term "'Coptic community' was appropriate in relation to the nature and philosophy of the Ottoman state which gave much weight to the community system as an intermediary through which the state dealt with society," he does so with some reservations. Guirguis illustrates that in the Ottoman period there were Copts who had no relation to religion or to the church.[3] The same is somewhat true today, although the current personal status law structure demands that Copts be defined as Christian. Just as there was a struggle between the church and the secular elite for leadership in the Ottoman period, a similar struggle continues today, with many Copts resisting

the church's move to represent them politically. The term "Coptic community" has a certain heuristic validity in that it is often used both by Copts
themselves and by Egypt's Muslims. Indeed, many Copts self-identify as a
separate community and emphasize the cultural and sometimes racial differences between Copts and Muslims, although others resist this position,
insisting that the emphasis upon difference is dangerous and that all Copts
and Muslims are Egyptians.

On many grounds it is erroneous to speak of a Coptic community. First,
Copts are extremely diverse from a socioeconomic perspective. They can be
found among the garbage collectors of Cairo and among the most wealthy
businessmen. Their social and political concerns are influenced as much by
their social and economic status as by their religious identity. Numerous different factions can be identified among Copts. There are Coptic radicals and
some human rights activists who tend to be uncompromising about Islam
and believe that change from within Arab-Islamic society is impossible. Such
Copts often employ varying types of polemical discourse. This uncompromising position can be found among the Coptic clergy and Coptic expatriates.
There are also Copts who emphasize the importance of dialogue with Muslims and participate in all political parties, although they tend to be secular Copts. There are still other Copts, many of them members of the Coptic
Church, who believe that the future of Oriental Christians lies in the Islamic
world and reject the secular atmosphere of the West.[4]

While the Coptic community is extremely diverse, the Copts as a religious
minority are referred to and discussed as a category within Egyptian political
debate. Copts also share some common issues. For example, they are united
in their concern about political Islam, the establishment of an Islamic state,
and the application of Islamic law. However, they hold varying views on how
these concerns should be addressed.

While literature on the religious revival of the latter half of the twentieth century has focused on the Islamic resurgence, a similar revival can be
identified among Copts, who since the 1952 Revolution have retreated from
the political sphere and have evidenced an increased religiosity. It has been
customary to see this as a product of the Islamization process. Such an interpretation juxtaposes Islamization with the secularism of the interwar period,
commonly referred to as a golden age for Copts, in which the secular Coptic
elite participated in the political sphere. This sense of national unity was symbolized in the 1919 Revolution when Muslims and Copts united against the

British. The golden age was undermined by the shift to Islamic themes in the 1930's and by the rise of sectarian tension in the 1940's.

While this characterization is true, it would be a mistake to see the reassertion of Coptic identity as simply a product of Egypt's Islamization. In fact, the revival of the Coptic Orthodox Church has its own internal factors; it is not simply the result of a reaction to political Islam.[5] The reform of the church and the increase in ethno-religious consciousness began with what is known as the Sunday School Movement, which had its origins among the clergy in the nineteenth century. Pope Kyrillos IV (1854–1861) tried to reform the church to counteract the influence of foreign, mostly Protestant, missionaries. He also tried to halt the dismantling of the *millet* system. The pope's reforms included the establishment of four modern schools with Western curricula, one of which was the first school for girls, to provide an alternative to missionary schools. A patriarchal college was also established.

However, these attempts at reform were set aside after Pope Kyrillos's death.[6] While the first Sunday schools were founded by laymen in 1898, it was not until the 1940's and 1950's that the reform movement of the church through the Sunday School Movement accelerated. The movement was largely led by educated laymen drawn from new urban upper-class university graduates of the 1940's and 1950's. They used the church as an outlet for their reform project. The movement emphasized Coptic identity based on indigenous cultural traditions, including legendary local figures. These educated laymen criticized the church patriarchs and wanted to moderate what they saw as a backward institution.[7] Many of them entered the patriarchal college, among them Nazīr Gayyid, who became the steward of the Sunday School Movement and went on to become Pope Shenouda III in 1971.[8]

In 1947 Gayyid became editor in chief of the *Sunday School Magazine*, which focused on church reform. The movement was becoming integrated into the church and provided the nucleus for reform.[9] At this time, a dissenting radical nonclerical group called the Coptic Nation (al-Umma al-Qibtiyya) was formed. It demanded the separation of religion and state in Egypt, although there are also indications that it imitated the Muslim Brotherhood and demanded a separate Coptic state.[10] The group's motto was "God is the king of the Copts, Egypt their country, the Gospels their law, and the Cross their insignia."[11] It aimed at reviving the Coptic language, and in 1916 the newspaper *al-Watan* suggested that the Copts reject Arabic and use Coptic again.[12] It also opposed the Orthodox religious establishment: in 1954 the Coptic Nation kidnapped and deposed Pope Yousab II (1946–1956). The group was dissolved shortly thereafter.[13] The *Sunday School Magazine* did not criticize the kidnapping, possibly indicating that Gayyid sympathized with the movement.[14]

In the 1950's President Nasser's policies strengthened the growth of Coptic cultural nationalism. Nasser's policy of land redistribution weakened the Coptic elite and led to a reduction in political participation for Muslims and Copts.[15] Before nationalization, Copts owned 75 percent of transport services, 44 percent of industry, 51 percent of banks, and 34 percent of agricultural land.[16] Like Egyptian Muslims, the Coptic community also experienced a surge in religious feeling after the defeat of 1967. In 1968 the Virgin Mary was seen at Zaytoun, a northern suburb of Cairo. It was believed that she had appeared to Egyptians to restore their faith in God and give hope to the defeated.[17] A boom in the construction of churches followed, and many new benevolent funds were created, some with money from Coptic emigrants abroad. There was also a surge in the number of Copts who became monks.

The Islamization process initiated by Sadat in the 1970's reinforced this trend and undermined the development of secular citizenship that had occurred in the interwar period. The political process became more religious and marginalized the Copts. There were more and more writings that discussed the position of Islam toward the *dhimmīs*.[18]

During this period, under the leadership of Pope Shenouda III (1971–), the Coptic Church emerged as the effective political representative of Coptic concerns and clashed with the state. In January 1977 the church convened a Christian religious conference, which issued a statement demanding that officials stop considering applying the *sharīʿa* to non-Muslims. It demanded an end to restrictions on the building of churches, an end to discrimination in high state positions, and the freedom to publish books on Christian history and heritage. These demands went unanswered. In March 1980 Pope Shenouda issued a statement objecting to Article 2 of the constitution, which states that the principles of *sharīʿa* law are the major source of legislation, and expressing anxiety that religion was replacing Egyptian nationalism.[19]

In response, Sadat initiated an anti-Coptic campaign. He declared that Pope Shenouda was planning to establish a Coptic state in Upper Egypt with Asyut as its capital.[20] S. S. Hasan argues that while such an accusation was not strictly wrong, Sadat failed to understand that this nation was not to be a geographical entity. Rather, the Copts were establishing a separate religio-cultural nation.[21] Pope Shenouda refused to pledge his loyalty to the regime, marking the end of the *millet* partnership. Pope Shenouda's predecessor, Pope Kyrillos VI (1959–1971), had based his relations with Nasser on the *millet* partnership by presenting the concerns of the community to Nasser and promoting Coptic loyalty to the regime. In return, he could expect the state to protect the Coptic community and to consider him the Copts' legitimate spokesman.[22] In response to Shenouda's statement, Sadat reminded the church that "he was a Muslim ruler of an Islamic country and that he would oppose any attempt to dilute the Islamic identity of Egypt."[23] In September 1981 Sadat arrested twenty-two priests and bishops and canceled the decree that had appointed Pope Shenouda.

This action served to reinforce the emergence of Pope Shenouda as the political leader of the Copts. Under him, the church has used the emphasis upon religious identity "to outbid the state for the loyalty of its beleaguered Christian citizens."[24] It is a position that Pope Shenouda makes no apology for, arguing that "the state can deal with one person and reach a result, rather than dealing with millions of persons, especially when it knows that those millions will listen to the word of the Pope."[25] In the presidential elections of 2005, Pope Shenouda supported President Mubarak, and many Copts followed suit. The extent to which Copts depend on the political advice of the church was illustrated during Munīr Fakhrī ʿAbd al-Nūr's first but unsuccessful run for the People's Assembly in 1995. ʿAbd al-Nūr, secretary general of the liberal secular Wafd Party, asked a Coptic pharmacist to vote for him and received the reply "I have to go back to the priest and he will give me the instructions."[26] It is frequently claimed that Copts are politically passive. These complaints generally come from the prominent secular political families of the 1930's and 1940's.[27]

The political leadership of Pope Shenouda has coincided with a growing sense of Coptic nationalism or ethnic consciousness. The younger generation of Copts increasingly emphasizes a religiously nationalistic sense of identity.[28] Hasan refers to this as "Coptic cultural nationalism," with clergy thinking of the Copts as a nation and referring to "Shaʿbina (our people)" or "al-Umma al-Qibtiyya (the Coptic nation)."[29] The kind of sentiment expressed by the radical group the Coptic Nation became more pronounced in the Sadat era. Some Copts emphasized that they were not Arabs but the true and pure descendants of pharaohs.[30] Despite the political explosiveness of such sentiments, they are still embraced by some church members. In 2007 Bishop Murqus of the Marī Girgis Church in the Cairene suburb of Shubra al-Khayma, former spokesman for Pope Shenouda and secretary of the Information Committee in the Coptic

Orthodox Church, stated that "Copts are the sons of Egypt and its proprietors."[31] In 2008 Bishop Thomas of al-Qussia in Upper Egypt made a presentation to the Hudson Institute in which he delineated a firm distinction between Coptic identity and Arab identity. He asked of Egypt's Muslims, "Are [they] really Copts or have they really become Arabs?" arguing that Muslims have adopted an "imported identity."[32] This attitude of separation is emphasized by many expatriate Copts, who lobby in support of Egypt's Copts from abroad through monetary contributions—including raising money in American churches during times of sectarian tension in Egypt—and by exerting political pressure.[33]

Secular Copts reject Coptic cultural nationalism. Munīr Fakhrī 'Abd al-Nūr and Samīr Murqus, who is a Coptic intellectual and frequently writes on Coptic affairs, stress that they are first and foremost Egyptians.[34] They emphasize Egyptian identity and argue that talking about the Copts as a separate community or a religious minority undermines the concept of citizenship and harms national unity.[35] They are critical of the church's involvement in politics. 'Abd al-Nūr describes the political role of Pope Shenouda as "catastrophic," since it means that Copts are perceived as a religious minority rather than as citizens of the Egyptian state.[36] Yūsuf Sidhum, who is the editor of the Coptic newspaper *al-Watanī*, says that such an approach is "political suicide" and that a secular state can never be possible as long as the Copts ask the church to represent them in front of the state. Copts, he argues, should never be represented by one political party.[37] The U.S. Copts Association is also critical of the fact that the church has emerged as the political representative of the Copts. Michael Munīr of that organization argues that while the state in many respects forced the church to emerge as the Copts' representative, many of the representatives of the church enjoy this role.[38] Secular Copts are not the only ones who are critical of the emergence of the church's political role. Monks from the monastery of Macarius also decry the church's involvement in politics.[39] Father Mattā al-Miskīn (1919–2006), spiritual director of the monastery, argued against the church's concern with politics. Many church members also criticize Pope Shenouda's authoritarian leadership style.[40]

While some are convinced that Pope Shenouda seeks to control the political life of Copts, others are not so condemnatory.[41] The argument is made that Pope Shendouda stepped into this role because there were no laymen to do so. In the 1970's, there was no secular elite to take on the leadership of the Copts during a turbulent time. For Muslims, political opposition became centered on the mosque, and it is therefore natural that Copts became focused on the church. In the view of Yūsuf Sidhum, editor of *al-Watanī*, the actions of the church were appropriate at that time but they are no longer so; the church is like a mother who naturally protects her baby but continues to do so when that baby becomes a teenager.[42] The church has defended itself against accusations that it wants to become a political representative of the Copts. Bishop Thomas says if "the church stays silent, who will demand their [Copts'] rights?"[43]

Similar arguments are made concerning the social services that the church provides for Christians, especially Christian youth. Among those services are private classes to supplement the substandard classes at public schools, child care, health care, and social activities such as picnics, sports, and plays. While some secular Copts argue that the church is happy to control Christian youth, the church's position is that it is filling a gap and that if the state provided social services the church would not have to.[44]

Regardless of the reason, the availability of such services has meant that the public space has become increasingly confessional. Thus, while sectarianism is not a policy, it is informally embedded. Copts and Muslims publicly express their religious identity. One indication of this is that specifically Muslim and Christian names are becoming more popular.[45] Reports of people being asked what their religion is have increased. There has also been a rise in the use of religious symbols, such as bumper stickers on cars, as identifying markers.[46] The veil acts as an important public symbol of religious difference as well, distinguishing Christian women from Muslim women.

Such confessional behavior applies more to lower- and middle-class Egyptians than to upper-class Egyptians. In prosperous areas like the Cairo suburb of Maʿadi there is much more interaction between Muslims and Christians than in poorer, rural areas. However, Munīr Fakhrī ʿAbd al-Nūr says that for most of Egyptian society "there is a major cut and break in the texture. . . . Muslims and Copts are not mixing together any more. . . . They don't mix in my constituency. I can see that I can feel that. I go and sit in the cafes in the small streets of the very, very popular quarter. There are no Copts. I go to the churches, you find all the Copts there where they do everything."[47]

SECTARIAN TENSION

Debates in the Western media often focus on questions such as these: Are Copts persecuted? Are Coptic Christians—particularly young women— forced to convert to Islam? To what extent are Coptic Christians targeted or attacked, and if so, are the perpetrators Islamist groups? What is the level of state protection available to Coptic Christians?

Understandably, getting to the truth of such issues is extremely difficult. Interpretations are often influenced by political agendas. The U.S. Copts Association speaks of discrimination and persecution. Within Egypt, the newspaper *al-Katība al-Tayyiba* extols such a view. The Wafā' Qustantīn event, which occurred when the wife of a priest who tried to convert to Islam was returned to the church, illustrates the Western media's capacity to frame events within the context of Christian persecution. According to the Center for Arab-West Understanding, an organization that closely monitors Muslim-Christian relations in Egypt, Christian persecution stories are impossible to validate, since they can be exaggerated interpretations of events. Rumors about persecution and discrimination can be spread for personal reasons. In addition, the Coptic Church takes pride in being a church of martyrs and emphasizes that suffering is part of being a Christian.[48]

Nevertheless, sectarian tension and discrimination against Copts are a problem. The debate is about the extent of the problem. The 1970's have been labeled the "Decade of Sectarian Conflict."[49] The majority of sectarian incidents during that decade occurred in Upper Egypt, where the percentage of Copts is relatively high. According to the contested 1976 census, the three governorates of Minya, Asyut, and Sohag in Upper Egypt had a Coptic population of 19.4 percent, 20 percent, and 14.6 percent, respectively, indicating a connection between the relatively high proportion of Copts and sectarian tension.[50] Other factors that contributed to the situation included difficult social and economic conditions and the fact that during this time Minya and Asyut were bases for al-Jamā'a al-Islāmiyya.

Militant Islamists found the large number of Copts in these areas a threat and used this for political ends. For example, Karam Zuhdī, leader of al-Jamā'a al-Islāmiyya, stated (in the 1970's and long before the group's reformation) that Christians in Minya and Asyut "take advantage of their numbers to hold demonstrations of strength and superiority."[51] Patrick Gaffney reports that there were insults, beatings, and acts of vandalism directed against the Copts. The situation in Minya was particularly tense. There, members of al-Jamā'a al-Islāmiyya expressed strong anti-Coptic sentiments, and preachers from the group often referred to Copts as "unbelievers" or "Crusaders." In 1977 al-Jamā'a al-Islāmiyya of Minya gained control of the student union, which resulted in a climate in which it was thought to be dangerous for a Christian to run in student elections.[52] In 1978 in Samalūt, a town in Minya, several churches were burnt, priests were attacked, and one priest was murdered.[53]

The pages of the Islamist magazine *al-Daʿwa* of the 1980's testify to this sectarian tension. The magazine accuses the Copts of trying to increase their progeny, dominate the country, and throw Muslims out. Christians are blamed for sectarian violence and accused of conspiring with Israel to separate Egypt from the Arab world.[54]

Sectarian incidents also occurred in the Nile Delta and in Cairo. In June 1981 one of Egypt's worst sectarian incidents occurred in al-Zawiya al-Hamra, a poor neighborhood in Cairo that contained a large number of new rural migrants from Minya.[55] There are conflicting reports as to how the violence started. According to one, it began as a personal dispute between a Christian and a Muslim. According to another, the militants of al-Jamāʿa al-Islāmiyya took over a plot of land owned by a Copt with the intention of building a mosque on it. The incident sparked intense violence between the Coptic and the Muslim communities. Men and women were killed, "babies were thrown from windows," and "bodies [were] crushed on the pavement below."[56]

A number of factors contribute to sectarian violence. Socioeconomic difficulties play an important role.[57] The al-Zawiya al-Hamra area was exceedingly poor, and by 1981 residents had been hit by spiraling increases in the cost of living as a result of Sadat's open-door economic policy. In Upper Egypt poverty and social deprivation were widespread. Economic factors played a large role in the Islamist condemnation of Christian "arrogance." The majority of Copts in Upper Egypt are, like Muslims, extremely poor. However, the relatively higher rate of urbanization among Copts and the higher proportion of them in certain professions (such as law and medicine), coupled with the collective perception that colonial domination and Christian missionaries served to economically advance them, inevitably contributed to socioeconomic tensions. The culture of vendettas and clan rivalry in Upper Egypt means that small conflicts can spiral into inter-religious ones.[58] According to Saad Eddin Ibrahim, one of the reasons behind sectarian tension is that "there is a folkloric belief that Copts are not full citizens and that their loyalties are suspect."[59]

Another important factor is that the Islamists attacked the Copts as a substitute for attacking the state. The disproportionately large number of Copts in Asyut and Minya provided the militants with immediate targets.[60] Gaffney argues that "because local Copts, as Christians, were associated with the Western world and its capitalist culture . . . radical Islamists displayed both political and confessional motives in attacking them."[61] By attacking the Copts, al-Jamāʿa al-Islāmiyya was trying to embarrass the regime, since protecting the Copts was considered a duty of the government.[62]

It can also be argued that the state's lack of response to sectarian violence fueled further incidents. When al-Jamāʿa al-Islāmiyya of Minya attacked a Coptic church at Easter in 1978, Gaffney points out, neither the police nor other civil authorities took steps to charge the perpetrators, who made no effort to hide their actions, and an unofficial policy of silence about confessional tensions was evident in the official media.[63]

While sectarian violence was particularly severe during the Sadat era, violence directed against Copts has continued. The years 1992 and 1993 were particularly turbulent, with sectarian violence occurring in Upper Egypt (mostly involving al-Jamāʿa al-Islāmiyya), Cairo, and Alexandria.[64] One of the most significant incidents in recent years occurred in al-Kosheh in 1998–1999 and 2000. While al-Kosheh is an extremely poor town in Upper Egypt, it had no previous history of sectarian problems and it was not a stronghold of al-Jamāʿa al-Islāmiyya. In 1998, a man from a gambling ring that was mostly composed of Christians was murdered. The police rounded up the suspects and subjected them to abusive methods of investigation. Coptic groups abroad and the foreign press claimed that the police were deliberately targeting Christians. A British newspaper published an article headlined "Egyptian Police 'Crucify' and Rape Christians."[65] The portrayal of the incident in the Western media created an atmosphere of distrust, although violence did not break out until two years later. In 2000 a dispute between a Coptic merchant and a Muslim client resulted in armed confrontation, which drew people from neighboring villages, turned into sectarian violence, and resulted in the death of twenty Copts and one Muslim. Copts were outraged when the court failed to find anyone among the ninety-six defendants guilty of murder. Coptic outrage was only partially rectified when two Muslims were found guilty of murder in February 2003.

Different interpretations exist to explain what happened and who was to blame. Yūsuf Sidhum, editor of al-Watanī, argues that the state is to blame, along with the secret service, which encourages extremists and turns a blind eye to these actions.[66] However, others deny that there is an institutionalized bias. It appears that the first al-Kosheh incident was a case of gross police brutality that was not specifically targeting Copts. While the first incident was not sectarian, the interference of organizations abroad contributed to the second

incident, which was sectarian. In the second incident, the absence of the security services for two days facilitated the escalation of violence.

There has been relatively little violence directed at Copts as a direct result of the U.S. invasion of Afghanistan and Iraq following September 11, 2001.
However, the absence of direct physical repercussions can be attributed to the
security services and not to good sentiments.[67] Bishop Thomas of al-Qussia
reports that just after September 11, in his diocese of Asyut, the villagers distributed a drink called *sharabāt*, which is drunk at weddings and other cel-
ebrations.[68] During this time, he says, Christians were afraid, which is why
so many Christian writers emphasized that President George W. Bush is not
a Christian.[69] Pope Shenouda has complained that he has "lost count of the
articles, books and publications attacking Christianity in Egypt."[70] Bishop
Murqus of the Marī Girgis Church in Shubra al-Khayma in Cairo complains
about the bad atmosphere, which manifests itself in insults to priests in the
streets.[71] Despite the above incidents, since 9/11 anti-Coptic discourse in
the public sphere has diminished, although this can be attributed partly to a
clampdown on anti-Coptic literature, possibly in response to U.S. pressure.

Periodic outbreaks of sectarian violence still occur. The years 2004 and
2005 were particularly turbulent ones for Muslim-Christian relations in
Egypt. In December 2004, an uproar erupted over the alleged conversion of
Wafā' Qustantīn, the wife of a priest. In October 2005 Egypt's worst outbreak
of sectarian violence in five years occurred in Alexandria when thousands of
Muslim demonstrators took to the streets after Friday prayers in outrage over
a play that was considered slanderous to Islam.[72] The attacks left sixty-three
people injured, about half of whom were police officers. One Coptic Orthodox
church and two Evangelical churches were attacked. The play, which had been
staged inside the Coptic Orthodox Church of St. George in Alexandria in 2003
and subsequently recorded and distributed on CD and DVD, was titled *I Was
Blind, But Now I Can See*. The plot reportedly revolves around a young Christian who converts to Islam, guided by a Muslim friend. The youth becomes
disillusioned with Islam and returns to the Christian faith. The intention was
to advise Christian youth not to convert to Islam.

Muslims viewed the play as an attack on Islam, and after an angry response from Muslims, the Holy Synod of Orthodox Copts in Alexandria issued a statement stressing its respect for Islam and stating that the play was
not intended as an insult. The Muslim reaction came two years after the actual
play, which was taken by some to indicate that protest over the play was a

calculated attempt to disrupt the 2005 elections and undermine the chances of Coptic candidates who were running for office: only one of the fifty Coptic candidates won a seat.

Most recently, violence has occurred in the southern town of Mallawī in the governorate of Minya, two hundred miles south of Cairo. While the violence had a sectarian dimension and many media sources presented it as a religious conflict, it was also about land, with both sides using religious arguments to elicit sympathy from people within their own religious circles.[73] In May 2008 the monastery of Abū Fānā was attacked. Muslims from neighboring villages burned monastic cells and a chapel in an area of disputed land. Three monks were kidnapped and ill-treated. The Coptic Ecclesiastical Council issued a statement urging President Mubarak to guarantee the safety of Christians in Egypt.

Tension over the land had been brewing for some time, with both villagers and monks attempting to reclaim desert land that belongs to the state. People who wish to purchase state land have to go to the government to obtain permission. However, to avoid difficult government procedures, the monks of the monastery of Abū Fānā, which has recently undergone great expansion, bought the land through 'urfī contracts, which are agreements between two parties that have not been officially registered. Much land in Egypt is bought through such agreements, and the procedure is commonly used as a step toward proper registration of the land. Egyptian authorities generally accept the agreements, but in this case Minya's governor rejected the 'urfī agreements.[74]

Accusations on both sides indicate considerable tension. Christians accused the government of favoring Muslim institutions and creating bureaucratic obstacles for Christian projects, while Christians are accused of always getting their way when news is published in the West. Though such conflicts can end up generating financial support for Copts in Egypt, they do considerable harm to the overall climate.[75] Though this incident was framed in a sectarian manner, it also had economic dimensions in the disparity between the monastery, which was perceived to be flourishing, and the poor Muslim village.[76]

One subject often reported by Western media is the allegation that Coptic girls are kidnapped and forced to convert to Islam.[77] The U.S. Copts Association and the American Coptic Union claim that such forced conversions occur.[78] However, many of the kidnapping cases are in fact runaway cases, and conversions are often motivated by social problems.[79] Coptic families will claim that the girl has been kidnapped in order to avoid the shame of her conversion. In many situations, the police are unhelpful. In cases of romantic attachments, Coptic girls disappear, it is claimed, with the cooperation and coordination of the police. Conversion is the easiest way for a girl to leave her family.[80]

The question of forced conversion indicates the complexity of the Coptic issue and illustrates that Copts themselves are not always passive victims but are often contributors to a tense situation. Some Copts argue that the social exclusivity of the Coptic community itself can lead to tensions.[81] Copts may also manipulate incidents for their own ends. Sometimes the Coptic Church uses the sentiments of the Coptic community in the U.S. and international media to impose its own will. The incident that occurred over the building of a wall around St. Anthony's monastery in 2003 is one example. Monks built a wall around the monastery and included land that was not their own. They had started building the wall in 1992, although it wasn't until 2003 that they finished it and government authorities took action to remove the wall. The monks then played on the sentiments of the Coptic community and the international community, pitting themselves against the security forces. The government gave in.[82]

The pages of *al-Katība al-Tayyiba* are full of claims of the persecution of Christians by Muslims. The church has some role in promoting distribution of the newspaper and allows a number of priests to write in it, even though it is not officially a church publication. Such claims about persecution, along with the fact that the church encourages the political retreat of Copts by arguing that "leaving the world is seen as a sign of religiousness," have contributed to the isolation of Coptic Christians in Egypt.[83]

The connection between the church and Coptic activists in the United States means that Copts in Egypt become associated with Coptic activist groups abroad. Such groups claim that Copts in Egypt are persecuted, and in the United States, they lobby the U.S. government accordingly. The Web sites of organizations such as the U.S. Copts Association, Free Copts, Copts United, and the Middle East Christian Association are a few examples of how the Internet is used to lobby opinion abroad.[84] YouTube is also an important forum, not only for these organizations but also for individuals to post incidents that are deemed illustrative of the persecution of Copts. For example, after the event at al-Kosheh, the U.S. Copts Association was the first to publish pictures of persecution, including, Michael Munīr claims, pictures of decapitations and people being burned alive. The U.S. Copts Association showed these images to members of the U.S. Congress and the British Parliament.

There is debate about the extent to which such activities of expatriate Copts are supported. Many Copts emphasize that issues should be dealt with internally, but Michael Munīr states that it is only rich Copts who are supported by the regime—and wish to speak for Copts as a whole—who make such claims and that the majority of poor Copts support the activities of organizations such as the U.S. Copts Association.[85]

While a siege mentality has increasingly defined the Coptic Church's approach, many Copts stress Egyptian nationalism, the links between Muslims and Christians, and the distinctiveness of Egyptian national identity tied not to religion but to the land. These Copts emphasize the strong relationship between Muslims and Christians and disagree with Copts who want to revive the Coptic language and depict Muslims as invaders.[86] Through his concept of the "seven pillars of Egyptian identity," Mīlād Hannā, a secular Coptic intellectual and the first Arab recipient of the Simon Bolivar Prize (in 1998), emphasizes the mosaic of Egyptian identity as opposed to a specifically Coptic or Muslim identity.[87] Many upper-class Copts state that they are not persecuted and are angry with Copts abroad and middle-class Copts within Egypt for making such claims, arguing that it does more harm than good and that any problem facing Egypt's Copts must be dealt with nationally as an Egyptian problem.[88]

THE ROLE OF THE STATE

One of the key aspects of the Coptic issue in Egyptian politics is that the Copts are caught between the Islamists and the state. Sectarian conflict occurred in the 1970's partly because an attack on Christians was considered an attack on the state, since from the Islamist perspective, the protection of non-Muslims is one of the roles and responsibilities of the state.[89] The Coptic issue is also central to the state's definition of itself, which is why the state avoids addressing the issue. The discourse on national unity, where one is either for or against national unity, has become a mechanism for avoiding a nuanced discussion of the challenges inherent in relations between Muslims and non-Muslims.

The al-Zawiya al-Hamra incident of 1981 illustrates how the Coptic issue is associated with the relationship between Islamists and the state. The incident precipitated an angry response from Coptic groups in the United States, which protested the treatment of Copts in Egypt during Sadat's visit to Washington in August 1981. Sadat then engaged in anti-Coptic discourse and manipulated Muslim stereotypes and conspiracy theories about Christians.

The incidents at al-Zawiya al-Hamra were also used by the regime to clamp down on al-Jamāʿa al-Islāmiyya, which by this time had become an extremely powerful force. A direct attack upon al-Jamāʿa al-Islāmiyya was impossible, as the regime might then have been accused of attacking Islam.[90] Instead, the regime accused al-Jamāʿa al-Islāmiyya of trying to destroy national unity and the Egyptian nation; the organization's infrastructure was severely damaged and many of its members were arrested.[91] Thus the regime used the Coptic issue to maintain its repressive stance.

The events surrounding the Ibn Khaldun conference of 1994 illustrate how the issue of commitment to national unity is used to stifle debate. The Ibn Khaldun Center for Development Studies organized a conference on minority affairs in conjunction with the Minority Rights Group in London, and the issue of the Copts in Egypt was put on the agenda. There was considerable protest, and the conference had to change its venue to Cyprus. The protest centered around two issues. First, there was uproar over the fact that the Copts had been described as a minority. Nationalist political commentator and former editor of *al-Ahrām* Muhammad Haykal (1923–) argued that the Copts were not a minority but an integral part of "Egypt's unbreakable fabric." He said that treating Copts as a minority was "false" and "dangerous" and would only serve the interests of Egypt's enemies.[92] The conference was therefore presented as a threat to Egypt's national unity. Haykal's attack was followed by other articles in the Egyptian press, most of which supported Haykal's position, including one by Pope Shenouda.[93] Tāriq al-Bishrī, one of the Wasatiyya (centrist) Islamist intellectuals, argued that "saying that the Copts in Egypt are an ethnic or cultural minority who are separated from the rest of the community is an affront to all Egyptians."[94] While Copts abroad welcomed the conference, Copts within Egypt protested it. Pope Shenouda rejected calling the Copts a minority, stating that they are "part and parcel of the Egyptian nation."[95]

Opposition to the conference also focused on the fact that it had received funding from abroad. Copts in Egypt felt that things should be resolved within the country and feared that they would become associated with activist Copts abroad. Muhammad Haykal used the issue of the conference's funding to claim that there was a foreign conspiracy to undermine Egyptian national unity. Such discourse was not new. The idea of a Western conspiracy formed the backbone of Egyptian nationalist discourse in the 1920's, and complaints about Western-funded research have been made since the 1980's.[96]

Much of the discourse in response to the conference emphasized unity between Muslims and Copts. This was either historically based, with its roots in the common fight of Muslims and Copts against colonialism, or ethnically based. Some discourse was Islamist. The leftist Islamist newspaper *al-Sha'ab* argued that Copts and Muslims belonged to the same cultural model but that this model was Islamist rather than nationalist.[97]

The conference provoked such a strong reaction because it raised the question of the role and status of the Copts within Egyptian society, which was embarrassing to the state since the state shares responsibility for anti-Coptic discrimination and marginalization.[98] The arguments surrounding the conference were an expression of "deep-rooted Egyptian concerns" regarding the religious/nationalist balance in Egypt. Ami Ayalon argues:

> Treating the Copts as a religious minority would define the Muslim majority as a religious community as well. And underscoring religion as the primary determinant of Egypt's collective identity would diminish the weight of its other parts. . . . Moreover granting religion such a leading status would signify reverting to pre-modern values "while minimising later developments that underlay Egypt's claim to modernity."[99]

The state was also keen to preserve the fragile status quo concerning its relationship with the Islamists and was eager not to provoke the Islamists by defending the Copts.[100] The state's desire to avoid confrontation with the Islamists was particularly acute at this time. During the early 1990's, al-Jamā'a al-Islāmiyya had become very powerful and had stepped up its violent activities, which included targeting the Copts.

The mobilization of the national unity discourse was designed to stifle the ramifications of discussing the status of the Copts.[101] The discourse served the political interests of the parties concerned and not the Copts themselves. The interest that was aroused about the conference was accompanied by the repression of real debate on the status and treatment of the Copts. At the same time, however, the increased curiosity was a sign that the issue could not be repressed forever.[102]

The invocation of national unity has continued to be used as a means by which the state has stifled debate. Paying lip service to national unity includes visits by state officials and national unity feasts. However, such actions hide tensions on the street. Mubarak frequently announces that there is no difference between Muslims and Copts in Egypt, and that according to the Egyptian Constitution they are all equal in rights and duties. He has denied that sectarian tension is an issue, often blaming it on sociocultural differences that are exaggerated by a hostile foreign media.[103]

This sensitivity has permeated many parts of Egyptian society. For example, al-Azhar shares the attitude. In the "dial-a-shaykh" service, set up in the early 1990s by al-Azhar, shaykhs will not answer certain problematic questions, including whether non-Muslims go to heaven or hell. While the state does censor a great deal of anti-Coptic material, many Copts feel that the state is not responsive to their difficulties and that it takes measures only when the tourist industry is threatened.[104] Yūsuf Sidhum of al-Watanī writes that whenever violence between Muslims and Christians erupts, discussion is avoided under the pretext of avoiding a topic that would stir up public opinion.[105] Some claim that the government has supported sectarian attacks. The light sentences of most of the Muslims involved in the events at al-Kosheh in 2000 seemed to confirm state apathy toward the plight of the Copts. Sidhum argues that the high level of anti-Coptic discourse in the 1990's made Copts "desperate" and indicated that the state was not doing anything to combat the Islamists.[106]

However, the waning influence of the radical Islamists has provided an opportunity for the state to be more conciliatory toward the Copts, and the government has made a number of minor concessions. Religious programs attacking Copts were stopped in 1991. State radio and television now carry live broadcasts of Christmas and Easter masses. In 2003 the Coptic Christmas Day was made an official holiday, although requests to make the Coptic New Year a holiday also have been rejected. The education minister has been purging schoolbooks of passages that incite hatred of Christians. In 1998 President Mubarak removed the requirement for presidential approval every time repairs need to be carried out on a church, and in 2004 he removed a similar requirement for the construction of new churches. Both are now the responsibility of the governor and the security services. While this is an improvement, Copts and Muslims still do not have equal access to places of worship.

Instruction in Coptic culture and history has recently been introduced into schools and into the Egyptian media. Some newspapers have started to publish articles by Copts and articles about Coptic history. Pope Shenouda has a platform in the newspaper al-Gumhuriyya.[107] His relationship with Mubarak is far better than his relationship with Sadat was. However, this improvement is based on what Paul Sedra defines as the "Mubarak-Shenouda

millet partnership," in which Shenouda represents the Copts and pragmati-
cally realizes that he needs to adopt a low profile, cooperate with the regime,
avoid confrontation, and embrace the rhetoric of national unity. This strategy
enables him to consolidate his power within the church.[108] Shenouda argues
that Mubarak is always receptive to his "demands."[109] A greater margin of
freedom under Mubarak means that Coptic issues are discussed and there is
more of an open atmosphere.[110]

These improvements should not be overestimated, however. Copts want
more concessions. Coptic rights lawyer Mamdūh Nakhleh comments that
"to say it is an improvement when we see a Copt on television" is a fantasy,
since Copts do not have the same rights as Muslims.[111] In the elections of 2005,
Copts were disappointed when the National Democratic Party announced
that only one Copt, Yūsuf Butrus Ghālī, would be on its list of candidates.[112] In
addition, in 2007, the regime broke a promise reportedly made to the church
that it would allocate a specific number of seats to Copts in the Shura Council
elections. As a result, it is reported that the church plans to escalate its actions
against the regime by, for example, encouraging foreign powers to intervene.[113]
The state's slaughter of pigs in May 2009, which hit Coptic pig farmers hard,
has been seen as an action that targeted Copts and incited religious tensions.

While the state is reluctant to interfere and push for more of an open discussion about Copts, that has in fact happened in discussions involving the
centrist Islamists. Increasing dialogue between Coptic and Muslim intellectuals since 1981 has meant, according to Murqus, that Egypt's Copts are in
the "stage of regaining citizenship."[114] In general, the atmosphere has become
more conducive to discussing the Coptic issue. In July 2008, for example, a new
comedy was released, *Hassan and Murqus*, in which a Coptic Christian priest
and a Muslim preacher are forced to go into hiding and change their religious
identities when they are threatened by extremists in their own communities.
This greater openness toward discussing relations between Copts and Muslims in Egypt is evident notwithstanding the fact that in the last couple of
years relations between Islamists and Copts have become more strained.

COPTIC CONCERNS

In 1992 the secular Coptic intellectual Samīr Murqus wrote an article titled
"Concerns of the Coptic Youth." In it Murqus argues that there were particular reasons for framing the Coptic issue in the context of concerns rather than
that of problems or persecution. The notion of "concerns" makes the point

that Copts are not guests in Egypt and they are not a minority. Rather they are Egyptian citizens, and therefore they have the right to talk about concerns that are shared. Using the word "concerns" also establishes a kind of sympathy with the other, with the implication that both parties accept that they are living together in the same context.[115]

One of Murqus's concerns, which is voiced by secularists more than by church members, relates to the confessional climate, which he states is a particular problem for Copts, although it concerns Egyptians in general. Murqus is concerned that since the 1970's the political process has become religious. This has meant, he argues, that the arena of political struggle has become an arena for rivalry not between various political trends but between Islam and non-Islam and between Muslims and non-Muslims. This shift has led to Copts being considered an independent confessional community that must be dealt with as if they were one bloc. In Murqus's view this approach threatens national unity. As long as there is political Islam, he argues, there will be a political Christianity, and as long as there are Islamic groups there will be Christian groups.[116]

Another of Murqus's concerns has to do with the lack of political participation of Egyptians. While the Egyptian Constitution gives all Copts the right to political representation, Copts complain that they are politically marginalized and underrepresented in a number of fields. The extent of underrepresentation is unclear because it is linked to the percentage of their population, which is disputed. Whatever their percentages, though, Copts are to a certain extent politically underrepresented—despite the fact that Pope Shenouda concedes that things are getting better.[117] There are hardly any high-ranking Copts in the military, police force, judiciary, or diplomatic corps. Copts are also drastically underrepresented in higher university posts. They tend to be excluded from the intelligence service and the presidential staff and are underrepresented among Egypt's regional governors. Copts are also excluded from al-Azhar, and there is no Coptic university. While the People's Assembly has 444 members, in the year 2000 Copts occupied only 6 seats, and only 3 were actually elected; the other 3 were appointed by the president. After the 2005 elections, there were only 3 Copts in the People's Assembly (only one of them was elected, Yusuf Butrus Ghālī). The highest Coptic representation in the parliament was in 1942, when Copts occupied 27 seats out of a total of 264.[118] Munīr Fakhrī 'Abd al-Nūr of the Wafd Party encountered considerable anti-Coptic polemic when he ran for election. Pope Shenouda argues that the reason 'Abd al-Nūr succeeded was because the government gave him assistance in order to avoid strife in his electoral district.[119] Maher Khella, the Coptic candidate in Alexandria, was pressured to withdraw his candidacy after the sectarian violence there. Copts also complain that Coptic events, affairs, and issues are not covered on Egyptian television. Except for an hour a year, no expression of the Christian faith is allowed on state television.[120] Pope Shenouda claims that Copts face problems in registering to vote, which means that while more than half of the residents of the suburb Shubra are Coptic, no Copt has been elected.[121]

However, Copts do obtain leading posts in Egyptian society—for example, Husnī Gindī is the editor of one of Egypt's most prominent newspapers, *al-Ahrām*—although the U.S. Copts Association says that the regime typically allies itself with a few rich Coptic families.[122] Copts are overrepresented in the fields of law, medicine, and journalism, but Pope Shenouda points out that they encounter considerable opposition when running in the physician and pharmacist syndicate elections.[123] Copts have a large presence in civil society associations,[124] and they owned 22.5 percent of all private investment companies that were founded between 1974 and 1993.

Some attribute the underrepresentation of Copts in Egyptian politics to the Copts themselves, who avoid politics and public life, although this attitude is partly connected to political apathy in Egyptian society as a whole. Many Copts do not even register to vote; to try to rectify this, Pope Shenouda issued a papal decree in early 2009 requiring a electoral card from all Copts who marry.[125] The marginalization of Copts can be attributed, in part, to the Coptic Church, which often encourages them to retreat to the church and to suffer difficult times. Their political passivity is also a result of the feeling that their citizenship rights have been eroded.[126]

The high rate of Coptic conversion to Islam is contributing to the decline of the Coptic population. According to Kamāl Zākhir Mūsā, a Coptic author, conversion to Islam has something to do with a reaction against the paternalistic nature of the church.[127] However, there are also considerable incentives to convert to Islam. Mixed marriages often result in conversion. Marriage between a Muslim woman and a non-Muslim man is conditional upon his conversion. While marriage between a Muslim man and a non-Muslim woman is not conditional upon her conversion, she often does convert because if she remains a Christian she cannot inherit from her husband or be buried next to him. Copts also convert to Islam because the Coptic Church makes divorce very difficult.

Requests by Copts for divorce have increased in the last decade, partly because Christian women are becoming more economically independent, but Vivian Fu'ād argues that the church is unresponsive to the new dynamics of society.[128] While the Administrative Judiciary, one of the many courts of the Egyptian judicial system, has granted some Copts the right to remarry, Pope Shenouda continues to refuse permission.

Emigration abroad also contributes to the decline in the Coptic population. According to the church, the 1996 census in the diocese of al-Qussia in Asyut in Upper Egypt (a former stronghold of radical groups and an area that has a larger proportion of Copts compared to the rest of the country) calculated that 31.6 percent were Christians. The 2006 census calculated that 24.7 percent were Christians.[129] While many are leaving for Cairo (although this includes Muslims too), a large number of those who leave this diocese are leaving the country.

One concern that is particularly important to the church has to do with the building of churches, which is regulated by the legal system inherited from the Hatti Humayun decree of 1856. The process of obtaining licenses to build and repair churches has become easier in the last couple of years, and a greater number of church building permits have been granted. However, sectarian violence is sometimes related to difficulties that Copts encounter when constructing or repairing churches. In May 2004 a priest and two other Copts died in a car crash while in police custody after trying to repair a church wall at night, claiming that they would have had to get permission from the security services to repair it. In May 2007 sectarian violence occurred in Bimha in the Ayat district, south of Giza, over Christians' alleged plans to convert a house owned by a Copt into a church. Eleven Copts had to be hospitalized and a substantial amount of property was destroyed. In this case, the state apprehended the culprits. The National Democratic Party and the security apparatus held reconciliation sessions, although with limited success.

This incident confirms the need for a unified law for places of worship, which is supported by many Muslims. In 2007 three bills proposing such a law were presented to the People's Assembly, but they have been indefinitely postponed. The first one was presented by a Muslim, and the second was presented by the National Council for Human Rights, which is made up of Muslims and Christians. Yusūf Sidhum argues that when such an issue is presented in the right framework for equal citizenship, many Muslims join with Copts.[130]

NON-MUSLIMS, THE CONSTITUTION, AND THE LAW

Ultimately any discussion of the Copts in Egypt must consider what rights Egyptian law bestows. How does Egyptian law define the political, legal, and social rights of non-Muslim minorities? In theory, the Egyptian Constitution establishes political, legal, and social equality between Muslims and non-Muslims. Article 40 of the constitution states that "all citizens are equal before the law. They have equal public rights and duties without discrimination due to sex, ethnic origin, language, religion or creed." Article 46 states that "the State shall guarantee the freedom of belief and the freedom of practicing religious rites." In addition, Article 8 states that "the State shall guarantee equality of opportunity to all Egyptians." Among the amendments to the constitution that were approved in March 2007 was an addition to Article 1 stating that "the Arab Republic of Egypt is a state with a democratic system that is based on citizenship."[131]

At the same time, however, Article 2 states that "Islam is the Religion of the State, Arabic is its official language and the principles of Islamic *shari'a* are the main source of legislation." Many have argued that there is a contradiction between Article 2 and the principle of citizenship. The notion of equality in Article 8 is also subject to qualifications. In 1971 the Supreme Constitutional Court stated:

> The principle of equality before the law does not mean a mathematically calculated equality applied to all people regardless of their different circumstances and legal status. The legislature, in the interests of the public, has the interest to set general and abstract standards by which equality before the law is determined. Consequently, only those people who meet these standards can exercise the rights guaranteed them by law.[132]

The issue of personal status law is fundamental to the relationship between religious minorities and the state. Article 9 of the constitution states that, "the family is the basis of the society founded on religion, morality, and patriotism." Egyptian legislation states that "the personal status law of *all* Egyptians, regardless of their religion, is governed by Islamic law." However, non-Muslims are given the freedom, under the abolition of the *shari'a* and *milli* courts of 1955, to apply non-Muslim personal status laws,[133] on the condition that these non-Muslims are of the same "sect and rite." The Christian community has three rites, twelve sects, and a total of six personal status laws. When a case involves two Christians of different sects and rites, Islamic law is applied.

The right of non-Muslims to apply their own personal status law extends only to officially recognized religious communities.[134] Muslims, Christians, and Jews can be governed by their own personal status laws, but a person without a religion or from a religion other than Judaism or Christianity, such as a Bahā'ī, is a legal nonentity and Islamic law is often applied.[135] In addition, the application of non-Muslim personal status law is limited to family law, i.e., marriage and divorce, circumscribed by the condition that no law can go against "public order."[136] The concept of public order has been used to protect the autonomy of non-Muslim religious communities from the application of some Islamic rules that are considered a violation of the essence of the Christian faith such as polygamy, on the basis that this would be against public order.[137] However, public order has also been used to increase the scope of Islamic law applied to non-Muslims. Capacity, guardianship, and inheritance for all Egyptians have come under "general law," and the concept of public order has been used to apply Islamic law to general law.[138] Thus Islamic law is applied to non-Muslims in personal status issues outside of family law, including inheritance issues. Non-Muslims are not allowed to legally adopt children, since adoption is not allowed in Islamic law. In cases in which one member of a married couple converts to Islam, the children are almost always given to the Muslim parent. Children of Muslims who have converted to Christianity remain officially Muslims. However, when a Christian becomes a Muslim, his children will automatically become Muslim by law.

The constitution states that Egyptians enjoy "freedom of belief and the freedom of practicing religious rites." However, there are areas in which this is restricted. Muslims face considerable restrictions when leaving the Muslim faith.[139] This is particularly important to Copts. A number of Copts convert to Islam for financial or personal reasons and wish to convert back to Christianity.

While there is no criminal punishment for apostasy, apostasy still has social and legal implications. In 1980 the High Administrative Court ruled that "it is completely acceptable for non-Muslims to embrace Islam but by consensus Muslims are not allowed to embrace another religion or to become of no religion at all." Through the use of Article 98f of the penal code, which prohibits the use of religion to "ignite strife, degrade any of the heavenly religions or harm national unity or social peace," the police detain and often mistreat Muslims accused of apostasy.[140]

From the perspective of personal status law, the apostate is punished, since apostasy is a legal impediment to almost all personal status rights because the apostate is considered a legal nonentity. Consequences of apostasy include the dissolution of the apostate's marriage, which prevents the apostate from entering into a new marriage and from inheriting. The apostate's legal ties with children are also broken.[141] This was illustrated in the case of Nasr Abū Zayd. Here, the *hisbā* procedure (referring to a lawsuit to protect Islam that can be initiated by any Muslim without having a direct interest in the case) was used to claim that Abū Zayd was an apostate and therefore his marriage should be legally dissolved. In this case, the Court of Cassation allowed a declaration of apostasy and ruled on its legal consequences.[142]

The state also puts up administrative barriers to those wishing to leave Islam. The Egyptian courts have one-way religious conversion documents. A person's religion is stated on his or her identity papers. It is easy to have a conversion to Islam officially recorded. In these cases, the birth certificate—it is often alleged—is thrown away. However, to have a conversion *from* Islam officially recorded has proved extremely difficult.[143] Complaints have been made that Christians have been defined as Muslims by bureaucratic clerks handling the shift from manually issued identity documents to computerized ones. Such individuals face the uphill—or even impossible—task of having their identity correctly recorded as Christian.[144]

Until early 2008 the apostate had the option of either falsely stating that he or she was a Muslim on his identity papers or of not having any identity papers, which can prove a significant impediment to daily life. On April 24, 2007, the High Administrative Court rejected the right of forty-five Christian converts to Islam to reconvert to Christianity. The court would not allow them to be defined as Christians on their identity cards and other official documents. It announced that while freedom of religion is an Islamic principle and while this implies full respect for other monotheistic religions, Islamic principles prevent someone from leaving Islam for other religions. The court went on to announce that "there is a difference between religious freedom that is provided by the law and Constitution, and the manipulation of religions that is considered a threat to orderly conduct."[145] This ruling contradicted a previous ruling of April 2, 2007, that granted Egyptians the full right to choose their faith and the right to reconvert to Christianity and to have this declared on all official documents.[146] In February 2008 the High Administrative Court ruled in favor of fifteen Christians who had converted to Islam and then reconverted to Christianity. The court ruled that the Ministry of Interior should change the official documents of Christian converts who had previously converted to Islam, and for whom the ministry had issued documents citing them as Muslims, to cite them again as Christians, but retaining the phrase "previously proclaimed Islam as their religion."[147] While this change was welcomed by many Copts and human rights activists, considerable reservations were expressed about the implications of retaining such a phrase. This ruling has been awaiting an appeal that—as yet—the High Administrative Court has refused to hear, thus prolonging the uncertainty for Copts who have re-converted to Christianity.

Restrictions on apostasy and freedom of religion also affect the Bahā'īs of Egypt. Because the state does not officially recognize any religion other than Islam, Judaism, and Christianity, Bahā'īs are currently not allowed to state their religious identity on their identity cards. Until recently, Bahā'īs had to be officially registered as Muslim, Jew, or Christian or have no identity card. This was reinforced in December 2006, when the High Administrative Court argued that the interpretation of Article 46 of the 1971 Constitution on the freedom to practice religious rites applies to the three divine religions only. It also stated that registering any religion other than the three divine religions is a breach of the law.[148] In January 2008, however, a High Administrative Court ruling gave Bahā'īs a small concession and allowed the religion box on identity cards to be left vacant or to have a dash in it. The court declared that the Ministry of Interior should not force citizens to officially belong to a religion that they do not believe in.[149] After an appeal, this ruling was confirmed by the High Administrative Court in March 2009.

Bahā'īs and others regarded as atheists have been convicted and imprisoned under Article 98 for opposing the basic principles of the ruling system of the country and promoting extremist ideas that disparage or belittle divinely revealed religions.[150] In theory they have the right to practice their religion freely, but not in a way that is offensive, so all expression has to be behind closed doors. While Nasser's charter appeared to invoke the idea that all religious faiths were in some way equal, in 1960 a presidential decree ordered that Bahā'ī communities should be dissolved and banned the practice of their religious ritual and the circulation of literature promoting their beliefs. Their assets were confiscated.[151] The concept of public order was invoked.[152]

In 1975 the Supreme Constitutional Court confirmed this interpretation and limited the religions protected by the constitution to the three divinely revealed religions: Islam, Judaism, and Christianity.[153] While the Bahā'ī community in theory allows intermarriage with Muslims and Christians, the guardian of Egypt's Bahā'īs has temporarily prohibited Bahā'īs from marrying Muslims or Christians. This is because, it has been argued, when Bahā'īs divorce their Christian or Muslim partners, the courts in Egypt side against Bahā'īs, which has meant that they lose their children and their property.

CONCLUSION

The case of the Bahā'īs in Egypt illustrates that even before the process of Islamization in the 1970's, Egypt was not fully secularized, for religious identity determined personal status law and therefore the social structure of Egypt. In Egypt individuals are born into the family, and the identity of the family and therefore of the individual is based on religious affiliation. Understanding the religiously conservative social structure of Egyptian society is important for situating Islamist conceptions of citizenship.

The process of Islamization has served to further entrench religious identity and to separate Egyptians along the lines of religion. While the growth of Coptic nationalism as focused on the leadership of the church has its own roots within the community, the Islamization of state and society has contributed to this process. The emphasis on the separation of Copts from other Egyptians, combined with the lobbying and support they get from Copts abroad, has potentially harmful implications for Coptic-Muslim relations in Egypt.

The question of the role and status of non-Muslims, particularly Copts, in Egyptian society is an important and sensitive one for the state. It is linked to the current struggle over what role religion should play. It is also related to the question of national identity within Egypt. The role of non-Muslims is central to how the state sees itself. The government's eagerness to preserve the status quo has involved not making a commitment on whether Egypt is an Islamic or a secular state. Directly addressing the issue of the Copts would mean defining Egypt as a religious or an Islamic state. The emphasis placed on national unity and calls to avoid stirring up confessional strife are used to avoid discussion on the issue.

The Coptic issue is also important from the perspective of the Islamists, and it is to be expected that the issue would feature prominently in Islamist thought. The question of the role of non-Muslims in an Islamic state runs parallel to many issues that emerge in discussions about Islamist thought in general, such as the Islamist positions on democracy, pluralism, and citizenship. It is for this reason that the question of the role and status of the Copts is so important. In the last decade, radical groups have renounced violence, and the Muslim Brotherhood has become more involved in the political process. As a result, they are increasingly being called upon to define their vision of an Islamic order and what an Islamic state is. The question of the Copts is central to these issues.

4 THE *DHIMMA*

CALLS FOR THE ESTABLISHMENT of an Islamic state and the application of Islamic law have strained Christian-Muslim relations in Egypt. Many Copts fear that the application of Islamic law will lead to the status of *dhimmī* being reimposed upon them. Whether Islamists think that the rights of non-Muslims should be defined according to the *dhimma* contract in contemporary Egypt is therefore a vitally important question not only for Muslim-Christian relations but also for Islamist thought and the Islamist movement in general. The role of non-Muslims is linked to fundamental questions about the place of the principles of freedom of religion, tolerance, and pluralism in Islamist thought.

An analysis of the Islamist position shows that while political Islam is characterized by the call for the unity of religion and state and the application of Islamic law, there is diversity in how the outcome of the application of Islamic law is envisioned and in how the call for the application of Islamic law relates to the status quo. This diversity involves many Islamists' rejecting the definition of non-Muslims as *dhimmīs*, an issue that will be addressed in subsequent chapters.

Nevertheless, Coptic concerns that they will be treated as *dhimmīs* are valid. For a number of Islamists, the *dhimma* contract would provide the framework for determining relations between Muslims and non-Muslims in an Islamic state. There is an assumption that no change can be made in the revealed law and that elements of the Islamic tradition are fixed. Islamic law in the sense of divine law as revealed in the Qur'an and the Hadith is conflated with Islamic jurisprudence, which was the product of the interpretation of Islamic law by Islamic scholars in a particular historical context.

While most mainstream Islamists claim that they want to re-create the relationship that non-Muslims had with the early Islamic Empire, in reality the underlying assumptions behind the *dhimma* that is invoked do undergo change. The *dhimma* is cast in a light that is more reflective of modern sensibilities and is equated with the concepts of tolerance and pluralism. Certain aspects of the *dhimma* are emphasized and other aspects are deemphasized. Just as the rights and duties entailed in the *dhimma* were historically contingent and varied, any expression of the *dhimma* in the contemporary context is inevitably influenced by that context.

Calls for the application of the *dhimma* raise the question of how this relates to the contemporary situation. How can the *sharīʿa*, which was formed in the context of the victorious premodern Islamic polity, accommodate the demands of the modern nation-state? How can the *dhimma* and the *millet* system, which were contingent upon the autonomy that non-Muslim communities had in the premodern context before the establishment of the centralized nation-state, be applied in this new context?

This chapter will address the question by looking at Islamist thinking that continues to emphasize the importance of the *dhimma*. This type of thought is represented by many members of the Muslim Brotherhood and by Islamist preachers and writers associated with the Brotherhood, such as the Islamist thinker Sayyid Qutb, Yūsuf al-Qaradāwī (the renowned Islamist thinker and writer and newly appointed member of al-Azhar's Islamic Research Academy), and Muhammad al-Ghazālī (former Azharite and popular Islamist preacher and writer). The writings of the Pakistani Islamic thinker Abū Al-ʿAlā al-Maudūdī (1903–1979) are also discussed.[1] While al-Maudūdī was Pakistani, his treatise on the role of non-Muslims is one of the few extended examinations of the subject and forms a frame of reference for many Islamic thinkers both in Egypt and throughout the Muslim world. The idea that the *dhimma* should define relations between Muslims and non-Muslims can also be found in the writings and actions of more radical groups such as al-Jamāʿa al-Islāmiyya and al-Jihād. This chapter will examine these positions. It will also look at radical views that call for some kind of departure from the idea of providing non-Muslims with the protection of the Islamic state.

ISLAMIC HISTORY AND LAW

Contemporary Islamist thought attaches considerable importance to historical precedents. This is not particular to the contemporary period; it has been an important characteristic of calls for social and political reform throughout Islamic history. For the majority of Muslims, the military and political success during the formative Islamic period was God's reward to his Muslim followers. In the modern period, the military and economic weakness of many parts of the Islamic world has been viewed as God's punishment of Muslims who have turned their backs on Islam. This position has resulted in an emphasis on the need to return to some golden age that is rooted in early Islamic history. While the notion of a golden age is a common theme in Islamist thought, the temporal and geographical boundaries of this golden age vary. Many Islamists, most notably the renowned reformists Rashīd Ridā (1865–1935) and Sayyid Qutb (1906–1966), accept only the very earliest part of the formative period, that of Muhammad and the first four rightly guided caliphs (610–661), as constituting the golden age. However, Muhammad al-Ghazālī, Azharite Islamist preacher and member of the Muslim Brotherhood, was less apathetic toward the period after the rightly guided caliphs and extended the golden age to include the 'ulamā' of the early classical period during the time of Abu Hanifa (d. 767).[2]

While many Islamist reformers are apathetic about the medieval period of Islamic history, and also about medieval Islamic jurisprudence, the Islamists whose work is analyzed in this chapter take more of a conservative view and emphasize looking back at all periods of Islamic history for normative models of social and political relations. Many Islamists regard the *sharī'a* (in the sense of divine law) as having been fulfilled in Islamic jurisprudence. Islamic jurisprudence, which was formed as a response to social and political circumstances, is seen by many Islamists as the correct interpretation of Islamic principles in the Qur'an and the Sunna.

Islamists who place emphasis on the validity of Islamic jurisprudence for today's Islamic society view the reenactment of the *dhimma* contract as an intrinsic part of the reestablishment of an Islamic order.[3] Their approach to the rights and role of non-Muslims "revolves around an orbit of the realities of Islamic history."[4] The founder of the Muslim Brotherhood, Hasan al-Bannā, argues that all necessary answers and models could be found in the Islamic texts. In his view, the sacred law and the decisions of the Islamic jurists were sufficient to supply every need of Muslim society and to cover every contingency. Al-Bannā emphasizes not only the Qur'an and Hadith but also jurisprudence, writing that Islam has "solved" the problem of interreligious relations and "its holy and wise institutions . . . contained a clear and unambiguous text concerning" their protection. The Qur'anic verse "Allah does not forbid you to deal with those who have not fought against you in religion" (60:8) is one example.[5]

This confident approach to the Islamic jurisprudence of the four schools of law is also held by more contemporary members of the Muslim Brotherhood such as Ma'mūn al-Hudaybī (supreme guide 2002–2004). Jurisprudence, he states, "left little room for the rulers to promulgate public laws out of character with the *shari'a*."[6] According to the independent reformed Islamist and former member of al-Jihād Kamāl al-Sa'īd Habīb (1957–), "There is no book of Islamic jurisprudence that does not guarantee the rules for how a non-Muslim should live under Islam and how he is to be protected."[7]

However, even those thinkers who advocate a close adherence to jurisprudence exhibit some recognition that a rigid approach to Islamic jurisprudence is neither necessary nor desirable. Hasan al-Bannā calls for a return to the Qur'an and Hadith and implies that the opinion of everyone except the Prophet is liable to change and modification. Every Muslim of a certain understanding, he argues, should investigate the legal deduction of jurists and decide which opinions attract him most.[8] Ma'mūn al-Hudaybī writes that "the fixed and unchangeable tenets of the Islamic shari'a are very few" and there is always the possibility of using independent reasoning (*ijtihād*) "to deduce views that are appropriate to global economic, and social changes."[9]

The question therefore is how Islamists who call for the application of the *dhimma* are able to strike a balance between these historical models and the demands of the particularist nation-state, which include the hegemony of universalist values such as human rights and democracy. While this tension is manifest throughout Islamist discussions on the role of non-Muslims, it is particularly the case with Islamists who wish to revive the *dhimma* as a model for defining relations between Muslims and non-Muslims.

TOLERANCE AND PLURALISM

While Islamic history provides the normative ideal for organizing Muslim society, mainstream Islamist thought on non-Muslims cannot simply be understood as a continuation of the *dhimma*. The *dhimma* concept is filtered through contemporary priorities, as illustrated by the use of the concepts of tolerance and pluralism. For the majority of Islamist thinkers, these two concepts form the foundation for the treatment and status of non-Muslims in a proposed Islamic state. In their view, tolerance and pluralism in Islam are manifest in Islamic history and the divine texts, for example, "and we made you into nations and tribes that you may know each other—(not that you may despise each other) (49:13)."[10]

The employment of the concepts of tolerance and pluralism in any discourse cannot be taken at face value. These concepts have their own histories or genealogies and have meaning in their own discursive contexts. Therefore, any analysis of Islamic articulations of tolerance and pluralism must be understood in light of the context within which they are used. In Arabic, the terms *tasāmuh* and *samāha*, which are often translated as "tolerance," both mean forbearance and treating kindly and forgivingly.[11] In classical Islam, both words can be found to mean "they acted in an easy or a gentle manner with one another."[12] The Arabic word for "pluralism," *ta'adudiyya*, is a modern construct coined from the word *ta'addud*, which means "to be numerous." Yvonne Haddad points out that the term was first used by Arab nationalists in the mid-1980's.[13]

Such terms are utilized within Islamist thought where they take on underlying assumptions that derive from the context within which they are used. The underlying assumptions behind the modern Islamist uses of the terms "tolerance" and "pluralism" are no compulsion in religion, the concept of the Abrahamic religions, and good treatment as rooted in Islamic history. While the term "pluralism" has been appropriated from Western political theory, contemporary Islamists are keen to show that such an appropriation does not involve the actual concept itself. Thus, it is argued that the idea behind it is essentially Islamic even if the term itself has been borrowed. Kamāl al-Sa'īd Habīb implies that Western thought took the notion of tolerance from Islam. Islam "taught mankind pluralism," so how can Muslims be accused of being against pluralism?[14]

One of the foundations of the notion of pluralism and tolerance is the principle of no compulsion in religion, which is expressed as an intrinsically Islamic, divinely ordained principle based on the Qur'an: "let there be no compulsion in religion (2:256)" and "to you be your religion; to me mine (109:6)."[15] God does not desire Muslims to force others to believe, since "if it had been the Lord's Will, They would all have believed (10:99)"[16] and "wilt thou then compel mankind against their will to believe (10:99)."[17]

It is argued that compulsion in religion has no intrinsic value for society or for Islam itself. For the popular Islamist preacher and writer Muhammad al-Sha'rāwī (1911–1998), compulsion in religion is pointless; it is destructive, harmful, and leads to hypocrisy. Faith is not valid, he argues, unless it is voluntary.[18] Ma'mūn al-Hudaybī, a former supreme guide of the Muslim Brotherhood, states that Muslims are allowed to be "preachers but not judges" of the Islamic message. They have no right to enforce God's judgment in this world. That is for the hereafter.[19]

However, the principle of no compulsion is understood within a specific framework, defined by interpretations of the *dhimma* in Islamic jurisprudence. It should not be confused with the principle of freedom of religion. The principle of no compulsion in religion is based on the principle of religious brotherhood for People of the Book (Jews, Christians, and Zoroastrians).[20] Much is made of the bond between the Abrahamic faiths. This freedom of religion cannot, it is argued, be stretched beyond the Abrahamic faiths to include Bahā'īs. Al-Hudaybī calls for the "freedom of establishing religious rites for all the known heavenly religions."[21]

Traditional attitudes toward apostasy also constitute boundaries to the concept of no compulsion in religion. While there is no criminal punishment for apostasy in Egypt, many, including Muntasir al-Zayyāt, a former lawyer for al-Jamā'a al-Islāmiyya who knew Ayman al-Zawāhirī, Osama Bin Laden's "right-hand man," imply that under an Islamic state this should be the case.[22] According to Ma'mūn al-Hudaybī, if you are quietly an apostate, no corporal punishment should be exacted. However, it becomes justified when the changing of religion is used as a "game." He mentions one such case: A Coptic woman who wanted to divorce her husband became a Muslim. Her husband also converted to Islam, and so she converted back to Christianity in order to divorce him.[23]

Islamists' understandings of no compulsion in religion also include restrictions on proselytism. While the Pakistani thinker Abū Al-'Alā al-Maudūdī took an unusually liberal view on this, arguing that non-Muslims could have a discretionary right to propagate their religion, his is not a mainstream view.[24] The majority hold that Muslims and non-Muslims do not have equal rights in propagating their religion or proselytizing: this includes a prohibition on non-Muslims' publicly displaying any religious activity.[25]

The principle of no compulsion in religion does not imply equality of access to places of worship. The Islamist magazine *al-Da'wa* argues that tolerance should never mean that Muslims should share in the building of churches or that "the Muslim state or any Muslim individual should undertake building churches or temples by financing them." This would put the church "on a footing of equality with the mosque," it says, which is impossible.[26] How is it possible, one writer for *al-Da'wa* asks, for the Muslim state to take part in the building of a church and to put a cross on it when the Qur'an denies that God was crucified?[27] Al-Jamā'a al-Islāmiyya saw *jihād* against the Copts as involving the prevention of church building.[28]

The principle of no compulsion in religion is also based on the underlying assumption that while Muslims should not force others to believe, the desired aim, conversion, is there all the same.[29] The fact that God himself created believers and unbelievers does not mean that God loves all of them equally. The existence of nonbelievers is a source of disappointment for Muslims.[30] For Muhammad al-Ghazālī, it is necessary for Muslims to "remind them [non-Muslims] that they have forgotten and show them the correct path."[31] However, this view is tempered by an emphasis by others upon fostering good relations with non-Muslims and not reminding them of the fact that they are unbelievers.[32]

One of the underlying assumptions behind the way tolerance and pluralism are used is the idea of good treatment. Good treatment is the concept of *ihsān*, derived from Qur'an 16:128, "for Allah is with those who restrain themselves, and those who do good." *Ihsān* refers to giving more than one owes and taking less than one is owed, i.e., a kindness toward someone that goes beyond justice.[33] It is emphasized that "good treatment" is an "Islamic obligation which no Muslim would dare to underestimate or take lightly."[34] The obligation to treat non-Muslims well requires that a practical distinction be made between theological disagreements and social and political relations. The position is taken that religious differences should not affect everyday relations between Muslims and non-Muslims in society. 'Isām al-'Aryān of the Muslim Brotherhood sees this as fulfilling the Islamic historical legacy.[35]

The concept of good treatment is based on both Qur'anic verses and anecdotal references to Islamic history. The injunction "Allah forbids you not, with regard to those who fight you not for (your) faith nor drive you out of your homes, from dealing kindly and justly with them (60:8)" has, it has been argued, been fulfilled throughout Islamic history. History confirms, *al-Da'wa* states, that Islam takes care of all who have lived in its shelter.[36] The actions of the Prophet and his companions illustrate Islam's good treatment. One frequently mentioned story is that of 'Umar Ibn al-Khattāb (caliph 634–644), who came across an elderly Jew who was tired and hungry. 'Umar took him to his house and gave him something to eat. Then he ordered that he be given money from the state treasury.[37]

Such an anecdotal approach to the notion of good treatment means that the concept is not engaged with on a level of rights and expectations, or with reference to the current constitution and law. For example, good treatment in the contemporary context takes the form of Muslim Brotherhood members greeting "Coptic brothers on the occasion of their feast."[38]

Few Islamist thinkers pass up the opportunity to compare Islam's historical record of religious tolerance with that of Christianity. This tolerance is manifested, it is argued, by the fact that one of the oldest churches in the world, the Hanging Church in Cairo, has never been attacked or destroyed.[39] Yūsuf al-Qaradāwī argues that Islamic history abounds with numerous instances whereby the religious jurists try to reinstate the rights of non-Muslims. He contrasts this to the religious intolerance of medieval Europe.[40]

Good treatment of the People of the Book is conditional upon their submission to Islamic political authority, through which the harmony and balance of the Islamic world are kept intact.[41] Thus there is no harm in having relations with People of the Book, but friendship at the "expense of religion is forbidden."[42] Sayyid Qutb argues that while it is not the intention of Islam to force its beliefs on people, Islam is not merely "belief." In an Islamic system, he says, "there is room for all kinds of people to follow their own beliefs, while obeying the laws of the country which are . . . based on the Divine authority."[43]

The idea that Islamic history provides the model for good treatment avoids the question of what constitutes "good treatment" in the contemporary Egyptian context. Is it a fixed concept or is it contingent upon contemporary standards? How can this be applied in a very different social and political context? What aspects of the classical vision of *dhimma* are to be re-created in the modern context?

NON-MUSLIMS AS *DHIMMĪS*

One of the challenges facing many contemporary Islamist theorists is a reluctance to address how their political ideas can be applied to contemporary situations and what legal implications they have. Beyond general statements about no compulsion in religion and tolerance, there is relatively little discussion about what the rights or freedoms of non-Muslims under contemporary Islamic rule would be. This problem is not specific to discourse about non-Muslims, although that subject is particularly sensitive.

The reluctance to relate the ideal Islamic model to the reality has its roots in classical Islamic thought, where there was a disconnection between two types of Islamic literature: the mirrors-for-princes genre, which was concerned with giving rulers practical advice, and the "God-given Islamic religio-political model" or the "paradigmatic model of the early *umma*." Carl Brown argues that this lack of integration helped protect the notion of the ideal early community.[44] The same applies to contemporary Islamists. Avoiding a discussion of how and in what way these ideal social models can be applied today means that the ideal behind the slogan of "Islam is the solution" remains protected.

The political discourse of the Muslim Brotherhood illustrates the problems involved in moving from these general ideals to a more specific program. Since the 1980's, the Muslim Brotherhood has become an integral part of the Egyptian political process. The question of its manifesto, agenda, and how it situates itself as a political party is particularly pressing, especially in light of the fact that it issued a draft party platform in 2007. One of the reasons that the Muslim Brotherhood has been slow to provide answers to issues such as its position on political pluralism and non-Muslims is that the group gave priority to political issues over the interpretation of Islamic law and to action over thought. This emphasis developed partly because the Brotherhood became so involved in political conflict with the regime.[45] However, recent manifestos illustrate that the Muslim Brotherhood is becoming more oriented toward political specifics, even though it continues to give insufficient attention to the role of non-Muslims.[46] One reason for the group's reluctance to discuss this issue is that the role of non-Muslims pertains to the fundamental issues of pluralism and citizenship, which have broader ramifications. Its positions on non-Muslims and on the concept of citizenship form an important part of its current conflict with the state.

Many Islamists, both radical and more mainstream, view the application of the *dhimma* contract and the payment of *jizya* as a necessary part of the revival of Islamic law.[47] Reformed former al-Jihād member Kamāl al-Sa'īd Habīb defines the *dhimma* as a continuation of pluralism, since while God did order pluralism, it was within the "framework of the political and social Islamic structure" and on the condition that non-Muslims "pay the *jizya* and accept the necessity of the rules of the *millet* and the promised covenant of the *dhimma*."[48] In the 1980's and early 1990's al-Jamā'a al-Islāmiyya forcibly extracted *jizya* from Copts in Upper Egypt. In 2003, after the group renounced violence, it condemned this practice. While it still emphasizes that accepting *jizya* and imposing the *dhimma* covenant on non-Muslims is part of the group's vision of an Islamic state, it has also stated that it is not permissible for individuals or groups to demand the *jizya* payment, because it is up to the Islamic state to establish this agreement with non-Muslims.[49]

Members of the Muslim Brotherhood tend to be more cautious about advocating the *dhimma* and the *jizya*, although clearly these concepts form a significant part of their thinking. In the mid-1980's Yūsuf al-Qaradāwī argued that non-Muslims should not serve in the army and should pay the *jizya* on the basis that the Islamic state is best protected by those who believe in it.[50] In 1997 the supreme guide of the Muslim Brotherhood, Mustafā Mashhūr (1996–2002), argued that Copts could not serve in the military, since their loyalty could not be trusted,[51] a position that caused uproar among Copts and members of the liberal intelligentsia. Mashhūr was forced to retract his statement. While it was argued that his statement had been taken out of context, other Islamists defended it, stating that he was expressing his own views and did not represent those of the Muslim Brotherhood as a whole. There is no doubt, however, that some members of the Muslim Brotherhood do hold this view, even though they make few public statements to this effect. It could be argued that the Brotherhood's draft party platform of 2007 on the religious functions of the state and on the protection of non-Muslims opens up the possibility for the imposition of the *jizya*:

> The state has basic religious functions and it is responsible for protecting the religion and the Islamic state must protect the non-Muslim in regard to his belief, worship, houses of worship and other things . . . the decision to go to war represents a decision according to Islamic law, that must be based upon the goals and fundamentals as defined by Islamic law.[52]

The Brotherhood is incredibly cautious about comments concerning the *jizya*, as was illustrated in an interview with former Supreme Guide Ma'mūn al-Hudaybī in 2003. At one point al-Hudaybī implied that the *dhimma* status is a privilege for non-Muslims. While he acknowledged that non-Muslims did fight for the Islamic army in Islamic history, he said that it would be inappropriate to ask non-Muslims to defend Islam. However, if they choose to defend the land out of nationalism, then that is all well and good. He also implied that this was all theoretical and that the *dhimma* no longer exists. Rather, he said, we now have the nation-state. In addition, he argued, Muslims are barely able to defend themselves, let alone take on the responsibility for defending non-Muslims.[53] Al-Hudaybī's statement illustrates that there is a tension between the ideal, the application of the *dhimma* as rooted in Islamic history, and the reality of the current situation in Egypt, whereby non-Muslims do serve in the army.

If Islamists call for applying the *dhimma* and the *jizya*, what does that mean and what implications will it have for the status of non-Muslims? In Sunni normative classical Islam, the *dhimma* was seen as a contract by which non-Muslims submitted to the Islamic authority, and the *jizya* was in general seen as a payment for unbelief or as a symbol of subjugation. In the 1940's, Mahmūd Shaltūt (the shaykh of al-Azhar, 1958–1963) defined the *jizya* as symbol of "submission to the authority of the Muslims and subjection to their laws" and a "distance from harmful acts and a contribution in carrying the burden of the state."[54] The idea of submission is a position that radical Islamists still maintain. Submission is seen as divinely ordained, as emphasized by the last part of Qur'an 9:29, "until they pay the *jizyah* with willing submission, and feel themselves subdued." Submission is sometimes expressed in vituperative terms emphasizing servility and humility. The Alexandrian cassette sermon preacher of the 1970's and 1980's Ahmed al-Mahallāwī states, "Verily Islam is and has always been tolerant with regard to *dhimmīs*, yet on the condition that they know their place."[55] Al-Jamā'a al-Islāmiyya still states that the *jizya* is, among other things, a payment for submission.[56]

However, while many contemporary Islamists advocate the *jizya*, they depart from the idea of submission and present the *jizya* in a light that is more palatable to modern sensitivities. Some, for example, present it as a social tax instead of the *zakāt* (the alms tax that is a religious requirement for Muslims), while others present it as a payment for not serving in the army.[57]

Though the *jizya* still forms an important part of Islamist thinking, some question whether payment of it is even necessary, since in the early days of the Islamic community non-Muslims did serve in the Muslim army. Kamāl al-Sa'īd Habīb, a reformed former al-Jihād member, criticizes Muslim Brotherhood members for not realizing that the idea of the *jizya* can be revised since, he argues, a non-Muslim can choose to serve in the army. He argues that some Muslim Brotherhood members do not understand that the texts in Islamic jurisprudence pertaining to the *jizya* are numerous and have different independent judgments.[58] His is a position that other more conservative Islamists, such as the members of al-Jamā'a al-Islāmiyya, show an openness to.[59]

At the same time, questions remain as to whether it is appropriate to allow a non-Muslim to serve in the military. Some, such as Mamdūh Ismā'īl, who is an Islamist defense attorney and a former member of al-Jihād, say that a non-Muslim can serve in the army but that he should not be forced to. The same applies, he argues, to Muslims in the West, where, for example, it would be inappropriate to ask American Muslims to defend Israel. Ismāʿīl argues that there is an orientalist bias toward the concept of *dhimma*. The West, he says, does not fully understand the meaning of Islamic jurisprudence and the meaning and implications of the term *dhimmī*, which is essentially a legalistic concept that defines rights and duties. He argues that the West mistakenly thinks of the *dhimmī* as discriminatory and restrictive.[60]

An examination of how the *dhimma* relates to the principle of equality reveals the conflicting pressures of reconciling tradition with modern realities. Equality is invariably framed in terms of references to the Hadith "They have what we have and their responsibilities are our responsibilities." Statements among contemporary Islamists about equality abound, and yet the question is how are Muslims and non-Muslims equal—in what spheres and on what terms?[61] A closer look illustrates the inconsistent ways in which the equality of non-Muslims is expressed.

Of course, not all Islamists feel the need to bow to the pressure of invoking the concept of equality. According to the editors of *al-Daʿwa*, the tolerance of Islam does not include putting Muslims and non-Muslims on an equal footing, since Islam is "the sole religion that is acceptable with God." *Al-Daʿwa*'s definition of tolerance is based upon Islam's historical record and is defined by the idea of the absence of violence toward the "other." It means disputing with the People of the Book and advising them about Islam as well as forgiving them despite the fact that "many of them wish to turn you away from your religion."[62]

Abū al-ʿAlā al-Maudūdī also does not attempt to equate Islamic notions of tolerance and pluralism with equality. He claims that the Islamic system will always ensure that the rights of minorities will not be subject to the "whims and caprices" of the majority and will be protected by a system that ensures that no curtailment of these rights is allowed. In a nation-state, he argues, the majority always has the power to curtail the rights of the minority: "In reality the minorities have nowhere any say in important matters of the state." However, he argues, the Islamic system, unlike nation-states, where equality is frequently violated, will not be hypocritical in its claims.[63] This position is similar to Sayyid Qutb's notion that legislation made by an individual or governing class cannot be free of self-interest.[64] It is for this reason that the Islamist writer Kamāl al-Saʿīd Habīb argues that non-Muslims should be happy with and feel secure under an Islamic system, since "the value of equality is a fantasy value that in reality is not possible except through justice."[65]

When Islamists do invoke equality, they do not do so in terms of individual equal rights but in terms of the maxim "They have the same rights and responsibilities as we have." The multiple-law system that gained its full expression in the *millet* system is advocated as the epitome of equality, as it provides equality of opportunity for religious communities, but not individuals, to live by their own religious beliefs and adopt their own laws.[66] Thus equality is defined in terms of equal access to communal rather than individual rights.

Communal rights for non-Muslim communities include not being obliged to abstain from anything that is lawful in their religion, such as drinking wine and eating pork.[67] Ma'mūn al-Hudaybī argues that non-Muslims can settle their disputes and litigation in their own courts and that "a Muslim judge cannot examine or pass verdicts in these cases unless they themselves refer these cases to him."[68] Al-Hudaybī seems to be envisaging a modern-day application of the *millet* system in which non-Muslims have their own courts. He does not explore how this idea can be reconciled with the current centralized court system that passes rulings in the name of the Egyptian state. Yūsuf al-Qaradāwī partly rectifies this issue by arguing that non-Muslims would have their own courts only in personal status issues. In other areas of law, what he terms as civil matters, non-Muslims would be subject to *sharī'a*.[69]

While the notion of communal autonomy figures prominently, it is limited to "religious" issues. Usury is not considered a religious issue and would therefore also be forbidden to non-Muslims.[70] The penal code is also not considered a religious issue but a general one and therefore, according to Ma'mūn al-Hudaybī, should be applied to non-Muslims.[71] One writer for *al-Da'wa* makes the claim that since both Islam and Christianity condemn fornication, for which there is a harsh penalty in the Islamic penal code, Christians have no reason not to apply the Islamic penalty for it. Nothing in the Islamic penalty for adultery, he argues, violates or restricts the rights of Christians.[72]

The problem of applying the concept of equality to Islamic jurisprudence becomes clear when looking at the issue of Islamic criminal law and the legal value of a non-Muslim. Regarding the legal value of the non-Muslim in cases of retaliation, the Hanafi position, which emphasizes equality in terms of criminal punishment involving retaliation, is generally adopted.[73] For example, al-Hudaybī states that even if a Muslim steals from a non-Muslim, he should have his hand cut off.[74] However, the equality of Muslims and non-Muslims in criminal law is not accepted by all. Radical Islamists argue that Christians and Jews are unequal to Muslims, legally, socially, and politically: Islam denies equality between a Muslim and an unbeliever.[75] Muntasir al-Zayyāt, lawyer to al-Jamāʿa al-Islāmiyya, argues that a Muslim cannot be killed for the death of a non-Muslim.[76] The more mainstream Yūsuf al-Qaradāwī does not take a specific position on this, arguing that the jurists agree that killing a non-Muslim is a great sin but differ in their opinions about whether it is as much a sin as killing a Muslim.[77]

The discussion of equality in different spheres highlights the challenge of applying this principle in the context of the centralized nation-state. This difficulty is illustrated by the question of the value of a Christian as a witness in court. For the lawyer Mamdūh Ismāʿīl, reformed member of al-Jihād, in some situations there is equality and in some there is not. When it comes to commercial and civil dealings, he says, the testimony of non-Muslims is equal. However, when it comes to the penal code, which is applicable to non-Muslims, then there is no equality between a Muslim and a non-Muslim. This is because, Ismāʿīl says, there are sides to the *sharīʿa* where faith is an important factor in reaching a judgment. This also applies to Muslims: a Muslim who does not abide by the *sharīʿa* is a sinner and his testimony is not acceptable.[78]

The emphasis upon communal identity is also reflected in ideas about the social status of non-Muslims in mainstream Islam. Perhaps the most noticeable example of this comes from Yūsuf al-Qaradāwī. In his view Islam, based on the Qurʾan and Sunna, "desires its followers to develop their own distinctive characteristics in appearance, as well as in beliefs and attitudes."[79] Other examples include Muhammad al-Shaʿrāwī's instructions stating that a Muslim cannot go to the funeral of a *kāfir*, in this case a Christian, and that a Muslim should not give alms to a non-Muslim at the end of Ramadan.[80]

In the early 1990's the Cairene preacher ʿUmar ʿAbd al-Kāfī became notorious for his comments inciting Muslims to limit their relations with non-Muslims. When asked in his Cairo mosque how one should greet Coptic neighbors and colleagues, he responded that one must not greet a Coptic neighbor with the peace greeting. He argued that one cannot congratulate a Christian at Easter, since it would sanction the idea of the resurrection of Christ and in turn imply a renunciation of Islam.[81] He is also reported to have said that it is not allowed for a Muslim girl to undress in front of a Coptic girl, stating, "It would be tantamount to a male gaze being set upon you; it is an affront to your chastity."[82]

Some Islamists take this further and justify a more extreme form of separation, using the Hadith of Bukhārī "Do not greet the People of the Book" to limit social interaction between Muslims and Christians.[83] For example, al-Jamāʿa al-Islāmiyya would not undertake trade with Christians in Upper Egypt and provoked students to mistreat Christians in order to "deepen the separation between them and the masses of Muslims." This position reflected the exhortation from the medieval thinker Ibn Taymiyya (1263–1328) for Muslims to avoid commercial partnerships with Christians, since "such a partnership may contribute to [their] the Christians' prosperity and consequently, perpetuate their infidelity."[84]

DHIMMĪS IN THE POLITICAL ENTITY

There is ambiguity with regard to how the concepts of equality and pluralism would be applied in the political sphere. This ambiguity is further compounded because these principles are framed not in terms of legal rights but in terms of Islamic history as a normative ideal. Discussions often revert to what the Prophet Muhammad did, but the challenge lies in relating these anecdotes to the contemporary Egyptian political situation.

Any consideration of the role of non-Muslims in the political sphere must be preceded by a discussion of attitudes toward democracy as a principle. A number of Islamist groups have condemned democracy, advocating instead a council of consultation, in which a select group, whose membership is determined by virtue only, rules in accordance with the *sharīʿa*.[85] Al-Jihād criticizes the Muslim Brotherhood for taking part in the democratic system, arguing that democracy usurps God's right of legislation and is therefore equal to *shirk* (associating something with God, the worst sin for a Muslim).[86] The group opposes democracy because it establishes equality between a Muslim and an unbeliever. Democracy is also unacceptable, al-Jihād argues, because it establishes the principle of equality for citizens and gives individuals the right to convert from Islam to another religion.[87]

While such groups have advocated a system of *shurā*, or consultation, this is envisioned as being available to only a select group of Muslims. Under such a system, few opportunities exist for communal Christian activity and institutional formation. Such limited prospects also apply to Muslims, who would be restricted by the idea that one's political trustworthiness is determined by religious virtue. Such ambivalence toward democracy was emphasized by Muslim Brotherhood thinkers Sayyid Qutb and Hassan al-Bannā, who called for ideological unity. For Qutb, a good society is one with unified political orientations. Minorities have no right to form political parties. He sees non-Muslim "institutions and traditions" as poisonous and argues that they distort human nature and curtail human freedom.[88]

While anti-democratic views were popular within the Muslim Brotherhood up until the 1980's, such a position has given way to a growing acceptance of democracy. This is presented not in terms of adopting Western values but in terms of reaffirming Islamic ones. Muntasir al-Zayyāt states: "Islam precedes the West in confirming democracy," since Islam accepts other opinions through the practice of consultation. He criticizes Islamists for being narrow-minded and for being against democracy just because they see it as something that comes from the West. However, he says, there must be differences in how democracy is applied.[89] Mamdūh Ismāʿīl agrees that Islam has democratic elements, such as freedom of opposition to the system, freedom of thought, and freedom of religion, but he says that "we are not required as Muslims and Arabs to be apes who mimic the West." Certain limits must be imposed to protect the faith. For example, the rights of homosexuals or the right to blaspheme cannot be tolerated.[90]

Some Islamists who accept democracy understand it in terms of majority rule as defined by the Muslim majority, which the Copts must respect. It is assumed that all Muslims will be united and will behave as a political unit. For al-Ghazālī, democracy is the right of the majority to choose Islamic rule; the same would apply to countries with majorities of another religion. Al-Ghazālī writes, "Protecting the rational interests for communities of every religious inclination does not, all by itself, destroy the right of the majority to express its sovereignty and carry out its program." Since 90 percent of the Egyptian population is Muslim, they must have the right to make the Egyptian state Islamic.[91]

For the Muslim Brotherhood, advocating democracy is an effective political strategy, since in an anti-democratic context, championing the people's right to choose is expedient. However, the problem is that there are doubts about whether this goes beyond the people's right to elect an Islamic system. The secular and liberal elite—both within Egypt and in the West—fear that the Muslim Brotherhood's approach to democracy is based on the idea of "one man, one vote, one time." The Muslim Brotherhood is constrained by the legacy of Hasan al-Bannā, who opposed ideological disunity and internal division.[92] Maʾmūn al-Hudaybī claims that Hasan al-Bannā's disapproval of a multiparty system was a product of political circumstances and "did not really mean rejecting the concept of political parties itself." In any case, al-Hudaybī argues, this is an issue that can be left to "*Ijtihad* [intellectual reasoning to derive a legal ruling from the sources of Islamic law] and it is not one of the fundamentals of Islam where *Ijtihad* has no place."[93] There is some flexibility in the system so that the Muslim Brotherhood can change its views to fit the circumstances, an idea that is drawn from al-Bannā's work.[94]

The majority of Islamists argue that democracy must be constrained by the Islamic framework. Irreligious or secular parties would contradict "the oneness of God" and therefore cannot be tolerated.[95] Difference of opinion is tolerated only if it is, as Ma'mūn al-Hudaybī writes, "far from the agreed upon fundamentals (of Islam) and falls into the circle of the individuals' actions, then there can be a difference of opinion."[96] How this framework is to be defined and maintained is key. According to the Muslim Brotherhood's 2007 draft party platform, the legislature must consult a body of senior religious scholars regarding clear texts in the Qur'an and the Sunna.[97]

The question of what political rights non-Muslims have within this democratic system is a contentious one. From a legal perspective, there is debate about whether Christians have a right to be politically autonomous and active within an Islamic state, particularly whether Christians can be political leaders of Muslims. This debate derives from the correct interpretation of the following two verses from the Qur'an: "And never will Allah grant to the Unbelievers a way to triumph over the Believers" (4:141) and "O ye who believe! Take not the Jews and the Christians for your friends and protectors [*awliyā'*]; they are but friends and protectors to each other. And he amongst you that turns to them (for friendship) is of them" (5:51).[98] The main debate focuses on the precise meaning of the concept of *wilāya* (rule or authority) connected to *awliyā'* (rulers or masters), which is explicitly mentioned in 5:51.

In classical Islamic jurisprudence, there is an understanding that Copts should not be in positions of authority over Muslims, something that was reflected in the frequent calls for *dhimmīs* to be demoted from positions of authority. Based on this, doubts have been raised about whether Copts can be political candidates in contemporary Egypt. Religious *fatāwā* (legal judgments) that question the right of Copts to run as candidates have been issued. Casting doubt on the right of Christians to run has become an effective means of discrediting Coptic candidates.[99] When the Coptic politician Munīr Fakhrī 'Abd al-Nūr ran for office in 1995 and 2000, his opponent distributed flyers that included Qur'anic verses containing theological polemic.[100]

The question of whether non-Muslims have a right to political rule was of particular concern to Abū Al-'Alā al-Maudūdī, who though he was a prominent Islamic thinker was also a Pakistani politician at the time of the establishment of the Pakistani state. In the first part of his treatise on the subject, he states that non-Muslims should have reduced political power and no role in policymaking. They should not occupy central posts in the state and certainly not leadership positions; neither should they participate in the election of the Shura Council or be members of it. The responsibility for running the state lies with Muslims who believe in Islamic ideology, and non-Muslims have "nowhere any say in important matters of the state," since, he argues, "the responsibility to run the state should rest primarily with those who believe in the Islamic ideology."[101]

However, the second part of his treatise takes a somewhat different approach. He argues that while non-Muslims cannot be members of the Shura Council in the traditional sense, this rule could be relaxed, and non-Muslims could be allowed to become members of parliament, since a parliament or legislature in the modern sense is considerably different from the Shura Council in its traditional sense. In this case, the sphere of influence of non-Muslim minorities would be limited to matters relating to the general problems of the country or to the interests of minorities. Their participation would not compromise the fundamental requirements of Islam. At the same time, and in possible contradiction to the idea that non-Muslims could become members of parliament, he also states that non-Muslims have the right to establish their own house of representatives, that this house would then submit their collective objections and suggestions to the parliament, and that the "Islamic Government would be bound to consider them sympathetically and justly."[102] Then again, Maudūdī argues that all offices except some key posts are open to *dhimmīs*. He does not define what those key posts are, but says that "all posts connected with the formulation of State-Policies and control of important departments should be treated as key-posts," which should be given only to those "who have fullest faith in its ideology and who are capable of running it according to the letter and the spirit of the ideology."[103] Maudūdī also argues that non-Muslims have the same rights as Muslims to free speech, including criticizing Islam, although that is "subject to the same limitations as are imposed by law on the Muslims."[104]

Maudūdī's ideas, while inconsistent and at times contradictory, are an example of the tension between the old system, represented in his idea of the

Shura Council, and the new system, represented by the parliament. Maudūdī's argument regarding the ban of non-Muslims from sensitive, powerful, or influential positions in the Islamic state certainly has weight in Islamic jurisprudence and support among many Islamists. For example, Islamist lawyer Mamdūh Ismāʿīl argues that non-Muslims can discuss the aspects of *sharīʿa* that are relevant to them. They can have an opinion. It is the duty of the Muslim ruler to protect non-Muslims, so he should listen to their opinions.[105] Ismāʿīl says that jobs connected with the symbolism of the state, creed, and national security cannot be occupied by non-Muslims. For example, they cannot serve in religious positions such as that of judge, and a non-Muslim certainly cannot become president.[106] Both Yūsuf al-Qaradāwī and Maʾmūn al-Hudaybī argue that non-Muslims have the right to occupy government positions that do not have a direct bearing on religion or that are "not related to enforcing the rulings of the Islamic *sharīʿa* in which they do not believe."[107] Thus the statement of Hassan al-Bannā that "there is no harm in employing non-Muslims in minor positions when necessary" still forms a part of the Muslim Brotherhood's thinking.[108]

Even Islamists who would like more involvement of non-Muslims in the political sphere place limits on that involvement. Yūsuf al-Qaradāwī draws on the ideas of eleventh-century jurist Abū al-Hasan al-Māwardī (974–1058) and argues that non-Muslims may run for elections but that the overwhelming majority must be Muslims. The same applies to women who are allowed to serve in parliament, but again the majority must be men. Non-Muslims can be governors in the ministry, "but under the general governance of Muslims." In the same way, a non-Muslim woman can have authority in running the home, since ultimately the Muslim husband is in control.[109]

The implication is that rights are given to non-Muslims by Muslims, a situation that creates an inherent inequality and positions the state as the monopoly of Muslims. The same implication is reflected in al-Qaradāwī's comment that a non-Muslim has the right to file a complaint when his rights are infringed upon, with the "guarantee offered by the widespread Islamic conscience instilled in Muslims by the Islamic creed."[110] Non-Muslims are not, however, allowed to publicly abuse Islam and should consider the "feelings of Muslims."[111]

The views of these conservative members of the Muslim Brotherhood illustrate the tension that exists between allowing greater non-Muslim involvement with traditional assumptions derived from the *dhimma*. While Maʾmūn al-Hudaybī, for example, argues that every Egyptian citizen (man or woman) has the right to take part in parliamentary elections and the right to become a member of parliament through elections, every citizen does not have equality in political terms.[112] Al-Hudaybī implies that some sort of representation is required for Christians, since there are five million of them in Egypt.[113] However, when pressed, he did not want to get into the specifics of this representation and would speak only of the "general principle" of representation.[114] As a principle, Copts should be represented in parliament, but details can be given later.[115] He argues that while they should be involved in discussing the matter and should be asked for their opinion, they should also be willing to accept the outcome of decisions.[116] According to al-Hudaybī, human rights are universal, but political rights always differ between the majority and the minority and it is the nature of democracy that the majority should rule.[117] He states that the Muslim Brotherhood would not reject having Copts as members in a political system "as long as these Copts do what they are required to do," which is to acknowledge the right of the Muslim majority to apply the *sharī'a*.[118]

CHRISTIANS IN THE EGYPTIAN NATIONAL PROJECT

Most contemporary Islamists who take the *dhimma* as a point of departure envision politics divided along the lines of religious community. Non-Muslims would be limited to representing themselves and to looking after their own interests, with their own particular representatives and voters.[119]

This communal vision of politics treats non-Muslims as a separate religious bloc and assumes that this bloc will act monolithically and that religious identity will determine political behavior. It raises the question of what role, if any, the notion of Egyptian identity plays in this approach. The Muslim Brotherhood has often rejected the "worldly concept of national identity," which coincides with general assumptions about Islamist antipathy to national feeling.[120] Hasan al-Bannā was apathetic toward the idea of the nation-state and wrote: "All Muslims in these geographically determined countries are our people and our brethren: we are concerned about them and we share their feelings and sensibilities . . . we seek power only that we may share in it together." Muslims must define patriotism according to belief, he argues, and not according to territorial borders and geography.[121] While al-Bannā did not deny love of the land, or that "Arabdom" has its distinct qualities and moral characteristics, his primary concern was with the unity of Muslims.[122]

This antipathy toward the idea of national identity was taken further by Sayyid Qutb, who argued that the relationship that binds Muslims together was the only relationship recognized by God and "all other relationships based on blood or other considerations become eliminated."[123] A Muslim has "no nationality except his belief" and "no relatives except those who share the belief in God."[124] This rejection of the nation-state was taken to its extreme by some of Qutb's followers, who held that the nation-state was a Western concept tantamount to unbelief. Al-Jamā'a al-Islāmiyya has, until recently, pushed for the reestablishment of the caliphate.[125] Mamdūh Ismā'īl, a former member of al-Jihād, still emphasizes the bond of faith as the only acceptable justification for loyalty.[126] The implication is that cultural unity between Christians and Muslims becomes devalued, and therefore Copts would have little opportunity for expressing a sense of national identity.

However, in the current context it is only a minority of Islamists who deny the concept of the nation-state. Most Islamists accept the nation-state as the framework for political action. This view has, in turn, influenced their ideology, although many are still ambiguous about the concept of national identity. Islamists are more pragmatic and acknowledge that a concept of Egyptian identity does exist, yet there is still some antipathy. While Ma'mūn al-Hudaybī has a firm attachment to the idea of the homeland (*watan*), he argues that one cannot value a member of one's nation above a fellow Muslim. For him, nationalism must be tempered by Islamic justice.[127] He writes that Christians are our "partners in the country" and were brothers in the long struggle to liberate the nation.[128] However, these thinkers still adhere to the overwhelming importance of the notion of the wider Islamic community. For them the religious bond is the strongest of all bonds.[129] Yūsuf al-Qaradāwī writes that "a Muslim is closer to his Muslim fellows than to any non-believer, even though the latter may be his father, son, or brother."[130]

The limitations of the Muslim Brotherhood's commitment to the concept of national identity was illustrated when Mahmūd 'Izzat Ibrahīm, of the Muslim Brotherhood's Guidance Office, stated that he would rather be ruled by a non-Egyptian Muslim than a Copt. This was in line with his statement that the ruler's job is to lead people in prayer and command them to pay the *zakāt*, which a non-Muslim cannot do.[131]

Such antipathy to Egyptian identity is also reflected in the idea that non-Muslims are guests. Al-Sha'rāwī refers to non-Muslims as guests who should be "satisfied to stay in our lands."[132] Al-Qaradāwī likens the security granted to *dhimmīs* to the "citizenship granted by a government to an alien who abides by the constitution, thereby earning all the rights of a natural citizen."[133]

THE END OF THE *DHIMMA*

Most classical jurists considered the *dhimma* a permanent contract. Though some, such as the historian al-Tabarī (839–923), thought that the *dhimma* contract could be revoked, theirs was a minority position. The majority of Islamists who call for the reestablishment of the *dhimma* emphasize the permanency and sacredness of the *dhimma* contract. Most see the *dhimma* as divinely ordained and hold that it would be a sin to revoke it. They argue that the *dhimma* is a trust and it is the religious responsibility of Muslims to adhere to that trust: Muslims are "bound to protect" the life and property of non-Muslims.[134] The conditions that deprive the *dhimmī* of his status are leaving the state and going over to its enemies, openly revolting against the state, or trying to overthrow it. Aside from that, according to Maudūdī, a *dhimmī* will always be entitled to his *dhimmī* status.[135]

However, a minority of Islamists do not agree with the sacred nature of the *dhimma* contract and emphasize its temporal nature. Al-Jamā'a al-Islāmiyya argues that the *dhimma* contract comes not from God but from the Muslim community. Temporality and revocability are also implied by the emphasis placed upon the necessity for *dhimmīs* to behave well. Karam Zuhdī, leader of al-Jamā'a al-Islāmiyya, has stated that Copts and Muslims have the same obligations and enjoy the same rights "provided that they do not do what the expatriate Christians do—attacking our country and trying to divide its citizens."[136] Emphasis is placed on the conditional nature of the covenant between non-Muslims and the Islamic state. The preacher 'Umar 'Abd al-Kāfī stated that non-Muslims can have "their rights," "as long as the non-Muslims have not committed hostile action against us and have not done wrong to us and have not cursed our religion and have not plunged into our affairs."[137] In one article in *al-Da'wa*, 'Umar al-Tilmisānī, a former supreme guide of the Muslim Brotherhood, claims that because of the current enmity of the Jews toward Islam, there is to be no protection for them and that the *dhimma* contract is void.[138]

Such discourse emphasizes temporality and opens the way for revoking the *dhimma*, echoing the approach of the classical jurist Ibn Taymiyya (1263–1328). Influenced by his antipathy toward non-Muslims, which resulted from the Crusades and the Mongol invasions, Ibn Taymiyya broke with tradition that held to the permanency of the *dhimma* pact and called for the revocation of the *dhimma*. This has also occurred in the contemporary period, as theological polemic has laid the foundation for arguing that the protected status of Christians should be revoked. Theological polemic, while not necessarily endowed with political implications, is in some situations used to undermine the belief that Christians are People of the Book who should be respected and protected as fellow monotheists.

Among radical Islamists, theological polemic picks up on common themes in medieval Islamic discourse. It focuses on accusations that Christians are guilty of *shirk* (associating something with God) for making Jesus into the Son of God and worshipping him. Christians are also accused of the distortion of scripture, and Christianity is accused of being an irrational religion because of such concepts as original sin and the Trinity. These accusations reflect the idea held by some medieval Muslims that only Christians who accepted Muhammad were to be considered as believers.[139] A distinction is also made between a pure Christianity and Christianity as it later developed. Qutb claims that Christianity was corrupted by the rulers of the Byzantine Empire so that *shirk* entered into it.[140] Muhammad al-Ghazālī argued that "Crusaderism" is different from original Christianity, which reflected the message of Jesus, which was then abandoned. It is therefore a new religion, with only remnants of the old Christianity.[141]

Such theological polemic can be found in medieval Islamic theological discourse, which under some circumstances had political implications for the treatment of non-Muslims. It can also have political implications in the current context. For example, theological polemic was used to undermine Coptic politician Munīr Fakhrī 'Abd al-Nūr's recent candidacy for parliament. To call someone an unbeliever has important social implications. In Egyptian culture, a faithful person is a good person, and thus the term "unbeliever" is used to describe an outsider. If you are not faithful, the implication is that you are not part of the community.[142]

This polemic also provides the theological foundation for arguing that Christianity is not really a celestial religion, which would mean demoting Christians from the revered status of People of the Book to the status of other unbelievers, or polytheists. It marks a departure from the traditional understanding that underlies the notion of the *dhimma*—i.e., that Jews and Christians were People of the Book and therefore had a far higher status than non-monotheists.[143]

The theological polemic combined with Sayyid Qutb's central and most influential concept of *al-jāhiliyya* serves to highlight the insecurity of the *dhimma*. Historically, *al-jāhiliyya* stands for the culture of pre-Islamic Arabia, a period of barbarism and paganism. For Qutb, however, *al-jāhiliyya* is ahistorical. It is no longer a past time in history but rather a condition or state.[144] All Jewish and Christian societies are *jāhilī* societies. So-called "Muslim societies" are also part of *al-jāhiliyya*, because they do not apply God's law and because "of the authority they give to human institutions."[145] Qutb's ideas imply confrontation with the forces of *al-jāhiliyya*. On one level, his ideas about *al-jāhiliyya* do not constitute a negation of the *dhimma*. Though he advocated the universalization of Islam, this did not imply the annihilation of non-Muslims, although any acceptance of Christianity or Judaism rested on the condition that it was under the authority of Islam. The *jizya* was for him a sign of submission from non-Muslims.[146]

However, Qutb's ideas also operate on another level. Implicit in his thought is the notion of a fixed, permanent struggle between Islam and People of the Book that is primarily religious in nature. He takes a number of verses in the Qur'an that refer to the Prophet's political disputes with the People of the Book, namely the Jews, out of their historical and political context. One such verse is this: "Quite a number of the People of the Book wish they could turn you (people) back to infidelity after ye have believed. From selfish envy, after the Truth hath become manifest to them (2:109)."[147] For Qutb, verses such as this describe a permanent and essential characteristic of the People of the Book. In his exegesis, he refers to the war that the People of the Book, "especially the Jews," conducted against the early Muslim community.[148] Qutb's criticism of the Jews is particularly vitriolic: writing in the 1960's, he had the state of Israel foremost in his mind.

Thus, just as the early Islamic community struggled against the People of the Book, contemporary Islamic society faces the same struggle. Qutb refers to the permanent renewed battle between Muslim society and its "traditional enemies who are still the same and their incentives are still the same."[149] He thus explains contemporary political concerns in terms of eternal historical truths.

Such ideas were reflected in both the rhetoric and the actions of al-Jamā'a al-Islāmiyya, which believed that the Copts embodied the eternal enmity of Christianity, which was intent on destroying Islam.[150] Karam Zuhdī, the group's leader, came from Upper Egypt, where there are a large number of Christians. Zuhdī argued that Christians were infidels and thus a proper target for *jihād*. He railed against the "Crusaders' manifestations of superiority" and their provocative behavior. He accused them of wanting to turn Egypt into a Coptic country.[151] 'Umar 'Abd al-Rahmān (1938–), former advisor to al-Jamā'a al-Islāmiyya and al-Jihād, argued that Christians, who, he says, follow

the laws of the devil, are part of a bloc of unbelievers that is intent on destroying Islam. One is either for or against Islam; there is either right or wrong,
belief or unbelief, since, he says, "what is after right, except error?"¹⁵² The notion of the eternal enmity of the People of the Book can also be found in the
pages of *al-Da'wa*.¹⁵³

The concept of a permanent struggle between Islam and Christianity is
also articulated through the concept of the Crusades. The preoccupation with
the Crusades is a relatively new phenomenon, arising in response to Western
influence in the region. In medieval Arab historiography, the Crusades were
never the object of special attention; Muslim historians did not even have a
specific term for them, other than describing them as "Frankish" invasions.¹⁵⁴
The term "Crusade" dates to the nineteenth century, and its use derives "from
belief in a certain parallelism" between the events of the period of the Crusades and the colonial era. The Crusades "became a symbol of its domination
as well as irrefutable proof of the innately malicious character of Western intentions toward the Arab-Islamic world."¹⁵⁵

The equation of the Crusades with colonialism means that, in many cases,
the Crusading spirit is viewed as a European characteristic rather than a Christian one. Qutb describes the Crusading spirit as being "latent in the European
mind."¹⁵⁶ Some of the rhetoric, however, has reached even further back in time
and linked the concept of the Crusade to the same historical enmity expressed
in the Qur'an and experienced by Muhammad. This connection is illustrated in
the literature of radical Islamists, in which little effort is made to distinguish
between Western and Eastern Christians. The concept of the Crusade is used
to justify and explain sectarian tension between Copts and Muslims.

A small number of Copts have worked toward and called for the establishment of a separate state and sought help from Copts in the United States and
the U.S. government, actions that easily lead to Copts' being viewed as part of
a broader conspiracy against Islam. The magazine *al-Da'wa* accused Coptic
leaders of encouraging Copts to maximize the number of children they have
and accused Coptic doctors of not treating Muslims.¹⁵⁷ After the violence of
al-Zawiya al-Hamra in 1981, *al-Da'wa* accused the Copts of spying and dissim-
ulation as a provocation for the violence. The violence that occurred was presented as an illustration of the Crusader conspiracy against Islam. *Al-Da'wa*
also accused Copts of scheming to eradicate Islam in Egypt and turn it into a
Christian state.¹⁵⁸ Much is made of the connections that Coptic Christians in
Egypt have with Copts in the United States. Sālim al-Rahhāl of al-Jihād states

that the Copts are part of this "Crusading hatred" that is in turn linked to the Palestinian-Israeli conflict.[159] For Kamāl al-Saʿīd Habīb, the Copts are part of and allies with the Crusading world and are a means by which the enemy imposes its values.[160]

Sheikh Kishk, a popular preacher of the 1980's and 1990's, employed similar tactics. In one sermon he opened a letter from a "non-Muslim citizen," which he said smelled of "wickedness." The letter was from a Christian asking critical questions about Islam, including why did the Prophet break his own law by having more than four wives and why did God say to the Prophet, "If you doubt what God has revealed, ask those who have read the book before you."[161]

Such associations are inevitable in times of political strife, but conflations like these have serious implications for Coptic-Muslim relations in Egypt. The political ramifications are strongly felt by Copts, who out of fear were eager to dissociate themselves from "Bush's Crusade." Thus the Coptic Church feels impelled to stand up and tell people that it is not associated with the Americans.

POLITICAL VIOLENCE

So what implications do the above attitudes have for Christians living in a modern Muslim state? Such ideas are used by radical Islamists to put Christians outside the protection of the *dhimma*. Members of al-Jihād do not explicitly mention military *jihād* against indigenous Christians under Islamic rule. However, the group condoned killing non-believers, who, in its view, are all the same.[162] ʿUmar ʿAbd al-Rahmān argues that conciliation with and acceptance of the *jizya* from Christians can be withdrawn if the Muslim leader so chooses. This view lays the groundwork for military *jihād* against them. He states that *jizya* is to be accepted only if it is in the Islamic state's interest to accept it.[163] He is reputed to have incited violence against Christians.[164] In response to the events of al-Zawiya al-Hamra, he also issued a *fatwā* stating that the wealth of non-Muslims was allowed, meaning that Muslims could expropriate the wealth of non-Muslims and killing them in the process was justified.[165] Thus the property rights of Christians could be violated, and— one example of the effect of the *fatwā*—in the late 1970's numerous Christian-owned jewelry shops in Upper Egypt were looted.

In the 1990's, al-Jamāʿa al-Islāmiyya claimed that it is not possible for Muslims to live amicably with Christians and stated that Christians must be fought because they are the enemies of Islam.[166] On a tape made at a mosque in Imbaba following the sectarian events of 1991, the group rejected "national unity." Karam Zuhdī, the leader of al-Jamā'a al-Islāmiyya, thought that *jihād* should be waged against Christians who posed an obstacle to spreading Islam. He used accusations of unbelief to justify political violence. Zuhdī used this designation of Christians as unbelievers on account of their belief that God is Christ the Son of Mary to justify violence against them and seize their property.[167] Not only did he and his followers consider the wealth of Copts as permissible spoil for Muslims, but Zuhdī is linked to the deaths of many Christians in the 1970's and 1980's.[168]

The case of Shukrī Mustafā, leader of Jamā'at al-Muslimīn (Society of Muslims), better known as al-Takfīr wa al-Hijra, illustrates such an attitude taken to its extreme conclusion. Mustafā came from Upper Egypt, where there is a relatively high percentage of Christians. He argued that Christians were to be targets of violent *jihād. Jihād* would not cease if non-Muslims surrendered; it would cease only upon conversion to Islam. Using the idea that God instructed Muslims to fight in stages, he argued that the final and most important stage was based on God's command to continue fighting until everyone became a Muslim. He stated that God had ordered him to fight and not stop fighting, quoting from the Qur'an: "Oh ye who believe fight the unbelievers who gird you about (9:123)." God's order was that Muslims should fight non-Muslims to the death. Mustafā argued that the obligation to fight non-Muslims derived from the fact that Christians wanted to turn Muslims against their religion.[169]

It is impossible to tell whether these ideas are held by anyone else besides Shukrī Mustafā and his small group of followers. There is no doubt that his is a fringe view. However, ideological unity was a common theme among some Islamist groups. Al-Jihād states: "Our aim is the establishment of the religion in its entirety in every soul and above every inch of the earth inside every house and in every institution and in every community"—a view based on the group's interpretation of the following Qur'anic verse: "And fight them on until there is no more tumult or oppression and there prevails justice and faith in Allah (8:39)."[170] While there are indications that this constituency is small, it does exist. A number of Islamic authors refer to and address such thought in their writings.[171]

The fact that al-Jamā'a al-Islāmiyya has revised some of its views and now categorically rejects violence against Christians is an indication that such opinions lack widespread credibility. The group has expressed sorrow for the violence they have committed against Copts and says that those who committed violence against Copts were interpreting the Qur'an incorrectly.[172]

The Copts faced considerable anti-Coptic sentiment from some quarters during the 1970's and 1980's, when Muslim extremists infiltrated the media. Preachers were allowed to operate freely, and religious programs attacking Coptic doctrines and creeds increased. Since September 11, 2001, however, the government has banned a great deal of the radical literature and cassette tapes. It has clamped down on radical preachers, so it is not possible to assess how many people hold such views. It is possible that these attitudes have simply gone underground. The Coptic intellectual and Islamist sympathizer Rafīq Habīb says that the harsh words of Karam Zuhdī toward Christians influence the "common" people and that these kinds of radical ideas still exist.[173]

The political context and the perception that there is a global conflict between Christianity and Islam fuel such radical views. Copts have been concerned that echoes of the "clash of civilizations" perception could reach Egypt and affect Muslim-Christian relations by implicating Copts. Many Egyptian Copts have found it necessary to publicly distance themselves from Western political activity. Egyptian Coptic intellectuals have condemned the Christian Coalition, an American umbrella organization of right-wing Christian groups that defend Israel's actions.[174] Rafīq Habīb stated that when "there is an external enemy that is Christian, the insider Christians are in trouble . . . because ordinary Muslims think O.K. it is the same Bible," so though "you are not saying it in public, you are with Israel."[175] It is not just radicals who talk of a Crusade. Habīb states that the masses are also saying this.[176] Certainly it is true that Copts were more supportive of the invasion of Afghanistan after 9/11. However, many Copts are equally anti-Western.[177] Amid the increasing concern about the possibility of anti-Christian violence, many churches are now guarded by police. Saad Eddin Ibrahim states that when the shaykhs talk about the Crusades, there is an unspoken question as to the position of the Copts.[178] This is not just a Muslim issue, though; negative views exist on both sides. Cornelis Hulsman reports that there are strong anti-Islamic sentiments among Copts. For example, he has witnessed Coptic youth expressing support for President Bush.[179]

CONCLUSION

Support for the reintroduction of the *dhimma* status to define relations between Muslims and non-Muslims is an important theme in contemporary Islamist thought, partly because of the enduring authority of Islamic history and Islamic jurisprudence. However, while the Islamists discussed in this chapter claim to return to a true Islam as rooted in Islamic history, their discourse is strongly influenced by modern concepts and priorities such as tolerance and pluralism. Although contemporary Islamists wish to ground their political discourse in the Islamic tradition, this tradition is altered by the context within which it is invoked.

This illustrates that contemporary Islamists are under considerable pressure to authenticate their vision of Islam within the Islamic tradition, yet at the same time to respond to the pressures of modernity. The struggle to balance the two has resulted in inconsistency and confusion. There is a problem with conveying medieval Islamic concepts by utilizing Western terms. The Arabic rendition of pluralism conveys more a sense of numerical variety than one of ideological diversity. Difficulty also arises in expressing the concept of equality between non-Muslims and Muslims in terms of communal rather than individual rights.

An overemphasis on Islamic history as having established a precedent for determining relations between Muslims and non-Muslims precludes concrete reference to current realities. There is relatively little reference to how the concept of tolerance relates to specific legal questions regarding non-Muslims in Egypt. There is a reluctance to anchor general principles to the contemporary context. For the Muslim Brotherhood in particular, the struggle to balance the need to base their ideas on Islamic tradition with a response to the modern political process, of which they are an important part, poses dilemmas. The Muslim Brotherhood, as Samīr Murqus has argued, "carries a double burden." It has the historical burden of the legacy of Hasan al-Bannā, who rejected democracy and called for ideological unity, and it also has the burden of opening up to the reality of the political process in which it is involved. It has yet to directly confront questions such as what its position is regarding Egyptian identity, cultural heritage, and national memory. It has yet to confront the question of what its position would be regarding political pluralism, *da'wa*, and the political rights of non-Muslims.[180]

While mainstream Islamists seek to reintroduce the *dhimma*, radical Islamists seek to provide utopian solutions to current political problems. They do not view Islamic tradition as something that needs to be emulated. They employ concepts such as the Crusade to establish the idea of continuous and permanent Christian enmity toward Islam, thus providing justification for claiming that Christians are no longer protected peoples. The emphasis upon Christians being unbelievers is used as a justification for violence and for revoking the *dhimma* contract. Christians are put on the same level as other unbelievers, and all unbelievers are considered the enemies of Islam. Thus the Islamic tradition, which reflected an environment within which Christians lived alongside Muslims, is denied.

There are indications that these utopian and radical ideas are no longer as prevalent as they were in the 1970's and 1980's. However, while the kind of literature that advocates such views has become difficult to obtain, especially after 9/11 and in the last few years, it may still exist: such dichotomizing and simplistic views have a powerful appeal. Nevertheless, a shift away from radicalism may have occurred as part of a broader movement within Egyptian society toward a more conciliatory and accepting position on non-Muslims.

5 TOWARD CITIZENSHIP

SINCE THE EARLY 1980's, an Islamist political discourse that seeks to break the connection between Islam's essential values and classical Islamic jurisprudence has evolved. This discourse has been applied to a number of different topics, including the questions of Islam's compatibility with democracy and the rights of women. It has also been applied to the concept of the *dhimma*. A group of centrist and moderate intellectuals known as the Wasatiyya (from the term *wasat*, meaning center, i.e., moderate) argues that Islamic history does not have to determine the formation of the contemporary Egyptian Islamic state. In their view, rejecting the *dhimma* and establishing the concept of citizenship for defining identity in an Egyptian Islamic state is compatible with *sharī'a*. Muslims, they say, must assess what Islam means for contemporary Muslims by employing *ijtihād* (intellectual reasoning to deduce Islamic law from its sources) to reinterpret the divine law. This reinterpretation must distinguish between the following: Islam in the sense of its essence—that is, the divinely ordained law found in the Qur'an and the Hadith—and Islam as Islamic jurisprudence, which was the historical product of human endeavors to interpret the divinely ordained law.

Calls for returning to the Qur'an and the Sunna and reinterpreting Islamic jurisprudence are not new. They date back to the early modern Islamic thinkers Jamāl al-Dīn al-Afghānī (1838–1897) and Muhammad 'Abduh (1849–1905), who called for rejecting tradition and employing *ijtihād* to reinterpret the Qur'an and the Hadith. However, the use of this approach to argue for citizenship as the basis for relations between Muslims and non-Muslims in Egypt is a relatively recent innovation. The Wasatiyya engagement with the concept of citizenship within an Islamic framework started in the early 1980's. During the 1980's and 1990's, defining Copts as citizens rather than as *dhimmīs* had little appeal within Islamist discourse and was limited to the writings of the Wasatiyya intellectuals. During the last ten years, however, arguments for citizenship have had considerable influence upon the ideas of contemporary Islamist movements, among them the Muslim Brotherhood and the al-Wasat (Center) Party.

While reliance on Islamic jurisprudence for defining the relationship between Muslims and non-Muslims is rejected, establishing the notion of citizenship is not achieved by breaking away from Islam. Citizenship is justified within an Islamic framework by appealing to the Qur'an and the Sunna to reinterpret the Islamic message. By so doing, Islam, in terms of its essence, is purged of the accretions of tradition. Establishing Islamic legitimacy is important when the advocates of citizenship face the danger of being accused of imposing Western values upon Islam.

This chapter examines how the concept of citizenship is articulated within an Islamic framework and justified as authentic from an Islamic perspective. It illustrates that citizenship is articulated by drawing on precedents found in early Islamic history. Islamic history is therefore not rejected, but the notion of a golden age during the time of the Prophet, which is presented as the true representative of Islamic values, is separated from the medieval period, in which the *dhimma* contract took its classical form. Thus a distinction is made between the early Islamic history of the Prophet and Islamic history as it evolved. Citizenship is projected back onto the time of the Prophet and expressed as a true fulfillment of his intentions.

Another approach to legitimizing citizenship is also taken. Establishing the principle of citizenship is expressed as a logical response to and acceptance of the status quo. Citizenship, it is argued, forms the basis of the current Egyptian state and is to be accepted. Islamic political theory is thereby sanctioning the status quo. This sanctioning of the status quo, it has been shown, dates back to medieval Islamic political thought.

CITIZENSHIP VERSUS THE *DHIMMA*

Classical Islamic society was constructed not on the basis of citizenship in the context of the nation-state but on the *dhimma* contract, which was developed in the context of the Umayyad and Abbasid empires. The *dhimma* contract was based on the idea of religious tolerance, although it was a tolerance that was articulated within the Islamic political framework and linked to Islam's inherent superiority. The premise behind it was that while the political supremacy and dominance of Islam were necessary, uniformity of religion was not. Coercion was condemned, and faith as a voluntary act was emphasized, although there were rare incidents of forced conversion.

The Islamic state granted religious tolerance to the *dhimmī* not as an individual but as a member of a protected community.[1] The absence of the principle that rights were attached to an individual as a human being also applied to Muslims. The rights of Muslims were created by the law and due to them as Muslims.[2] This became more institutionally entrenched under the *millet* system, which gave religious communities authority over the individuals in the community. It can be argued that there was no concept of an individual's direct relationship with the state. Certainly it was not believed that a relationship to a particular geographical area brought rights.[3] However, non-Muslims were allowed the protection of the Islamic polity. This protection was perceived to be divinely ordained and protected by the law. Since the state existed to enforce the law, it was the obligation of the Islamic polity to protect non-Muslims. Beyond the promise of protection, however, the non-Muslim individual functioned as a member of a relatively autonomous religious community. This arrangement precluded the development of citizenship notions: children, for example, were educated by their religious communities and not as citizens of a nation-state.

One of the challenges facing the Islamist movement today is the growing legitimacy of concepts such as human rights, democracy, and citizenship. In response, many Islamist groups have argued for the compatibility of Islam with citizenship, equality, and human rights. Many Islamists now take the view that not only are democracy and citizenship compatible with Islam but these concepts are also an expression of its very essence. The idea that they are particular to the Western historical experience is therefore rejected. This marks an important shift in Islamist discourse, away from the radical ideas of the 1970's and 1980's, which rejected such concepts as citizenship and democracy, characterizing them as imported ideologies. It also marks an important shift away from arguments that call for the application of the *dhimma*. The challenge of departing from this position lies in articulating the concepts of citizenship and human rights through the use of legitimate methods and forms of argumentation. These methods need to remain within the framework of Islamic thought while at the same time remaining committed to the concept of citizenship that they invoke.

The term "citizenship" is a relatively new concept in Islamic thought. Historically, the term "citizen" did not exist in Islamic political language.[4] The Arabic translation for "citizenship" is *muwātana*, which derives from the word *watan*, "homeland" or "fatherland."[5] In classical usage, *watan* meant one's place of abode or residence.[6] Bernard Lewis argues that the concept of the *watan* did not have any political implications and that it was not until the concepts of nationality and citizenship were introduced in the Islamic world that a term "was needed and was found."[7] The Egyptian scholar Rifa'a Rafi' al-Tahtāwī (1801–1873) introduced the concepts of fatherland (*watan*) and patriotism (*wataniyya*) into Arabic, from which the term *muwātana* for "citizenship" evolved.[8] This form, coming from the verbal noun of the sixth form of the verb, implies some kind of reciprocity—i.e., the notion of sharing a homeland. It must be remembered that "citizenship" is merely a translation of the concept of *muwātana* and the concept of *muwātana* must be understood by the way in which it is articulated in Islamist discourse.

THE WASATIYYA AND THE REVISION OF ISLAMIC JURISPRUDENCE

The emergence of moderate Islamists or the Wasatiyya (centrist) intellectuals has had a significant impact on the discussion of citizenship in Egypt. The concept of citizenship has been appropriated by the centrist Islamist intellectuals, who question the assumption that citizenship is best guaranteed within a secular framework.

The Wasatiyya intellectuals include Dr. Muhammad Salīm al-'Awwā, Fahmī Huwaydī, Tāriq al-Bishrī, and Dr. Muhammad 'Imāra.[9] Muhammad Salīm al-'Awwā (1942–) is a prominent Egyptian lawyer, a professor of comparative law, and an independent Islamic scholar. He has recently served as secretary general of the International Union of Muslim Scholars and as head of the Egyptian Association for Culture and Dialogue.[10] Fahmī Huwaydī (1936–) is a columnist who writes on Islamic affairs in the semi-official newspaper *al-Ahrām* and the London-based newspaper *al-Sharq al-Awsat*. He is also a member of the International Union of Muslim Scholars. Tāriq al-Bishrī (1933–) is a historian, a retired judge, and a former head of Egypt's State Council.[11] Muhammad 'Imāra (1931–), perhaps the most conservative of the group, is a prolific and highly renowned Islamic writer who is a member of the Islamic Research Academy, an important wing of the Egypt's religious institution al-Azhar. He is a former Marxist turned Islamist. All four are laymen who received a secular education, and none of them except 'Imāra belongs to an official religious institution.

This group of intellectuals has strong nationalist sympathies. They seek to combine elements of nationalist ideology and Islam, they embrace the notion of Egyptian-ness, and they do not question the legitimacy of the Egyptian nation-state. It is this embrace of the Islam-based nation-state that has provided the inspiration for moderate Islamist groups, such as the al-Wasat Party and the pragmatists of the Muslim Brotherhood.

Other individuals associated with the Wasatiyya intellectuals include Yūsuf al-Qaradāwī (1926–), one of the most important contemporary Islamic scholars. He was professor and dean at the Faculty of Islamic Studies, University of Qatar, and was nominated as a member of al-Azhar's Islamic Research Academy in 2009. He also has considerably popularity and is one of the most respected thinkers in the contemporary Islamic world. Chapter 4 discussed his writings from the mid-1980's. Since then his views have become closer to those of the Wasatiyya.

Perhaps one of the most interesting individuals associated with the Wasatiyya movement is Rafīq Habīb, who is a Protestant Copt and a former member and founder of the al-Wasat Party. He is director of the Coptic Evangelical Association for Social Services and son of the Rev. Samuel Habīb, the late head of the Evangelical *Millet* Council. Rafīq Habīb is not representative of Coptic opinion. He has only a few Coptic sympathizers, among them Hanī Labīb and Gamāl Asad. The fact that he is a Copt who supports the Islamist agenda means that for the Wasatiyya Islamists, he represents a vindication of their ideas.

Like all Islamists, the Wasatiyya intellectuals insist on the application of Islamic law and are firmly opposed to secularism. They see Islam as a universal ideology for state, society, and government. They argue that Islam is a superior system and the best way to guarantee the rights of Christians. However, they feel that imposing Islamic jurisprudence in the context of the contemporary Islamic state is no longer appropriate. They call for *ijtihād* to renew Islamic jurisprudence, and their ideas constitute a revision of Islamic jurisprudence.[12] They have made considerable progress in articulating citizenship by using Islamic principles and drawing on Islamic precedents. They make a firm distinction between Islam's values and principles (found in the Qur'an and the Hadith) and the classical Islamic historical model for the treatment of non-Muslims.

The articulation of the concept of citizenship within the Islamic movement is, to a certain extent, new. However, it still lies within the framework of modern Islamist thinking. Muhammad Salim al-'Awwā situates his ideas on citizenship within the methodology of more conservative Islamic thinkers. In his most recent work, he argues that he is not alone in his position, and he even rejects the idea that the Wasatiyya are particularly new. He is eager to argue that his position regarding the *dhimma* and citizenship is the same as that of the "general public of old." In his view, many modern *'ulamā'*, such as former shaykh of al-Azhar Mahmūd Shaltūt (1893–1963), Jadd al-Haqq 'Alī Jadd al-Haqq (former mufti and grand imam of al-Azhar 1982–1996), Muhammad al-Ghazālī (1916–1996), and Yūsuf al-Qaradāwī (1926–), also take this position.[13] The fact that al-'Awwā has chosen to associate himself with more conservative Islamic scholars indicates that he is under some pressure to avoid being described as someone who departs from Islamic tradition.

While the articulation of citizenship is in itself new, the methods employed are not. These thinkers belong to the broader tradition of Islamic thought that rejects the blind imitation of tradition and advocates *ijtihād*. The interpretation of Islamic history forms the foundation for the new Islamic jurisprudence and for the articulation of citizenship. A less idealized and apologetic view of Islamic history is adopted, marking a departure from mainstream Islamism. Al-'Awwā criticizes the kind of Islamic thought discussed in chapter 4 for "revolv[ing] around an orbit of the realities of Islamic history" and for selecting either the most- or the least-favorable periods and using them to generalize about Islamic history as a whole.[14]

The Wasatiyya take a markedly different approach to Islamic history. They distinguish between two periods of history: the golden age of the Prophet and the subsequent development of Islamic history in the medieval or post-Rāshidūn period. They argue that the medieval period of Islamic history can be cast aside and one can return to an original Islam as embodied in the model established by the Prophet. Islam as divinely revealed law is therefore distinguished from the way it evolved historically. History, in Fahmī Huwaydī's view, produced circumstances by which Islam became estranged from its spirit, just as a seed that is not planted in fertile earth fails to "bring forth the hoped-for yield." One of the main reasons for this estrangement, he argues, was the influence of the Hanbalī school of law, which caused relations between Muslims and Christians to become characterized by tension and fanaticism, and as a result, Muslims as well as non-Muslims were oppressed.[15] For al-'Awwā, Islamic history contains positive and negative moments. While this should be a source of warning and advice, it should not bind us in the sense that it must be adhered to.[16] The idea that old historical formulas that defined relationships do not apply in the modern context means that the status of non-Muslims in the medieval period of Islamic history does not need to be replicated. Even Yūsuf al-Qaradāwī and Muhammad ʿImāra, who retain some of the attitudes toward history discussed in chapter 4, adopt a less idealized view of history, paving the way for the possibility that contemporary Islamic society can distance itself from the need to reapply Islamic historical models.[17]

Islamic jurisprudence is distinguished from the true Islam, which is the Qur'an and the Hadith. Jurisprudence is seen not as the essence of Islam but as a product of history. Muhammad Salīm al-ʿAwwā writes against the use of tradition, arguing that to cling to the "books of the ancients" is politically harmful.[18] In the case of non-Muslims, he denies that Islamic jurisprudence should define how non-Muslims are treated today. Fahmī Huwaydī explains that Islamic jurisprudence has been historically conditioned. The formulation of jurisprudence toward non-Muslims within the Islamic Empire was influenced by the enmity that non-Muslims outside the Islamic world displayed toward Islam. Huwaydī points out that the term *ahl al-dhimma* (the People of the *dhimma*) was used by Arab tribes before the coming of Islam. He argues that the term is not mentioned in the Qur'an and was projected onto the Prophet through the Hadith.[19]

While the distinction between the golden age and history forms one of the foundations for citizenship, reinterpretation of the Qur'anic verses through the use of *ijtihād* forms another. Muhammad Salīm al-ʿAwwā calls for a pragmatic approach: *ijtihād* must be applied in a way that reconciles the present Islamic state with Islamic principles. This contemporary Islamic state represents a new kind of Islamic order that had not been envisioned by Muslim jurists.[20] *Ijtihād* includes examining the historical context or the occasions of revelation of the Qur'an in order to understand its contemporary relevance. Al-ʿAwwā argues that an analysis of a verse of the Qur'an must take into account the literal meaning of the words along with the eternal value of the Qur'an, which is a book that is valid for each generation. The Muslim community does not have to adhere to one explanation; interpretations of the Qur'an can be appropriate for the time. Thus the problem with intolerant attitudes being advocated does not lie with Islam or Islamic law, but instead "is a problem of individual Muslims who understand things as they wish."[21] Fahmī Huwaydī takes this flexible approach by distinguishing between temporary and lasting stipulations in the Qur'an. The text of the Qur'an has two levels. One level contains rules pertaining to the relation of a person to God. These rules relate to details of worship and have to be obeyed. Verses that relate to relations between people and government can be interpreted to reflect differences in context. Verses that relate to determining the relations between people can be interpreted to reflect contemporary demands.[22]

The verses that refer to relations between Muslims and non-Muslims are subject to this flexibility. Verses that have been used to justify the social and political exclusion of non-Muslims are interpreted contextually in a way that allows the reader to arrive at a different conclusion from that of a more literal reading. For al-'Awwā, the verses that have been taken to mean forbidding friendship with non-Muslims (e.g., "Thou wilt not find any people who believe in Allah and the Last Day, loving those who resist Allah and His Messenger, even though they were their fathers or their sons, or their brothers, or their kindred" [58:22]) refer only to those non-Muslims who harbor enmity toward the Islamic community.[23] Such verses were revealed as a way to protect the Islamic community from its enemies.[24] The other, more positive, verses are interpreted as conveying universal principles for Islam's treatment of non-Muslims.

CITIZENSHIP

It is argued that Islam can be separated from the idea of imposing the *dhimma* contract and the *jizya* payment, paving the way for the establishment of citizenship. Fahmī Huwaydī points out that the Islamic justifications for the *dhimma* are weak and that the *dhimma* was not an Islamic invention but one that existed before Islam.[25] Muhammad Salīm al-'Awwā argues that the early Islamic community adopted the *dhimma* as a way of defining relations between the Muslim conquerors and their non-Muslim subjects; they modified it to mean the protection of God and the Prophet rather than simply the protection of a certain tribe.[26] Therefore the *dhimma* was a political institution rather than a religious one. The domination of Muslims over non-Muslims is also historicized. Tāriq al-Bishrī states that in the early Islamic community Muslims were numerically inferior and it was therefore necessary for them to hold leadership. It would have been natural, he says, for Muslims to fear the political participation of non-Muslims and insist on their subjugation.[27]

The *dhimma* can therefore be discarded. In fact, it is argued, the *dhimma* was discarded when the nation-state was established. This, Huwaydī states, abolished the contract of protection as the basis for determining relations between non-Muslims and the state.[28] Thus the status quo is legitimate: there is no contradiction between the establishment of the nation-state and Islam.

In the form of retroactive justification, al-Bishrī argues that the *dhimma* was a political concept that has been overtaken by the concept of citizenship.[29] With the nation-state, a new kind of relationship and a new constitution, with equal citizenship as its basis, exist. Al-'Awwā argues that we no longer take the references in Islamic jurisprudence to slavery as being relevant in the modern context, and likewise we should not consider the references to the institution of *dhimma* as being relevant today.[30]

The same applies to the *jizya*, which, in Huwaydī's view, was not an Islamic invention, and, further, he states that there is no agreement in Islamic jurisprudence about its precise definition and meaning.[31] Others also deny that the *jizya* was a symbol of submission to a superior Islamic authority, or that it was a payment for lack of faith.[32] Huwaydī argues that interpretations of the phrase at the end of 9:29 to mean "humiliation and degradation," "fight those who believe not in Allah nor the Last Day, nor hold that forbidden which hath been forbidden by Allah and His Messenger, nor acknowledge the Religion of Truth, from among the People of the Book, until they pay *Jizyah* with willing submission, and feel themselves subdued" is mistaken.[33] Such an interpretation separates the verse from the fundamental principles of Islam, principles that include the dignity of human beings and respectful treatment of the People of the Book. Huwaydī claims that this interpretation was emphasized by jurists in response to both the aggression of non-Muslims toward Islam during the period of the Crusades and the invasion of the Mongols. It reflects the enmity between Muslims and Byzantines when the verse was revealed. In his view the correct interpretation of the idea of submission is that it means subjection to Islamic law. Thus the submitter is one who accepts the authority of Islam and desists from fighting the Muslim ruler.[34]

Despite recognition of the multiplicity of meanings the *jizya* has taken historically, it is emphasized that the correct interpretation was that it was a substitute for taking part in the defense of Islamic territories. Al-'Awwā reports that the *jizya* was not always a necessary part of the *dhimma* contract and that the Shāfi'ī scholar Ibn Hajar (1372–1448) regarded it as a substitute for *jihād*.[35] An emphasis on this interpretation undermines the religious rationale behind the *jizya*, which justifies the argument that the *jizya* should no longer be enforced. In the same way, al-Bishrī argues that *jizya* was a substitute for fighting *jihād*, which was initially an act of worship. However, he says that now Christians are being conscripted for military service and fight for the state, there is no point in extracting *jizya*. In the current Egyptian state, non-Muslims can serve in the army and therefore do not have to pay the *jizya*.[36] Al-'Awwā also argues that the *jizya* was a payment for defense, one of the obligations of the *dhimma* contract, but that since this contract is now dead, the *jizya* can be discarded.[37] 'Imāra argues that the classical texts contain a justification for non-Muslims serving in the army: under the community commanded by Muhammad, non-Muslims were able to serve in the army or pay *jizya*. If non-Muslims chose to do military service, the *jizya* was not taken and the booty was divided equally.[38] Thus, it is argued, there is historical precedent for non-Muslims undertaking military service.

By advocating that the *dhimma* is a historical institution, which is not intrinsically linked with the principles of Islam, these Islamists are saying that there is no difficulty in reconciling citizenship with Islamic law.[39] However, they go further and give both Islamic and historical rationales for the principle of citizenship.

Despite the fact that a less deterministic attitude is taken toward history, history and historical models still provide a powerful source of legitimacy, although they make a distinction between the golden age of the Prophet Muhammad and the subsequent development of Islamic history. Employing the "liberal *shari'a*" approach, which "takes liberal positions as being explicitly sanctioned by the *shari'a*," Muhammad Salīm al-'Awwā argues that the Constitution of Medina established the foundation for citizenship in the Islamic state, with the idea that religion, as opposed to tribal lineage, formed the basis of citizenship. He argues that citizenship was extended to the Jews who resided in Medina and that the constitution "makes non-Muslims living in the state of Medina citizens," who have the same rights and duties as Muslims.[40] 'Imāra argues that Islam established citizenship because it recognized the concept of rights and duties: in the Constitution of Medina, Muhammad established equality despite religious differences.[41] Al-'Awwā argues that if the Jewish tribes had not reneged on this contract, it would have remained valid and non-Muslims would have been full and equal citizens[42] and that diverse political and social circumstances encountered by succeeding Muslim generations, along with the fact that the Prophet left general rules rather than specific regulations, meant that changes inevitably occurred to the political system established by the Prophet.[43]

Al-'Awwā also employs the "silent Sharī'a" argument: the silence of the Qur'an on an issue, such as democratic and pluralistic political governance does not mean that it is not allowed. The Qur'an and the Hadith defined not a particular system of rule but rather Islamic values or principles. Therefore it is wrong to assume that there is only one form of political system that can be considered Islamic.[44] The caliphate, for example, was a concept for ruling that was devised by the companions of the Prophet and was not determined by God; instead it was values like justice, consultation, freedom, and equality that were divinely inspired.[45]

It is also argued that circumstances have changed and have produced the appropriate conditions for the establishment of citizenship. A unified Islamic state no longer exists today, and therefore future political systems should not be determined on the basis of this. Manifesting his legal background, Muhammad Salīm al-'Awwā argues that the *dhimma* was a historical contract that is no longer valid, since colonialism brought with it the destruction of one of the parties, the Islamic caliphate. The new state is not a successor to the old state. The new state is a new type of Islamic order that is based on a Muslim majority rather than conquest by a minority. It is a state that both Muslims and non-Muslims have participated in establishing.[46] The anticolonialist movement was vital in establishing the new political order. Both Muslims and Christians took part in the 'Urābī Revolt in 1881 and the 1919 Revolution against British rule in Egypt. Thus new states were founded on a new type of sovereignty that was based on a kind of social contract; this differed from the kind of rule that was based upon conquest.[47]

Tāriq al-Bishrī concurs, arguing that the struggle against the occupation was essential in making everyone a citizen of Egypt and in the evolution of the collective Egyptian psyche. He shows that through the historical process, Muslims and Copts have evolved a national identity. The 1919 Revolution against the British was a key moment in the evolution of this national identity. It symbolized political unity between Copts and Muslims and the establishment of a common national identity, which played a crucial role in the formation of an Egyptian political entity. It was not just a reaction to the discriminatory policies of British rule, but illustrated that Christians and Muslims were mixing in the political arena.[48] Al-Bishrī insists that Copts are full members of the Egyptian nation and emphasizes the necessity for the absolute independence of the Egyptian nation.

SHARING IN AN ISLAMIC CIVILIZATION

One of the underlying assumptions behind citizenship is the direct relationship between a citizen and the state along with the recognition of an individual's contribution to society. This direct relationship was not present in classical

Islam when a small or premodern state existed and the relationship between the Islamic polity and its subjects was a distant one. The *millet* system further entrenched this with the idea that one's identity was linked to the member-ship of one's own religious community. This applied to Muslims as well as non-Muslims, although the emphasis that the political order was defined by the *umma*, which was seen in a religious sense, was inevitably more inclusive of Muslims than non-Muslims.

One of the challenges facing Islamist arguments for citizenship is avoiding a situation in which the Islamic nature of the state becomes a tool for exclud-ing non-Muslims. Clearly this is the case when the notion of the *umma* is un-derstood as the religious community of all Muslims to the exclusion of other forms of religious identity. A common theme in Islamist thought is an apathy toward national identity. Additionally, there is the challenge of reconciling the importance of the *umma* with the concept of the nation-state. It is often assumed that such forces are opposed to one another.

The state, particularly when defined in individualist and secularist terms, is a Western concept, and the "Arab state is not a natural growth of its own socio-economic history or its own cultural and intellectual tradition."[49] And yet the nation-state has been remarkably durable in the region. The majority of Islamists use and have come to accept the state as the framework for action, a development that is clearly evident with Islamists in Egypt. As a result, their political priorities are determined by the nation-state even if broader priori-ties associated with the *umma* are not renounced.

The Wasatiyya Islamists adopt a practical outlook and accept the reality of the nation-state. They accept the breakup of the Islamic order, the disso-lution of the caliphate in 1924, and the subsequent establishment of nation-states. They are comfortable with writing about Islamic political theory in this new political framework. Al-'Awwā argues that since the anticolonial effort involved both Muslims and Christians, the contemporary Egyptian state is a product of combined efforts. According to him, since the new state has been established, the payment of the *jizya* can be discarded. The importance of the Egyptian nation-state is indicated by his support for Copts serving in the army. The obligation to pay the *jizya* has been replaced with the obligation to defend the nation and serve in the army.[50]

While these Islamists accept the importance of the nation-state, they do not understand the nation-state in a secular sense and they maintain the re-ligious identity of the state. The concepts of national and religious identity can exist side by side. Al-Bishrī argues that with *ijtihād*, there is no contra-diction between religious and national rule.[51] He understands that there are different levels of loyalty—region, city, nation, and individual—and he says that "you can enter into the citizenship conviction with your religion and values." There can be contradictions, he says, but the question is how to keep the balance.[52]

The Wasatiyya intellectuals argue that the two elements, nationalism and Islamism, can be synthesized. Central to al-Bishrī's thought is the notion that Islamic and nationalist elements can be unified through the *sharīʿa*, which should be the source for the revival of Islamic civilization.[53] This uni-fication is accomplished through the concept of an Islamic civilization that, it is argued, provides the source of national identity so that nationalist loy-alty can exist along with loyalty to the Muslim *umma*. It is through the idea that non-Muslims share in an Islamic civilization that non-Muslims can be citizens.

Al-Bishrī argues that by employing *ijtihād*, religious and national rule can be reconciled.[54] He advocates unifying nationalism with Islam. In his most important work, *The Muslims and Copts in the Framework of the National Community*, written in 1980, he discusses the history of the period before 1952 from the perspective of intercommunal relations. His primary motivation for writing the book was his concern for national unity and for the continued cohesiveness of Egyptian society. In his view unity and cohesiveness have been undermined in part by the colonial experience, but in particular since the Revolution of 1952 and Egypt's defeat by Israel in 1967.[55] There has been a split in society between two competing political trends: the indigenous, refer-ring to the Islamic trend, and the introduced, referring to the Westernized nationalist trend. Al-Bishrī does not argue that a choice must be made be-tween these two trends, but he advocates that the rift should be mended and that they should be unified. This would, he says, create a cohesive and unified Egyptian national community.[56]

Emphasizing that the concept of an Islamic civilization is not exclusive to Copts, the Wasatiyya intellectuals argue that the Islamic civilization, while religiously inspired, is the historical product of all people who live in its lands. Al-Bishrī says that the Islamic civilization is the heritage of both Muslims and Copts: it is a synthesis of shared and accumulated customs and a product of shared historical experience involving *jihād*.[57] It is necessary to accept that contemporary Egypt has been formed as a result of a blend of civilizations between Muslims and Copts in Egypt if a national community for all Egyptians is to be formed.[58]

For the Wasatiyya Islamists, non-Muslims have evolved to be part of the *umma*, which is the historical product of the cooperative efforts of all religious groups that have lived and worked together. They embrace the contribution of non-Muslims to this community. For Huwaydī, non-Muslims and Muslims together form a single community. There are many references to this, he argues, in the Qur'an, the Hadith, and the Constitution of Medina.[59] 'Imāra argues that non-Muslims are an essential and intrinsic part of the community and that they have had a role in helping to build Islamic civilization. The Islamic marriage laws, which include People of the Book, are a means by which this one *umma*, in which non-Muslims are unified with Muslims, is established. More importantly, friendship and allegiance between Muslims and non-Muslims are seen as vital for the unity of the *umma*. The other, Muhammad 'Imāra argues, is part of the *umma*'s religious essence.[60]

A distinction is made between Islamic civilization as a culture and the religious community. *Sharī'a* viewed as a source of cultural unity is not exclusive but inclusive. According to Muhammad 'Imāra, Christians share in *sharī'a* since the principles of *sharī'a* are a reflection of the values and morals held by both Muslims and non-Muslims. The *sharī'a* takes a strict approach to moral issues such as adultery. This reflects, 'Imāra says, the common beliefs held by Muslims and non-Muslims, which place importance on religion in daily life, family values, and tradition.[61]

Central to Tāriq al-Bishrī's thought is the notion that Islamic and nationalist elements can be unified through the *sharī'a*. He defines the *sharī'a* as a unifying force, one in which the two trends, the religious and the nationalist, can meet. The *sharī'a* would help to create an Egyptian national consciousness, which emphasizes national unity between Copts and Muslims but which is also rooted in the Islamic tradition. He argues that *sharī'a* is capable of providing a religious formulation for granting equal political rights to Copts in an Egyptian nation-state that is also Islamic.[62]

An enthusiastic proponent of this Islamic nationalist project is the Coptic intellectual Rafīq Habīb, who holds that the Arab-Islamic world is currently facing a "civilization crisis." Habīb calls for a revival of the Arab-Islamic civilization: together Muslims and Christians should struggle to rebuild it. He refers to this Arab-Islamic civilization as the civilization of moderation. It appears, however, that he is talking specifically about Egypt when he argues that this civilization of moderation originates in the contributions of three different eras: the Pharaonic, the Christian, and the Islamic.[63] The implication is that this historical experience has contributed to a specifically moderate and tolerant culture.

For Habīb, the values and traditions of this civilization are key to its revival. Its values are dependent upon the importance of religion, and this includes Islam and Christianity. The culture is characterized by the believing community with its sense of justice and righteousness. Habīb writes, "The Arab-Islamic civilization is based on the values of religion and is considered a religious civilization." The civilizational revival that he calls for cannot begin "except through a revival of religion and religious values."[64]

This Arab-Islamic civilization is a product of the accumulated efforts of Muslims and Christians. It is inclusive of Coptic Christians. For Habīb, "the fight for democratization must be an indigenous and joint struggle between Christians and Muslims, rather than the secular rights discourse popular in the West. . . . Our culture is religious—not biased towards Islam or Christianity—but a joint expression of both."[65] Al-Qaradāwī argues that Arab Christians are Muslims from a cultural perspective in that they contributed to the Arab culture that mixed with Islam.[66]

Habīb, like the other Wasatiyya intellectuals, emphasizes that the principles of sharī'a are a reflection of common values that are not particular to Muslims. In Egypt, he says, "morals and ethics are religiously derived, unlike the secular and humanist tradition which prevails in the West."[67] He argues that the unit of the religious family forms the basis of the social system in Egypt. In Egypt, he says, discipline comes from the family through religion, whereas in the West, discipline comes more from the law than from the family. Copts—like Muslims—are vested in this system, because "here in Egypt" religion has two meanings: "one is belief in God and the other is social."[68]

Habīb denies that the revival of an Arab-Islamic civilization would marginalize Christians, maintaining that the idea that the concept poses a problem for Christians is not valid. Through an emphasis on Islam as a religious culture, there is room, he says, for Coptic involvement and expression. He says, "We want for the future . . . two integrated groups, Christians and Muslims."[69] He distinguishes between the umma as a religious concept and the umma as a cultural concept. While there is a strong connection between the two, Muslims who live outside of this Arab-Islamic civilization do not see themselves as belonging to it, although they would relate to Islamic values.[70] The same is true of Eastern Christians, who would relate to the values and traditions of the Arab-Islamic civilization, and not to Western civilization.

The idea that Christians and Muslims have together contributed to the Arab-Islamic civilization is notably different from other types of Islamist thought, which emphasize that Christians constitute the other or guests. It is also very different from the idea that the political involvement of Christians is accepted as long as they behave as a separate group, as described in chapter 4. Fahmī Huwaydī, for example, disagrees with this communal approach and argues that non-Muslims should not be treated as an entity that is separate from society.[71]

FRIENDSHIP AND LOYALTY

A core element of citizenship is the concept of loyalty or civic friendship, which constitutes mutual concern as a basis for communal and political relations. This idea relates to the concept of *muwāla* or *walā*,'—friendship, goodwill, and loyalty. It derives from the contract of clientage in Islamic law. In pre-Islamic poetry, *walā'* refers to an egalitarian relationship of mutual help, an idea that is also found in the Qur'an and some later literature. However, in most later works, *walā'* refers to an unequal relationship of assistance, a meaning that is also derived from the Qur'an. It is in this sense that it was used to refer to the non-Arab Muslims who were treated as inferior to Arab Muslims, particularly during the Umayyad period (661–750).[72]

Chapter 4 showed that some Islamists interpret "O ye who believe! Take not the Jews and the Christians for your friends and protectors [*awliyā'*]; they are but friends and protectors to each other. And he amongst you that turns to them (for friendship) is of them" (5:51) as an indication that, in the words of Huwaydī, "Islam decisively forbids becoming friends with Jews and Christians, makes cutting off relations with them necessary and makes the Muslim who befriends them afraid that he will be thought to have separated himself from Islam and joined Judaism or Christianity." However, Huwaydī, like many of the Wasatiyya, speaks out against this, stating that the verse was directed at hypocrites who, with their allies (who included People of the Book), opposed Islam. It therefore refers to Jews and Christians who were fighting Muslims, and thus the verse advises cutting off relations at this time as a form of self-defense for the Muslim community.[73]

The concept of friendship between Muslims and non-Muslims is central to the Wasatiyya approach to citizenship. The Wasatiyya advocate friendship and loyalty as a basis for relations between Muslims and non-Muslims in Egypt. The idea of communal solidarity is reflected in an emphasis upon the experience of anticolonialism, in which Muslims and non-Muslims came together in 1919 to fight the British. At that time Muslims and Copts fought together and shaykhs and priests met in churches and mosques.[74] Therefore, for the Wasatiyya, the 1919 Revolution became an expression of the collective experience of living side by side with one another.

The idea of communal solidarity between Muslims and Copts is also evident in the concept of an Islamic civilization in which Muslims and Copts have shared values. Emphasis is put upon the shared interests that Muslims and Christians have in prioritizing religion and the family and in combating atheism and materialism. There is a recognition that non-Muslims have contributed to the development of the Islamic civilization, which is the historical product of cooperative efforts.

The concept of communal solidarity is also expressed through an emphasis on the experience of Muslims and Christians living in close proximity to one another. Muhammad 'Imāra emphasizes the extent to which Muslims and Christians live side by side as neighbors in Egyptian communities.[75] He argues that "the unity of the *umma* cannot be realized except through the friendship of all who live in it and their membership in its state and in the components of its identity and its national and civilizational security."[76]

The Islamic marriage laws are emphasized as a means by which Muslims and Christian families become united. 'Imāra argues that the laws are a means by which this one *umma*, in which non-Muslims are unified with Muslims, is established. Therefore, non-Muslims are an intrinsic and essential part of the community.[77] In Muhammad Salīm al-'Awwā's view, the fact that the Qur'an allows Muslims and non-Muslims to share food and allows Muslim men to marry Jewish and Christian women signifies the value placed upon friendship between Muslims and Christians.[78] He argues that it is a religious requirement for people of different religions to be neighbors and engage in human brotherhood.[79]

This experience of living together means that significance is attached to the idea of national brotherhood. The popular Islamic thinker Yūsuf al-Qaradāwī states that while "religious brotherhood has great importance, this does not negate the existence of other brotherhood," referring to "our Christian brothers inside the Islamic nation."[80] Tāriq al-Bishrī refers to the multiple forms of loyalty and loyalty to fellow Egyptians, and one's neighbor forms part of this.[81] Emphasis upon this kind of communal solidarity means that the social distinction and differentiation expressed by other Islamists is rejected. The Wasatiyya do not emphasize Muslims and Christians' physically distinguishing themselves.

In fact, the Wasatiyya also express concern that communal solidarity between Muslims and non-Muslims has been undermined because of the increasingly sectarian nature of Egyptian society and that national identity has been weakened. Huwaydī laments that "in the absence of democracy they [Muslims and Christians] do not share their dreams as Egyptians." He says that because of the weakness of the government, they do not think as Egyptians but as Muslims and as Copts.[82]

CITIZENSHIP IN CONTEMPORARY POLITICAL DISCOURSE

In chapter 4, it was shown that many members of the Muslim Brotherhood are committed to the reestablishment of the *dhimma* for organizing relations between Muslims and non-Muslims and the Islamic state. However, in recent years, the discourse of the Wasatiyya Islamists on citizenship has had a significant impact on mainstream Islamist political discourse, including that of members of the Muslim Brotherhood. For most of the twentieth century, Islamists associated citizenship with the prerevolutionary secular order and viewed it as a particularly Western concept. Citizenship, along with values such as democracy, was rejected by the Islamists of the 1970's. However, there has been a shift toward accepting the idea that citizenship is, on some level, compatible with the Islamic revival. This change is illustrated by the fact that political groups such as the Muslim Brotherhood and the al-Wasat Party have been using the discourse of citizenship to define relations between Muslims and non-Muslims in Egypt.

The political group that has been most influenced by the ideas of the Wasatiyya intellectuals is the al-Wasat Party.[83] Members of this party have maintained that the Wasatiyya ideas helped them to establish their party. For example, Abū al-'Ilā Mādī, the leader and founder of al-Wasat, says that the *jizya* "is not an Islamic innovation." He distinguishes between the permanent aspects of Islam and the things that are changeable. He also argues that the colonial experience was vital to the establishment of citizenship.[84] The al-Wasat Party has talked of its commitment to citizenship for non-Muslims, and it is this issue, along with the rights of women, through which it has sought to distinguish itself from the Muslim Brotherhood. Some of the founding members of the party were Copts. In the most recent edition of the party's political program, Abū al-'Ilā Mādī states that "citizenship determines the rights and duties of all Egyptians and is the basis of the relations between all Egyptians. There should be no discrimination between citizens on the basis of religion, gender, color or ethnicity in terms of their rights, including the right to hold public office."[85] He accepts the current Egyptian Constitution based on equality for citizens and rejects calls for a return to the *dhimma* era.[86]

Abū al-'Ilā Mādī denies the primacy of religious loyalty, marking a significant departure from mainstream Islamism. Mādī argues that "citizenship," as a term, expresses the link between the citizen and the citizen's homeland. He sees the Constitution of Medina as having regulated "the relation among citizens of the same state based on the idea of belonging to the state rather than religious belief, tribal, color or ethnic racism." He is aware of the multiplicity of identities and loyalties but prioritizes the nation. The *umma* functions on three levels: the country, Egypt the Arab nation, and the Islamic religion. The *umma* as a nation is the most important. Mādī argues that he feels more loyalty toward an Egyptian Christian than a Pakistani Muslim.[87] In the party's recent program, the idea that non-Muslims share in an Islamic civilization is clearly expressed:

> Islam is not only the religion of Muslims: it is also for both Muslims and non-Muslims, the cultural framework within which Egypt's creative intellectuals, scientists and leaders have made their contributions, and Arabic, the language of Islam is the language in which Egyptian religious leaders, whether Muslim or Christian, have preached. Islamic culture is the homeland of all Egyptians, Muslim and non-Muslim.[88]

Mādī compares the concept of an Islamic civilization to the concept of a Western civilization. He says that Muslims along with members of other religions currently have a role. The Islamic civilization, he says, is similar. The fact that it has been influenced by Islam does not preclude non-Muslims from being part of that civilization.[89]

Such ideas can also be found among the pragmatists of the Muslim Brotherhood. According to Huwaydī, his views are accepted in the Muslim Brotherhood, although he does not know to what extent. In many seminars, he says, "when they want a moderate Islamic view" represented they usually "invite one of us," but he does not know how much of an influence they have."[90]

'Isām al-'Aryān, prominent spokesman for the Muslim Brotherhood, shares many of the Wasatiyya perspectives on non-Muslims and citizenship.[91] 'Abd al-Mun'im Abū al-Futūh, former member of the Muslim Brotherhood

Guidance Office and general secretary of the Arab Physicians' Union, has been influenced by the ideas of the Wasatiyya intellectuals. At one point he was rumored to be Mashhūr's successor as supreme guide, although now as a pragmatist he is less influential since the conservatives have gained the upper hand. Secularists know and respect Abū al-Futūh for his sincerity and, unlike the conservative members of the Muslim Brotherhood, for his commitment to a democratic culture within the organization.[92]

For Abū al-Futūh, other non-Muslims have citizenship rights, since citizenship—rather than religion—forms the basis for the determination of rights and duties. The nation-state is the new reality, and citizenship has superseded the *dhimma* for organizing the modern state.[93] In his view, while in the West citizenship required the separation of religion and state and the rejection of any interference from religious institutions, this is not the situation with Islam from both a historical and an ideological perspective whereby "the presence of religious institutions in the relationship between the individual and the sultan was always, in curbing the power of the sultan, for the good of the individual." He states that citizenship, which is characterized by the full presence of the individual in general life and includes taking part in the legislation of the state, has become a reality of life in the modern era, and the rights and duties of citizenship "irrespective of religion or of race" have become one of the most virtuous systems of our time. Citizenship, he argues, "is connected to the legal, political, and constitutional reality of the Islamic *umma* that is distributed into a number of nations and this does not—in any sense—contradict belonging to the Islamic *umma*."[94]

Abū al-Futūh confirms that citizenship involves "complete equality in rights and duties."[95] His commitment to this is illustrated by the fact that he confirms that Christians should continue to be in the Egyptian army. He justifies this position by arguing that wars are fought for the state and not for Islam. Wars for the expansion of ideology are no longer necessary, since ideology can now be spread through the Internet and books. Fighting is in defense of the nation, and non-Muslims can be involved.[96] He also argues that Islamic civilization belongs to all Egyptian people, Muslims and Christians. Non-Muslims have had a role in helping to build the Islamic civilization. Neither religious nor national identity is more important. Both can function side by side.[97]

Muhammad Habīb, who resigned from his position as deputy supreme guide after the Guidance Office elections in January 2010, argues that Copts are citizens of the "first level" and that the *jizya* is a historical obligation that should no longer be applied. Non-Muslims must be in the army because *jihād* now involves defending the nation and non-Muslims must take part in that.[98] When asked about the recent amendment to Article 1 of the Constitution and its compatibility with Article 2, he took the position that the concept of citizenship contains ambiguity and needs definition. He accepted citizenship in terms of the following: eradicating discrimination between citizens with regard to color, religion, ideology, and gender, as well as establishing equality in rights and duties before the law.[99]

This approach to citizenship is also reflected in the Muslim Brotherhood's 2007 draft party platform, which states: "Our Islamic program for reform of the state . . . is based on the principle of citizenship. Egypt is a state for all those citizens who enjoy Egyptian nationality and all citizens enjoy equal rights and duties provided by the law according to the principles of equality and equal opportunity."[100] It confirms commitment to freedom that "provides for justice and equality between individuals and safeguards their freedom of belief, action, property, freedom of opinion and expression."[101]

However, critics of the platform point to parts of it that emphasize the religious nature of the state, whereby "the decision to launch war is a religious decision" that is based on the rules of *sharī'a*. It also states that the "principle framework for Islamic *sharī'a* is the consensus of Muslim jurists." Critics have argued that this effectively renders the regime envisioned by the Muslim Brotherhood a "totalitarian theocratic regime" that counteracts the principle of citizenship.[102] They also point to earlier statements by the Muslim Brotherhood that avoid the principle of citizenship. The 2004 platform did not mention citizenship and claimed only that "Copts are a part of the fabric of the Egyptian society. They are partners of the nation and destiny."[103]

Certainly not all members of the Muslim Brotherhood share the same perspective on citizenship. Former Supreme Guide Muhammad Ma'mūn al-Hudaybī argued that Christians in Egypt are citizens, that Copts "have the same rights and duties as us," and that they "enjoy all rights of citizenship." At the same time, however, he still referred to the *dhimma*.[104] "Citizens" do not have equal political rights, since, he says, "human rights have to be for everyone, but political rights differ." When asked if his ideas on *jizya* or the *dhimma* contradict the concept of citizenship, he replied, "But in what country in the world does the minority have the full political rights like the majority?"[105]

Further ambiguity is evidenced by some members of the Muslim Brotherhood who argue that there is considerable continuity between the concept of the *dhimma* and citizenship. Even the pragmatist 'Isām al-'Aryān draws a parallel between *dhimma* and "equality between Muslims and non-Muslims."[106] Yūsuf al-Qaradāwī makes this same conflation, writing that "in modern terminology, *dhimmis* are 'citizens' of the Islamic state."[107] He implies that citizenship is just another way of expressing the concept of the *dhimma* and does not accept that the two are conceptually different:

> The *fuqahā'* stated that the *ahl al-dhimma* are of (the people of *dār al-Islām*) and the expression (the people of the *dār*) means that we express in our contemporary language that they are citizens and they have the right of citizenship in all its attributes just as Muslims.[108]

Muhammad Habīb also argues that there is no actual conflict between citizenship and *dhimma*. One should use only the concept of citizenship because "our Coptic brothers get upset with the term *dhimma* and imagine that it makes them second class citizens."[109]

This conflation between the *dhimma* and citizenship is also made by Islamists with more radical associations. For example, Kamāl al-Sa'īd Habīb, an independent reformed Islamist and former member of al-Jihād, argues that "citizenship does not negate the idea of differentiation." He therefore illustrates that for many, citizenship is simply another way of articulating the common assumptions behind the *dhimma*. He sees citizenship in the Western context as inappropriate in an Islamic state. An Islamic state should not be based upon the concept of the "melting pot," he argues, where everyone is equal and diversity is not recognized. Rather, the state should be based on the *millet* system, which recognizes differences.[110] The concept of the *millet* defines the relationship between the citizen and the state, while recognizing that the citizen belongs to a community to which he owes his primary allegiance.[111] For al-Sa'īd Habīb, citizenship means that there is equality in law, "but the differences continue." Mamdūh Ismā'īl, an Islamist lawyer who was refused permission to set up an Islamic law party in 1999, also makes this distinction between citizenship in a "Western understanding" and "Islamic citizenship." He argues that Islamic citizenship comes from within the Islamic heritage of jurisprudence and of *sharī'a*.[112]

Such statements illustrate the problems involved in assessing Islamist discourse on citizenship, particularly the discourse of politically active groups. Likening citizenship to the *dhimma* must be seen in a particular context in which it has become politically controversial to argue that the *dhimma* should form the basis for the treatment of non-Muslims. The issue of citizenship for non-Muslims has become caught up in relations between the Islamists and the state. The government uses the question of the Muslim Brotherhood's commitment to citizenship to delegitimize the group by accusing it of undermining national unity. As a result, the statement of one's commitment to citizenship becomes a defensive mechanism. It has become very difficult to say that you are not committed to citizenship on some level, and in some circumstances references to citizenship have become empty slogans that deflect attention away from a frank discussion of the issue.

The inconsistencies and tensions in Islamist statements on citizenship have been used as examples of their duplicity, particularly in the case of the Muslim Brotherhood. It is often argued that there is a difference between the Brotherhood's written postulations and its actual practice or underlying intentions.[113] Many secular Christians and Copts doubt the sincerity of the organization's commitment to citizenship.[114] According to the Coptic intellectual Samīr Murqus, calling Copts "partners of the nation" is a way of avoiding the concept of citizenship. In his view the Brotherhood resorts to the term "citizenship" when members are under pressure or attack; the term merely constitutes "a kind of cosmetics." But when they feel strong, Murqus says, they define non-Muslims as partners.[115] Secular human rights activists clearly see a disconnect between the Muslim Brotherhood's commitment to citizenship and its commitment to a state based on *sharī'a*.

However, such inconsistencies and tensions should not mean that Islamist references to citizenship must be taken less seriously. The Muslim Brotherhood's statements must be understood as coming from a political group that works within a complex political context and whose ideology is in a state of flux. In addition, such statements must be understood in the context of the different ideological positions that exist within the organization itself. While the *dhimma* is still an important part of the Muslim Brotherhood's understanding of the proposed relationship between the Muslim majority and religious minorities, some of the organization's members have very different views, which get articulated in multiple and often contradictory ways.[116] Like any political group, the Muslim Brotherhood is made up of competing interests and ideologies, and any such statements must be viewed accordingly.

Statements on citizenship also reflect considerable caution. The Coptic intellectual with Islamist sympathies, Rafīq Habīb, explains the Muslim Brotherhood's reluctance to commit to the concept of citizenship. He argues that while the organization is deliberately cautious about statements referring to citizenship, it is not because the Brotherhood wants to reenact the discriminatory policies of the *dhimma*. While the Muslim Brotherhood is committed to citizenship in terms of equality, it is not committed to citizenship in terms of secular values. Ḥabīb says that the group is fearful of giving the wrong impression; it is not committed to a secular understanding of citizenship, and it is cautious about expressing its commitment to the concept in general.[117]

CONCLUSION

Islamist statements on citizenship illustrate that Islamist ideology is in a state of flux as it adjusts its ideology to the context of the Egyptian state and to the hegemonic concepts of citizenship and pluralism. Assessing individual intentions concerning untested claims regarding citizenship is an impossible task. The important issue is that citizenship is being articulated within the context of the renewal of Islamic jurisprudence and that this has had a significant impact on political discourse.

The Wasatiyya intellectuals have made considerable advances toward the establishment of a theoretical basis for the concept of citizenship within Islamic thought. Central to this is the distinction between Islamic jurisprudence as a historical product and divine law. At the same time, citizenship is justified by drawing on the Egyptian political experience. The fact that both Copts and Muslims participated in the establishment of the Egyptian nation-state is, it is argued, central to the foundation of modern Egyptian citizenship. It also articulates a sense that Muslims and Christians belong to the community as expressed through the concept of an Islamic civilization that is made up of the experience of Muslims and Christians living together.

The Wasatiyya have laid important theoretical foundations for citizenship within an Islamic framework. These ideas have had a substantial impact on current political debate and are being embraced by political groups. References to non-Muslims as citizens are made by the Muslim Brotherhood and Islamist parties such as al-Wasat. However, statements on citizenship are made by groups within the political context. This means that Islamist discourse on citizenship is often articulated in complex ways, since the term "citizenship" has become one that is utilized in conflicts between the state, the Islamists, and secularists, resulting in a range of meanings for it. While the Wasatiyya Islamists argue that citizenship is distinct from the *dhimma*, some more-conservative Islamists express it as a continuation of the *dhimma*.

Tensions and contradictions within Islamist articulations on citizenship should not, however, mean that Islamist statements on citizenship are disregarded. Such tensions are not necessarily evidence of Islamist duplicity but rather an indication that Islamist discourse on citizenship is in a state of flux and is subject to political debate. The important point is that the "citizenship" concept within an Islamic framework has been established as legitimate, even if the range of assumptions behind it varies.

These tensions and contradictions apply not only to the Muslim Brotherhood but also to the Wasatiyya intellectuals themselves. In early 2007, controversy erupted over a new book by Muhammad ʿImāra, *The Sedition of Takfīr between the Shiʾa ...and Wahhabism ...and Sufism*, in which ʿImāra quoted the medieval thinker Abū Hāmid al-Ghazālī's definitions of "unbelief" and "belief." Al-Ghazālī, and therefore by association ʿImāra, allegedly encouraged killing non-Muslims. After a public uproar ʿImāra subsequently apologized and stated that he had blindly quoted from al-Ghazālī's book. He argued that it was not possible for a great imam like al-Ghazālī to have written something that was against the spirit of Islam, and therefore a printing error must have occurred when al-Ghazālī's work was originally published in 1907.[118]

For Copts, this exchange seemed to contradict all of ʿImāra's talk on citizenship. Whether it should be viewed as an illustration of his duplicity is debatable. Muhammad ʿImāra's writings and statements on non-Muslims and citizenship constitute an important contribution to Wasatiyya ideas on citizenship. This controversy reveals the complexity and difficulty that Islamists face when attempting to reconcile Islam's foundational texts and authoritative figures with contemporary realities.

It is also significant that the public reacted so strongly and that the book was subsequently removed. The response to the book indicates that a shift in public expectations has occurred. Citizenship is no longer considered an imported secular ideology but has gained legitimacy within the Islamist framework. As a result, the boundaries of what is or is not acceptable in the mainstream press have shifted, and this, in turn, determines the range of behavior and treatment that become publicly acceptable. Islamist discourse on citizenship sets up certain expectations and in itself brings about an important shift. The very fact that the constitutional amendment of 2007 established that the Egyptian state is based on the principle of citizenship while existing alongside Article 2 is one indication of this shift.

6 CITIZENSHIP IN AN ISLAMIC STATE

THE WASATIYYA INTELLECTUALS have made a significant contribution to the articulation of a theoretical basis for citizenship in Islamic thought. The Wasatiyya discourse on citizenship emphasizes the notion of membership, belonging, and community through the anticolonial experience and sharing in an Islamic civilization.

However, it is important to move beyond the theoretical justifications for citizenship and look at its underlying assumptions or limitations. How is citizenship articulated and understood by the Wasatiyya Islamists? What social and political rights are accorded therein? What are the political, social, and legal implications of the concept of citizenship in an Islamic state? What does being a citizen mean in this context? How is citizenship connected with religious identity?

Islamist discourse on citizenship is full of references to the complete equality of non-Muslims. It is argued that non-Muslims are politically, socially, and economically equal in terms of rights and duties.[1] In classical Islamic society, relations between Muslims and non-Muslims were not based on the principle of equality, which was not prioritized as a concept. While in theory Muslim male believers were politically equal under the law, under the *dhimma* non-Muslims were tolerated, although they were not equal.[2] In theory the non-Muslim had restricted political responsibility: non-Muslims were exempt from the duty put upon Muslims "to enjoin the good and forbid evil."[3] In practice, however, many non-Muslims did serve in government positions. In addition, non-Muslims did not have legal parity with Muslims. There was no concept of natural rights, although this is not to say that there was no concept of rights as such. Certain rights or expectations were given to the *dhimmī*, not due to the individual as a human being but on account of the individual's membership in a religious community under the *dhimma* contract. The absence of the idea that rights were attached to an individual because of any essential human nature applied to Muslims as well, whose rights created by the law were due to them as Muslims.[4]

While contemporary Islamists provide theoretical justifications for citizenship, the question of what kind of citizenship remains. How will this principle of equality be applied in a practical sense, and what are the limitations to it? What are the underlying assumptions, boundaries, or responsibilities involved in this kind of citizenship? Islamists emphasize that citizenship must be exercised within an Islamic framework or within Islamic boundaries so that the political system is a reflection of the public order. The concept of public order is used to invoke limitations to individual religious autonomy and lack of equality in personal status law. These discussions focus primarily on the understanding of the rights of non-Muslim men. The issue of the rights of non-Muslim women is a whole other topic. For Coptic intellectual Vivian Fu'ād, the question of whether, for example, a Muslim woman could become prime minister is far more challenging than whether a non-Muslim man could do so.[5] The discussions here focus on how the rights of non-Muslim men relate to those of Muslim men.

POLITICAL INVOLVEMENT AND THE CONCEPT OF *WILĀYA*

The Wasatiyya intellectuals (Muhammad Salīm al-ʿAwwā, Fahmī Huwaydī, Tāriq al-Bishrī, and Muhammad ʿImāra) advocate the compatibility of democracy and political pluralism with Islam. They deny that democracy is a violation of God's sovereignty, arguing that pluralism is a natural phenomenon that is supported by the Qurʾan.[6] For Muhammad Salīm al-ʿAwwā, since the Qurʾan establishes pluralism in general (49:13) and since the original Islamic state was based on a plurality of religions, pluralism in the political sphere must be recognized. Islam has been falsely accused of opposition to political pluralism. Al-ʿAwwā argues that since the *sharīʿa* established only general rules, the majority of Islamists today are wrong in assuming that there is only one form of political system that can be considered Islamic.[7] In his view, the Prophet left the details of the system for Muslims to decide, "according to their interest, the requirements of the time, the place, and changing circumstances. Nothing was binding on them except for the general rules of Islamic law." Islam in the Qurʾan and the Sunna, he states, did not define a specific system of rule, but it did define Islamic values that the *umma* had to adhere to and the rulers had to rule by. The silence of the *sharīʿa* on matters of political democracy does not necessarily mean that democracy is not permitted.[8] Fahmī Huwaydī argues that a distinction must be made between the position of Islam and the position of Muslims toward democracy. The position of Muslims has been confused and "has to a large extent been burdened by history and memory which has played a decisive role in arousing suspicions and misgivings." One of these, he argues, is the association of democracy with a Western plan to oppress and degrade the rights of Arabs and Muslims. He calls for democracy and a plurality of parties, quoting Yūsuf al-Qaradāwī's *fatwā* that states there is no legal provision for prohibiting a plurality of parties. He argues for freedom, political participation, and pluralism, although such values should not be modeled on Western democracy.[9]

The Wasatiyya intellectuals call for a multiparty democratic system, in which citizens would have the right to participate on an equal basis.[10] They argue for the political agency and self-determination of Copts. As citizens, Copts would have considerable opportunity for political involvement. The right of Copts to vote and be voted for would be supported.[11] They would have the right to participate in elections and in governing the Muslim state, and this right would extend to leadership roles. For Huwaydī, the right of Copts to vote and to have political representation is connected to their dignity as human beings.[12]

The foundation of this argument in support of the political autonomy of non-Muslims is linked to the Qur'an. The contextual approach to the interpretation of certain Qur'anic verses makes this kind of political participation compatible with the divine texts. Jurists have traditionally interpreted the following verses to mean that non-Muslims should be restricted in their political and professional involvement:

> Oh ye who believe! Take not the Jews and the Christians for your friends and protectors [*awliyā'*]; they are but friends and protectors to each other. And he amongst you that turns to them (for friendship) is of them (5:51).

> And never will Allah grant to the Unbelievers a way (to triumph) [*sabīlan*] over the Believers (4:141).

While *awliyā'* is often interpreted to refer to friendship, it can refer to master or proprietor, since the Arabic can mean either. It is often argued that this verse refers to non-Muslims who are aggressive toward Muslims and therefore it should not be taken as a general prohibition against either friendship with non-Muslims or against their being in positions of authority.[13] Verse 4:141 has also been used by a number of Islamists to argue for the political disenfranchisement and subjugation of non-Muslims. While it does not explicitly mention the concept of *wilāya* (rule or power) of Muslims over non-Muslims, it is taken to refer to the question of authority. The Wasatiyya intellectuals argue that the verses have been misinterpreted, misused, and taken out of context. In their view such verses refer only to non-Muslims who harbor enmity toward the Islamic community and have a religious, not a political, application.[14]

Muhammad Salīm al-'Awwā maintains that in the current political environment, nomination and election do not constitute requests for sovereign authority or *wilāya*. He states that it is permissible to nominate and vote for Copts in the People's Assembly, since members of the People's Assembly are representatives of the *umma* and are nominated by the *umma*. A representative works for those who have nominated him. He does not have ultimate authority over them. *Wilāya*, he argues, refers to power and a kind of leadership or conception of authority that no longer exists.[15]

Tāriq al-Bishrī adopts a similar stance, arguing that the nature of the modern state is different from the kind of government envisaged by medieval theorists. Today, institutions have taken over decision-making roles that were once occupied by individuals. The framework for governmental organization is therefore different. Individuals are now part of the collective decision-making process and are not themselves the decision makers. The modern system is based upon a distribution of sovereignty, and no one has ultimate legislative authority. The eleventh-century jurist Abū al-Hasan al-Māwardī (974–1058) wrote that non-Muslims were entitled to occupy executive but not jurisdictional positions. However, al-Bishrī argues that contemporary systems of government are different from those of al-Māwardī's time, which means that the restriction on non-Muslims occupying jurisdictional positions is no longer applicable.[16]

This distinction lays the foundation for an important shift in views on political leadership. There has been considerable debate in recent years about the question of the presidency or head of state.[17] The level of attention that this issue has received is perhaps surprising, since any debate about it is theoretical in the current political context—President Mubarak has been president since 1981. The question of whether a non-Muslim can, from an Islamic perspective, be elected as president, has become a recurring topic in discussions concerning the extent to which Islamists are committed to the rights of non-Muslims.

The issue is very politically charged, and the Muslim Brotherhood's party platform of 2007 was negatively received in the press because it claimed that women and non-Muslims cannot serve as head of state. Muhammad 'Imāra is skeptical about the validity of such a discussion. He argues that there is a kind of sophistry surrounding this issue.[18]

Nevertheless, even if the election of a Copt to the presidency is unlikely, symbolically it is important whether a Copt is allowed, from an Islamic legal perspective, to be head of state, because if he is not, some level of religious discrimination is revealed. This question has become a symbol for how committed Islamists are to the rights of the Copts. It is currently one of the issues on which the al-Wasat Party distinguishes itself from the Muslim Brotherhood. Al-Wasat's most recent statement affirms

> complete equality between men and women in terms of political and civil rights. Competency, professional background and the ability to undertake the responsibility should be the criteria for holding of public office, for example in the judiciary, or for the presidency.[19]

The Coptic intellectual Rafīq Habīb is skeptical about al-Wasat's commitment to this, maintaining that while the party's members say that a Copt can be a candidate for the presidency, they do not say that al-Wasat would ever put forward a non-Muslim candidate.[20]

Al-'Awwā argues that a non-Muslim can be prime minister or president, even though he cannot have religious duties. He can be part of all professions except specifically religious ones—although this raises the question of the whether positions in the judiciary would be religious. Interestingly, it implies, however, that the post of prime minister or president is not a specifically religious one.[21] Al-Bishrī also argues that a non-Muslim could be the head of state precisely *because* such a post is very different from the caliphate described by medieval theorists.[22]

Not all of the Wasatiyya intellectuals and politicians go this far. Muhammad 'Imāra thinks the head of state should be a Muslim.[23] Fahmī Huwaydī agrees, saying, "It is not logical to have a leader or head of state who does not believe in the *sharī'a.*"[24] He argues that such a restriction does not violate the concept of citizenship, but he also says, "If the majority votes for a non-Muslim then I would accept [it]."[25]

Influenced by the fact that the political leadership of Copts has become a litmus test for commitment to national unity, the Muslim Brotherhood has affirmed its commitment to allowing non-Muslims to occupy all posts except that of head of state. While nothing was mentioned in the Muslim Brotherhood's platform of 2004 concerning the legality of Copts' taking up political posts, the party platform of 2007 affirmed that it was the function of the prime minister or president to protect and preserve Islam and to allow Muslims to practice their religion. Thus the modern president is charged with the duty of preserving religion, a duty that the caliph once had. The Muslim Brotherhood argues that the duty of the prime minister would go against the belief of non-Muslims and that therefore they should be exempt from this position.[26] Rafīq Habīb argues that not allowing a non-Muslim to be head of state is not a violation of citizenship. In his view, the state has the responsibility to protect Islam because in Islam there is no institution like the church in Christianity. If there were such an institution, then the head of state would not have the responsibility to protect Islam and a Copt could become president.[27]

In making such an argument, Rafīq Habīb bypasses the question of whether al-Azhar constitutes an institution that protects religion. He then goes on to illustrate the problem involved in making such an argument: distinguishing between those posts that involve the protection of religion and those that do not. He argues that it might also be difficult to have a Coptic foreign minister because the foreign minister would also be responsible for making decisions that impinged upon religious issues.[28] Muhammad Habīb, former deputy to the supreme guide of the Muslim Brotherhood, avoids affirming this and argues that these are details that can be worked out.[29]

However, this stance against a non-Muslim becoming the head of state is not supported by all members of the Muslim Brotherhood. In 2003 'Abd al-Mun'im Abū al-Futūh, a prominent pragmatist member of the organization, did not object to a Christian becoming president of Egypt.[30] In October 2007 there were rumors from an unnamed Muslim Brotherhood source that a commitment to the right of a non-Muslim to be elected president would be forthcoming. Now Abū al-Futūh is more cautious, stating that there is "no reason to stipulate this [i.e., the religious identity of the president] when the existing Egyptian constitution makes no reference to the issue."[31]

PUBLIC ORDER

These progressive views on leadership are tempered by an underlying conservatism. While political involvement of non-Muslims in the Egyptian state is advocated, it is implied that ultimate political authority, *wilāya*, should rest with Islam. The concept of *wilāya* is used to ensure the integrity of the Islamic state as an Islamic state. It is argued that political pluralism should not contradict the basis of Islam. Therefore, there are restrictions not only on the political freedom of non-Muslims but also on that of Muslims. Thus while these Islamists argue for a democratic system, it is a system that has certain restrictions expressed in the concept of "constants."[32] This concept of restrictions or limits is articulated by the concept of public order, or *ordre public*, which is expressed by the Arabic term *al-nithām al-'āmm*.

The concept of public order is of European origin.[33] The first European code to adopt the expression *ordre public* was the French Civil Code of 1804 (Art. 6), which reads, "Private agreements cannot derogate from laws which affect *ordre public* and good morals."[34] The concept is, of course, vague and variable. According to Gerhart Husserl, "*Ordre public* is a function of time and place."[35] It stands for certain principles that are considered essential to a society and that may not be altered by any rules of that society. Public order was used to decide on the admissibility of a foreign law, the application of which may be rejected if it violates domestic public order.[36]

The concept of public order was introduced into the Egyptian legal system around the end of the nineteenth century.[37] It has been utilized by the Court of Cassation in several rulings and has been defined as "the social, political, economical or moral principles in a state related to the highest (or essential) interest . . . of society" or as "the essence . . . of the nation."[38] In 1979 the same court defined public order as being based on secular doctrine. However, it was also argued that public order is "sometimes based on a principle related to religious doctrine in the case when such a doctrine has become intimately linked with the legal and social order, deeply rooted in the conscience of society."[39]

The utilization of this concept in contemporary Islamist discourse is interesting, given its secular origins, although the idea of secular origins should not be overstated. Any concept of public order has inevitably been influenced by religious norms and practices. What is interesting is that the utilization of the concept has a clear role in the notion of defense against encroaching Western values and the erosion of intrinsically Islamic ones. For Rafīq Habīb, public order invokes the idea that the political process cannot go against Egyptian values, since "if it is against the Egyptian values it will not be democratic, [and] if it is democratic it will be with Egyptian values."[40] For Muhammad 'Imāra, it is the public order that imposes limits on freedom: there is no absolute freedom. This applies in the West where, he argues, there is no freedom to betray the state.[41]

The concept of public order is used as a mechanism for conceptualizing limits to the democratic system. For example, while non-Muslims would have the right to criticize the formulation of *shari'a*, that right would obtain only on condition that respect be shown.[42] 'Imāra argues that it is possible to have Christian members of parliament as long as the majority of the members are Muslim. It is also possible, he argues, for a Christian to lead the army and take part in all legal and legislative institutions as long as the majority of the members that make up those institutions are Muslim.[43]

The concept of public order thus becomes a mechanism for defining differences between some archetypal Western democracy, which, it is argued—questionably—has no limits, and democracy in the Egyptian Islamic state. It is also a mechanism for arguing that democracy, when limitations are imposed, does not have to be inimical to Islam. The public order is defined by the people, the majority of whom are Muslims, and is therefore understood as a democratic concept.

In this way Fahmī Huwaydī rejects what he calls Western-style democracy. Democracy in Egypt, he argues, must be formulated on the basis of the Islamic civilization. According to Huwaydī, all parties "must accept and acknowledge Islam, both ideologically and legally and not oppose it or deny it." It is therefore not possible "to establish a party that calls for apostasy, freethinking, or atheism, or that discredits the heavenly revealed religions in general or Islam in particular, or makes light of the sacred things of Islam: its creed, its law, its Qur'an and its Prophet." He likens the possible parties to the diversity of schools in Islamic jurisprudence.[44] Thus there are limits, but he argues that these are particular to every society. Islam provides the constitution, and since Islam is the official religion of the state, how can it be legally allowed to propagate violation of that constitution? In Huwaydī's view, you have a right to be an unbeliever, but you have no right to change the system, since that would be against the constitution and the public order.[45] Yūsuf al-Qaradāwī agrees, and refuses to advocate Western democracy, which he says "has no principles by which it abides, nor virtues which regulate its behavior."[46]

Muhammad Salīm al-'Awwā argues that this concept of a public order is not just for the protection of Islam. While non-Muslims must abide by the values of Islam and respect its provisions, Muslims would also not be able to attack any other religion. Neither Muslims nor non-Muslims would be able to defend atheism, because it is anti–public order. Al-'Awwā argues that this is not because it is anti-Islam or anti-Islamic law but because it is anti the morale of a Muslim state, which is composed of religious people.[47] The lawyer and prominent member of al-Wasat 'Isām Sultān argues that the rule to respect religion applies to Christians and Muslims.[48]

Tāriq al-Bishrī is more tentative about enforcing these kinds of limitations, indicating the variety of ways in which they can be viewed. However, he does say that such limitations must be kept in mind, because you must have a frame of reference, just as liberal societies do.[49] Such reticence is also expressed by Muhammad 'Imāra, although he says that it would be difficult to have an atheist party in a Muslim state.[50]

Whether the concept of public order is used in a restrictive or a more liberating way depends on how its relationship to the democratic process is envisaged. Different groups view the relationship between the public order and the will of the people in different ways. The Muslim Brotherhood—or at least the group's conservatives—takes a quite rigid approach. It argues for a more text-based notion of public order that would clearly adhere to Islam as it has been traditionally interpreted. This position was illustrated in the Muslim Brotherhood's party platform of 2007, which stated that the frame of reference for the *sharī'a* is the consensus of Muslim jurists and that the legislative authority must seek their opinion in matters related to the clear texts of the Qur'an and the Sunna.[51]

Perhaps the most liberal approach to the question of the relationship of the public order to the will of the people is that of al-Wasat. 'Isām Sultān, a prominent party member, argues that the public order constitutes values such as freedom, dignity of the human being (both of which are contextually resonant), and the protection of general and private wealth. In his view the public order is a flexible concept, many aspects of which can be revised by the will of the people. He even sees flexibility in the penal code, an element that most Muslims regard as explicitly stated in the Qur'an and therefore unnegotiable. In fact, he goes so far as to say that there are no texts, just values.[52] Abū al-'Ilā Mādī, leader of al-Wasat, argues that when al-Wasat members talk about the *sharī'a*, they are referring to general principles such as justice and take a very general and non-literal interpretation of the *sharī'a*. According to him, their task is to select "interpretations of Islamic law which contribute toward, rather than obstruct the development of Egyptian society," and he states that the interpretations they offer are "illuminated by the general goals of *sharī'a* and its fundamental principles." Even these are human interpretations, and as such may or may not be correct.[53] The important thing is that there is considerable room for the people to determine the public order. This indicates a significant shift away from the belief that Islam is fixed. Thus the concept of public order does not have to be a mechanism for conservatism, although Abū al-ʿIlā Mādī situates the party in the middle between those who want to limit the concept of Islamic "constants" to nothing and those who see them in a broad sense.[54]

This flexible approach to defining the public order represents a departure from the party's ideological roots. It has been argued that such liberalism on the part of al-Wasat results from its need to distance itself from the Muslim Brotherhood. The area in which al-Wasat can establish itself as a distinct party is becoming narrower as the discourse of some members of the Muslim Brotherhood continues to become more conciliatory.[55] Like Rafīq Habīb, Fahmī Huwaydī argues that such flexibility has gone too far. While he grants that people are free to establish an Islamic state if they wish to, once this happens, he would impose limits. While these limits are not rigid and are not many, they do exist. He makes a firm distinction between rules relating to worship and those dealing with relations between human beings. The former should be respected, but the latter are flexible. Huwaydī argues that there is considerable flexibility, that the things that have been decided in the *sharīʿa* are few, and that 95 percent are open to the people's judgment.[56]

INDIVIDUAL RELIGIOUS AUTONOMY

The concept of public order has been utilized to justify retaining some Islamic laws, although the possibility of flexibility is present. Egypt's religious nature is viewed by some as one of the principal characteristics of the Egyptian public order.[57] This includes the religious and social structure based on personal status law. Rafīq Habīb argues that since Egypt is a religious society and the basic unit is the family, which is not civil but religious, the current system of personal status law, barring changes in details, must be maintained.[58] This choice would mean that non-Muslims could function only on a certain level within the confines of their own religious communities, and there are of course important implications for the concept of citizenship with respect to how the principle of individual autonomy is applied. The issue of equality regarding one's right to marry is one example.

The inequality between men and women and Muslims and non-Muslims in terms of the right to marry is upheld. This is related to the question of *wilāya*, or authority to rule. In the view of Muhammad Salīm al-ʿAwwā, leadership and guardianship in marriage belong to the man.[59] The rationale behind the marriage law is that a non-Muslim man should not have *wilāya* over a Muslim woman. Moderate Islamists present this idea as connected to the idea that Islam demands respect for Christian and Jewish beliefs but not vice versa. Since a man is the head of the family, he is able to fulfill his religious command by respecting his wife's beliefs.[60] Yet the underlying implication is that *wilāya* should remain with Muslims and that non-Muslims should not have ultimate authority over Muslims. Thus while the Wasatiyya Islamists can conceive of a non-Muslim being in a position of authority over a Muslim in the political sphere, the same cannot be countenanced in the religious or, more specifically, the familial sphere.

Tāriq al-Bishrī argues that while there might be a contradiction between personal status provisions and equal citizenship from a rational perspective, from a historical or contextual perspective this is not necessarily the case.[61] Muhammad Salīm al-ʿAwwā argues that no contradiction exists, since this inequality also exists between Christians if they are not from the same church. Thus it is not about inequality between Muslims and non-Muslims.[62] Indeed, it is accepted that in the field of personal status, Muslims and Christians are not necessarily unequal, but equality is not viewed in individualistic terms. Thus an individual is not able to move freely from one religious community to another without social and legal repercussions. Equality on an individual level is accepted in the political sphere, but in the area of the family, equality is still viewed in terms of the community's right to apply its own laws.

There are therefore limits to the concept of individual autonomy. Much of the discussion of citizenship in the Egyptian context focuses on the question of the Copts as a community and on minority rights rather than individual rights. Some ambiguity is expressed toward the precise status of individuals who do not belong to a religious group. While there is greater openness toward other religions, the idea of the heavenly revealed religions remains a fundamental assumption behind Islamist conceptions of citizenship. Though al-ʿAwwā states that the "Qurʾanic constitution" includes non-Muslims "whatever their religion," People of the Book "have more detailed provisions concerning the reverence that is due to them."[63] It is argued that Muslims are religiously compelled to have good relations with People of the Book.[64] Muhammad ʿImāra holds that the unity of God, which is a fundamental principle of the heavenly religions, is one of the fundamental constants of Islam.[65]

The prioritization of the concept of the heavenly revealed religions results in some antipathy, for example, toward non-Muslims who are not Jews or

Christians. However, there is an acknowledgment that citizenship applies to all Egyptians. Some Islamists are beginning to use more universal and open language, advocating respect for the dignity of humankind. They talk of the nobility of humankind and the spirit of human brotherhood. Muhammad Salīm al-'Awwā speaks of human brotherhood as being a Qur'anic principle for defining relations between Muslims and others.[66] Fahmī Huwaydī argues that Islam takes pride in a human being as divinely created and that he or she should be honored, regardless of his or her creed. An individual is, above all, a "human being who has dignity which must be preserved, since the human being in the true Islamic understanding is a chosen creation of God." Huwaydī argues that it is the fundamental duty of Islamic society to defend the dignity of human beings.[67]

The concept of the divine religions does still influence the thought of the Wasatiyya intellectuals and that of al-Wasat, while at the same time it is argued that non-Muslims should have their rights as Egyptian citizens and as human beings.[68] In 'Imāra's view, that pluralism extends beyond the People of the Book. Equal treatment was and still should be applied to other man-made positivist religions.[69] Indicating the flexible nature of this issue, in 2003 Fahmī Huwaydī expressed some defensiveness about the precise status of non-Muslims such as Bahā'īs, who are said to believe in an "anti-Islamic religion." He argued that Bahā'īs constitute only a small number in Egypt and so do not deserve the attention they get. However, he also affirmed that other non-Muslims should have their civil rights guaranteed because they are human beings.[70] In 2007 Huwaydī stated that the beliefs of all non-Muslims, including Bahā'īs, should be respected and that they should have the right to build their own temples, although he conceded that this is a complicated legal issue. He also argues that they should have their own personal status law and follow instruction according to their own belief (which happened informally in the Ottoman Empire). While the current Egyptian Constitution restricts any formal recognition of religions that are not deemed to be divinely revealed, that does not necessarily have to be the case. He argues that while the Islamists are currently in no position to deal with revising this constitutional position, he does not automatically preclude such a move.[71] Rafīq Habīb takes a more conservative line, saying that Bahā'īs should have the right to do whatever they want in their own homes but that such freedom cannot extend to the right for Bahā'īs to build their own temples and have their own personal status law.[72]

While it is argued that non-Muslims who are not Jews or Christians should have their civil rights, the problem lies in the question of their official recognition. Rafīq Habīb argues that they should not be allowed to have their own personal status law or their religion recognized on their national identity cards.[73] Muhammad 'Imāra agrees, arguing that officially recognizing them would go against the public order. He says that you can do what you want in your own home, but to do it in front of the general public is wrong because it would "harm the feelings and creed of the general public." Thus, he goes on, "the freedom of the human being is limited by respect" for the public order. This is the same as with homosexuality, which, though practiced, cannot be officially recognized. There is a difference, according to 'Imāra, between individual freedom and official recognition of that freedom.[74] What 'Imāra fails to mention is that if that freedom is not officially recognized, the law can be used to curtail the freedom.

The Muslim Brotherhood is unwilling to acknowledge the civil rights of Bahā'īs. Former Deputy Supreme Guide Muhammad Habīb argues that Bahā'īs clash with the public order and that the 'ulamā' consider them apostates. When asked what the solution is, he responds that there is no Islamic law that needs to be put into effect and that the party is concerned with other issues.[75] The Muslim Brotherhood commits itself only to the "freedom of practicing religious rites for all acknowledged divine religions."[76]

This uneasiness is also manifested by al-Wasat. Despite al-Wasat's commitment to citizenship and to the liberal interpretation of texts, the party affirms "the freedom of belief of worship for all members of revealed religions."[77] Abū al-'Ilā Mādī also argues against official recognition of Bahā'īs and says that they should have their own personal status law provisions determined by sharī'a. This would mean that members of religions other than Judaism, Christianity, and Islam would have to organize their personal status affairs and identify themselves as members of one of those three religions. For example, someone who wants to get married and to have that marriage officially recognized would have to do so as a Muslim, a Jew, or a Christian.[78]

Limitations to individual autonomy can also be discerned in the consequences imposed for apostasy, although there is a significant difference from the mainstream Islamic position: the Wasatiyya categorically reject the death penalty for apostasy. Muhammad Salīm al-'Awwā argues that there is no mention in the Qur'an that punishment by death for apostasy should be enforced in this world. Apostasy is only a discretionary punishment and not a penal punishment that has been defined in the Qur'an. The penalty should be exacted by

God in the hereafter. The death penalty also contradicts the principle of "no compulsion in religion" (2:256).[79] However, it is argued that apostates should be penalized in terms of the restriction of their rights under personal status laws.[80] Tāriq al-Bishrī states that the current legal system accepts Islam as the essential definition of the general order and therefore it cannot accept individual acts like apostasy. Thus while an apostate would still have his legal rights as a citizen, he should be socially punished. Al-Bishrī states that an apostate should be socially punished because apostasy constitutes an act against society and Islam.[81] This, Fahmī Huwaydī argues, is similar to the punishments that the Coptic community imposes upon its own apostates.[82]

The concept of public order is also invoked to impose restrictions on the freedom to express one's religious feelings. While people have a right to change their religion, an individual is not allowed to publicly express his change of religion or to encourage others to do so. For Muhammad Salīm al-'Awwā, encouraging apostasy would be against the public order of Islam. Non-Muslims must respect the feelings of Muslims, since "it is not allowed for [non-Muslims] to curse Allah or his Prophet or his religion and his book openly or to spread rumors of ideas that contradict the ideology of the state." However, he also states that Muslims are obliged to respect the religions that went before Muhammad—i.e., Judaism and Christianity.[83] Huwaydī takes a more liberal approach and argues that a Muslim has the right to persuade and argue for his religion—as does a Jew or a Christian, although this prosyletism (actively going out and speaking to the people) would not extend to other non-Muslims.[84]

CIVIL VERSUS RELIGIOUS SPHERES

Such inequalities as those mentioned above illustrate the particular parameters within which Islamic discussions on citizenship are understood. There are limitations to equality, of which the rule concerning marriage is one example. One of the mechanisms used for justifying inequality in certain areas, such as personal status law, is a distinction between the civil and the religious spheres. The religious sphere is narrowly conceptualized and limited to issues of personal status law and personal worship.

Classical Islam did not recognize the distinction between civil and religious per se, although in practice there was a distance between the representatives of Islam, the *'ulamā'*, and the political institutions of the Islamic polity. Nevertheless, the concept of religion has existed since the foundation of Islam:

the term "religion" used to denote a system of ideas as distinct from others is found in the Qur'an. Wilfred Cantwell Smith states that "Islam, it could be argued, may well in fact be characterized by a rather unique insistence upon itself as a coherent and closed system, a sociologically and legally and even politically organized entity in the mundane world and an ideologically organized entity as an ideal."[85] This has opened the space for a distinction between the worldly and the religious, which can be seen in Ibn Khaldūn's (1332–1406) distinction between royal authority and the caliphate, the duty of which was to protect the religion.[86] While the concept of the civil to denote the non-religious field is a relatively recent import from Western thought, conceptualizing the religious or spiritual (dīn) as opposed to the non-religious or temporal (dunyā) has its own roots in classical Islamic thought.[87]

Contemporary Islamists use the terms "civil" and "religious" to distinguish the public, political sphere from the religious sphere, which they argue constitutes the family and religious worship. It is a particularly modern construction and is related to the very establishment of the category of personal status law in the late nineteenth century. The concept of personal status law is readily accepted. The distinction between the religious sphere, with the definition of the religious as pertaining to personal status law, and the civil sphere has become a mechanism for legitimizing the level on which equality between Muslims and non-Muslims applies. It is the distinction between the civil and the religious that enables these Islamists to argue that non-Muslims can be included in an Islamic civilization. A distinction is made between an Islamic order as a platform for politics and culture and a religious one. Muhammad 'Imāra argues that in Islamic jurisprudence, there is a civil law that is for the whole community, including non-Muslims, and is separate from religious law, which applies to Muslims only.[88]

It is therefore argued that equal citizenship applies to the civil political sphere, even if equality of citizenship does not apply to religious law. The normative classical rules relating to a non-Muslim not having authority over a Muslim do not apply in the political sphere, but they do apply in the context of marriage. As Muhammad Salīm al-'Awwā states, "You have equal citizenship everywhere except when this contradicts religious teaching where you keep equality between people of the same religion and you cannot extend it from this religion to another."[89]

The distinction between the civil and the religious is extended to the definition of the Islamic state itself. It is argued that the Islamic state is a civil state and not a religious one. A civil Islamic state is distinct from a religious state because a religious state derives from Western notions based on the church, which claimed to represent God's will. A religious state is one in which the ruler is sacrosanct and claims to represent the divine; thus there is a direct relationship between God and the state. The Islamic state is a civil state, in which the source of power is the people. The Wasatiyya intellectuals argue that this model is similar to the democratic system in the West, although in an Islamic democracy the people do not have absolute power; they have power as long as they do not go beyond the Islamic framework. Thus there is no institution in Islam that can claim that it has the right view and the best *ijtihād*.[90] Non-Muslims are equal in the Islamic state precisely because it is a civil one. Yūsuf al-Qaradāwī writes that the Islamic state is not "one based on theology alone. Instead, it is a civilian State based on choice agreement and consultation."[91] Tāriq al-Bishrī makes a distinction between "the existence of Islam as religion and state and religious government," stating that he does not want "religious government in the sense that the government becomes an intermediary between land and sky and rules in the name of God."[92]

This distinction has been emphasized by al-Wasat and more recently by the Muslim Brotherhood. 'Abd al-Mun'im Abū al-Futūh of the Muslim Brotherhood argues that *sharī'a* is not a dogma or creed relating to faith, differentiating between a body of religious law and *sharī'a* as a civil code.[93] Therefore, the phrase "a civil party with an Islamic reference" has become a common frame of reference, employed both by al-Wasat and, more recently, by the Muslim Brotherhood.[94]

CONTEXTUALIZING CITIZENSHIP

It has been shown that the Wasatiyya intellectuals have made a significant contribution to articulating a relationship between Muslims and non-Muslims in a proposed Islamic state that is not defined by the *dhimma* but is based on citizenship. This conception of citizenship also retains recognition of certain Islamic values, although the degree of contingency and openness to the democratic process varies. These Islamic values include issues relating to freedom of religion, individual autonomy, and personal status law, as well as references to the Islamic nature of the state.

Various mechanisms are used to establish this difference and to conceptualize boundaries within which both Muslims and non-Muslims are allowed to be politically active. First, the concept of public order provides a framework within which political expression is maintained. Second, the difference between the religious sphere and the civil sphere distinguishes areas in which Egyptians are equal citizens from areas in which they are primarily members of religious communities. While non-Muslims have political equality, it is argued, they do not have equality in the religious sphere, which applies to personal status law.

One of the problems in this approach to citizenship is that the emphasis upon personal status law has the potential to undermine the concept of citizenship by forcing the individual to be linked to a religious community. In addition, when the religious community takes on a political role, the danger is that the individual is identified in the public sphere not as an Egyptian but as a Muslim or a Christian. The importance of religious affiliation in Egypt has increased in the last few decades and consequently the concept of citizenship has been weakened.

However, the Wasatiyya Islamists argue that the religious community's taking on a political role is not necessarily a result of a religious social structure based on personal status law. In their view a unified political community based on citizenship can coexist with a religious social structure, and it is possible for multiple forms of identity to exist side by side.

Another issue that constitutes a challenge for the concept of citizenship is the belief that the Islamic nature of the state must be maintained, a belief that is arguably problematic, since the implication would be that Muslims (or indeed a particular group of Muslims) would have a monopoly on defining what Islam is and what its provisions are. In the view of many theoreticians, citizenship is unworkable in the context of a confessional state, since if the institutions in which rights and obligations are exercised favor one group over another, citizenship is diminished. However, this result is not inevitable: protecting the Islamic nature of the state could be a liberal or an illiberal force, directed against Muslims and non-Muslims alike. In the same way secular states can be liberal or illiberal.

The same can be said about the idea that Islam cannot be transgressed, which is represented by the concept of public order. Such a principle could be used to justify authoritarianism and to restrict freedom of speech. However, whether this is an inevitable consequence is debatable. It would of course depend on how Islam is applied in the public sphere and on the kind of consensus, if any, that evolves concerning the nature of Islamic values. It is contingent upon the majority's understanding of public order. As Tāriq al-Bishrī points out, an Islamic frame of reference can yield a range of approaches just as a secular frame of reference can.[95]

Another potentially problematic issue with the Wasatiyya conception of citizenship is the pragmatic nature of the arguments used to justify it. Such arguments, based on expediency, might be unsettling for those who wish for an articulation of citizenship, based on a priori principles, that clearly delineates the rights and role of non-Muslims. However, the idea of pragmatism is actually well established in Sunni thought. Such an approach is in line with classical Sunni Islam, which has often evolved political theory to justify the status quo rather than establishing fixed principles for future application.

It might be argued that this conception of citizenship simply constitutes a more modernized and contextualized form of the *dhimma* itself. While there are overlaps, there has been a shift toward the ethic of participation and inclusion and an emphasis on communal solidarity between Muslims and non-Muslims. Also, significant distinctions exist, particularly in the tone, the language, the level of commitment to the political participation of non-Muslims, the nation-state, and the flexibility applied to Islamic law. These Islamists, by breaking away from the *dhimma*, have laid the theoretical foundations for citizenship and for flexibility in the interpretation of Islamic jurisprudence and the religious texts. The thinkers themselves perceive that they are departing from the *dhimma*, although some vestiges of it remain in the approach to personal status law and freedom of religion. Even Fahmī Huwaydī argues that organizing one's life according to personal status law is a historical issue that does not necessarily derive from Islamic law. Thus he categorizes personal status law as a changeable thing. Tāriq al-Bishrī, however, says it would be very difficult to allow non-Muslim men to marry Muslim women.[96]

The majority of these intellectuals and activists accept that there are important differences between the type of citizenship they envisage and citizenship broadly conceived in the West. Rafīq Habīb argues that "*muwātana* as citizenship as any Western person understands it has no place in Egypt."[97] While 'Imāra argues that in the West citizenship is not known except in the context of secularism, he holds that it is an intrinsically Islamic concept, confirmed because Islam established the concept of equality in rights and duties.[98]

Islamist conceptions of citizenship are evolving, just as citizenship in any context is a constantly evolving concept. It is not monolithic, nor is it perfectly applied. In the United Kingdom, the queen as head of state takes a vow to protect the Protestant faith. In the United States, while in theory religion and state are separated, religion has come to be an integral part of the political process and of social relations, which can result in excluding or including people on the basis of religious belief.

One must also not forget that citizenship is a translation, and therefore an approximation, of the concept *muwātana*, which implies a level of reciprocity among various groups living in the same homeland. While these thinkers use the term in both Arabic and English, it refers to a kind of compatriotism and sense of community, and not necessarily to citizenship in the modern liberal sense of the word, which is assumed to be contingent upon the indifference of the state to religion. While Islamists appropriate the concept of citizenship, they articulate a religiously rooted citizenship, and do so in a way that accords with the cultural and legal context.

Differing approaches to citizenship raise interesting questions about its universality and flexibility as a concept. Islamists argue that one should not judge Islamic conceptions of citizenship from the perspective of secularism. Tāriq al-Bishrī says that the Islamist articulation of citizenship should "pull the carpet from under the feet of the secular point of view." Citizenship and equality do not have to exclude religious thinking.[99] Pulling the carpet would involve posing questions such as whether a citizen's relationship to the state that is not mediated through a religious community is necessarily a violation of citizenship. It would also involve asking whether religious toleration and citizenship are necessarily predicated upon the indifference of political authorities to religion.

Citizenship and equality are not fixed entities; they are contingent upon the community in which they are exercised. Any consideration of citizenship must involve an examination of the conditions that make it meaningful. It is not a political decision to be imposed from above, but a process that reflects the needs of the community, and the boundaries of the rights contained in citizenship must be determined contextually.

7 COPTIC RESPONSES

WHILE ISLAMISTS HAVE MADE A CASE for citizenship in an Islamic state, any discussion of citizenship in Egypt must take into consideration the response of different sectors of the Coptic community. The Copts are not passive recipients of an Islamist agenda set by Muslims. They are part of an ongoing debate within Egypt concerning the relationship between religion and the state and secular and Islamist conceptions of citizenship. Are there points at which a contextualized, culturally Islamic citizenship does in fact take into account the Egyptian social and political culture? Are there points at which an Islamically oriented conception of citizenship is, as Rafīq Habīb and the Wasatiyya intellectuals claim, more responsive to the needs of the Copts? How do Copts understand the relationship between citizenship and religious identity?

ARTICLE 2

It is commonly assumed that Eastern Christians support a secular state. The interwar period (1918–1939) was a golden age for Copts, in part because of its secular atmosphere. Certainly many Copts call for a secular state. Coptic opposition to the application of Islamic law and the idea that a secular state would be in their best interests were evident after the Muslim Brotherhood successes in the 2005 elections.[1] However, an analysis of Coptic discourse and debates in contemporary Egypt illustrates that the picture is far more complex. The majority of Copts are united in their reservations with regard to an Islamic state where *sharīʿa* is the sole source of legislation. However, their responses to the question of Article 2, which states that "the principles of Islamic *sharīʿa* are *the* main source of legislation," vary, indicating that not all Copts call for a secular state.

An effort to assess Coptic responses to Article 2 illustrates the problem of referring to such an entity as the Coptic community. Copts are present across the Egyptian geographical and socioeconomic spectrum. Politically, they represent a number of different positions—despite the fact that the Coptic Church has emerged as the Coptic community's effective political representative and has eclipsed the secular Coptic elite. The different agendas and positions represented by Copts were manifest during the early 2007 debate about Article 2 of the constitution. Just as Islamist debates on citizenship are influenced by the political context, so are Coptic statements concerning Article 2, because a tense and charged atmosphere surrounds discussions of Article 2. During the debate about the constitutional amendments, many Copts felt that objection to Article 2 would be perceived by Muslims as an assault on Islam.[2] As a result, there was some criticism that Copts did not object strongly enough to Article 2.[3]

As would be expected, many Copts oppose Article 2. The strongest opposition comes from Coptic expatriates.[4] For example, in July 2006 the Fourth International Coptic Conference, held in New Jersey, called for the abolition of Article 2.[5] Michael Munīr of the U.S. Copts Association refers to Article 2 as "racist."[6] Such opposition to Article 2 is to be expected from expatriates, since they tend to be more alarmist about Islamist agendas—and they feel more free to express their political opinions.

There are also voices within Egypt that call for the abolition of Article 2. One argument made is that Article 2 goes against the idea of a civil state, which is necessary for the principle of citizenship.[7] Another view states that Article 2 divides the Egyptian nation into believers and non-believers.[8] Many Copts oppose it because they fear that it will facilitate the establishment of a religious state.[9] Secularists such as Munīr Fakhrī ʿAbd al-Nūr, secretary general of the Wafd Party and member of a veteran political family; Yūsuf Sidhum, a Coptic intellectual and editor in chief of the periodical *Watanī*; and ʿAbd al-Munʿim Saʿīd, the head of the al-Ahram Center for Political and Strategic Studies call for the abolition of Article 2, although they emphasize that it is not appropriate to push for its abolition now.[10]

However, many Copts call for simply amending the article.[11] Some suggest that such an amendment should take into account that Egypt is a multireligious country, for example by inserting a reference to Christians and Christianity as partners in the Egyptian homeland.[12] The Cairo Institute for

Human Rights Studies sent a demand to President Mubarak that Article 2 be amended to mention the religious neutrality of the state and to take into account that not only the Islamic but also the Pharaonic and Coptic civilizations contributed to the formation of Egypt. The appeal had 185 signatories.[13] The Egyptian Union of Human Rights Organization (EUHRO) recommends amending Article 2 to state that "it will not interfere with the principle of citizenship, and would not influence the beliefs of others."[14]

There have also been calls for replacing the definite article "the," in the part of Article 2 stating that the "principles of Islamic *shari'a* are *the* principal source of legislation" with the indefinite article "a," thus allowing for other sources of legislation beside the *shari'a*.[15] Such a request came from Bishop Marqus, the bishop of Shubra al-Khayma and official spokesman for the Coptic Orthodox Church at the time.[16] Pope Shenouda publicly criticized Bishop Murqus, who then lost his position as spokesman.

Pope Shenouda's reaction to Bishop Murqus's comments reveals the political sensitivities surrounding Article 2. Pope Shenouda has been careful not to voice opposition to Article 2. In early 2007 he rejected calls by Coptic expatriates for its omission and pointed to the danger of amending it.[17] Such statements might well hide a deeper antipathy, since Pope Shenouda strongly opposed the 1980 amendment of Article 2 that made the *shari'a* the main source of legislation.

Some Copts argue that Article 2 does not pose a problem and that the *shari'a* actually allows Copts to have their personal status law. Nabīl Luqā Bibāwī, a Coptic author and vice-chairman of the Shura Council Information and Culture Committee, argues that Article 2 allows for the Bible to be a source of legislation in cases of personal status law for Copts.[18] Rafīq Habīb, a Coptic intellectual with Islamist sympathies, argues that without Article 2, "the Christian personal status laws become unconstitutional as they violate the principle of equality before the law as mentioned in Article no. 40 from the constitution."[19]

While most secular Copts and Muslims oppose Article 2, many Copts who are associated with the government have issued statements of support for it. Arguments are made to the effect that the *shari'a* does not deprive Christians of their rights.[20] Amīn Iskandar, a Coptic intellectual and political analyst, took the position that the article is logical, since the majority of the Egyptian people are Muslim. Copts do not need to be afraid of this article, nor are they in any way oppressed because of it.[21]

PERSONAL STATUS LAW

One of the important features of Islamist discourse on citizenship in an Islamic state is the emphasis upon citizenship existing alongside the religious social structure of Egyptian society. An analysis of Coptic responses to personal status law indicates that the majority of Copts themselves also envisage a kind of citizenship that preserves religious identity and religious community.

When *sharī'a* was replaced by Western law in many legal spheres, it was not abolished but was limited to the area of personal status law. It was at this time, around 1875, that personal status law was first established as a legal category, thereby marking a significant shift toward the family as a legal category. The family was never strictly secularized, since it remained inextricably linked to its religious identity. It has been argued that the maintenance of personal status law, which is contingent upon the religious family and upon the mediation of religious authorities, has been an impediment to the development of the secular nation-state. One of the important features of the modern secular state is secular personal status law, i.e., secular marriage, including the ability to marry without having one's civil status mediated by one's affiliation with a particular religion (although no marriage is completely secular—it is inherently a religious concept). Citizens can theoretically organize themselves as neutral members who have a direct relationship with the state that is not contingent upon religious identity. Other markers of secularism related to the religious family include the right to freely convert from one religion to another.

While the maintenance of personal status law has served to restrict the secularization of Egyptian society, it is a system that many Copts wish to keep intact. Copts who are committed to the secularization of personal status law constitute a minority.[22] Vivian Fu'ād and Samīr Murqus, who are Coptic researchers and writers, Munīr Fakhrī 'Abd al-Nūr, who is the secretary general of the Wafd Party, and Milād Hannā, who is a Coptic writer and winner of the International Simon Bolivar Prize, are a few examples. The concept of secular personal status law also has some support from the U.S. Copts Association.[23]

Such Copts claim that "secularism never died" and that secularism is there among writers, university professors, and intellectual groups.[24] However, the influence of secular Copts is questionable, and Cornelis Hulsman, director of the Center for Arab-West Understanding, argues that Milād Hannā is "probably one of the very last" secularists.[25] The strength of the secular Coptic elite was weakened both by Gamal Abdul Nasser's nationalization policies and by Pope Shenouda's control of the church.[26] Michael Munīr, of the U.S. Copts

Association, complains that the problem is that elitists have taken up the cause of secularism but they have not been able to transform it into a grass-roots movement.[27]

Secular Copts who advocate the establishment of civil personal status law know that such a change is unlikely. The vast majority of Egyptians would not accept turning matters concerning social status over to a centralized and secular body of law. Having a unified civil personal status law could be "very difficult," from the perspectives of both Muslims and Christians.[28] In general, there are no calls for a civil solution; the current system is viewed as something that Copts can live with.[29] Munīr Fakhrī 'Abd al-Nūr says that when he suggested such an idea to the National Council for Human Rights, he received an incredulous response and said, "Just forget it. At this stage it is very far from the common culture."[30]

This situation is very different from that of prerevolutionary Egypt, when the concept of civil personal status law was on the agenda. Then, secular Muslim and Christian politicians worked to establish a unified civil law, although they encountered resistance from the Copts. At the time, the Muslim politician 'Abd al-Hamīd Badawī (1887–1965) argued that religious differences in Egypt were fading away, and he expressed hope that all matters relating to social status would be incorporated in one legal system under a civil code.[31]

Indeed, Coptic discussions about Article 2 and citizenship do not include questioning the current personal status law. This omission reflects the power of the church over the Coptic community and the increasing confessional nature of Egyptian society. The conflicts over personal status law issues do not indicate that the community is struggling for a civil secular state. Rather, the church as de facto leader of the Coptic community is trying to protect itself and the community by reinforcing its own authority.

Three issues relating to personal status—marriage, divorce, and inheritance—illustrate the point. Today, Christians marry under the patronage of the church. In addition, they have to have the state's sanction of the marriage. For the Coptic Church, marriage is a sacrament, and therefore the concept of civil marriage draws opposition for religious reasons.[32] The church would not recognize the children of a civil marriage, and that would have social and legal implications.[33]

However, in theory Bishop Thomas, whose diocese is in al-Qussia in Upper Egypt, does not see an impediment to a civil marriage that is accompanied by the sacramental blessing of the church.[34] Thus it would seem that the reasons for resisting civil marriage also relate to the Coptic community's sense of self-preservation. From the perspective of the church, civil marriage would diminish the church's control over the community, and that, it is feared, would lead to the dissolution of Coptic identity.[35] Civil marriage also provides easier paths to conversion, which would further undermine the Coptic community. The same fear surrounds mixed marriages, which, while rare, are often associated with conversion and are therefore considered a loss.[36] Thus there are vested interests: for Christians, keeping the religious identity of the marriage helps preserve the balance between the Coptic and the Muslim communities.

A similar situation exists with regard to divorce. The church resists allowing Christians to divorce. The Coptic personal status law, which was issued by the Coptic *millet* council in 1938, gave fifteen justifications for divorce, and it is this law that has been applied by the national courts since 1955. In the 1970's, Pope Shenouda III issued a papal decree that limited justifications for divorce to one, adultery.[37] However, according to the Egyptian Constitution, personal status law must be passed by the People's Assembly before it is applied by the national courts. Pope Shenouda's papal decree has not been discussed in the People's Assembly. So a dilemma exists: the state accepts the 1938 law as valid, but the church has refused to accept that law and the church's new law has not been sanctioned by the People's Assembly. Thus Copts can still get a divorce in the national courts under the Coptic personal status law of 1938, and since 98 percent of judges are Muslim, a liberal approach to the law is taken.[38] The problem is that Copts who divorce in such a way lose their right to remarry in the church. In 2006 Pope Shenouda appealed an administrative court ruling that obligates the church to allow Christians who obtain divorces from civil courts to remarry. This ruling was seen as interference with the church's teachings.[39] He continues to refuse to marry Christians who obtain divorces from civil courts except in circumstances of adultery and impotence. Najīb Jabrā'īl, a Coptic personal status law attorney and director of the Egyptian Union of Human Rights Organization (EUHRO), is closely associated with the church, and he argues that the administrative court's ruling is a dangerous precedent and a violation of the church's religious authority. In his view, such a ruling applies only to civil institutions and has no influence over the pope.[40]

Clearly there are religious reasons for this approach to divorce. However, there are other reasons as well, one of which is resisting the application of Islamic law within the Christian community. Many would argue that from the perspective of the church, it would be in its best interest to be more lenient about divorce. The church's intransigent position on divorce causes many Copts either to convert to Islam or to convert to another Christian denomination in order to obtain a divorce. Making divorce easier for Copts would reduce conversion. However, for the church, the issue of divorce symbolizes the growing encroachment of Islamic law upon its teachings and upon the Christian way of life. In early 2009, the Dār al-Iftā', the institution responsible for issuing *fatwās* (or legal opinions), issued a *fatwā* stating that polygamy is not prohibited in Christianity. This pronouncement caused an uproar among Copts, who considered it an "unacceptable interference" in Christian affairs. The church stated that al-Azhar is not entitled to issue *fatwās* for Christians.[41] Such an appropriation of authority was viewed as a threat to Christian personal status law. Defending Christian marriage by not allowing divorce is seen as a way of protecting the community. It is for this reason that the church is pushing for a unified personal status law for all Christians. A unified law would prevent the application of Islamic law to a case involving Christians from different denominations. It would also prevent Christians from gaining a divorce by changing denomination, although such a development might result in more Christians converting to Islam to obtain a divorce.[42] The draft law was presented to the People's Assembly several times, the last time in 2000, but the assembly has not yet placed the item on its agenda.

Not only has effort been put into resisting the encroachment of Islamic law, but church members and others connected to the church wish to extend the Coptic Church's control over personal status law so that everything connected with the family, including guardianship, inheritance, and adoption, which is currently ruled according to Islamic law, would come under Christian law.[43]

The question of inheritance is an interesting example. Traditionally, the church has not had a position on inheritance and has applied Islamic law. The Coptic Orthodox Church did not oppose any civil law as long as it did not interfere with the church's sacraments.[44] It is only as far back as the fourteenth and fifteenth centuries that any evidence that inheritance was dealt with by the church can be found. So Copts used *sharī'a* not because they were forced to but because they did not come up with an alternative.[45]

Most families do not oppose the application of Islamic law for inheritance, indicating that it is a cultural issue rather than a religious one. In a patriarchal society, many Coptic families are happy with giving men a greater share of inheritance.[46] Copts accept the submission to Islamic law on some personal status issues because it is part of their overall cultural heritage and, according to Mīlād Hannā, constitutes "an unwritten pact," in return for which the penal code is not applied.[47] Hannā argues that "Egypt is another type of cultural life," by which Copts live with Muslims without feeling significantly different. "We live with the events," he says. "We live with the laws, we live with the present cultural concepts."[48]

However, there are indications that the degree of acceptance of the status quo is exaggerated. For example, many Coptic women feel it is unfair, and in many rural areas Islamic inheritance law is used to exploit women and give them even less inheritance than they are entitled to.[49] Because of such unfair practices, many Coptic families, including that of Yūsuf Sidhum (editor of the Coptic newspaper al-Watanī), have chosen to redistribute the money equally within the family.[50] This change occurs, of course, only if all family members agree, and it is done after the state distributes the estate according to Islamic law.

Opposition to Islamic inheritance law also exists within the church,[51] expressed in religious terms on the basis that equality of the sexes is in the Christian texts.[52] Bishop Murqus states that many people ask the church for advice about how they should distribute their inheritance and, he says, "we now respond from the Bible itself."[53] What is noticeable here is that opposition to inheritance does not involve the employment of a secular human rights discourse. It largely follows the Islamic line that inheritance is due to one's family. The shift involves reacting against the supposed gender inequity. This position is framed as being opposed to "Christian law."

A particular proponent of this stance is Bishop Thomas. Contrary to the belief that reformation of the inheritance law is not a priority for Copts, he argues that it is in fact an important issue because one must look at it from a holistic perspective. He says that the application of Islamic inheritance law to Copts means that Copts are not free to do what they believe in. Such a lack of freedom could spread to other things, he argues, saying, "It kills the inner dignity [when] you are pushed to apply something on your own self and your own family that conflicts with your faith." It goes against the beliefs of the church and because of that, he argues, it puts pressure on the church to implement the concept of equality. This in turn puts pressure on individual Christians to decide between their faith and the norms of society. It also puts pressure on church leaders to persuade men to sell or give their property to their daughters, with the possibility that the uncles will raise a court case against the daughters. This in turn creates a bigger conflict in the family, and then, he argues, the church has to go in and make peace between the uncles and the daughters.[54]

What is interesting here is the articulation of a new conflict between Islamic law and Christian values, even though the Coptic community has not previously had a position on inheritance. Here the church is stepping in and presenting Islamic inheritance as an encroachment on the right of Copts, not as individuals but as a religious community that wishes to live its life according to the Bible under the jurisdiction of the church.

Another issue that is important to consider when analyzing Coptic views on citizenship has to do with the question of freedom of religion and conversion. The Wafā' Qustantīn event illustrated that attitudes toward conversion are culturally influenced, and that conversion brings great shame to both the Muslim and the Christian communities. The right to change one's religion is culturally challenging to both Muslim and non-Muslim communities in Egypt.[55] Rafīq Habīb argues that this reflects the common Egyptian culture: "We don't think of it in terms of being my right to change my religion, in our values, it is a kind of obligation to be faithful to your religion all your life" and "in our culture you can be against the state, but you cannot be against religion because religion is sacred."[56]

In a study commissioned by the Center for Arab-West Understanding that examined more than one hundred conversions to Islam and a few conversions to Christianity, all the converts' families were convinced that the conversion was due to duress.[57] Shame over conversion is also behind many of the stories about the forced kidnapping of Christian girls. Father Mattā al-Miskīn has stated that if Egypt was a country with 90 percent Christians and 10 percent Muslims, then Egyptian culture would be quite similar, with Christians as a majority behaving similarly to Muslims as a majority.[58] Such a statement is impossible to assess, but it does suggest that attitudes toward issues such as conversion cannot be understood in terms of Christian versus Muslim. Secular Copts and secular Muslims have a more tolerant attitude toward conversion than do conservative Copts and conservative Muslims. Yūsuf Sidhum reflects the Coptic secular position and states that while the church does not bless losing a Christian to the Islamic faith, it should be "the right of every citizen to shift from one faith to another" without pressure or harassment.[59] This is not a position that the church has consistently taken.

While the church clearly resists the conversion of Copts to Islam, it would not be expedient for the church to take the same approach to conversion as the majority of Muslims. For example, Copts are not against the right of Copts who have converted to Islam to convert back.

The Coptic approach to the Bahā'ī question is instructive here. Again, the Coptic position is mixed and complex. The U.S. Copts Association, for example, is strongly supportive of improving the rights of Bahā'īs.[60] However, the church on the whole is not concerned with the establishment of a legal position for Bahā'īs in Egypt.[61] Rafīq Habīb claims that Copts share the concept of the heavenly religions, saying that "if there is a space for non-religious ideas then our people, our sons, or Christians will be in excess." He says that such a person would not be a Jew, Christian, or Muslim, but he would "be something else and this something else has no space in Egypt." You cannot deal, he says, with someone who does not belong to a religion because the social system won't support that: "If you are outside these rules you are outside the social system, so how can we deal with you?"[62]

Of course, Habīb is reflecting a particularly Islamist perspective—and he is one of the more conservative Wasatiyya—and his intent is to show that because there are strong cultural similarities between Copts and Muslims, Islamic law is therefore appropriate for Copts. The response of Copts to the issue of Bahā'īs tends to be less theologically based and more politically oriented than Habīb makes out. For example, Bishop Thomas says that according to his own personal opinion, the government should give the Bahā'īs their civil rights, since the status of the Bahā'īs is linked to that of a Christian who has converted to Islam and wishes to convert back, and therefore will be considered an apostate.[63] Nevertheless, the church as a whole does not prioritize human rights and the issue of the Bahā'īs.[64] There are political reasons for this: the church could never call for the official recognition of Bahā'īs, since that would involve coming out against the majority of Muslims, against state bodies, and against court rulings.[65] The church's response to the question of the Bahā'īs is derived from the fact that it feels the need to defend the Coptic community. The integrity of the community, rather than the freedom of individuals, is prioritized. Just as Muslims wish to protect their community from Bahā'īs, Christians wish to protect their community from other forms of Protestantism, such as Mormons and Jehovah's Witnesses.[66] Greater freedom for Bahā'īs would open up the possibility of greater freedom being given to Protestant groups that threaten the Coptic Orthodox Church.

One can see this in the attitude the church takes toward national identity cards. Secular Copts and Muslims support the removal of religious affiliation on identity cards, viewing it as the key to establishing a human rights–based culture, increasing Egyptians' sense of national affiliation, and putting an end to religious discrimination.[67] The church, on the other hand, wishes to keep religious affiliation on identity cards since it fears that removing that designation could result in illegal marriages between Muslims and Christians.

The church's position on freedom of speech is also instructive,[68] as illustrated by two recent events. One incident concerned the screening of the film *The Da Vinci Code*, where the church successfully lobbied the parliament and the media to ban the film. The other incident concerned *Bahib al-Sīmā (I Love Cinema)*, a film aired in 2004 that was written and directed by Christians. The plot traces the daily life of a Coptic family in 1960's Cairo. The father of the family is a teacher who takes an extreme approach to his religion, considering procreation the sole purpose of sex. His wife struggles with her frustrated sexual life. The whole story is told from the view of their son, a six-year-old boy who adores the cinema despite the fact that his father considers it a sin.

Even before the film was aired there were rumors that the church might be consulted on the film. Such an idea was rejected by the censorship authority. After its release, many Coptic laymen and clergymen opposed the film and demanded that the church be consulted on any works that relate to religion. A lawsuit was filed against the film on the grounds that it was demeaning to the Orthodox Christian faith and demeaning to the church because of certain sexual scenes that take place inside the church.[69] Leaflets asking Christians to boycott the film were distributed in some areas. Rafīq Habīb argues that this incident illustrates that Copts are behaving not as individuals but as an institution.[70] Vivian Fu'ād, director of the Coptic Centre for Social Studies, based at the Centre of St. Mark for Social Services in Cairo, argues that incidents like this allude to the cultural similarities between Copts and Muslims.[71] More recently, an advisor to the Coptic Church filed a lawsuit to prevent the publication in 2008 of a novel by Yūsuf Zaydān called *'Azāzīl* that is accused of offending Christianity and has won the Arabic Booker Prize.

The above attitudes toward marriage, divorce, inheritance, and freedom of religion and speech indicate that while Copts oppose Egypt as an Islamic state they also see citizenship in terms that make it possible to preserve the centrality of the church. They are interested in maintaining the integrity of the Coptic community, and because the Christian family is the core of the Coptic community, the best way to do so is through the personal status law.

The emphasis on personal status law reinforces the church's emergence as a political and social representative of the Copts. For secularists, this in itself constitutes a significant impediment to the concept of citizenship. Many members of the Coptic community are critical of the church's taking on such a role. Yūsuf Sidhum states that allowing the church to represent Copts is "political suicide" and that citizenship is not possible as long as Copts leave society, retreat to the church, and ask the church to represent them in front of the state.[72] He argues:

> We as Christians carry for His Holiness [Pope Shenouda] the feelings of love and respect. However, we are first, Egyptians. We are the citizens of the state like all Egyptians. We are no separate ethnic group. We are not an immigrant society in this country. We will never become like Red Indians who are looked at as a part of a past history and extinct culture. . . . No, a thousand no's. We are Egyptians. We have inherited the Egyptian culture like all Egyptians we live on the Egyptian land. Egyptian blood runs in our veins. We carry in our feelings Egyptian cultures that have formed along the years . . . if we suffer some forms of discrimination, our way to conquer that is to put our problems on the Egyptian social problems table. We would call for the love that gathers us all to confront these problems on the national level and not by giving it a sectarian form.[73]

Sidhum says that Christians should be encouraged to intermix with Muslims and that while it was appropriate for the church to deal with the social needs of the Copts at a certain period of time, it has deprived Copts of a chance to intermix healthily with their Muslim counterparts. He argues that the church should encourage Christians to return to society.[74] This is a choice that the Copts cannot afford not to make, he says, arguing, "How can we preserve our identity and culture by putting ourselves in a confrontation with 90 percent [of the population]. As one of our Muslim friends said if you play it this way you will be crushed."[75]

In the church's defense, this political role is not something that all members of the church have necessarily chosen to take upon themselves. The church has taken this stance because of the inequality that Copts encounter. There is a feeling that if the church stays silent no one will demand their rights. Bishop Thomas argues that the church prioritizes not politics but justice and that "if something is not fair for our people we have to stand up for them." There is no secular Coptic organization, he states, that can fulfill this role. In terms of the approach to personal status law, while Bishop Thomas argues that in theory he is not opposed to a civil personal status law, he takes the position that the current approach to personal status law has been influenced by the contemporary social and political situation.[76] The Coptic community is shrinking because of conversion to Islam and Christian emigration. Thus it is natural for the church to fear the withering away of the community.

CONTRADICTION?

It has been argued that there is a contradiction between Coptic opposition to an Islamic state and the approach of the church to personal status law, human rights, freedom of speech, and political representation.[77] It is central to Rafīq Habīb's Islamist agenda that there is a contradiction and that Copts are mistaken in thinking they want a secular state. Islamic law, he argues, with its multiple law system, is more appropriate for Copts. The basic unit in Egyptian society is the family and not the individual, and having a civil law for marriage and divorce would be a "dangerous thing," since to establish the concept of the civil family would be to destroy the family. The unit of the religious family rules the social system, and Habīb argues that Copts—like Muslims—are vested in this system, because in Egypt religion has two meanings: one is belief in God and the other is social.[78]

To overcome this supposed contradiction, some make a distinction between a civil state that is neutral but respects religion on the one hand and secularism on the other.[79] Bishop Murqus also argues for a "neutral" state that retains Egypt's structure of religious communities.[80] However, Rafīq Habīb argues that you cannot have a neutral state, since there is in fact no neutrality in the political field. It is a mistake to think that society can be based on two religious communities while the state is neutral. It will, he says, not be neutral; rather it will be secular and it will rearrange the legal system and constitution according to secular ethics.[81] Habīb again uses this to bolster his argument that the multiple-law system of an Islamic order would be more beneficial to Copts than secular law would.[82] Habīb says that Christians and Muslims have the same social values and that *sharīʿa* has guaranteed the followers of other religions the right to have their own faith and has given Copts the right to have their own marriage laws. But secularism, according to Habīb, presupposes that all religious faiths have the same law.[83]

Secular Copts also question whether the majority of Copts really want a secular state in terms of freedom of expression and in terms of personal status law, pointing out that the majority of Copts reject secular ethics.[84] Samīr

Murqus argues that there is in fact a contradiction between the implications of a secular state and the power of the church and religiously based personal status law.[85] However, he rejects Rafīq Habīb's solution, saying that it is the very social conservatism focused on personal status law that is impeding the development of citizenship and that the church's approach is part of the problem.[86] In his view a contradiction exists between the concept of citizenship that is used in current political discourse and the idea of minority rights and religious rights. Murqus argues that people cannot behave as citizens while behaving as a religious community. One of the steps in achieving a secular state is to emphasize a wider sense of belonging, since the "concept of citizenship transcends the notions of sect or religious community, as well as the notion of minority and its ramifications."[87]

Thus the problem that is impeding the development of citizenship in Egypt is that Christians are acting collectively in the public sphere rather than as individual citizens. According to Mīlād Hannā, this practice of collective action is particular to Egyptian culture; in the West, he writes, "human rights mainly safeguard the individual's freedom. In Egypt, precedence is given to collective rights."[88] He argues that in Egypt the sense of belonging to a religious group is one of the most powerful forms of association.[89] As a secularist, Hannā advises moving away from collective emotions connected with religion. He argues that Copts have no affiliation to any other country except Egypt, so "if Copts founded a political party based on religion then that immediately means that Egypt has been divided." Very few would join this party, because they "know that whoever stands in the ranks of this political party would be killed, especially under current conditions."[90]

CITIZENSHIP IN AN ISLAMIC STATE

It has been shown that Rafīq Habīb uses the political discourse and behavior of the Copts concerning personal status law, freedom of speech, the notion of religious authority, and freedom of religion to bolster the claim that Copts are best suited to a kind of Islamic citizenship. Habīb argues that while Copts think there is a conflict between them and the Wasatiyya, in fact the two are very similar.[91] But what do Copts in fact think about the ideas of the Wasatiyya? Are there any grounds for arguing that there is an overlap between Islamist and Coptic conceptions of citizenship?

In 2003 signs suggested that many secular or intellectual Copts had some respect for the ideas of the Wasatiyya. They were not entirely dismissive of this kind of thinking.[92] Samīr Murqus acknowledges that the dialogue of the mid-1990's established by people like the Wasatiyya intellectual Tāriq al-Bishrī was positive for discussions in Egypt on citizenship.[93]

However, further analysis illustrates that openness to their views does not mean acceptance. While there are areas in which the two positions are similar, broader concerns remain.[94] For example, with regard to the Islamist concept of an Islamic civilization, the fact that Copts and Muslims share similar cultural characteristics does not necessarily vindicate the concept of an Islamic civilization. It is of course accepted that Copts and Muslims are culturally similar and that Arab culture has influenced the culture of Copts.[95] During a project that involved teaching priests and shaykhs about reproductive health and women's rights, Vivian Fu'ād, director of the Coptic Centre for Social Studies, discovered that both priests and shaykhs had a patriarchal attitude toward women's rights and they used their respective religious texts to support their point of view. She argues that religious leaders become a reflection of what people need, and that this, as opposed to religious discourse, is what influences the formation of culture.[96]

However, accepting that Christians and Muslims have similar cultural practices does not mitigate the fact that the Islamic civilization project appears to exclude Christians. While those who expound this project argue that it includes the contributions that non-Muslims have made to this civilization, nevertheless the danger is that it would favor the contributions of Islam and of Muslims.[97] Samīr Murqus argues that there is an implicit problem in the concept of the Arab-Islamic civilization, because while it accepts the non-Muslim contributions, it necessarily prioritizes Islam. He argues that you have to accept that civilization is complex and that it is not derived just from Islam. There is not simply an Islamic identity, but a cultural identity. He calls on the Wasatiyya not to base their approach on numbers but to give Copts, despite their small numbers, the opportunity to be part of the "cultural complex" with Muslims.[98] This does not deny the Islamic influence, he argues, but it is a kind of citizenship based on the Egyptian national community that is in turn based upon Muslims and Christians living together. This national community was, he argues, a strategic choice despite the difficulties that Egyptians have encountered.[99]

The idea of a culturally defined citizenship that respects religion but is distinct from an Islamic state also coincides with the ideas of Mīlād Hannā, who argues that Egypt possesses the quality of acceptance of the other.[100] In his book *The Seven Pillars of Egyptian Identity*, he emphasizes that Egypt is made up of different notions of belonging, which are complementary and harmonious; Egypt has a Sunni face, Shi'ite blood, a Coptic heart, and Pharaonic bones. While he recognizes that currently Egyptians give precedence to their sense of belonging to religion, whether to Islam or to Christianity, there are other feelings of belonging which should make the Egyptian proud. This, he argues, helps to balance the emphasis on religion. The Copts, he writes, "as an integral part of Egypt—have all the characteristics of the Egyptians."[101]

The response of Wasatiyya intellectual Fahmī Huwaydī to Mīlād Hannā's conception of a particularly Egyptian identity is indicative of the gulf that exists between Copts and Wasatiyya Islam. Huwaydī does not take Hannā's ideas seriously, saying, "If I want to behave as a Pharaonic [person] what can I do?"[102] Some more conservative members of the Wasatiyya, like Muhammad 'Imāra, seem unwilling to acknowledge that the Copts have anything to be concerned about regarding the application of Islamic law. 'Imāra argues that in 1982, 98 percent of Muslims and 70 percent of Christians agreed with the application of *sharī'a*.[103] At the time, Pope Shenouda argued:

> Copts under Islamic *sharī'a* will be happier and more secure: they were so in the past when *sharī'a* prevailed. We are happy for Muslims to exist under the maxim of "they have the same rights and duties as we have." Egypt imported law from outside and applied it on us and as a result we do not have the same separate laws that we had under Islam. So how could we be satisfied with imported laws and not be satisfied with the laws of Islam?[104]

According to Yūsuf Sidhum of *al-Watanī*, when Pope Shenouda was asked what he thought about the application of *sharī'a*, the pope, in turn, asked how non-Muslims would be treated. His questions included how Copts would be regarded in Islamic law, how their faith would be regarded, and what the positions of Islamic law would be on women's rights, banking, Coptic witnessing, and freedom of shifting from one faith to another. Answers to these questions have not been received.[105]

Secularists dispute that the concept of citizenship can be applied in an Islamic state. The concern is that an Islamic state will emphasize that the Copts are a minority, which, Samīr Murqus argues, contradicts the concept of citizenship, which "means surpassing the ideas of sect, denomination or *dh[imma]*, where the nation absorbs all this." Citizenship, he argues, also surpasses the idea of minorities.[106] He argues that though Egyptians are using the terminology of citizenship, they are in fact talking about minority rights and religious rights.[107] Dialogue on the basis of citizenship cannot include reference to the Copts as a minority. Therefore those "who try to defend the rights of Copts on the basis of minority rights, ethical and religious [sic] and who see Copts as one homogenous block" are going against the concept of citizenship.[108] Since the political system is permeated by references to religion, Murqus argues, there is a danger that the political process will degenerate into a situation in which one is either for or against Islam. For example, if politicians try to tackle the problem of poverty and an Islamic solution is provided and it is opposed, this means that anyone who opposes it is in danger of being labeled as anti-Islam.[109] Other secularists agree.[110] Nabīl ʿAbd al-Fattāh, writer for the al-Ahram Center for Political and Strategic Studies, argues that the problem lies in the disputes over terminology and that such debates stand in the way of developing an agenda to tackle Egypt's problems.[111] He also mentions that Arabic dictionaries omit the word muwatāna. This is of great significance, he says, since it leads to confusing the concept of citizenship with other concepts like nationality or national loyalty, illustrating the ambiguity of such a concept.[112]

MORE REVOLUTIONARY THAN THE REVOLUTION

One of the other major reservations that the Copts have concerning the Wasatiyya intellectuals in general, and the Muslim Brotherhood and al-Wasat in particular, is that they lack a clear agenda. It is suspected that these groups do have a hidden agenda that is based on applying the dhimma. Lack of commitment to a clear articulation of citizenship is seen as a political strategy that gives these groups flexibility.

With regard to the Muslim Brotherhood and its commitment to citizenship, Samīr Murqus rejects the Muslim Brotherhood's stance on citizenship rights as "ambiguous" and asked former Deputy Supreme Guide Muhammad Habīb to define the concept of citizenship in a written document.[113] He argues that the Muslim Brotherhood still has not faced reality and outlined what its position is on fundamental questions, including the rights of non-Muslims and the relationship between the religious and civil spheres. Despite the fact that the Brotherhood declared that it would announce a detailed position regarding the Copts and citizenship rights, this has not happened.[114] The opaque nature of statements such as the claim that the Muslim Brotherhood is a "civil party with an Islamic framework" is another cause of concern.[115]

The Muslim Brotherhood is accused of engaging in *taqiyya*, which is a Shi'a concept of not revealing one's "true" political intentions for reasons of self-preservation.[116] Mīlād Hannā argues that this vagueness is a political strategy and that "they are very clever not to push the events." The Muslim Brotherhood, he argues, does not want to scare the Copts and push them into a corner whereby their only option would be to convert to Islam or leave the country. Thus, Hannā argues, Egyptians would rather leave things flexible as they are now and accept the idea that the Copts and the Muslim Brotherhood are "deceiving each other."[117]

Many Copts fear the ramifications of the full application of *sharī'a*. They oppose the penal system, and they think that under *sharī'a* they will be considered *dhimmīs* and be forced to pay the *jizya*, that while they will be accepted and tolerated, they will not be treated equally and will be politically marginalized.[118] There is also concern that Egyptian national identity will be undermined, which will have dangerous implications for Copts.[119] Others fear being thrown out of the country.[120]

Copts are not the only ones who have serious misgivings about the Islamists: women (e.g., Nawāl al-Sa'adāwī and Naglā' al-Imām), secularists, civil society supporters, leftists, and other advocates of democracy share the concern. For example, Fouad Zakariyya, an Egyptian Arab intellectual, is critical of the Islamist movements and argues for the "depoliticization of religion in contemporary Muslim societies in order to avoid political exploitation and to keep religious ethical and normative values alive."[121] Nabīl 'Abd al-Fattāh, of the al-Ahram Center for Political and Strategic Studies, argues that the majority of the Muslim Brotherhood members subscribe to a rigid ideology and that the predominant culture in the organization is undemocratic and based on patterns of obedience.[122]

The above suspicions also apply to the Wasatiyya and to al-Wasat. Yūsuf Sidhum argues that the Wasatiyya move from the left to the right. At one moment they appear moderate and at another fundamentalist.[123] Munīr Fakhrī 'Abd al-Nūr invokes the experience of the French Revolution and argues that the Islamists will be more "revolutionary than the revolution." It is very difficult, he says, once you are within the framework of political Islam, to remain moderate. You can be moderate outside but not within. He wonders if there is such a thing as Wasatiyya Islam.[124] 'Abd al-Nūr is convinced that the solution lies in Egyptian nationalism and not in Christianity or Islam.[125] It is due to this lack of trust that many Copts feel that it is better to live with the current regime than an Islamist one. This even applies to a Wasatiyya Islamist regime, because of the potential for it to become more restrictive of the rights of non-Muslims.[126]

Such suspicions seemed to be vindicated in early 2007 with the publication of Muhammad 'Imāra's new book, in which he allegedly justified the killing of non-Muslims. The very fact that this book was published by the Waqf Ministry, which is a government institution, seemed to indicate state-sponsored animosity toward Copts. Bishop Thomas argues that he expected that al-Azhar would issue a statement that what 'Imāra wrote was against "Islam."[127] Expecting that response was not realistic, especially since it involved denouncing the writings of a renowned classical scholar. Nevertheless, the incident seemed to confirm the bleak prospects for Copts in an Islamic state. For many Copts it indicated that a regression had occurred among the Wasatiyya intellectuals.

While there is little evidence to support the idea that the Wasatiyya intellectuals have become extremist or fundamentalist, it is true that the positive dialogue and attitudes that existed in 2003 have broken down, especially since 2004. A difference in tone can be found in al-'Awwā's recent work, which manifests an attitude of "them and us."

Two events were primarily responsible for this. First, the debates about the constitutional amendments in 2007 contributed to growing mistrust. Copts who criticized Article 2 were perceived to be attacking Islam.[128] Second, the deterioration of relations dates back to 2004 and the Wafā' Qustantīn incident, during which the Wasatiyya intellectuals criticized the role of the church and the relationship between the state and the church.[129] The church was accused of illegally and unconstitutionally detaining Wafā' Qustantīn.[130] The church's political role in general and Pope Shenouda's political role in particular were criticized. It was argued that the pope had no right to express his political opinions in public or to deliver his political opinion to the Egyptian authorities.[131] Muhammad Salīm al-'Awwā, who has since given up dialogue with the church, called upon it to return to its spiritual mission. Muhammad 'Imāra has argued that the political role that the church has adopted is an "unchristian" aberration. Referring to the maxim "My kingdom is not of this world," he argues that the message of the church is spiritual, and that throughout Egyptian history the Coptic Church did not enter politics.[132] Tāriq al-Bishrī has also attacked a Coptic priest for attempting to separate Coptic history from Muslim history and for claiming that Copts do not enjoy equality with Muslims.[133] He also complains that Pope Shenouda seems to be beyond criticism, though even the president and his family, the ministers, and the shaykh of al-Azhar are regularly criticized.[134]

This view is shared by Rafīq Habīb, who takes Pope Shenouda to task for encouraging the Christian community to view the church as the focal point for its revival.[135] Habīb argues that the Qustantīn incident was detrimental for the balance between the state and the church. He writes: "If Wafā's Islam was genuine, then the state's dignity, in the eyes of its subjects, was flushed down the toilet, and if it was not, then the state acknowledged the church's power over the Copts of Egypt and lent legitimacy to the church to represent the Copts."[136] While he criticizes the increasing political role of the church, he acknowledges that the church must have an important social role. However, he says, "When the church becomes the political party of all Christians, then we will go into [a] denominational political style like Lebanon."[137]

The Wasatiyya intellectuals, like the secularists, see the political role of the church as an impediment to citizenship. They call upon Christians to be fully involved in the institutions of the state, in political parties, and in parliament. When a Muslim has a problem he goes to the parliament or the state, Muhammad ʿImāra argues. He does not go to the mosque or to al-Azhar. Thus, he continues, the entry of Christians into the church is not in their interest.[138] In the view of Fahmī Huwaydī, it is due to the weakness of government that Egyptians have started thinking like Muslims and Copts rather than like Egyptians. He argues that Copts have to think like native Egyptians, not like religious people.[139]

While secularists and Islamists are united in their disapproval about the political behavior of the church, their solutions are very different. The secularist position argues that the neutrality of the state will provide a neutral space enabling Copts to become more active in the political sphere. The Islamist position argues that an Islamic state does not preclude the full involvement of Copts within that state. Yet this argument lies at the crux of the obstacles facing Islamic conceptions of citizenship. There is a tension between Islamist opposition to Coptic political behavior and the very Islamist agenda that seeks to create an Islamic state. While there are a number of factors that have contributed to the retreat of Copts from the political sphere, the process of Islamization is one of them. Islamists expect to invoke religion in the political sphere, yet they criticize Copts for acting politically as Christians, when it is the very invocation of Islam in the political sphere that has contributed to the retreat of Copts. Samīr Marqus argues that invoking religion in the public sphere will only lead to a counterreligious invocation.[140] In his view the fact that competition in the political sphere has turned into a competition between the Islamic and the non-Islamic, between Muslims and non-Muslims rather than between differing trends, currents, and ideas, is an impediment to citizenship.[141] The fact that these Islamists fail to see the Islamic nature of the state and the government as a hindrance to Christian involvement poses fundamental challenges for Islamist conceptions of citizenship.

CITIZENSHIP AS A PROCESS

The disconnection between Islamist criticism of the political retreat of the Copts and calls for an Islamic state illustrate the challenge Islamists face in articulating the concept of citizenship in an Islamic state. While Islamist conceptions of citizenship and notions of community and solidarity might be theoretically possible, it is difficult to see, within the current context, a situation in which Copts find the Islamized political space one which they would wish to enter. While there are indications that some secular Copts have been responsive to the Wasatiyya ideas, this is no longer the case, since relations between the Wasatiyya and many Copts have deteriorated since the Wafā' Qustantīn event in 2004. From this perspective, it is difficult to see how a Wasatiyya Islamic state, which is based on the state favoring one religion, would achieve the kind of citizenship that it claims it advocates. It could be argued that the idea of an Islamic cultural revival in which non-Muslims could take part is idealistic. Since this cultural revival would primarily be Islamic, the further marginalization of the Copts is a real danger.

It is on these grounds that secular and religiously conservative Copts associated with the church reject the Wasatiyya position and argue for some kind of neutral or secular state. At the same time, many of their positions indicate that they are not necessarily advocating a neutral or secular state, partly because the prospects for one evolving are unlikely. Many religiously conservative Copts do call not for abolishing Article 2, but for amending it. Many secular Copts do argue not for a complete secularization of the law and the state but instead for a contextualized approach to citizenship. While they reject the position that Egypt should be defined as an Islamic state in which Islamic law is the sole source of legislation, they accept the idea that religion should still have an important role. While Murqus rejects the viewpoint of Rafīq Habīb and the concept of an Islamic citizenship, he argues that establishing citizenship is a process and involves a struggle.[142] This process, he says, began under Muhammad ʿAlī, and while citizenship was enhanced and undermined during different historical periods, the evolution continues today.[143] Murqus also argues that citizenship is not an ideal value that is fixed: rather it expresses the situation of citizens in a particular context.[144] He calls for the concept of cultural citizenship. He accepts that there should be a space for religion in everyday life, but argues that religion should not enter the political sphere.[145] Cultural citizenship would not exclude Christian culture, since Egypt is a "cultural complex" containing various cultures and it is "a fatal mistake to deal with the Egyptian cultural complex as a simple culture."[146]

While Murqus remains skeptical about the Wasatiyya and the Islamist agenda, he implies that Article 2 is not the major issue and that he approaches Article 2 from a cultural perspective. For him it is the political apathy of Egyptians in general, in particular that of the Copts, that constitutes an impediment to citizenship.[147] Such a situation has been created in part by an overemphasis on religious identity in the political sphere. For citizenship to be achieved, Murqus argues, the identities of tribe and kin must give way to national community.[148]

Mīlād Hannā agrees with Murqus; he does not view Article 2 as the major problem. For him, the answer to Egypt's dilemma concerning citizenship does not lie in defining Egypt as either a secular or an Islamic state. It is better to live with the ambiguity that currently exists, he says. He accepts *sharīʿa* for personal status law, arguing that it is part of the overall culture and that the submission of Christians to Islamic law in some areas constitutes "an unwritten pact."[149] However, Hannā sees a big difference between accepting Egypt as a religious state, on the one hand, and on the other, accepting that religion constitutes one of the guidelines for the law. While the constitution states that *sharīʿa* is one of the principal sources of legislation, Hannā considers this to be broad and flexible, since it is not written that *sharīʿa* is the only source. Rather, he argues, it is applied with great flexibility and there is no clear line between being secular and being religious in Egyptian society.[150] Therefore this ambiguity suits the condition of Egypt. He says, "We don't want to push the events. This is a cultural mechanism or an unwritten formula that we live with."[151]

However, in Yūsuf Sidhum's view it is this very flexibility that is problematic, since such ambiguity could open the way for the imposition of a more conservative interpretation of *sharīʿa*. It could result in the imposition of the *dhimma* status upon non-Muslims and would therefore have important implications for the rights of Copts and other non-Muslims.[152] However, Sidhum concedes that one must accept that religion still has to play an important role in the life of Egyptians, although he argues that the Egyptian state should not be of a certain religious identity. He sees this as a first step, since the prospect of Egypt's becoming a completely secular state in the near future is extremely unlikely. This means that for the time being, religious identity would still influence civil relations and civil law. However, the first step is to separate religion from state and religion from politics.[153]

These secular Copts therefore call for a more contextualized approach to citizenship. While they reject the idea of an Islamic state, they do not reject an important position for religion. Accepting some place for religion would involve finding religious solutions to the challenges facing contemporary Egypt. Munīr Fakhrī 'Abd al-Nūr acknowledges that the time is not right for the imposition of secular values. For example, rather than advocating the imposition of secular human rights values, he says that what is needed to address the problem of rights for Bahā'īs is a theological development that would accept, Islamically speaking, religions other than Judaism, Christianity, and Islam.[154]

The fact that even secular Copts recognize that in contemporary Egypt, citizenship cannot exclude religious thinking or religious identity indicates that citizenship has to develop from a process that is contextually responsive and reflective of the current reality. Thus, while the Wasatiyya Islamist conception of citizenship has not gone far enough for Copts, there is a consensus that the issues have to be worked out contextually, taking into account the religious makeup of Egypt, of which personal status law forms an important part.

CONCLUSION

In the current political climate, Article 2 is unlikely to be revised in favor of a secular approach to legislation. The majority of Egyptian Muslims think that Article 2 is an important expression of their religious beliefs. In this case, from the perspective of the rights of non-Muslims, the best-case scenario would lie in struggling to form legislation that would reconcile Article 2 with a more liberal approach to the rights of non-Muslims and the principle of citizenship. While some would argue that there is a contradiction between Islamic law and citizenship, an analysis of different Islamist positions indicates that this is not necessarily the case. It depends on what interpretation of Islamic law is taken and what understanding of citizenship is implied. There are grounds for arguing that the concept of citizenship within an Islamic state could be realized even though at this juncture some problematic issues remain. Change of this sort would mean viewing citizenship as a struggle that would involve demonstrating that there is no contradiction between Article 2 and citizenship. The Wasatiyya intellectuals are engaged in such an effort, and it is possible that in the current political climate, the Wasatiyya conception of citizenship in an Islamic state may be the most salutary option from the perspective of non-Muslims.

Grounds also exist for arguing that a contextual approach to citizenship would be more responsive to the Coptic position. On some issues many Copts' conceptions of religious community, personal status law, and freedom of speech converge with the liberal Islamist position. This point is central to Rafiq Habīb's argument that the interests of Copts lie in the *sharīʿa*, which allows for a kind of multiple law system in which religious communities are free to follow their own religious law. However, by and large, Habīb's ideas are rejected by Copts, as is the idea that there is any convergence between this position and that of the Wasatiyya. Many Copts and secular Muslims have significant reservations about the Islamist agenda and about the implications of an unmodified Article 2. They fear that Islamists will revert to more traditional understandings of *sharīʿa* once they are in power.

Notwithstanding the climate of fear that surrounds the idea of an Islamic state, certain problems and issues remain with Islamic conceptions of citizenship. It is true that the idea of convergence between the Wasatiyya and the Copts can go only so far. However, it is arguable that the idea of convergence is what offers the most positive prospects for the development of a concept of citizenship that synthesizes nationalist elements with Islam, precisely because any formation of Egyptian citizenship cannot exclude either Islamic thinking or the Egyptian political experience. Thus the concept of citizenship in Egypt must be engaged contextually. Such an approach to citizenship involves asking what an appropriate conception of citizenship within the current context would be. Citizenship in this context would involve struggling to define what citizenship rights are in an Islamic state. The ideas of the Wasatiyya open up the possibility of greater convergence between Copts and Muslims, including the possibility that previously taboo issues, such as the rights of Bahāʾīs, could be addressed. It is within the realm of possibility that the evolution of a contextualized citizenship that takes into account the Egyptian religious and cultural context could be achieved.

CONCLUSION

TO CONCLUDE, I turn to the title of this book, *The Challenge of Political Islam: Non-Muslims and the Egyptian State*. One could, of course, problematize the whole concept of "challenge" because it implies that political Islam necessarily faces a problem that must be solved regarding its position on religious tolerance and the rights of non-Muslims. Regardless of the veracity of such an assumption, many Islamic thinkers and activists endeavor to define their perception of the position of "Islam" on the rights and role of non-Muslims precisely because of these assumptions.

This book has described how Islamist thinkers have responded to this challenge and have articulated the concepts of tolerance, pluralism, and citizenship. While political Islam calls for the unity of religion and state and for an Islamic state based on *sharī'a*, Islamist individuals and organizations represent a wide range of positions on what kind of political system this approach would create and what it would mean for the rights and role of non-Muslims. The fact that many Islamists have taken a conciliatory approach to issues such as the nation-state, democracy, human rights, and citizenship points to the diversity within contemporary Islamist ideology. This diversity counteracts the assumption—often reinforced by Islamic discourse itself—that Islamism is a rigid ideology that seeks to apply a fixed and transhistorical body of law.

This is not to say that there are no grounds for such an assumption. For many Islamists, including more-conservative members of the Muslim Brotherhood, the *dhimma* contract is presented as an integral part of a proposed Islamic order. Calls for the revival of the *dhimma* are accompanied by discourse about protection and Muslims giving non-Muslims their rights. It is assumed that Christians form one bloc and that they are entitled to political involvement as a bloc but only in relation to issues that affect them. Accompanying this assumption is another: that non-Muslims are protected guests of the Muslim majority. At the same time, the *dhimma* status is—somewhat opportunistically—conflated with citizenship without any real intellectual attempt to examine the implications and the differences. Such views illustrate that Islamists like the conservative members of the Muslim Brotherhood face considerable challenges in reconciling the historical model that they are invoking with the modern centralized state.

The emphasis upon the application of the *dhimma* is not shared by all Islamists. Some radical groups disregard the *dhimma*. They deny the Islamic historical experience by turning non-Muslims into the enemy, thereby undermining the idea that non-Muslims should be protected by the Islamic state. Such Islamists gain legitimacy for this position from ambiguous texts and some historical precedents. They are largely going against the Islamic historical experience, which is one that was defined by Christians and Muslims living together. This experience forms an integral part of Egyptian historical memory and is one of the greatest threats to the legitimacy of such a position.

It is this historical experience that is integral to the Wasatiyya conception of citizenship, which implies a sense of inclusion in the wider Egyptian community and recognizes the contribution of non-Muslim individuals to the community. The concept of an Islamic civilization to which Muslims and non-Muslims have contributed and in which they share cultural values implies that theological differences can be kept separate from notions of cultural identity. The concept of an Islamic civilization as distinct from the Islamic religion provides some foundation for inclusiveness. The Wasatiyya claim that they are committed to the political participation of non-Muslims. The fact that Islamists argue that citizenship is a right of all Egyptians and that this citizenship was earned by Muslims and Christians who established the modern Egyptian state is very different from the idea that protection is given by Muslims to non-Muslims. The concept of public order and the distinction between the civil and religious spheres are utilized to provide a conceptual structure for this system. It maintains the distinction between the social and political sphere and the religious or, more specifically, familial sphere and preserves the importance of the religious community. The distinction between the civil and religious spheres within the Islamic framework provides a mechanism for reconciling religious differences with the concept of civil equality. The concept of public order helps to conceptualize and justify social and religious conservatism in a democratic framework. At the same time, it lays the foundations for a certain dynamism or flexibility in the political sphere. The concept of public order is contingent and changeable, and therefore it can be a force for conservatism or for change.

Such articulations of a religiously based citizenship cast doubt on the assumption that Islamism simply calls for the application of the normative *sharīʿa* position that evolved within classical Islamic jurisprudence. Like any tradition, Islamic thinking is evolving and changing, as illustrated by the articulation of political concepts and ideas in the Egyptian context. When Islamists invoke traditions in claiming to return to an earlier practice, they in fact reinvent those traditions. In addition, Islamists are not responding to this tradition monolithically: they differ over how the foundational texts should be interpreted and over the role that Islamic heritage should play in the contemporary context. Therefore, modern Islamic thought on non-Muslims cannot be understood by the continuity of such historical institutions as the *dhimma*. This realization also casts doubt on the assumption that the way certain concepts were understood at particular historical junctures somehow determines how they are, can be, and will be understood. It would be a mistake to explain the meaning of words in today's discourse by reference to their classical roots or the lack thereof. Historically, classical Islamic political theory—and Islamic societies in practice—had notions of community, belonging, and solidarity.

The fact that the varying Islamist attitudes toward Copts do not correspond to a singular, determining interpretation of Islamic law raises a number of questions, including whether Islamist thinking can form the foundation for coexistence between Copts and Muslims that is not based on the indifference of the state toward religion. Another question raised is whether the Wasatiyya conceptions of belonging and citizenship provoke rethinking the notion of triumphant secularism.

Secularists argue that citizenship cannot be achieved in the Islamic framework and that citizenship for all Egyptians is contingent upon a secular context. They point to the fact that the constitution of 1923, which made no formal commitment to *sharīʿa*, opened up a golden age for the political involvement of the Copts. This position is argued not only by many Copts but also by Muslim secularists themselves, who are strongly skeptical about the Islamist agenda. Of course, accommodating religious difference is also a challenge for secular states. The occurrence of religious intolerance and violence in the context of the Islamic revival does not necessarily mean that violence is particular to that context or an inevitable development from it.

The recent discourse on citizenship should make us question the assumption that Islamism can only lead to discrimination. The Wasatiyya approach offers the beginnings of an articulation of religious coexistence that is not contingent upon secularism. Tāriq al-Bishrī argues that one should pull the carpet out from under the secular point of view: the Wasatiyya employment of *ijtihād* to formulate a new Islamic jurisprudence indicates that this is happening. The relationship between Muslims and non-Muslims that the Wasatiyya envisage is very different from the *dhimma* which is distinguished from "true" Islamic values and the early model established by the Prophet. The strength of the Wasatiyya approach is that it draws on Islamic principles, precedents, and texts at the same time as it accepts the status quo and embraces the idea of Egyptian identity. It also, in theory, seeks to improve on that status quo and increase the political involvement of non-Muslims. It takes account of contemporary realities and pressures, yet frames them in a way that establishes continuity with Islamic values.

Many would argue that one of the pressures upon the Islamist movement is the need to establish its own authenticity, an undertaking that will force it to adhere to an interpretation of Islamic law that is more rooted in the historical, normative *sharī'a* position. In addition, they point out that large parts of the Muslim Brotherhood, for example, are conservative and have non-democratic patterns of obedience and that the al-Wasat Party has failed to gain significant support. While these observations are true, other possibilities of interpretation exist. The ideas of the Wasatiyya have had a significant impact upon the thought of the more pragmatic members of the Muslim Brotherhood and have forced them to moderate their platform. It is also arguable that in the current context, the most salutary prospect for non-Muslims lies in the Wasatiyya model. In a context in which the Islamist agenda has become the status quo and Article 2 remains largely supported, many would suggest that an entirely secular agenda has no future.

In addition, grounds exist for arguing that Copts have an interest in seeking a definition of citizenship that also emphasizes religious community. An analysis of the Coptic debates on citizenship suggests that the majority of Copts have similar understandings of the relationship between citizenship and religious identity and that this is a type of citizenship that respects religious difference and is not indifferent to it. Thus, though Copts reject the Islamist agenda, there is in fact some convergence between the Wasatiyya vision of citizenship and Coptic conceptions of religious community, individual autonomy, and personal status law.

The idea of convergence can only go so far, however. The Islamist views on citizenship encounter a number of obstacles. Citizenship is potentially impeded by the tension between the rights of people as citizens and their rights as members of recognized religious communities. Despite the emphasis upon civil rights for all, there are questions about how this citizenship applies to non-Muslims who are not Jews or Christians, particularly Bahā'īs. While the Wasatiyya emphasize citizenship, they still emphasize minority rights as opposed to the rights of the individual citizen. In addition, the state would always favor one religion over another. Ultimately, if the political system is based on Islamic law, the political process becomes religious, and this development can lead to counterreligious movements.

The emphasis on minority rights in a state that is religiously defined fosters a danger that religious communities also become political communities and that political activity becomes focused on a religious leader. One of the factors impeding the exercise of citizenship in the current context is the political behavior of the Coptic Orthodox Church. The role of the church is important in maintaining the unit of the religious family, which is seen as integral to the social structure of Egypt. However, both secularists and Islamists consider the church's position as the political representative of the Copts to be antithetical to citizenship, since it impedes the Coptic citizen's direct relationship with the state and that citizen's involvement in state institutions.

Secularists argue that any reversal of this trend and any future for citizenship in Egypt can be realized only in the context of a religiously neutral state that would open up the public sphere to all Egyptian citizens regardless of their religion. However, the Wasatiyya Islamists insist that the Islamic state does not preclude the involvement of non-Muslims and that it is a mistake to think that the state can be neutral. They also argue that it is possible to maintain the Egyptian social structure based on religion in such a way that the Copts would not necessarily come to rely on the church to represent them politically. Islamists argue for the importance of the church in maintaining the unit of the family, but they resist the church's acting as the political representative of the Copts.

Such tensions illustrate the challenge, both theoretically and practically, facing the concept of citizenship in the framework of the contemporary Egyptian Islamic state. From this perspective, the concept of citizenship as a struggle and as a process is relevant. In this sense it is not a matter of accepting or rejecting the Islamist debates on citizenship. Accepting the idea that citizenship is a process means that the current contributions of the Wasatiyya toward the conception of citizenship is part of this process. The Wasatiyya position is not a static one. While the Wasatiyya have laid important conceptual foundations for citizenship, the specifics of how this citizenship is applied can be subject to struggle in the political arena. Fahmī Huwaydī, for example, suggests that it is possible to rethink the personal status law by saying that it is a historical rather than a religious phenomenon. In the same way, he says, it is possible to conceive of allowing Bahā'īs to have their own temples. So while the ideas of the Wasatiyya might not have resolved certain issues, it is possible that those issues can be addressed within an Islamic framework such that their ideas open up the possibility for greater convergence between Islamists and Copts.

Even secular Copts recognize that citizenship is a process and that in the Egyptian context citizenship cannot exclude religious thinking. Secularists imply that the problem with citizenship in Egypt is not necessarily Article 2. For them, it is the political apathy of the Egyptians in general and the Copts in particular that constitutes an impediment to citizenship. While the Islamization of Egyptian society has contributed to the apathy of the Copts, the disinterest among Egyptians in general has resulted from Egypt's undemocratic political system since the 1952 Revolution.

Any form in which citizenship is understood and articulated within an Islamic framework depends on the kind of road the Islamist movement will take in the next two decades. One possibility is that the movement will continue to grapple with the political reality on the ground and shift away from utopian slogans to adopt more pragmatic approaches. Despite the current ascendance of the conservatives within the Muslim Brotherhood, some interesting dynamics are discernible within the organization. Islamist parties may become increasingly "secular," while at the same time, the legitimacy of Islamic law, in terms of reference to both law and values, has and may continue to be the status quo, so that liberal secular parties become increasingly Islamic in their outlook. It is likely that such a convergence trend will continue, thereby rendering radical distinctions between the Islamist and the secular approaches increasingly problematic. It will not necessarily be a matter of whether or not to apply Islam; rather the question will be what kind of Islam, considering different conceptions about what constitutes religious authority, about the role of al-Azhar in the state, and about the relationship between the religious and the temporal spheres.

There are also other forces that could lead to the increasing polarization between the secular and Islamist perspectives, with the latter retreating to the historical normative *shari'a* position as the ideal (a position that was often ignored in practice). There is considerable pressure not to be seen as too Westernized and to be authentically "Islamic." In the context of global events and tensions, there might possibly be a shift toward a more conservative form of Islam. Ideas gain resonance in certain contexts, and political events help give life to certain ideas. One cannot prevent this from happening nor can the possibility of its having a detrimental effect on Muslim-Christian relations in Egypt be denied. In addition, certain concepts and themes within the Islamic discursive tradition provide opportunity for modern-day political conflicts to be projected onto Muslim-Christian relations in Egypt with exclusivist implications. Though it seems that this approach has little traction, it would nevertheless be wrong to underestimate the possibility that such exclusivist behavior might occur. The danger exists, especially since relations between Copts and Muslims are so linked to global conflicts and tensions. As this book goes to press in January 2010, the recent eruption of Muslim-Christian violence in Upper Egypt points to the continuing fragility of the situation.

The possibilities discussed above indicate that for all the discussion of the issue, the challenge facing citizenship in an Egyptian Islamic state is not simply a conceptual one. On a conceptual level significant progress has been made toward the articulation of an Islamic model of citizenship that is inclusive of non-Muslims. Ultimately, however, the challenge lies in putting the model into effect and in testing these ideas.

NOTES

Introduction

1. Sawsan Hulsman, "Escalations following the Alleged Conversion of a Priest's Wife to Islam," special for *Arab-West Report*, December 15–21, 2004.

2. ʿAmr al-Masriī, "Wafāʾs Conversion to Islam Was Due to Social Marital Problems," press review for *Arab-West Report*, January 5–11, 2005.

3. Michael Munīr, interviewed by the author, Virginia, 2009. The USCA is a Washington-based organization that was established by Michael Munīr in 1996. Munīr grew up in Minia in Upper Egypt and moved to the U.S. when he was twenty to study mechanical engineering.

4. Gihan Shahine, "Jumbled Reactions," *al-Ahram Weekly*, August 18–24, 2005.

5. Sana al-Saʾid, "Pope Shenouda in an Interview with al-Wafd: Wafāʾ Costantine Was Not Forced to Convert Back to Christianity," *al-Wafd (Arab-West Report)*, January 6, 2005; ʿAmr al-Misrī, "Wafaa Costantine 'The Woman Who Set the Coptic Church on Fire,'" press review for *Arab-West Report*, December 8–14, 2004.

6. Muhammad Salīm al-ʿAwwā, "The Church and Politics," *al-Usbūʿ (Arab-West Report)*, February 21, 2005, 4; Muhammad ʿImāra, interviewed by the author, Cairo, 2007.

7. Yvonne Haddad, "Christians in a Muslim State: The Recent Egyptian Debate," in *Christian-Muslim Encounters*, ed. Yvonne Yazbeck Haddad and Wadi Zaidan Haddad, 381–399 (Gainesville: University Press of Florida, 1995); Yvonne Haddad, "Islamist Depictions of Christianity in the Twentieth Century: The Pluralism Debate and the Depiction of the Other," *Islam and Christian-Muslim Relations* 7, no. 1 (1996): 75–93; Amira Shamma Abdin, "Modernist Interpretations of the Status of Non-Muslims in Muslim Society" (master's thesis, School of Oriental and African Studies [SOAS], 1995).

8. Talal Asad, "Q & A AsiaSource Interview with Talal Asad," AsiaSource (2002).

9. Talal Asad, "Reflections on Laïcité and the Public Sphere," *Social Science Research Council Items and Issues* 5, no. 3 (2005): 3.

10. Ahmed Moussalli, *The Islamic Quest for Democracy, Pluralism, and Human Rights* (Gainesville: University Press of Florida, 2001), 2–3.

11. Asef Bayat, *Making Islam Democratic* (Stanford, CA: Stanford University Press, 2007), 4.

12. Talal Asad, "The Idea of an Anthropology of Islam," Occasional Papers (Washington, DC: Center for Contemporary Arab Studies, Georgetown University, 1986), 14.

13. Robert W. Hefner, *Civil Islam: Muslims and Democratization in Indonesia* (Princeton, NJ: Princeton University Press, 2000).

14. Theodore Gabriel, *Christian Citizens in an Islamic State: The Pakistan Experience* (Aldershot: Ashgate, 2007), 72–73.

15. Paul Sedra, "Class Cleavages and Ethnic Conflict: Coptic-Christian Communities in Modern Egyptian Politics," *Islam and Christian-Muslim Relations* 10, no. 2 (1999): 219–235; Febe Armanios, "'The Virtuous Woman': Images of Gender in Modern Coptic Society," *Middle Eastern Studies* 38, no. 1 (2002): 110–130; S. S. Hasan, *Christians Versus Muslims in Modern Egypt* (Oxford: Oxford University Press, 2003).

16. Peter Makari's book looks at the rhetoric of the government, official religion, political parties, and NGOs, and argues that there is cooperation in the context of conflict, and that this rhetoric "encourage[s] and attempt[s] to foster a vibrant spirit of tolerance." Peter E. Makari, *Conflict and Cooperation: Christian-Muslim Relations in Contemporary Egypt* (Syracuse, NY: Syracuse University Press, 2007), xvii.

17. Gilles Kepel, "Islamism Reconsidered: A Running Dialogue with Modernity," *Harvard International Review* 22, no. 2 (2002): 22.

18. For an in-depth discussion of the diversity within and the concept of "contemporary Islamic thought," see Ibrahim M. Abu-Rabi', "Contemporary Islamic Thought: One or Many?" in *The Blackwell Companion to Contemporary Islamic Thought*, ed. Ibrahim M. Abu-Rabi' (Oxford: Blackwell, 2006).

19. It is reported that two surveys conducted by the National Centre for Social and Criminological Research and the Gallup Organization indicate that a majority of Egyptians support the application of *sharīʿa*. ʿAbd al-Munʿim Munīb, "If the People Want It, Why Not Apply Sharīʿah in Egypt," *al-Dustūr (Arab-West Report)*, October 22, 2008.

20. Gilles Kepel, *The Trail of Political Islam* (London: I.B. Tauris, 2002).

21. Kepel, "Islamism Reconsidered," 26. Asef Bayat also uses the term "post-Islamism" to describe a movement where Islamism has become forced to reinvent itself. Bayat, *Making Islam Democratic*, 11.

22. Arskal Salim, *Challenging the Secular State: The Islamization of Law in Modern Indonesia* (Honolulu: University of Hawai'i Press, 2008), 79–80.

23. Clark Lombardi, *State Law as Islamic Law in Modern Egypt: The Incorporation*

of the Sharī'a into Egyptian Constitutional Law, Studies in Islamic Law and Society (Leiden: Brill, 2006), 2.

24. Central Agency for Public Mobilization and Statistics, http://www.capmas .gov.eg/.

25. Robier al-Faris, "The Figure That Brings on a Headache," *Watani International (Arab-West Report)*, May 13, 2007.

26. Mamdūh Ramzī, interviewed by the author, Cairo, 2003.

27. Hamdī Rizq, "15 Million Copts," *al-Misrī al-Yawm (Arab-West Report)*, July 7, 2007; Cornelis Hulsman, "Interview with Dr. Philippe Fargues about Coptic Statistics," *Arab-West Report*, December 20, 2008; Michael Munīr, interviewed by the author, 2009.

28. Saad Eddin Ibrahim, *The Copts of Egypt: Freedom to Worship* (London: Minority Rights Group International, 1996), 2; *CIA World Factbook*, https://www.cia.gov/ library/publications/the-world-factbook/geos/eg.html.

29. Cornelis Hulsman, "Freedom of Religion in Egypt," *Arab-West Report*, September 4, 2003; Cornelis Hulsman, interviewed by the author, Cairo, 2003. This claim is supported by Philippe Fargues, former professor at the American University of Cairo, who argues that the official claims are correct. Hulsman, "Interview with Dr. Philippe Fargues about Coptic Statistics."

30. http://pewforum.org/docs/?DocID=450.

31. It is difficult to ascertain exactly when the first Bahā'īs arrived in Egypt, although there are reports that a man named Abū Fadl came to Egypt in 1910 to spread the faith.

32. Marshall Hodgson, *The Venture of Islam: Conscience and History in a World Civilization*, vol. 3, *The Gunpowder Empires and Modern Times* (Chicago: University of Chicago Press, 1974), 419, 411.

33. Ibid., 411.

34. Dale Eickelman and James Piscatori, *Muslim Politics* (Princeton, NJ: Princeton University Press, 1996), 26, 28.

35. Ibid., 25–26.

36. Ibid., 29–30.

Chapter 1

1. Nazih Ayubi, *Political Islam: Religion and Politics in the Arab World* (London and New York: Routledge, 1991), 1.

2. Abū Hāmid al-Ghazzālī (1058–1111): "necessity makes legal what would otherwise not be legal," cited in Albert Hourani, *Arabic Thought in the Liberal Age, 1978–1939* (Cambridge: Cambridge University Press, 1984), 14.

3. The Arabic for these terms is *nizām shāmil, dawla, watan, hukūma*, and *umma*.

Hasan al-Bannā, *Majmūʿat Rasāʾil al-Imām al-Shahīd Hasan al-Bannā* (Beirut: Dār al-Andalus, 1965), 7.

4. Arskal Salim, *Challenging the Secular State: The Islamization of Law in Modern Indonesia* (Honolulu: University of Hawai'i Press, 2008), 16.

5. Kate Zebiri, *Muslims and Christians Face to Face* (Oxford: Oneworld, 1997), 22.

6. Asma Afsaruddin, *The First Muslims: History and Memory* (Oxford: Oneworld, 2007), 184, 187–189.

7. Ira Lapidus, "The Separation of State and Religion in the Development of Early Islamic Society," *International Journal of Middle East Studies* 6, no. 4 (1975): 382.

8. Knut S. Vikør, "The Sharīʿa and the Nation State: Who Can Codify the Divine Law?" in *The Middle East in a Globalized World: Papers from the Fourth Nordic Conference on Middle Eastern Studies, Oslo, 1998*, ed. Bjørn Olav Utvik and Knut S. Vikør, 222–224 (Bergen, Norway: Nordic Society for Middle Eastern Studies, 2000).

9. Nadav Safran, *Egypt in Search of Political Community: An Analysis of the Intellectual and Political Evolution of Egypt, 1804–1952* (Cambridge, MA: Harvard University Press, 1961), 28.

10. Historians also tend to agree that this was the normative Sunni position from the mid-ninth century, although the nature of religious and political authority before the ninth century is debated.

11. Bernard Lewis, *The Political Language of Islam* (Chicago: University of Chicago Press, 1988), 31.

12. Muhammad Ibn Khaldun, *The Muqaddimah: An Introduction to History*, trans. Franz Rosenthal, ed. N. J. Dawood (Princeton, NJ: Princeton University Press, 1967), 155, 158, 172.

13. Sami Zubaida, *Islam, the People and the State: Political Ideas and Movements in the Middle East* (London: I.B. Tauris, 1993), 42.

14. Safran, *Egypt in Search of Political Community*, 14–15.

15. Najwa al-Qattan, "*Dhimmis* in the Muslim Court: Documenting Justice in Ottoman Damascus (1775–1860)" (Ph.D. diss., Harvard University, 1996), 111.

16. Vikør, "The Sharīʿa and the Nation State," 227.

17. Ayubi, *Political Islam*, 2.

18. Safran, *Egypt in Search of Political Community*, 15, 17–18.

19. Albert Hourani, *A History of the Arab Peoples* (Cambridge, MA: Harvard University Press, 1991), 118.

20. C. Cahen, "*Dhimma*," in *The Encyclopaedia of Islam²* (Leiden: Brill, 1965), 227.

21. Yohanan Friedmann, *Tolerance and Coercion in Islam: Interfaith Relations in Muslim Tradition* (Cambridge: Cambridge University Press, 2003), 199.

22. Cahen, "*Dhimma*," 227.

23. The technical terms for these were *dār al-Islām* (abode of Islam) and *dār al-harb* (abode of war). Historically speaking, *dhimma*, from which the term *dhimmī* is

derived, was not even "Islamic" in its origin. The *dhimma* developed from existing practices and was based on the position of the non-citizen groups in the Eastern Roman Empire. Noel Coulson, *A History of Islamic Law* (Edinburgh: Edinburgh University Press, 1964), 27.

24. Ibn Khaldun, *The Muqaddimah*, 183.

25. Ibn Rushd, "The Legal Doctrine of Jihad: The Chapter on Jihad from Averroes' Legal Handbook *al-Bidāya*," in *Jihad in Classical and Modern Islam*, ed. Rudolph Peters, 40 (Princeton, NJ: Princeton University Press, 1996).

26. "How (can there be such a league) seeing that if they get an advantage over you, they respect not in you the ties either of kinship or of covenant? With (fair words from) their mouths they entice you, but their hearts are averse from you; and most of them are rebellious and wicked . . . in a believer they respect not the ties either of kinship or of covenant. It is they who have transgressed all bounds."

27. There is some dispute over whether the whole document was completed in this period or whether it was added to later on.

28. Ibn Ishaq, *The Life of Muhammad: A Translation of Ishaq's Sirat Rasul Allah*, trans. A. Guillaume, ed. Ibn Hisham (Lahore, Pakistan: Oxford University Press, 1968), 231–233.

29. C. E. Bosworth, "The Concept of *Dhimma* in Early Islam," in *Christians and Jews in the Ottoman Empire: The Functioning of a Plural Society*, ed. Benjamin Braude and Bernard Lewis, 41 (New York: Holmes and Meir Publishers, 1982).

30. Ishaq, *The Life of Muhammad*, 232.

31. Bosworth, "The Concept of *Dhimma* in Early Islam," 41.

32. "If one amongst the Pagans ask thee for asylum *(jiwār)*, Grant it to him, So that he may hear the Word Of Allah; and then escort him to where he can be secure. That is because they are men without knowledge" (9:6). Ann Lambton, *State and Government in Medieval Islam: An Introduction to the Study of Islamic Political Theory* (Oxford: Oxford University Press, 1981), 202.

33. Montgomery Watt, "al-Hudaybiyya," in *The Encyclopaedia of Islam²* (Leiden: Brill, 1965), 539.

34. al-Tabarī, *History of the Prophets and Kings (Tā'rīkh al-Rusul wa al-Mulūk)*, trans. Michael Fishbein, vol. 8, *The Victory of Islam* (Albany: State University of New York, 1997), 123, 130. Another Hadith reports that 'Umar heard the Prophet saying "I will expel the Jews and Christians from the Arabian peninsula and will not leave any but Muslims." Ibn Hajjaj al-Qushayri Muslim, *Sahīh Muslim: Being Traditions of the Sayings and Doings of the Prophet Muhammad as Narrated by His Companions and Compiled under the Title al-Jāmi'-us-sahīh*, trans. 'Abdul Hamīd Siddīqī (Lahore, Pakistan: Kashmiri Bazar, 1971), 2:1767, 240. However, some jurists argue that the Jews and the Christians cannot be turned out of the land of Arabia merely for difference of religion and that it applies only to those who are hostile to the state.

35. Antoine Fattal, *Le Statut Légal des Non-Musulmans en Pays d'islam*, vol. 10, *Recherches Publiées sous la Direction de L'institute de Lettres Orientales de Beyrouth* (Beyrouth: Imprimerie Catholique, 1958), 22–23; al-Tabarī, *History of the Prophets and Kings (Tā'rīkh al-Rusul wa al-Mulūk)*, trans. Ismail Poonawala, vol. 9, *The Last Years of the Prophet* (Albany: State University of New York, 1998), 87.

36. Bosworth, "The Concept of *Dhimma* in Early Islam," 40.

37. Ibid., 39–40.

38. Friedmann, *Tolerance and Coercion in Islam*, 32.

39. Bruce Masters, *Christians and Jews in the Ottoman Arab World: The Roots of Sectarianism* (Cambridge: Cambridge University Press, 2001), 20.

40. Marshall Hodgson, *The Venture of Islam: Conscience and History in a World Civilization*, vol. 1, *The Classical Age of Islam* (Chicago: University of Chicago Press, 1974), 242–243.

41. Ibn Rushd, *The Distinguished Jurist's Primer (Bidāyat al-Mujtahid wa Nihāyat al-Muqtasid)*, trans. Imran Ahsan Khany Nyazee, vol. 1, *Great Books of Islamic Civilization* (London: Garnet Publishing, 1994), 483; Ibn Rushd, "The Legal Doctrine of Jihad," 40.

42. Afsaruddin, *The First Muslims*, 107.

43. Ayubi, *Political Islam*, 18–19.

44. 'Alī Ibn Muhammad al-Māwardī, *The Ordinances of Government: A Translation of al-Ahkām al-Sultāniyya w'al-Wilāyat al-Dīniyya*, trans. Wafaa H. Wahba, Great Books of Islamic Civilization (London: Garnet Publishing, 1996), 159.

45. Ibn Rushd, "The Legal Doctrine of Jihad," 40; Muhammad Ibn Ismail al-Bukhari, *Sahih al-Bukhari* (Riyadh: Darussalam, 1997), 4:241–242; Friedmann, *Tolerance and Coercion in Islam*, 198–199.

46. Ibn Rushd, "The Legal Doctrine of Jihad," 40; al-Māwardī, *The Ordinances of Government*, 159.

47. Ibn Rushd, "The Legal Doctrine of Jihad," 40.

48. Richard Bulliet, *The Case for Islamo-Christian Civilization* (New York: Columbia University Press, 2004), 22.

49. Ibid., 40.

50. Ibn Taymiyya, *Answering Those Who Altered the Religion of Jesus Christ*, trans. Bayan Translation Services (Al-Mansura, Egypt: Umm al-Qura, 2003), 259; Ismail Ibn Umar Ibn Kathir, *Tafsir Ibn Kathir (Abridged)*, trans. Shaykh Safiur-Rahman al-Mubarakpuri (Riyadh: Darussalam, 2000), 4:408.

51. The concept of *tahrīf* is used here. Ibn Taymiyya, *Answering Those Who Altered the Religion of Jesus Christ*, 144.

52. Ibn Kathir, *Tafsir Ibn Kathir*, 1:249.

53. Mahmud Shaltut, "A Modernist Interpretation of Jihad: Mahmud Shaltut's

Treatise *Koran and Fighting,*" in *Jihad in Classical and Modern Islam*, ed. Rudolph Peters, 77 (Princeton, NJ: Princeton University Press, 1996).

54. Fattal, *Le Statut Légal des Non-Musulmans en Pays d'islam*, 267.

55. Edward Lane, *Manners and Customs of Modern Egyptians* (New York: Cosimo, 2005), 546, 535.

56. al-Tabarī, *History of the Prophets and Kings (Tā'rīkh al-Rusul wa al-Mulūk)*, trans. Khalid Blankinship, vol. 11, *The Challenge to Empires* (Albany: State University of New York, 1993), 4, 6, 46, 96.

57. Fattal, *Le Statut Légal des Non-Musulmans en Pays d'islam*, 266–267.

58. Ibid., 266; Ibn Kathir, *Tafsir Ibn Kathir*, 4:405–406; Ibn Naqqash, "The Jizya's Meaning: Edict of Caliph Al-Amir Bi-Ahkam Illah (1101–1130)," in *The Dhimmi: Jews and Christians under Islam*, ed. Bat Ye'or, 188 (Rutherford, NJ: Fairleigh Dickinson, 1985).

59. *'adl* or *'adala*. Ayubi, *Political Islam*, 24.

60. Mohammad H. Kamali, "Fundamental Rights of the Individual: An Analysis of *Haqq* (Right) in Islamic Law," *American Journal of Islamic Social Sciences* 10, no. 3 (1993): 340–341. Although the Mu'tazilites claimed that human reason could provide a valid basis for legal rulings.

61. Patricia Crone, *God's Rule: Government and Islam* (New York: Columbia University Press, 2004), 281–282.

62. Lambton, *State and Government in Medieval Islam*, 204.

63. Safran, *Egypt in Search of Political Community*, 23–24.

64. al-Māwardī, *The Ordinances of Government*, 159.

65. Bat Ye'or, *The Dhimmi: Jews and Christians under Islam* (Rutherford, NJ: Fairleigh Dickinson University Press, 1985), 215.

66. Only the Hanafī school believed that both *dhimmīs* and Muslims must suffer the same penalty for similar crimes. The Hanbalī, Shāfi'ī (most of Egypt), and Mālikī schools stated that there is no equality in *qisās*. See Fattal, *Le Statut Légal des Non-Musulmans en Pays d'islam*, 115–116.

67. Ibn Rushd, *The Distinguished Jurist's Primer*, 2:427.

68. Cahen, "*Dhimma*," 229.

69. Donald Little, "Coptic Conversion to Islam under the Bahri Mamluks 692–755/1293–1354," *British Society for Oriental and African Studies* 39, no. 3 (1976): 552.

70. al-Bukhari, *Sahih al-Bukhari*, 9:46; Muslim, *Sahīh Muslim*, 3:898, ch. 1673; al-Māwardī, *The Ordinances of Government*, 61; Fattal, *Le Statut Légal des Non-Musulmans en Pays d'islam*, 165.

71. Friedmann, *Tolerance and Coercion in Islam*, 199.

72. Fattal, *Le Statut Légal des Non-Musulmans en Pays d'islam*, 165.

73. Ibn Rushd, *The Distinguished Jurist's Primer*, 2:427.

74. Fattal, *Le Statut Légal des Non-Musulmans en Pays d'islam*, 165–167.

75. Ibid., 165.

76. A. S. Tritton, *The Caliphs and Their Non-Muslim Subjects: A Critical Study of the Covenant of 'Umar* (London: Frank Cass, 1970), 136.

77. Ibn Rushd, *The Distinguished Jurist's Primer*, 2:427; al-Bukhari, *Sahih al-Bukhari*, 8:399.

78. "And never will Allah grant to the Unbelievers a way (to triumph) over the Believers (4:141)" and "Oh ye who believe! Take not for friends Unbelievers rather than Believers" (4:144). The Hanafī school made some concessions, but this did not receive approval of most other schools of the *sharī'a*, which held that non-Muslims are not allowed to assume any position which might bestow them any authority over a Muslim.

79. Abu Hamid al-Ghazzali, *Imam Gazzali's Ihya Ulum-Id-Din*, trans. al-Haj. Maulana Fazul-Ul-Karim (Lahore, Pakistan: Sind Sagar Academy, 1978), 2:232.

80. Benjamin Braude and Bernard Lewis, Introduction to *Christians and Jews in the Ottoman Empire: The Functioning of a Plural Society*, ed. Benjamin Braude and Bernard Lewis (New York: Holmes and Meier Publishers, 1982), 7.

81. Norman A. Stillman, "Dhimma," in *Medieval Islamic Civilization: An Encyclopedia*, ed. Josef W. Meri (New York: Routledge, 2006), 206.

82. Ibn Taghribirdi, "Dismissal of Christian Officials in Egypt (1410)," in *The Dhimmi: Jews and Christians under Islam*, ed. Bat Ye'or, 198–199 (Rutherford, NJ: Fairleigh Dickinson University Press, 1985); Ibn Naqqash, "The Jizya's Meaning," 193.

83. Stillman, "Dhimma," 206.

84. Delegated (*tafwīd*) and executive (*tanfīdh*). al-Māwardī, *The Ordinances of Government*, 26–29, 144, 130.

85. Joel L. Kraemer, *Humanism in the Renaissance of Islam: The Cultural Revival during the Buyid Age* (Leiden: Brill, 1992), 75.

86. Donald Richards, "Dhimmi Problems in Fifteenth-Century Cairo: Reconsideration of a Court Document," *Studies in Muslim-Jewish Relations* 1 (1993): 128.

87. Ibn Kathir, *Tafsir Ibn Kathir*, 4:406–407; Tritton, *The Caliphs and Their Non-Muslim Subjects*, 37–38, 59.

88. al-Bukhari, *Sahih al-Bukhari*, 4:417, 4:415, 8:23.

89. Ibn Qayyim al-Jawziyya, "Places of Worship, Clothes, and Behavior of Dhimmis," in *The Dhimmi: Jews and Christians under Islam*, ed. Bat Ye'or, 196 (Rutherford, NJ: Fairleigh Dickinson University Press, 1985).

90. Leila Ahmed, *Women and Gender in Islam: Historical Roots of the Modern Debate* (New Haven, CT: Yale University Press, 1992), 120–121.

91. Lewis, *The Political Language of Islam*, 78–79; al-Bukhari, *Sahih al-Bukhari*, 8:155.

92. Ibn Kathir, *Tafsir Ibn Kathir*, 3:204.

93. Ibid., 4:407.

94. Ibid.

95. al-Māwardī, *The Ordinances of Government*, 161.

96. Stillman, "Dhimma," 205.

97. Ibid., 206.

98. al-Qattan, *"Dhimmis* in the Muslim Court," 166.

99. Cahen, *"Dhimma,"* 227–228.

100. Ayubi, *Political Islam*, 32.

101. Hourani, *A History of the Arab Peoples*, 118.

102. Stillman, "Dhimma," 206.

103. Seth Ward, "A Fragment from an Unknown Work by Al-Tabari on the Tradition 'Expel the Jews and Christians from the Arabian Peninsula (and the Lands of Islam),'" *Bulletin of the School of Oriental and African Studies* 53, no. 3 (1990), 412–413.

104. Khan Qamaruddin, *The Political Thought of Ibn Taymiyya* (Islamabad, Pakistan: Islamic Research Institute, 1973), 124.

105. Ward, "A Fragment from an Unknown Work by Al-Tabari," 414.

106. Doris Behrens-Abouseif, *The Political Situation of the Copts, 1798–1923*, ed. Benjamin Braude and Bernard Lewis, vol. 2, *Christians and Jews in the Ottoman Empire: The Functioning of a Plural Society* (New York: Holmes and Meier Publishers, 1982), 188.

107. Robert Brenton Betts, *Christians in the Arab East: A Political Study* (Atlanta: John Knox, 1978), 120.

108. Youssef Courbage and Philippe Fargues, *Christians and Jews under Islam* (London: I.B. Tauris, 1998), 74.

109. Lewis, *The Political Language of Islam*, 38–39.

110. Benjamin Braude, "Foundation Myths of the *Millet* System," in *Christians and Jews in the Ottoman Empire: The Functioning of a Plural Society*, ed. Bernard Lewis and Benjamin Braude, 69 (New York: Holmes and Meier Publishers, 1982).

111. Braude and Lewis, Introduction to *Christians and Jews in the Ottoman Empire*, 12–13.

112. Courbage and Fargues, *Christians and Jews under Islam*, 100, 102.

113. Lewis, *The Political Language of Islam*, 39.

114. al-Qattan, *"Dhimmis* in the Muslim Court," 151–152.

115. Magdi Guirguis, "The Organization of the Coptic Community in the Ottoman Period," in *Society and Economy in Egypt and the Eastern Mediterranean, 1600–1900: Essays in Honor of André Raymond*, ed. Nelly Hanna and Raouf Abbas, 204–209, 211 (Cairo: Cairo University Press, 2005).

116. Coptic Orthodox, like other Orthodox monophysites, believe that Christ has only one nature, which is divine; they differ from the Chalcedonians, who believe that Christ has two natures, human and divine.

117. Lane, *Manners and Customs of Modern Egyptians*, 528.

118. A. S. Atiya, "Kibt," in *Encyclopaedia of Islam²* (Leiden: Brill, 1986).

119. Ira Lapidus, "The Conversion of Egypt to Islam," *Israel Oriental Studies* 2 (1972): 248–249, 251.

120. Ibid., 260.

121. Little, "Coptic Conversion to Islam under the Bahri Mamluks," 569.

122. Lane, *Manners and Customs of Modern Egyptians*, 33, 522.

123. Ibid., 130–131, 535.

124. Ibid., 534, 523, 535.

125. Albert Hourani, *Minorities in the Arab World* (Oxford: Oxford University Press, 1947), 46; Lane, *Manners and Customs of Modern Egyptians*, 524, 546, 535–536.

126. B. L. Carter, *The Copts in Egyptian Politics* (London: Croom Helm, 1986), 3.

127. Braude and Lewis, Introduction to *Christians and Jews in the Ottoman Empire*, 1.

128. Will Kymlicka, *Contemporary Political Philosophy: An Introduction*, 2nd ed. (Oxford: Oxford University Press, 2002), 231.

129. Hourani, *Minorities in the Arab World*, 22.

130. Kemal Karpat, "*Millets* and Nationality: The Roots of the Incongruity of Nation and State in the Post-Ottoman Era," in *Christians and Jews in the Ottoman Empire: The Functioning of a Plural Society*, ed. Benjamin Braude and Bernard Lewis, 141, 166 (New York: Holmes and Meier Publishers, 1982).

131. Rifa'a Badawi Rafi al-Tahtāwī, "Fatherland and Patriotism," in *Islam in Transition: Muslim Perspectives*, ed. John J. Donohue and John L. Esposito, 11–12 (New York: Oxford University Press, 1982).

132. Friedmann, *Tolerance and Coercion in Islam*, 4.

133. Abdullahi Ahmed An-Na'im, *Islam and the Secular State: Negotiating the Future of Shari'a* (Cambridge, MA: Harvard University Press, 2008), 131.

134. Bosworth, "The Concept of *Dhimma* in Early Islam," 46–47.

135. Tritton, *The Caliphs and Their Non-Muslim Subjects*, 16.

136. Ayubi, *Political Islam*, 2.

Chapter 2

1. Yūsuf al-Qaradāwī, *Al-Shaykh al-Ghazālī Kamā 'Ariftuhu Rihlat Nusf Qarn* (Cairo: Dār al-Shurūq, 2000), 13.

2. Knut S. Vikør, "The Sharī'a and the Nation State: Who Can Codify the Divine Law?" in *The Middle East in a Globalized World: Papers from the Fourth Nordic Conference on Middle Eastern Studies, Oslo, 1998*, ed. Bjørn Olav Utvik and Knut S. Vikør, 230–231 (Bergen, Norway: Nordic Society for Middle Eastern Studies, 2000).

3. Leonard Wood, "Shari'ah Revivalist Thought in the First Years of the Shari'ah Lawyers' Bar Association Journal, 1929–1931," *Maghreb Review* 32, no. 2–3 (2007): 205.

4. Talal Asad, *Formations of the Secular: Christianity, Islam, Modernity* (Stanford, CA: Stanford University Press, 2003), 206.

5. Ibid., 209.

6. Ibid., 206, 208–209, 248.

7. Nazih Ayubi, *Over-Stating the Arab State: Politics and Society in the Middle East* (London: I.B. Tauris, 1999), 3, 7, 15, 21–22.

8. Nadav Safran, *Egypt in Search of Political Community: An Analysis of the Intellectual and Political Evolution of Egypt, 1804–1952* (Cambridge, MA: Harvard University Press, 1961), 32.

9. Robert Brenton Betts, *Christians in the Arab East: A Political Study* (Atlanta: John Knox, 1978), 122.

10. Albert Hourani, *Minorities in the Arab World* (Oxford: Oxford University Press, 1947), 24.

11. Ibid.

12. Gilles Kepel, *The Prophet and Pharaoh: Muslim Extremism in Egypt*, trans. Jon Rothschild (London: al-Saqi, 1985), 157.

13. Charles Issawi, "The Transformation of the Economic Position of the *Millets* in the Nineteenth Century," in *Christians and Jews in the Ottoman Empire: The Functioning of a Plural Society*, ed. Benjamin Braude and Bernard Lewis , 264 (New York: Holmes and Meier Publishers, 1982).

14. Bruce Masters, *Christians and Jews in the Ottoman Arab World: The Roots of Sectarianism* (Cambridge: Cambridge University Press, 2001), 138.

15. Ibid.

16. Safran, *Egypt in Search of Political Community*, 36.

17. Roderic Davison, "The *Millets* as Agents of Change in the Nineteenth-Century Ottoman Empire," in *Christians and Jews in the Ottoman Empire: The Functioning of a Plural Society*, ed. Benjamin Braude and Bernard Lewis, 333 (New York: Holmes and Meier Publishers, 1982).

18. Kemal Karpat, "*Millets* and Nationality: The Roots of the Incongruity of Nation and State in the Post-Ottoman Era," in *Christians and Jews in the Ottoman Empire: The Functioning of a Plural Society*, ed. Benjamin Braude and Bernard Lewis, 164–165 (New York: Holmes and Meier Publishers, 1982).

19. Ibid., 163.

20. Paul Sedra, "Class Cleavages and Ethnic Conflict: Coptic-Christian Communities in Modern Egyptian Politics," *Islam and Christian-Muslim Relations* 10, no. 2 (1999): 224.

21. Gudrun Kramer, "*Dhimmi* or Citizen? Muslim-Christian Relations in Egypt," in *The Christian-Muslim Frontier: Chaos, Clash, or Dialogue?* ed. N. J. Nielsen, 37 (London: I.B. Tauris, 1998).

22. Karpat, "*Millets* and Nationality," 165, 144, 163.

23. Maurits Berger, "Public Policy and Islamic Law: The Modern *Dhimmī* in Contemporary Egyptian Family Law," *Islamic Law and Society* 8, no. 1 (2001), 94.

24. Safran, *Egypt in Search of Political Community*, 27.

25. Ibid., 110.

26. Hourani, *Minorities in the Arab World*, 41.

27. Berger, "Public Policy and Islamic Law," 92.

28. B. L. Carter, *The Copts in Egyptian Politics* (London: Croom Helm, 1986), 95–96.

29. Taha Hussein, *The Future of Culture in Egypt*, trans. Sidney Glazer (Ann Arbor, MI: American Council of Learned Societies, 1954), 3.

30. Carter, *The Copts in Egyptian Politics*, 102–103.

31. Wood, "Shari'ah Revivalist Thought in the First Years of the Shari'ah Lawyers' Bar Association Journal,"

32. Betts, *Christians in the Arab East*, xv.

33. Chase F. Robinson, *Islamic Historiography* (Cambridge: Cambridge University Press, 2003), 86.

34. Al-Bannā was a graduate of Dār al-'Ulūm. Hasan al-Bannā, *Majmū'at Rasā'il al-Imām al-Shahīd Hasan al-Bannā* (Beirut: Dār al-Andalus, 1965), 13, 7.

35. Ayubi argues that it "owes its origins to the alarmed reaction in Muslim circles to the final abolition of the caliphate" in 1924. Nazih N. Ayubi, "Islamic State," in *The Oxford Encyclopædia of the Modern Islamic World*, ed. John Esposito (New York: Oxford University Press, 1995), 321. However, according to the German scholar Reinhard Schulze, it dates from the nineteenth century. Fred Halliday, "'Orientalism' and Its Critics," *British Journal of Middle Eastern Studies* 20, no. 2 (1993): 155.

36. Gamāl 'Abd al-Nāsir, *Draft of the Charter* (Cairo: United Arab Republic Information Department, 1962), 63–64, 9–10.

37. Rafīq Habīb, interviewed by the author, Cairo, 2003.

38. Saad Eddin Ibrahim, *The Copts of Egypt: Freedom to Worship* (London: Minority Rights Group International, 1996), 15–16.

39. Carter, *The Copts in Egyptian Politics*, 109, 263, 258, 296.

40. Ibid., 236.

41. Ibid., 238–239.

42. Berger refers to the concept of "public order" as "public policy." Berger, "Public Policy and Islamic Law," 94–96.

43. Makram Samaan and Soheir Sukkary, "The Copts and Muslims of Egypt," in *Muslim-Christian Conflicts: Economic, Political, and Social Origins*, ed. Suad Joseph and Barbara L. K. Pillsbury, 140 (Boulder, CO: Westview, 1978); Najīb Jabrā'īl, interviewed by the author, Cairo, 2007.

44. Fouad Ajami, *The Arab Predicament* (Cambridge: Cambridge University Press, 1993), 4.

45. Qutb was born in Upper Egypt. He completed his education in Cairo and

graduated from the Dār al-ʿUlūm, then worked for the Ministry of Information. In 1949 he went to the United States, and on his return he joined the Muslim Brotherhood and became chief editor of *al-Daʿwa*. His most famous works include *Social Justice in Islam*, *Milestones*, and his Tafsir of the Qurʾan. He was sentenced to fifteen years' imprisonment in 1955, and in 1966 he was hanged on suspicion of plotting against the government. Kepel, *The Prophet and Pharaoh*, 37.

46. Ibid., 27.

47. Ibid., 92–95.

48. Barbara Zollner, *The Muslim Brotherhood: Hasan al-Hudaybi and Ideology* (London: Routledge, 2009), 4.

49. Kepel, *The Prophet and Pharaoh*, 127.

50. ʿUmar al-Tilmisānī, "Manhaj Allah . . . aw . . . al-Damār!!" *al-Daʿwa*, January 1979.

51. Kepel, *The Prophet and Pharaoh*, 111.

52. al-Jamāʿa al-Islāmiyya, Cairo University, "Lessons from Iran," in *Islam in Transition: Muslim Perspectives*, ed. John J. Donohue and John L. Esposito, 247–248 (New York: Oxford University Press, 1982).

53. Clark Lombardi, *State Law as Islamic Law in Modern Egypt: The Incorporation of the Sharīʿa into Egyptian Constitutional Law*, Studies in Islamic Law and Society (Leiden: Brill, 2006), 124–125.

54. Ibid., 128.

55. Ibid., 135.

56. Kepel, *The Prophet and Pharaoh*, 71.

57. al-Tilmisānī, "Manhaj Allah . . . aw . . . al-Damār!!"; Hilmī al-Qāʿūd, "Istirāha . . . Thumma Mādhā," *al-Daʿwa*, July 1978.

58. *al-Farīda al-Ghāʾiba*. Al-Jamāʿa also claimed responsibility; Talʾat Fuʾad Qasim, "What Does the Gamaʾa Islamiyya Want? An Interview with Talʾat Fuʾad Qasim," *Middle East Report* 198 (January–March 1996): 40. While al-Jamāʿa al-Islāmiyya and al-Jihād are often described as two separate groups, they were closely connected before 1984. Karam Zuhdī was the leader of both al-Jamāʿa al-Islāmiyya and the Upper Egyptian branch of al-Jihād in the early 1980's.

59. E.g., the Society of Repudiation and Renunciation, the Islamic Vanguards, Those Saved from the Fire, Shabāb Muhmmad, Jund Allah, and Jamʾiyyāt al-Tabligh and Hizb al-Tahrīr al-Islāmī. The last, a direct descendant of the group that was established in 1974, wishes to reestablish the caliphate.

60. Hishām Mubārak, *al-Irhābiūn Qādimūn: Dirāsat Muqārana bayn Mawqif al-Ikhwān al-Muslimīn wa Jamāʿāt al-Jihād min Qadiyya al-ʿUnf (1929–1994)* (Cairo: Kitāb al-Mahrūsa, 1995), 386–387.

61. Muhammad Salāh, interviewed by the author, Cairo, 2003.

62. ʿImād Shahīn, interviewed by the author, Cairo, 2003; Karam Zuhdī et al.,

Hurmat al-Ghulwūw fī al-Dīn (Cairo: Maktabat al-Turāth al-Islāmī, 2002); Karam Zuhdī et al., *al-Nash wa al-Tabyīn fī Tashīh Mafāhīm al-Muhtabasīn* (Cairo: Maktabat al-Turāth al-Islāmī, 2002); Karam Zuhdī et al., *Taslīt al-Adwā' 'Alā mā Waqa' fī al-Jihād min Ikhtā'* (Cairo: Maktabat al-Turāth al-Islāmī, 2002); Karam Zuhdī et al., *Mubādarat Waqf al-'Unf Ru'ya Wāq'iyya wa Nathara Shar'iyya* (Cairo: Maktabat al-Turāth al-Islāmī, 2002).

63. Explosion of Riyadh: Judgments and Impacts and River of Memories: Fiqh Revisions of the *al-Jamā'ā al-Islāmiyya*.

64. Zuhdī et al., *Hurmat al-Ghulwūw fī al-Dīn.*

65. Ibid.

66. See *al-Sharq al-Awsat*, July 15–17, 2003.

67. Nabīl 'Abd al-Fattāh, interviewed by the author, Cairo, 2003.

68. Mustafa Rajab, "The End of the Jamā'at al-Islāmiyah," *Rose al-Yūsuf (Arab-West Report)*, September 18, 2006.

69. Al-Jamā'ā al-Islāmiyya, http://www.egyig.com/.

70. Hossam al-Hamalawy, "Wannabes," *Cairo Times*, January 9–15, 2003.

71. Mamdūh Ismā'īl, interviewed by the author, Cairo, 2003.

72. 'Abd al-Hāfiz Sa'īd, "Will the Jihad Organization Announce from Tura Prison That It Has Abandoned Violence?!" *Sawt al-Umma (Arab-West Report)*, March 15, 2004; 'Abd al-Fattāh 'Abd al-Mun'im, "The Cease-Violence Initiative Is a Final Choice for Aboud Al-Zomor," *al-'Arabī (Arab-West Report)*, March 14, 2004. 'Abd al-Hāfiz Sa'īd, "Applying Islamic [Rules] in All Affairs of Life Is Something Impossible Now," *Sawt al-Umma (Arab-West Report)*, August 30, 2004.

73. *Wathīqat Tarshīd al-'Aml al-Jihādī fī Misr wa al-'Ālam (Document of Right Guidance for Jihad Activity in Egypt and the World).*

74. "Major Jihadi Cleric and Author of Al-Qaeda's Shari'a Guide to Jihad: 9/11 Was a Sin," *Memri*, December 14, 2007.

75. Umayma 'Abd al-Latīf, interviewed by the author, Cairo, 2003.

76. Hossam al-Hamalawy, interviewed by the author, Cairo, 2003.

77. 'Abd al-Fattāh 'Abd al-Mun'īm, "'Awdat Tanthīm Shukrī Mustafā," *al-'Arabī*, September 14, 2003.

78. al-Hamalawy, "Wannabes"; Hossam al-Hamalawy, "Fear of the Beard," *Cairo Times* 7, no. 7 (2003).

79. Amr Elshoubaki, "Old Jihad, New Jihad," *al-Ahram Weekly*, February 28–March 5, 2008.

80. Amr Hamzawy, "The Muslim Brotherhood's Party Platform," *Carnegie Endowment for International Peace* (2007), http://carnegieendowment.org/events/?fa=event Detail&id=1076&prog=zgp&proj=zted.

81. al-Tilmisānī was imprisoned under all three of Egypt's presidents.

82. Kepel, *The Prophet and Pharaoh*, 63.

83. Mustafa Mashhour, *Provisions of the Soul* (Cairo: al-Falāh, 2000), 188–189; Muhammad Ma'mun el-Hodaiby, "Upholding Islam," *Harvard International Review* 19, no. 2 (1997): 26; Muhammad Mahdī 'Ākif, "Muslim Brotherhood Initiative on the General Principles of Reform in Egypt" (Cairo, 2004).

84. Joshua Stacher, interviewed by the author, Cairo, 2008.

85. Muslim Brotherhood, "The Muslim Brotherhood's Program," http://www.ikh wanweb.com/Article.asp?ID=812&SectionID=70.

86. el-Hodaiby, "Upholding Islam," 25; Muhammad Ma'mun al-Hudaibi, *A Quiet Discussion on Heated Issues* (Cairo: al-Falāh, 2000), 30.

87. Ma'mūn al-Hudaybī initially pursued a judiciary career, and then became head of the Court of Cassation. He joined the Brotherhood's political wing at an early age and was arrested for the first time in 1965. After spending some time in Saudi Arabia, he returned in the mid-1980's and became more heavily involved with the Muslim Brotherhood. He was deputy supreme guide under former Supreme Guide Hamid Abu al-Nasr (1913–1996).

88. Muhammad al-'Asīrī, "Murshid Al-Ikhwān Yahkum Misr Siran," *Sawt al-Umma*, August 11, 2003.

89. Umayma 'Abd al-Latīf, interviewed by the author, 2003; Hossam al-Hamalawy, interviewed by the author, 2003.

90. Joshua Stacher, "The Brothers and the Wars," *Middle East Report* 250 (Spring 2009).

91. Yaroslav Trofimov, "Muslim Brotherhood Falters as Egypt Outflanks Islamists," *Wall Street Journal*, May 15, 2009.

92. Hossam Tammam, "Mb Goes Rural," *al-Ahram Weekly*, October 23–29, 2008. Hossan Tammam, "Too Old School to Strike," *al-Ahram Weekly*, April 2–8, 2009.

93. Trofimov, "Muslim Brotherhood Falters as Egypt Outflanks Islamists."

94. Israel Elad Altman, "The Egyptian Muslim Brotherhood after the 2005 Elections," *Current Trends in Islamist Ideology* 4 (2006): 5.

95. Ibid., 10.

96. Hamzawy, "The Muslim Brotherhood's Party Platform."

97. Munīr Fakhrī 'Abd al-Nūr, interviewed by the author, Cairo, 2003; Umayma 'Abd al-Latīf, interviewed by the author, 2003; Rif'at al-Sa'īd, "Hikayāt al-Irhābī al-Muta'silim fī Misr: Al-Ikhwān al-Muslimīn," *al-Ahālī*, August 20, 2003.

98. Mashhour, *Provisions of the Soul*, 157, 188.

99. al-Hudaibi, *A Quiet Discussion on Heated Issues*, 33.

100. a.n.m., "Tharwat al-Kharabawy Broke from the Muslim Brotherhood and Reveals Secrets: Al-Hudaiby Dreams of Ruling Egypt," *al-Ahrām al-'Arabī (Arab-West Report)*, June 12–18, 2003.

101. Khairat al-Shatir, "No Need to Be Afraid of Us," *The Guardian*, November 23, 2005.

102. Saad Eddin Ibrāhīm, interviewed by the author, Cairo, 2003.

103. Hamzawy, "The Muslim Brotherhood's Party Platform."

104. Stacher, "The Brothers and the Wars."

105. Joshua Stacher, interviewed by the author, Cairo, 2008.

106. Marc Lynch, "The Muslim Brotherhood's Party Platform," *Carnegie Endowment for International Peace* (2007), http://carnegieendowment.org/events/?fa=eventDetail&id=1076&prog=zgp&proj=zted.

107. Ibid.

108. Emmanuel Sivan, *Radical Islam: Medieval Theology, and Modern Politics* (New Haven, CT: Yale University Press, 1985), 130.

109. Charles Hirschkind, *The Ethical Soundscape: Cassette Sermons and Islamic Counterpublics* (New York: Columbia University Press, 2006), 6–8, 59.

110. Ibid., 11.

111. Ibid., 58–59, 61, 203, 178, 128. For a more detailed discussion of Kishk and his sermons, see ibid., 156–167.

112. Ibid., 138.

113. Ibrahim M. Abu-Rabiʿ, *Contemporary Arab Thought: Studies in Post-1967 Arab Intellectual History* (London: Pluto Press, 2004), 224. See this source for a good overview of Muhammad al-Ghazālī's thought.

114. Ibrahim M. Abu-Rabiʿ, *Intellectual Origins of Islamic Resurgence in the Modern Arab World* (Albany: State University of New York Press, 1996), 62.

115. Raymond Baker, *Islam without Fear: Egypt and the New Islamists* (Cambridge, MA: Harvard University Press, 2003).

116. *al-tayār al-islāmī al-wasat.*

117. Fahmī Huwaydī, interviewed by the author, Cairo, 2007.

118. Samīr Murqus, interviewed by the author, Cairo, 2003.

119. Hossam al-Hamalawy, interviewed by the author, 2003.

120. Baker, *Islam without Fear*, 36–37.

121. Joshua Stacher, "Post-Islamist Rumblings in Egypt: The Emergence of the Wasat Party," *Middle East Journal* 56 (Summer 2002): 416.

122. Ibid., 417.

123. Muhammad Al-Bāz, "Abū Al-ʿAlā Mādī: al-Hudaybī Khatr ʿAlā al-Ikhwān," *Sawt al-Umma*, September 1, 2003; Mohammed el-Dubaa, "Essam Sultan the Leader of the West Party Talks about Mamoun El-Houdeibi Though This Causes Family Embarrassment. He Says, 'If the Muslim Brotherhood Had a Martial Court, They Would Have Sentenced Us to Death by Hanging,'" *Arab-West Report*, December 5, 1997.

124. Stacher, "Post-Islamist Rumblings in Egypt," 421.

125. Ibid., 422.

126. Muhammad Heikal, *Autumn of Fury* (London: Andre Deutsch, 1983), 219.

127. Lombardi, *State Law as Islamic Law in Modern Egypt*, 138.

128. Majdī Sālih, "What Does the Prime Minister Mean by Saying 'Egypt Is Secular'?" *al-Usbū' (Arab-West Report)*, May 29, 2006.

129. Lombardi, *State Law as Islamic Law in Modern Egypt*, 138.

130. Fauzi Najjar, "Book Banning in Contemporary Egypt," *Muslim World* 91 (Fall 2001): 403, 420.

131. Umayma 'Abd al-Latīf, interviewed by the author, 2003.

132. L. Azuri, "As Part of Its Struggle against the Muslim Brotherhood, the Egyptian Regime Comes Out against the Concept of a Cleric-Led State," http://www.memri.org/bin/opener_latest.cgi?ID=IA34107.

133. Lombardi, *State Law as Islamic Law in Modern Egypt*, 159–160.

134. Ibid., 2.

135. Ibid., 5–6.

136. Badouin Dupret, *A Return to the Shariah: Egyptian Judges and Referring to Islam*, ed. John Esposito and Francois Burgat (London: Hurst, 2003) , 126.

137. Sami Zubaida, *Law and Power in the Islamic World* (London: I.B. Tauris, 2005), 170.

138. Fahmī Huwaydī, interviewed by the author, Cairo, 2003; Muhammad Salīm Al-'Awwā, interviewed by the author, Cairo, 2003.

139. Rafīq Habīb, interviewed by the author, Cairo, 2007.

140. 'Abd al-Mun'im Abū al-Futūh, interviewed by the author, Cairo, 2003.

141. Mashhour, *Provisions of the Soul*, 188.

142. el-Hodaiby, "Upholding Islam," 13.

143. E.g., Muhammad Salāh, "Brotherhood Leader Resigns and Attacks the Guidance Bureau (Misr: Qiyādī Yastaqil min al-Ikhwān wa Yahmīl 'Alā Matkab al-Irshād)," *al-Hayāt*, September 14, 2003.

144. 'Ākif, "Muslim Brotherhood Initiative on the General Principles of Reform in Egypt," 17, 27–29; al-Hudaibi, *A Quiet Discussion on Heated Issues*, 8–9.

145. el-Hodaiby, "Upholding Islam," 24–25.

146. Zubaida, *Law and Power in the Islamic World*, 161; 'Isām Sultān, interviewed by the author, Cairo, 2007.

147. 'Ākif, "Muslim Brotherhood Initiative on the General Principles of Reform in Egypt," 11, 20–22, 27–29.

148. Ibid., 14–16.

149. Muslim Brotherhood, "Barnāmij al-Hizb" (2007), 16.

150. Ibid., 10–11.

151. Hamzawy, "The Muslim Brotherhood's Party Platform." Diane Singerman, "The Muslim Brotherhood's Party Platform," *Carnegie Endowment for International*

Peace (2007), http://carnegieendowment.org/events/?fa=eventDetail&id=1076&prog=
zgp&proj=zted.

152. 'Abd al-Mun'im Abū al-Futūh, interviewed by the author, Cairo, 2008; 'Isām
Al-'Aryān, interviewed by the author, Cairo, 2008; Abū Hamīd al-Ghāzalī, interviewed
by the author, Cairo, 2008.

153. Muhammad 'Alī 'Ibrāhīm, "About Their New Program," *al-Gumhūrriyya*,
September 15, 2007.

154. Asad, *Formations of the Secular*, 248.

Chapter 3

1. According to André Raymond, as cited in Magdi Guirguis, "The Organization
of the Coptic Community in the Ottoman Period," in *Society and Economy in Egypt
and the Eastern Mediterranean, 1600–1900: Essays in Honor of André Raymond*, ed.
Nelly Hanna and Raouf Abbas, 201 (Cairo: Cairo University Press, 2005).

2. Maggie Morgan, "Samir Morcos: The Mirror of the Copt," *al-Ahram Weekly*,
June 23–29, 2005.

3. Guirguis, "The Organization of the Coptic Community in the Ottoman Period," 202.

4. Cornelis Hulsman, "Different Middle Eastern Christian Responses to Living in
a Muslim Environment," special for *Arab-West Report*, December 5, 2006.

5. S. S. Hasan, *Christians versus Muslims in Modern Egypt* (Oxford: Oxford University Press, 2003), 3.

6. Paul Sedra, "Class Cleavages and Ethnic Conflict: Coptic-Christian Communities in Modern Egyptian Politics," *Islam and Christian-Muslim Relations* 10, no. 2
(1999): 224.

7. Hasan, *Christians versus Muslims in Modern Egypt*, 3–5.

8. Sedra, "Class Cleavages and Ethnic Conflict," 225.

9. Wolfram Reiss, abridged by Cornelis Hulsman, "Renewal in the Coptic Orthodox Church; Notes of the Ph.D. Thesis of Revd. Dr. Wolfram Reiss" (Cairo: Arab-West
Report, 2001), 6–7, 14.

10. a.n.m., "Muwājaha ma'a al-Rajl alathī 'Azal al-Bābā Munthu Nusf Qarn," *al-
Musawwār*, July 4, 2003, 52–54.

11. Hasan, *Christians versus Muslims in Modern Egypt*, 60.

12. B. L. Carter, *The Copts in Egyptian Politics* (London: Croom Helm, 1986), 97.

13. a.n.m., "Muwājaha ma'a al-Rajl alathī 'Azal al-Bābā Munthu Nusf Qarn."

14. Reiss, "Renewal in the Coptic Orthodox Church," 15. Kamāl Zākhir Mūsa also
argues that there was some contact between the Sunday School Movement and the
Coptic Nation, but he is not sure how far this went. Cornelis Hulsman, "Interview
with Kamāl Zākhir Mūsa about His Conviction in the Need for Church Reform," special for *Arab-West Report*, November 8–14, 2006.

15. Samīr Murqus, interviewed by the author, Cairo, 2003.

16. Saad Eddin Ibrahim, *The Copts of Egypt: Freedom to Worship* (London: Minority Rights Group International, 1996), 23.

17. Cynthia Nelson, "Religious Experience, Sacred Symbols, and Social Reality: An Illustration from Egypt," *Humaniora Islamica* 2 (1974): 260.

18. Alī al-Fātih, "Samīr Murqus: Munthu 1952 wa Jamī'a al-Tayārāt al-Fikriyya Rahīna al-Sirā'a Bayn al-Dawla wa al-Ikhwān al-Muslimīn," *al-Qāhira*, February 10, 2004; Samīr Murqus, interviewed by the author, 2003; Samīr Murqus, "Our Experience: Dialogue Based on Citizenship," *al-'Ākhar . . . al-Hiwār . . . al-Muwātana* (Cairo: Maktabat al-Shurūq al-Dawliyya, 2005), 166.

19. Ibrahim, *The Copts of Egypt*, 18–19.

20. Ibid., 19.

21. Hasan, *Christians versus Muslims in Modern Egypt*, 10.

22. Sedra, "Class Cleavages and Ethnic Conflict," 225–226.

23. Hamied Ansari, "Sectarian Conflict and the Political Expediency of Religion," *Middle East Journal* 38 (Summer 1984): 404.

24. Hasan, *Christians versus Muslims in Modern Egypt*, 201.

25. a.n.m., "Muqābalat al-Usbū' fī Dair Anbā Bishoy," *al-Musawwar*, October 10, 2003, 16–36, 64–65.

26. Munīr Fakhrī 'Abd al-Nūr, interviewed by the author, Cairo, 2003.

27. Cornelis Hulsman, interviewed by the author, Cairo, 2007.

28. Cornelis Hulsman, interviewed by the author, Cairo, 2003.

29. Hasan, *Christians versus Muslims in Modern Egypt*, 201, 204.

30. Vivian Fu'ād, interviewed by the author, Cairo, 2003.

31. Usāma Salāma, "Waiting for a Law That Will Criminalize Discrimination between Muslims and Christians," *Ruz al-Yūsuf (Arab-West Report)*, February 10–16, 2007; Bishop Murqus, interviewed by the author, Cairo, 2007.

32. Bishop Thomas, "The Experience of the Middle East's Largest Christian Community during a Time of Rising Islamization" (paper presented at the Hudson Institute, July 18, 2008).

33. Cornelis Hulsman, "Interview with Munīr Fakhrī 'Abd Al-Nūr," *Arab-West Report*, January 21, 2009.

34. Samīr Murqus is a scholar and writer. In November 2006, he and Vivian Fu'ād received a prize from the Norwegian Academy for Arts and Freedom of Expression in recognition of his role in Muslim-Christian relations and inter-religious dialogue. Murqus was born and brought up in Shubra in Cairo in the 1950's. In 1994 he and Vivian Fu'ād set up the Coptic Centre of Social Studies and then moved to the Middle East Council of Churches. He now works for al-Fustāt, a major development research center. Munīr Fakhrī 'Abd al-Nūr is a prominent Coptic politician and economist. His father was Fakhrī 'Abd al-Nūr, a close colleague of the nationalist leader Sa'ad Zaghlūl.

35. Samīr Murqus, interviewed by the author, 2003; Munīr Fakhrī ʿAbd al-Nūr, interviewed by the author, Cairo, 2007.

36. Munīr Fakhrī ʿAbd al-Nūr, interviewed by the author, 2003.

37. Yūsuf Sidhum, interviewed by the author, Cairo, 2007.

38. Michael Munīr, interviewed by the author, Virginia, 2009.

39. Cornelis Hulsman, interviewed by the author, 2003.

40. Viola Fahmī, "The Truth behind the Coptic Wrath against Church Leadership," *al-Ahālī (Arab-West Report)*, April 9, 2008.

41. Munīr Fakhrī ʿAbd al-Nūr, interviewed by the author, 2003.

42. Yūsuf Sidhum, interviewed by the author, 2007.

43. Bishop Thomas, interviewed by the author, Anafora, near Cairo, 2007.

44. Munīr Fakhrī ʿAbd al-Nūr, interviewed by the author, 2003; Sana al-Saʿid, "Pope Shenouda in an Interview with Al-Wafd: "Wafāʾ Costantine Was Not Forced to Convert Back to Christianity," *al-Wafd (Arab-West Report)*, January 6, 2005; Bishop Thomas, interviewed by the author, 2007.

45. Fadi Habashi, "Resorting to Religious Names in Times of Crises!" *Sawt al-Umma (Arab-West Report)*, January 10, 2005.

46. a.n.m., "'Awdat Thāhira al-Mulsiqāt al-Dīniyya ʿAlā al-Sayyārāt," *Ruz al-Yūsuf*, January 9, 2004.

47. Munīr Fakhrī ʿAbd al-Nūr, interviewed by the author, 2003.

48. Cornelis Hulsman, "Do Not Claim Something That Cannot Be Proven; The Origin of Some Christian Persecution Stories," *Arab-West Report*, November 17–23, 2004.

49. http://www.cawu.org/. Samīr Murqus and Vivian Fuʾād, "Our Experience Dialogue Based on Citizenship," in *al-ʾĀkhar . . . al-Hiwār . . . al-Muwātana*, ed. Samīr Murqus, 151 (Cairo: Maktabat al-Shurūq al-Dawliyya, 2005).

50. Gilles Kepel, *The Prophet and Pharaoh: Muslim Extremism in Egypt*, trans. Jon Rothschild (London: al-Saqi, 1985),157.

51. Ibid., 207.

52. Patrick D. Gaffney, *The Prophet's Pulpit: Islamic Preaching in Contemporary Egypt* (Berkeley: University of California Press, 1994), 103, 86, 97.

53. Ibrahim, *The Copts of Egypt*, 19.

54. ʿAlī al-Qādī, "Tahdīd al-Nasl Bayn Islām wa al-Misīhiyya," *al-Daʿwa*, June 1981; al-Jamāʿa al-Islāmiyya, "al-Abʿād al-Haqīqiyya lil-Fitna al-Tāʾifiyya," *al-Daʿwa*, June 1980; a.n.m., "Al-Naʿara al-Tāʾifiyya Allati Yathiruhā al-Nasārā," *al-Daʿwa*, June 1980.

55. Gaffney, *The Prophet's Pulpit*, 256.

56. Kepel, *The Prophet and Pharaoh*, 166.

57. Ibrahim, *The Copts of Egypt*, 17.

58. Francois Burgat, *Face to Face with Political Islam* (London: I.B. Tauris, 2002), 84–85, 82.

59. Saad Eddin Ibrāhīm, interviewed by the author, Cairo, 2003.

60. Gaffney, *The Prophet's Pulpit*, 254.

61. Ibid., 86.

62. Muhammad Salāh, interviewed by the author, Cairo, 2003.

63. Gaffney, *The Prophet's Pulpit*, 98–99, 103.

64. Ibrahim, *The Copts of Egypt*, 21–22.

65. Christina Lamb, "Egyptian Police 'Crucify' and Rape Christians," *Sunday Telegraph*, October 25, 1998.

66. Yūsuf Sidhum, interviewed by the author, Cairo, 2003.

67. Cornelis Hulsman, interviewed by the author, 2007.

68. Bishop Thomas, interviewed by the author, 2007.

69. Cornelis Hulsman, interviewed by the author, 2007.

70. Hossam al-Hamalawy, "Stuck in the Middle," *Cairo Times* 6, no. 35 (2002).

71. Bishop Murqus, interviewed by the author, Cairo, 2003.

72. Amr al-Masri, "The Alexandria Demonstrations . . . What's Next?," press review for *Arab-West Report*, October 17, 2005.

73. Cornelis Hulsman, editorial in *Arab-West Report*, July 10, 2008.

74. Ibid.

75. Cornelis Hulsman, "Egyptian Villagers Resist Monastery's Growth," *Free Copts*, July 25, 2008.

76. Hulsman, "Interview with Munīr Fakhrī 'Abd al-Nūr," *Arab-West Report*, January 21, 2009.

77. Usāma Khālid, "Haqīqat Ightisāb al-Fatayyāt fī Mahalāt al-Tawhīd wa al-Nūr wa Awlād Rajab," *Sawt al-Umma*, March 22, 2004.

78. http://www.copts4freedom.com/english.htm.

79. Cornelis Hulsman, "Special for Arab-West Report," *Arab West Report*, August 9, 2003.

80. Yūsuf Sidhum, interviewed by the author, 2003; Bishop Murqus, interviewed by the author, 2007.

81. Vivian Fu'ād, interviewed by the author, 2003.

82. Cornelis Hulsman, "Dangerous Developments," *Arab-West Report*, September 6, 2003.

83. Hulsman, "Interview with Kamāl Zākhir Mūsa about His Conviction in the Need for Church Reform."

84. *http://www.copts.com/; http://freecopts.net/english/; www.coptsunited.com; http://www.Uppereasternchristian.org/*

85. Michael Munīr, interviewed by the author, 2009.

86. Sharīf Dūs, "'Āshat Misr," *al-Ahkbār*, December 16–23, 2003.

87. Mīlād Hannā, *The Seven Pillars of the Egyptian Identity* (Cairo: General Egyptian Book Organisation, 1989).

88. Gamāl Asʿad, "Mahākamat Aqbāt al-Mahjar," *Sawt al-Umma*, February 23, 2004.

89. Murqus and Fuʾād, "Our Experience Dialogue Based on Citizenship," 154–155.

90. Kepel, *The Prophet and Pharaoh*, 165.

91. Ibid., 129.

92. Karim al-Gawhary, "Copts in the 'Egyptian Fabric,'" *Middle East Report* (1996): 21; Ami Ayalon, "Egypt's Coptic Pandora's Box," in *Minorities and the State in the Arab World*, ed. Ofra Bengio and Gabriel Ben-dor, 64 (Boulder, CO: Lynne Rienner Publishers, 1999).

93. Christian Van Nispen Tot Sevenaer, "Changes in Relations between Copts and Muslims (1952–1991) in the Light of Historical Experience," in *Between Desert and City: The Coptic Orthodox Church Today*, ed. Nelly Van Doorn-Harder and Kari Vogt (Oslo: Novis forlag, 1997), 22.

94. Ayalon, *Egypt's Coptic Pandora's Box*, 64.

95. al-Gawhary, "Copts in the 'Egyptian Fabric,'" 21.

96. Dina al-Khawaga, "Le Debat sur les Coptes: Le Dit et le Non-Dit," *CEDEJ: Egypte Monde Arabe* 20, no. 4 (1994): 68–69.

97. Ibid., 70.

98. al-Gawhary, "Copts in the 'Egyptian Fabric,'" 22.

99. Ayalon, *Egypt's Coptic Pandora's Box*, 66.

100. al-Gawhary, "Copts in the 'Egyptian Fabric,'" 22.

101. al-Khawaga, "Le Debat sur les Coptes: Le Dit et le Non-Dit," 67.

102. Ibid., 74.

103. Bāhir al-Salīmī, "Laysat Qunbulat Mauqūta: al-ʿAlāqat Bayn Mashākil al-Aqbāt wa Tawāzanāt al-Hukūma," *al-Midān*, July 24, 2003; Ayalon, *Egypt's Coptic Pandora's Box*, 62.

104. Gaffney, *The Prophet's Pulpit*, 262. Two sermons of Sheikh Kishk—"Kishk Responds to the Conspiracies of the Copts" and "Will Jews and Christians Enter Heaven?"—are unavailable in Egypt.

105. Yūsuf Sidhum, "Ahdāth Qariya Jirzā Fasl Jadīd fī Musalsal Karīh," *al-Watanī*, November 23, 2003.

106. Yūsuf Sidhum, interviewed by the author, 2003.

107. Nabīl ʿAbd al-Malik, "al-Hiqba al-Qibtiyya . . . wa Kayfa Nuthahhiruhā?" *Ruz al-Yusuf* 34 (2003).

108. Sedra, "Class Cleavages and Ethnic Conflict," 227.

109. a.n.m., "Muqābalat al-Usbūʿ fī Dair Anbā Bishoy."

110. Samīr Murqus, interviewed by the author, 2003; a.n.m., "Muqābalat Al-Usbūʿ fī Dair Anbā Bishoy."

111. Odai Sirri, "Improving Trend," *Cairo Times* 6, no. 32 (2002).

112. Muhammad Ali, "The Copts Forewarn: Mubarak Deceived Us and Sectarian Sedition Might Be Back," *Sawt al-Umma (Arab-West Report)*, October 17, 2005.

113. Sharif al-Dawakhili, "Coptic Church Made a Plan to Escalate against the Regime after Copts Were Excluded from the Shura Council," *al-Dustūr (Arab-West Report)*, June 22, 2007.

114. Murqus and Fu'ād, "Our Experience Dialogue Based on Citizenship," 161, 166

115. Samīr Murqus, interviewed by the author, 2003.

116. Samīr Murqus, "Humūm al-Shabāb al-Qibtī," *al-Qāhira* 121 (1992): 64–69.

117. a.n.m., "Muqābalat al-Usbū' fī Dair Anbā Bishoy."

118. Shaymā' 'Ādil, "Statistics: 27 Copts in the Parliament in 1942, No Copts in the Parliament in 1957, and Three in 2005," *al-Misrī al-Yawm (Arab-West Report)*, May 20, 2009.

119. a.n.m., "Muqābalat al-Usbū' fī Dair Anbā Bishoy."

120. Bishop Murqus, interviewed by the author, 2003.

121. a.n.m., "Muqābalat al-Usbū' fī Dair Anbā Bishoy."

122. Cornelis Hulsman, editorial in *Arab-West Report*, August 12, 2003; Michael Munīr, interviewed by the author, 2009.

123. a.n.m., "Muqābalat al-Usbū' fī Dair Anbā Bishoy."

124. Vivian Fu'ād, interviewed by the author, 2003.

125. Muhammad Nūr, "The Electorial Card . . . A Basic Condition for Coptic Marriage," *Ākhir Sā'a*, January 28, 2009; a.n.m., "Should Copts Have a Quota of Parliamentary Seats?" *al-Jumhurriyya*, October 13, 2005.

126. Hossam al-Hamalawy, interviewed by the author, Cairo, 2003; Hulsman, "Interview with Kamāl Zākhir Mūsa about His Conviction in the Need for Church Reform"; Yūsuf Sidhum, "On the Shura Elections," *al-Watani International (Arab-West Report)*, June 17, 2007.

127. Hulsman, "Interview with Kamāl Zākhir Mūsa about His Conviction in the Need for Church Reform."

128. Vivian Fu'ād, interviewed by the author, Cairo, 2007.

129. Bishop Thomas, interviewed by the author, 2007.

130. Yūsuf Sidhum, interviewed by the author, 2007.

131. "The Egyptian Constitution."

132. Cited in Kevin Boyle and Adel Omar Sherif, eds., *Human Rights and Democracy: The Role of the Supreme Constitutional Court of Egypt*, vol. 3, Cimel Book Series (London: Kluwer Law International, 1996), 232.

133. Maurits Berger, "Public Policy and Islamic Law: The Modern *Dhimmī* in Contemporary Egyptian Family Law," *Islamic Law and Society* 8, no. 1 (2001): 92, 89.

134. a.n.m., "Qānūn al-Ahwāl al-Shakhsiyya al-Jadīd," (2000).

135. Berger, "Public Policy and Islamic Law," 88.

136. Ibid., 94; a.n.m., "Qānūn al-Ahwāl al-Shakhsiyya al-Jadīd."

137. Berger, "Public Policy and Islamic Law," 118–121.

138. Ibid., 94–95, 103, 112. This has included the application of the provision that non-Muslims and Muslims may not inherit from each other. It has also resulted in testimony discrimination. In addition, when the national courts were established, *sharīʿa* judges were transferred to the national courts, but no such arrangement was made for the judges and lawyers of non-Muslim courts. Ibid., 114, 127.

139. Hulsman, "Interview with Kamāl Zākhir Mūsa about His Conviction in the Need for Church Reform."

140. Maurits Berger, "Apostasy and Public Policy in Contemporary Egypt: An Evaluation of Recent Cases from Egypt's Highest Courts," *Human Rights Quarterly* 25 (2003): 722.

141. Ibid., 723–724.

142. Ibid., 731, 740.

143. Bishop Murqus, interviewed by the author, 2003.

144. Yūsuf Sidhum, "Civil Register Victims," *al-Watani International (Arab-West Report)*, June 5, 2007.

145. Tamir Shukri, "The Administrative Court: Moving from One Religion to Another Abuses Islam," *Arab-West Report*, May 2–8, 2007.

146. Magdy Malak, "Converts in Court," *Watani International*, May 13, 2007.

147. a.n.m., "The Supreme Administrative Court Ruled in Favor of Reverted Converts," press review for *Arab-West Report*, February 17, 2008.

148. a.n.m., "The Baha'i Case as an Ordeal of Citizenship and Freedom of Belief in Egypt," *Cairo Institute for Human Rights Studies*, January 16, 2007.

149. a.n.m., "Muhammad Hijāzī, Bahāʾīs, and Freedom of Creed in Egypt," press review for *Arab-West Report*, April 2, 2008.

150. Kevin Boyle and Juliet Sheen, *Freedom of Religion and Belief: A World Report* (London: Routledge, 1997), 27.

151. Ibid., 29.

152. a.n.m., "The Baha'i Case as an Ordeal of Citizenship and Freedom of Belief in Egypt."

153. Boyle and Sheen, "Freedom of Religion and Belief," 29.

Chapter 4

1. Abū al-ʿAlā al-Maudūdī was founder of al-Jamāʿa al-Islamiyya, which tried to establish an Islamic state in Pakistan. The group influenced the formulation of the Pakistani constitution.

2. Muhammad al-Ghazālī, *al-Islām al-Muftarā ʿAlayhi Bayn al-Shuyūʿiyīn wa al-Raʾsmāliīn*, 7th ed. (Cairo: Nahdat Misr, 2006), 146–147.

3. Abū al-ʿIlā Mādī and Shaykh Fawzi Fadil al-Zefzaf, "Citizenship within the New Religious Address" (paper presented at the Egyptian German Dialogue Forum Evan-

gelical Academy, Hanover, Germany, April 9–13, 2003); Yūsuf al-Qaradāwī, *Non-Muslims in Islamic Society*, trans. Khalil Muhammad Hamad and Sayed Mahboob Ali Shah (Indianapolis: American Trust Publications, 1985), 2; Kamāl al-Saʿīd Habīb, *al-Harakat al-Islāmiyya min al-Muwājaha ilā al-Murājaʿa* (Cairo: Maktabat Madbūlī, 2002), 192, 161, 141. Muhammad Maʾmūn al-Hudaybī, interviewed by the author, Cairo, 2003.

4. Muhammad Salīm al-ʿAwwā, "al-Taʿaddudiyya al-Siyāsiyya min Manthūr Islāmī," *Minbar al-Hiwār* 6, no. 20 (1991): 130.

5. Hasan al-Bannā, *Six Tracts of Hasan al-Bannā: A Selection from the Majmūʿat Rasāʾil al-Imām al-Shahīd Hasan al-Bannā* (Accra-Ghana: Africa for Publishing and Distribution, 2006), 108, 138–139.

6. Muhammad Maʿmun el-Hodaiby, "Upholding Islam," *Harvard International Review* 19, no. 2 (1997): 6, 20.

7. al-Saʿīd Habīb, *al-Harakat al-Islāmiyya min al-Muwājaha ilā al-Murājaʿa*, 141.

8. al-Bannā, *Six Tracts of Hasan al-Bannā*, 6.

9. el-Hodaiby, "Upholding Islam," 21.

10. Muhammad Maʿmun al-Hudaibi, *The Principles of Politics in Islam*, 2nd ed. (Cairo: Islamic, Inc., 2000), 29.

11. Hans Wehr, *A Dictionary of Modern Written Arabic*, ed. Milton Cowan (Beirut: Librairie du Liban, 1980).

12. Edward Lane, *An Arabic-English Lexicon* (Beirut: Librairie du Liban, 1874), 4:1423.

13. Yvonne Haddad, "Islamists and the Challenge of Pluralism," Occasional Papers (Washington, DC: Center for Contemporary Arab Studies, Georgetown University, 1995), 3.

14. al-Saʿīd Habīb, *al-Harakat al-Islāmiyya min al-Muwājaha ilā al-Murājaʿa*, 141.

15. Shaykh Muhammad Mutawallī al-Shaʿrāwī, *Min Fayd al-Rahmān fī Tarabiyyat al-Insān: Min Qawl al-Imām al-Shaykh Muhammad Mutawallī al-Shaʿrāwī* (Cairo: Kitāb al-Dhahabī, 1986), 150.

16. Ibid., 152.

17. al-Shaykh Mahmūd Fāyid, "Samāhat al-Islām maʿa Ghayr al-Muslimīn," *al-Daʿwa*, October 1980.

18. al-Shaʿrāwī, *Min Fayd al-Rahmān fī Tarabiyyat al-Insān: Min Qawl al-Imām al-Shaykh Muhammad Mutawallī al-Shaʿrāwī*, 147.

19. al-Hudaibi, *The Principles of Politics in Islam*, 28.

20. al-Bannā, *Six Tracts of Hasan al-Bannā*, 138.

21. Shaykh Muhammad Mutawallī al-Shaʿrāwī, *Jamīʿa Fatāwā al-Shaʿrāwī* (Cairo: Dār al-Jalīl, 1999), 1:147. Muhammad al-Ghazālī, *Min Hunā Naʿlam . . . !*, 6th ed. (Cairo: Nahdat Misr, 2006), 120; ʿAbd al-Halīm ʿAuwīs, "Masīrat al-Taʾrīkh bayna al-Islām wa al-Misīhiyya," *al-Daʿwa*, September 1978, 12–14; al-Hudaibi, *The Principles of Politics in Islam*, 35.

22. Muntasir al-Zayyāt, interviewed by the author, Cairo, 2003. Al-Zayyāt has written a book about al-Zawahiri: Montasser al-Zayyat, *The Road to al-Qaeda: The Story of Bin Lāden's Right-Hand Man* (London: Pluto Press, 2004).

23. Muhammad Ma'mūn al-Hudaybī, interviewed by the author, 2003.

24. Abul A'lā Maudūdī, *Rights of Non-Muslims in Islamic State*, trans. Khurshid Ahmad (Lahore, Pakistan: Islamic Publications, 1961), 26.

25. This view ranges from al-Qaradāwī to al-Jamā'a al-Islāmiyya; al-Qaradāwī, *Non-Muslims in Islamic Society*, 25; Hishām Mubārak, *al-Irhābiūn Qādimūn: Dirāsat Muqārana bayn Mawqif al-Ikhwān al-Muslimīn wa Jamā'āt al-Jihād min Qadiyyat al-'Unf (1929–1994)* (Cairo: Kitāb al-Mahrūsa, 1995), 378.

26. Muhammad 'Abd al-Qudūs, "Limāthā Nu'ārid Fikr Majma' al-Adyān," *al-Da'wa*, January 1980, 20–21.

27. Ibid.

28. Mubārak, *al-Irhābiūn Qādimūn*, 378.

29. Yūsuf al-Qaradāwī, *The Lawful and the Prohibited in Islam*, trans. M. Siddiqi, K. al-Hilbawi, and S. Shukri (Cairo: al-Falah, 2001), 57.

30. al-Sha'rāwī, *Min Fayd al-Rahmān fī Tarabiyyat al-Insān*, 151.

31. Muhammad al-Ghazālī, *Jihād al-Da'wa bayn 'Ajz al-Dākhil wa Kayd al-Khārij* (Cairo: Dār al-Nahda, 2001), 47.

32. Most notably Ma'mūn al-Hudaybī and Yūsuf al-Qaradāwī. Hilmī al-Namnam, "Hal la Tazāl Bilād al-Gharb Dār al-Kufr wa 'Anād?" *al-Musawwar*, November 23, 2001, 52.

33. Edward Lane, *An Arabic-English Lexicon*, 2:570.

34. al-Hudaibi, *The Principles of Politics in Islam*, 29; al-Ghazālī, *Jihād al-Da'wa bayn 'Ajz al-Dākhil wa Kayd al-Khārij*, 21.

35. 'Isām al-'Aryān, interviewed by the author, Cairo, 2003.

36. Fāyid, "Samāhat al-Islām ma'a Ghayr al-Muslimīn."

37. Ibid.

38. Muslim Brotherhood, "Mb Parliamentary Bloc Wishes Christians Merry Christmas," http://www.ikwanweb.com/article.php?id=668.

39. Muhammad Ma'mūn al-Hudaybī, interviewed by the author, 2003.

40. al-Qaradāwī, *Non-Muslims in Islamic Society*, 16, 52.

41. al-Sa'īd Habīb, *al-Harakat al-Islāmiyya min al-Muwājaha Ilā al-Murāja'a*, 192.

42. al-Ghazālī, *Jihād al-Da'wa bayn 'Ajz al-Dākhil wa Kayd al-Khārij*, 21.

43. Sayyid Qutb, *Milestones*, trans. n.m. (Delhi: Millat Book Center, n.d.), 61.

44. Carl Brown, *Religion and State: The Muslim Approach to Politics* (New York: Columbia University Press, 2000), 49–50. However, it is arguable that there was more of an overlap between the two genres.

45. Samīr Murqus, "The Religious Revival/Awakening . . ." (paper presented at a conference, Germany, 2006), 6.

46. Muslim Brotherhood, "The Muslim Brotherhood's Program," http://www ikhwanweb.com/Article.asp?ID=812&SectionID=70.

47. Abū al-ʿIlā Mādī, interviewed by the author, Cairo, 2003; Nabīl ʿAbd al-Fattāh, interviewed by the author, Cairo, 2003; Muhammad Salāh, interviewed by the author, Cairo, 2003; Qutb, *Milestones*, 73; ʿAbūd al-Zumur, "Manhaj Jamāʿāt al-Jihād," in *al-Nabī al-Musallih-al-Rāfidūn*, ed. Said Ahmed Rifʿat, 122 (London: Riyad al-Rayyes, 1991); Muhammad ʿAbd al-Salām Faraj, "The Neglected Duty," in *The Neglected Duty*, ed. Johannes Jansen, 172 (London: Macmillan, 1994).

48. Kamāl al-Saʿīd Habīb was a political science and economics graduate of the University of Cairo; he wrote his master's thesis on minorities in the Ottoman period and earned a Ph.D. in political science. He was a prominent member of al-Jihād and served ten years in prison for his involvement in the events of 1981. He now calls for intellectual revisions inside the Islamic *jihād* movement. He is a current member of the journalists' syndicate; al-Saʿīd Habīb, *al-Harakat al-Islāmiyya min al-Muwājaha ilā al-Murājaʿa*, 192; Kamāl al-Saʿīd Habīb, *al-Aqaliyāt wa al-Siyāsa fī al-Khibra al-Islāmiyya* (Cairo: Maktabat Madbūlī, 2003), 83.

49. Karam Zuhdī et al., *Mubādarat Waqf al-ʿUnf Ruʾya Wāqʿiyya wa Nathara Sharʿiyya* (Cairo: Maktabat al-Turāth al-Islāmī, 2002), 82–86.

50. al-Qaradāwī, *Non-Muslims in Islamic Society*, 2, 19; Maudūdī, *Rights of Non-Muslims in Islamic State*, 20, 10.

51. It must be noted that there is some debate about whether he really said this. Omayma Abdel-Latif, "The Iron Sheikh," Obituary of Mustafa Mashour, 1921–2003, *al-Ahram Weekly*, November 21–27, 2002. Muhammad Salāh has said that he did not say this and that he was misquoted. See Muhammad Salāh, interviewed by the author, Cairo, August 17, 2003. He argues that "the words were taken out of their context" and that he "was talking historically and about the Qurʾan." However, Samīr Murqus argues that it is certain that he said this.

52. Muslim Brotherhood, "Barnāmij Al-Hizb" (2007), 14.

53. Muhammad Maʾmūn al-Hudaybī, interviewed by the author, 2003.

54. Mahmud Shaltut, "A Modernist Interpretation of Jihad: Mahmud Shaltut's Treatise *Koran and Fighting*," in *Jihad in Classical and Modern Islam*, ed. Rudolph Peters, 77–79 (Princeton, NJ: Princeton University Press, 1996).

55. Emmanuel Sivan, "Eavesdropping on Radical Islam," *Middle East Quarterly* (March 1995): 14.

56. Zuhdī et al., *Mubādarat Waqf al-ʿUnf Ruʾya Wāqʿiyya wa Nathara Sharʿiyya*, 82–86.

57. Shaykh Muhammad Mutawallī al-Shaʿrawī, *al-Shaykh al-Imām Muhammad Mutawallī al-Shaʿrawī fī al-Hukm wa al-Siyāsa* (Egypt: Dar al Asmāʾ, 1990), 22; Yusuf Kamāl, "al-Jizya: Qāʿidat al-Takāful Lighayr al-Muslimīn," *al-Daʿwa*, January 1980.

58. al-Saʿīd Habīb, *al-Harakat al-Islāmiyya min al-Muwājaha ilā al-Murājaʿa*, 205.

59. Muntasir al-Zayyāt, interviewed by the author, 2003; Mamdūh Ismāʿīl, interviewed by the author, Cairo, 2003.

60. Mamdūh ʿIsmāʿīl, interviewed by the author, Cairo, 2003. Mamdūh Ismāʿīl was imprisoned for three years following the assassination of Anwar Sadat. He was arrested in March 2007 and accused of complicity in an "Egyptian project" of al-Qaeda. He was presumably released, because he is now assistant secretary general of the Islamic Lawyers' League and the group's spokesman. In June 2009 the group announced that it intends to set up a political party called the Sharīʿa Party to advocate the implementation of Islamic law in Egypt.

61. Muslim Brotherhood, "The Muslim Brotherhood's Program."

62. ʿAbd al-Qudūs, "Limāthā Nuʿārid Fikr Majmaʿ al-Adyān."

63. Maudūdī, *Rights of Non-Muslims in Islamic State*, 4–5.

64. Sayyid Qutb, *Hādhā al-Dīn* (Kuwait: Maktabat al-Faysal, 1989), 19.

65. al-Saʿīd Habīb, *al-Harakat al-Islāmiyya min al-Muwājaha ilā al-Murājaʿa*, 192, 208.

66. Ibid., 141.

67. al-Hudaibi, *The Principles of Politics in Islam*, 7–8; al-Qaradāwī, *Non-Muslims in Islamic Society*, 23; Maudūdī, *Rights of Non-Muslims in Islamic State*, 13.

68. al-Hudaibi, *The Principles of Politics in Islam*, 8.

69. al-Qaradāwī, *Non-Muslims in Islamic Society*, 18.

70. Ibid., 11; Maudūdī, *Rights of Non-Muslims in Islamic State*, 13.

71. Muhammad al-Bāz, "al-Hudaybī—Nurīd an Natafāhum maʿa al-Dawla . . . Lakin la Ahad Yurīd an Yasmaʿ Lanā," *Sawt al-Umma*, August 25, 2003.

72. a.n.m., "al-Masīhiūn fī Misr wa al-Hukm Yashra Allah," *al-Daʿwa*, February 1977.

73. Sayyid Qutb, *Social Justice in Islam*, trans. John Hardie (New York: Octagon Books, 1970), 47. He is taking the Hanafi view since in the Hanbali, Shafiʿi, and Maliki view non-Muslims are not equal in *qisās*. Maudūdī, *Rights of Non-Muslims in Islamic State*, 12–13.

74. Muhammad Maʾmūn al-Hudaybī, interviewed by the author, 2003; Maudūdī, *Rights of Non-Muslims in Islamic State*, 13.

75. Mubārak, *al-Irhābiūn Qādimūn*, 345. Jamāʿat al-Jihād al-Islāmī, "Wathīqat Muhākamat al-Nithām al-Siyāsī al-Misrī—1982," in *al-Nabī al-Musallih-al-Rāfidūn*, ed. Said Ahmed Rifʾat, 190 (London: Riyad al-Rayyes, 1991).

76. Muntasir al-Zayyāt, interviewed by the author, 2003.

77. al-Qaradāwī, *Non-Muslims in Islamic Society*, 5.

78. Mamdūh Ismāʿīl, interviewed by the author, 2003.

79. al-Qaradāwī, *The Lawful and the Prohibited in Islam*, 92, 161–162.

80. al-Shaʿrāwī, *Jamīʿa Fatāwā al-Shaʿrawī*, 1:252, 1:111.

81. ʿUmād Nāsif, *Duktūr ʿUmar ʿAbd al-Kāfī . . .* (Cairo: Dār al-Hadaf lil Nashr, 1993), 105–108.

82. Sivan, "Eavesdropping on Radical Islam," 16.

83. Muhammad Shibl, "Who Says That You Represent the True Religion (Man Alathī Qāl Innakum Tumaththiilūn Sahīh al-Dīn)," *al-Qāhira*, July 22, 2003. al-Azhar refutes the understanding that the Hadith means that it is *harām* to greet Jews and Christians.

84. Mubārak, *al-Irhābiūn Qādimūn*, 379, 390. Mubarak states that the government was happy to divide the authority, so in some areas the Jamāʿāt imposed its own rules, 382. Victor E. Makari, *Ibn Taymiyya's Ethics: The Social Factor*, American Academy of Religion Series 34 (Chico, CA: Scholars Press, 1983), 131.

85. Muhammad Salāh, interviewed by the author, 2003.

86. al-Jihād al-Islāmī, "Wathīqat Muhākamat al-Nithām al-Siyāsī al-Misrī—1982," 276; Mubārak, *al-Irhābiūn Qādimūn*, 343–344; ʿUmar ʿAbd al-Rahmān, *Kalimat al-Haqq* (Cairo: Dar al-ʾItisām, n.d.), 29.

87. al-Jihād al-Islāmī, "Wathīqat Muhākamat al-Nithām al-Siyāsī al-Misrī—1982," 189; Mubārak, *al-Irhābiūn Qādimūn*, 345.

88. Qutb, *Milestones*, 75.

89. Muntasir al-Zayyāt, interviewed by the author, 2003.

90. Mamdūh Ismāʿīl, interviewed by the author, 2003.

91. al-Ghazālī, *Min Hunā Naʿlam . . . !*, 122–123.

92. Hasan al-Bannā, *Majmūʿat Rasāʾil al-Imām al-Shahīd Hasan al-Bannā* (Beirut: Dār al-Andalus, 1965), 18; al-Bannā, *Six Tracts of Hasan al-Bannā*, 73.

93. Muhammad Maʾmun al-Hudaibi, *A Quiet Discussion on Heated Issues* (Cairo: al-Falāh, 2000), 15.

94. Ibid., 15; Yūsuf al-Qaradāwī, *State in Islam* (Cairo: al-Falāh, 1998), 240; al-Bannā, *Six Tracts of Hasan al-Bannā*, 6.

95. al-Ghazālī, *Min Hunā Naʿlam . . . !*, 130.

96. al-Hudaibi, *A Quiet Discussion on Heated Issues*, 68.

97. Muslim Brotherhood, "Barnāmij al-Hizb," 10–11.

98. Yusuf Ali has chosen to translate *awliyāʾ* as "friends or protectors," but it could also be translated as "rulers or masters."

99. Murqus, "The Religious Revival/Awakening . . . ," 19.

100. 5:72 and 5:73, Muhammad Shibl, "Islam and the Kitabis," *October Magazine (Arab-West Report)*, November 30–December 5, 2000.

101. Maudūdī, *Rights of Non-Muslims in Islamic State*, 1–4.

102. Ibid., 27–28.

103. Ibid., 30.

104. Ibid., 29.

105. Mamdūh Ismāʿīl, interviewed by the author, 2003.

106. al-Saʿīd Habīb, *al-Harakat al-Islāmiyya Min al-Muwājaha Ilā al-Murājaʿa.*, 208; Kamāl al-Saʿīd Habīb, interviewed by the author, Cairo, 2003.

107. al-Qaradāwī, *Non-Muslims in Islamic Society*, 12; al-Hudaibi, *The Principles of Politics in Islam*, 8.

108. al-Bannā, *Majmūʿat Rasāʾil al-Imām al-Shahīd Hasan al-Bannā*, 13.

109. al-Qaradāwī, *State in Islam*, 299–300.

110. al-Qaradāwī, *Non-Muslims in Islamic Society*, 14.

111. Ibid., 25.

112. al-Hudaibi, *The Principles of Politics in Islam*, 36; Maʾmūn al-Hudaybī, interviewed by the author, 2003.

113. al-Hudaibi, *A Quiet Discussion on Heated Issues*, 57.

114. Muhammad Maʾmūn al-Hudaybī, interviewed by the author, 2003.

115. al-Hudaibi, *A Quiet Discussion on Heated Issues*, 57; al-Bāz, "al-Hudaybī—Nurīd an Natafāhum maʿa al-Dawla . . . Lakin la Ahad Yurīd an Yasmaʿ Lanā."

116. al-Hudaibi, *A Quiet Discussion on Heated Issues*, 57.

117. Maʾmūn al-Hudaybī, interviewed by the author, 2003.

118. al-Bāz, "al-Hudaybī—Nurīd an Natafāhum maʿa al-Dawla . . . Lakin La Ahad Yurīd an Yasmaʿ Lanā."

119. Muntasir al-Zayyāt, interviewed by the author, 2003; ʿIsām al-ʿAryān, interviewed by the author, 2003.

120. Mashārī al-Dhaydī, "Ayna Yaqif al-Islāmiyyūn min Mafhūm al-Wataniyya?" *Al-Sharq al-Awsat*, October 14, 2003.

121. al-Bannā, *Six Tracts of Hasan al-Bannā*, 66.

122. Ibid., 70–71.

123. Qutb, *Milestones*, 117.

124. Ibid., 118–119.

125. Muhammad Salāh, interviewed by the author, 2003.

126. Mamdūh Ismāʿīl, interviewed by the author, 2003.

127. Muhammad Maʾmūn al-Hudaybī, interviewed by the author, 2003.

128. al-Hudaibi, *The Principles of Politics in Islam*, 29.

129. al-Qaradāwī, *Non-Muslims in Islamic Society*, 46; Fāyid, "Samāhat al-Islām maʿa Ghayr al-Muslimīn"; Muntasir al-Zayyāt, interviewed by the author, 2003.

130. al-Qaradāwī, *Non-Muslims in Islamic Society*, 46.

131. Usāma Salāma, "Egypt Torn Apart by Extremist Muslim Brotherhood Members and Copts," *Ruz al-Yūsuf (Arab-West Report)*, January 27, 2007. ʿIzzat is sixty-two years old and is a professor of medicine at Zaqaziq University.

132. al-Shaʿrawī, *al-Shaykh al-Imām Muhammad Mutawalli al-Shaʿrawī fī al-Hukm wa al-Siyāsa*, 22.

133. al-Qaradāwī, *Non-Muslims in Islamic Society*, 2.

134. Muhammad Ma'mūn al-Hudaybī, interviewed by the author, 2003; al-Qaradāwī, *Non-Muslims in Islamic Society*, 6–7.

135. Maudūdī, *Rights of Non-Muslims in Islamic State*, 15.

136. Karam Zuhdī, "The Leader of al-Jamā'a al-Islāmiyya Speaks inside the High-Security Prison," *al-Sharq al-Awsat*, July 16, 2003.

137. Nāsif, *Duktūr 'Umar 'Abd al-Kāfī . . .* , 85.

138. 'Umar al-Tilmisānī, "Hā'ulā'i al-Jahūd: Lā 'Ahd Lahum wa Lā Dhimma," *al-Da'wa*, October 1979.

139. Qutb, *Hādhā al-Dīn*, 17; Qutb, *Milestones*, 82–83; Quoting the Qur'an (9:30, 5:73, and 5:18), Qutb condemns Christians for distorting original beliefs; 'Abd al-Qudūs, "Limāthā Nu'ārid Fikr Majma' al-Adyān"; Shaltut, "A Modernist Interpretation of Jihad," 77; Ahmad al-Mahallāwī, *Khutub al-Shaykh Ahmad al-Mahallāwī Hawla Kul ma Yuhim al-Muslim fī Dīnihi wa Dunyahi* (Cairo: Dār al-'Itisām, n.d.), 2:147.

140. Sayyid Qutb, *al-Islām wa Muskilat al-Hadāra* (Cairo: Dār al-Shurūq, 1983), 58–59.

141. Muhammad al-Ghazālī, *Humūm Dā'iyya* (Cairo: Dār al-Bashīr, n.d.), 73, 77–88.

142. Vivian Fu'ād, interviewed by the author, Cairo, 2003.

143. However, there is a distinction to be made between *fiqh* and *tafsīr*: for practical purposes and in *fiqh*, Christians and Jews were given the status of *ahl al-kitāb* and enjoyed the protection of *dhimma* status. In *tafsīr*, the distinction between *ahl al-kitāb* and pagans was not so clear cut.

144. Sayyid Qutb, *Fī Zilāl al-Qur'ān* (Beirut: Dār al-Shurūq, 1982), 4:557.

145. William Shepard, "Sayyid Qutb's Doctrine of Jahiliyya," *International Journal of Middle East Studies* 35, no. 4 (2003): 527.

146. Qutb, *Milestones*, 70. This is also implied by al-Zumur, "Manhaj Jamā'āt al-Jihād," 122.

147. Qutb, *Milestones*, 113. In addition to "Oh you who believe! If ye listen to a faction among the People of the Book, they would (indeed) render you apostates after ye have believed! (3:100)"; Qutb, *Milestones*, 113. "Oh ye who believe! Take not for friends Unbelievers rather than Believers (4:144); Qutb, *Fī Zilāl al-Qur'ān*, 554–556.

148. Qutb, *Fī Zilāl al-Qur'ān*, 566.

149. Ibid.

150. Mubārak, *al-Irhābiūn Qādimūn*, 378.

151. Gilles Kepel, *The Prophet and Pharaoh: Muslim Extremism in Egypt*, trans. Jon Rothschild (London: al-Saqi, 1985), 207–208.

152. 'Abd al-Rahmān, *Kalimat al-Haqq*, 6, 58, 62. Shaykh 'Umar 'Abd al-Rahmān had close associations with al-Jamā'a al-Islāmiyya and al-Jihād and was the former group's *muftī*. 'Abd al-Rahmān was not convicted for his involvement in the assassination of Sadat, but was expelled from Egypt and went to Afghanistan and then on to the

United States. He is currently in prison in the United States for his involvement in the World Trade Center bombings in 1993.

153. 'Abd al-Qudūs, "Limāthā Nu'ārid Fikr Majma' al-Adyān."

154. Emmanuel Sivan, *Interpretations of Islam, Past and Present* (Princeton, NJ: Darwin Press, 1985), 3; Amin Maalouf, *The Crusades through Arab Eyes* (London: al-Saqi, 1984), i.

155. Sivan, *Interpretations of Islam, Past and Present*, 5, 7, 9.

156. Qutb, *Social Justice in Islam*, 235.

157. 'Alī al-Qādī, "Tahdīd al-Nasl Bayn Islām wa al-Misīhiyya," *al-Da'wa*, June 1981; a.n.m., "Haqā'iq Nuqadimuha lil-Mas'ūlīn Hawl Ahdāth al-Zawiya al-Hamra," *al-Da'wa*, July 1981, 20–21.

158. al-Jamā'at al-Islāmiyya, "Al-Ab'ād al-Haqīqiyya Lil Fitna al-Tā'ifiyya," *al-Da'wa*, June 1980.

159. Sālim al-Rahhāl, "Amrīka wa Misr wa al-Haraka al-Islāmiyya," in *al-Nabī al-Musallih-al-Rāfidūn*, ed. Said Ahmed Rif'at, 183 (London: Riyad al-Rayyes, 1991).

160. Kamāl al-Sa'īd Habīb, "Min Manthūr Jamā'at al-Jihād al-Islāmī," in *al-Nabī al-Musallih-al-Rāfidūn*, ed. Said Ahmed Rif'at, 204 (London: Riyad al-Rayyes, 1991).

161. Shaykh Kishk, *al-Munāthara* (Cairo: Nur Lil Intāg wa al-Tawzi'a al-Islāmī, n.d.).

162. 'Abd al-Salām Faraj, "The Neglected Duty," 174; Ibn Abdul Wahhab also saw Christians as *mushrikūn* who would lead Muslims to *shirk*. See Elizabeth Sirriyeh, "Wahhabis, Unbelievers, and the Problems of Exclusivism," *British Society for Middle East Studies* 16, no. 2 (1989): 126; 'Abd al-Rahmān, *Kalimat al-Haqq*, 47–48; al-Jamā'a al-Islāmiyya al-Jihādiyya, "Safhāt Min Mithāq al-'Amal al-Islāmī," in *al-Nabī al-Musallih-al-Rāfidūn*, ed. Said Ahmed Rif'at, 169 (London: Riyad al-Rayyes, 1991).

163. 'Abd al-Rahmān, *Kalimat al-Haqq*, 127.

164. Mubārak, *al-Irhābiūn Qādimūn*, 16.

165. Hamied Ansari, "Sectarian Conflict and the Political Expediency of Religion," *Middle East Journal* 38 (Summer 1984): 415.

166. Mubārak, *al-Irhābiūn Qādimūn*, 378.

167. Ibid., 380–381.

168. Ibid., 378.

169. Shukrī Mustāfa, "al-Nas al-Kāmil Li Aqwāl wa I'tirāfāt," in *al-Nabī al-Musallih-al-Thā'irūn*, ed. Said Ahmed Rif'at, 85–87 (London: Riyad al-Rayyes, 1991).

170. al-Jihādiyya, "Safhāt Min Mithāq al-'Amal al-Islāmī," 168.

171. al-Ghazālī, *Jihād al-Da'wa Bayn 'Ajz al-Dākhil wa Kayd al-Khārij*, 20; Yūsuf al-Qaradāwī, *al-Sahwa al-Islāmiyya Min al-Murāhaqa Ilā al-Rushd* (Cairo: Dār al-Shurūq, 2002), 224; Shaltut, "A Modernist Interpretation of Jihad," 78.

172. a.n.m., "al-Aqbāt fī Murāj'āt Qādat al-Jamā'āt al-Islāmiyya," *al-Midān*, August 21, 2003.

173. Rafīq Habīb, interviewed by the author, Cairo, 2003.

174. Abdul Latif, Omayma, "Defending the Faith," *al-Ahram Weekly*, October 24–30, 2002.

175. Rafīq Habīb, interviewed by the author, 2003.

176. Ibid.

177. Cornelis Hulsman, "Freedom of Religion in Egypt," *Arab-West Report*, September 4, 2003; Hānī Labīb, "Amrīka . . . wa Muhawalāt al-Saytara ʿAlā Misīhī Misr Munthu al-Qarn 19," *al-Midān*, August 21, 2003.

178. Saad Eddin Ibrāhīm, interviewed by the author, Cairo, 2003.

179. Cornelis Hulsman, interviewed by the author, Cairo, 2007.

180. Murqus, "The Religious Revival/Awakening . . . ," 6.

Chapter 5

1. Ann Lambton, *State and Government in Medieval Islam: An Introduction to the Study of Islamic Political Theory* (Oxford: Oxford University Press, 1981), 204.

2. Nadav Safran, *Egypt in Search of Political Community: An Analysis of the Intellectual and Political Evolution of Egypt, 1804–1952* (Cambridge, M.A.: Harvard University Press, 1961), 23–24.

3. This began to change with the concepts of *watan* and *wataniyya* as introduced by Rifāʿa al-Tahtāwī (1801–1873).

4. Bernard Lewis, *The Political Language of Islam* (Chicago: University of Chicago Press, 1988), 63.

5. Hans Wehr, *A Dictionary of Modern Written Arabic*, ed. Milton Cowan (Beirut: Librairie du Liban, 1980), 1079.

6. Edward Lane, *An Arabic-English Lexicon* (Beirut: Librairie du Liban, 1874), 8:3056.

7. Lewis, *The Political Language of Islam*, 40, 63.

8. Rifa'a Badawi Rafi al-Tahtāwī, "Fatherland and Patriotism," in *Islam in Transition: Muslim Perspectives*, ed. John J. Donohue and John L. Esposito, 11–12 (New York: Oxford University Press, 1982).

9. Sometimes the thought of Ahmed Kamāl Abū Magd is also included. See Ahmed Kamāl Abū Magd, *Hiwār al-Muwājaha* (Cairo: Dār al-Shurūq, 1988), although he is not mentioned in Muhammad Salīm al-ʿAwwā's list: Muhammad Salīm al-ʿAwwā, *Lildīn wa al-Watan Fusūl fī ʿAlaqat al-Muslimīn bi Ghayr al-Muslimīn* (Cairo: Nahdat Misr, 2006).

10. Al-ʿAwwā graduated from law school in 1963 and went on to receive diplomas in Islamic law and general law. He then received a Ph.D. in comparative law at London University in 1972.

11. Al-Bishrī is a 1953 graduate of Cairo University Law school.

12. Fahmī Huwaydī, *Muwātinūn lā Dhimmiūn: Mawqiʿ Ghayr al-Muslimīn fī*

Mujtama'a al-Muslimīn, 3rd ed. (Cairo: Dār al-Shurūq, 1999), 8; Tāriq al-Bishrī, interviewed by the author, Cairo, 2003.

13. al-'Awwā, *Lil dīn wa al-Watan Fusūl fī 'Alaqat al-Muslimīn bi Ghayr al-Muslimīn* (Cairo: Nahdat Misr, 2006), 21–22.

14. Muhammad Salīm al-'Awwā, "al-Ta'addudiyya al-Siyāsiyya min Manthūr Islāmī," *Minbar al-Hiwār* 6, no. 20 (1991): 130.

15. Fahmī Huwaydī, "Taqdīm Fahmī Huwaydī," in *al-Aqbāt: al-Kanīsa am al-Watan; Qissat al Bābā Shanūda al-Thālith*, ed. Abdul Latīf al-Manāwī, 9, 11 (Cairo: Dār al-Shabāb al-'Arabī, 1992).

16. al-'Awwā, "al-Ta'addudiyya al-Siyāsiyya min Manthūr Islāmī," 131.

17. Muhammad 'Imāra, *al-Islām wa al-'Aqaliyāt: al-Mādī, wa al-Hādir, wa al-Mustaqbal* (Cairo: Maktabat al-Shurūq al-Dawliyya, 2003), 21.

18. al-'Awwā, "al-Ta'addudiyya al-Siyāsiyya min Manthūr Islāmī," 131.

19. Huwaydī, *Muwātinūn lā Dhimmiūn*, 7–8, 110–111.

20. Muhammad Salīm al-'Awwā, *Fī al-Nithām al-Siyāsī lil Dawla al-Islāmiyya* (Cairo: Dār al-Shurūq, 1989), 257.

21. Muhammad Salīm al-'Awwā, interviewed by the author, Cairo, 2003.

22. Fahmī Huwaydī, interviewed by the author, Cairo, 2003. The terms he uses are *'ibādāt* for rules relating to worship and *mu'amālāt* for rules relating to relations between people.

23. al-'Awwā, *Fī al-Nithām al-Siyāsī lil Dawla al-Islāmiyya*, 251.

24. Tāriq al-Bishrī, *Bayn al-Jāmi'a al-Dīniyya wa al-Jāmi'a al-Wataniyya fī al-Fikr al-Siyāsī* (Cairo: Dār al-Shurūq, 1998), 28.

25. Huwaydī, *Muwātinūn lā Dhimmiūn*, 111; Fahmī Huwaydī, interviewed by the author, 2003.

26. Muhammad Salīm al-'Awwā, "Ahl al-Dhimma fī al-Nithām al-Huqūqī al-Islāmī," *al-Hayāt al-Tayyiba*, no. 11 (4th year) (2003): 181; al-'Awwā, *Fī al-Nithām al-Siyāsī lil Dawla al-Islāmiyya*, 256; Muhammad Salīm al-'Awwā, interviewed by the author, 2003.

27. Tāriq al-Bishrī, *al-Muslimūn wa al-Aqbāt fī Itār al-Jamā'a al-Wataniyya*, 2nd ed. (Cairo: Dār al-Shurūq, 1988), 680; al-Bishrī, *Bayn al-Jāmi'a al-Dīniyya wa al-Jāmi'a al-Wataniyya fī al-Fikr al-Siyāsī*, 38.

28. Huwaydī, *Muwātinūn lā Dhimmiūn: Mawqi' Ghayr al-Muslimīn fī Mujtama'a al-Muslimīn*, 125.

29. Tāriq al-Bishrī, interviewed by the author, 2003.

30. Muhammad Salīm al-'Awwā, interviewed by the author, 2003.

31. Huwaydī, *Muwātinūn lā Dhimmiūn*, 129, 131.

32. Tāriq al-Bishrī, interviewed by the author, 2003; 'Imāra, *al-Islām wa al-'Aqaliyāt*, 15.

33. The Arabic for this phrase is *'an yadin wa-hum sāghirūn.*

34. The *sāghir*. Huwaydī, *Muwātinūn lā Dhimmiūn*, 139–141.

35. al-ʿAwwā, *Fī al-Nithām al-Siyāsī Lil Dawla al-Islāmiyya*, 256; Muhammad ʿImāra, interviewed by the author, Cairo, 2003; al-ʿAwwā, "Ahl al-Dhimma fī al-Nithām al-Huqūqī al-Islāmī," 181–182.

36. Tāriq al-Bishrī, interviewed by the author, 2003.

37. Muhammad Salīm al-ʿAwwā, interviewed by the author, 2003; al-ʿAwwā, "Ahl al-Dhimma fī al-Nithām al-Huqūqī al-Islāmī," 182.

38. ʿImāra, *al-Islām wa al-ʾAqaliyāt: al-Māḍī, wa al-Hāḍir, wa al-Mustaqbal*, 15.

39. Muhammad Salīm al-ʿAwwā, interviewed by the author, 2003; al-Bishrī, *al-Muslimūn wa al-Aqbāt fī Itār al-Jamāʿa al-Wataniyya*, 681; Bisan Hassab, "Tariq al-Bishri: The Application of Sharʾiah in Egypt Will Not Affect the Rights of Copts because the Principle of Citizenship Is Fundamentally Rooted Therein," *al-Dustūr (Arab-West Report)*, May 14, 2007.

40. Charles Kurzman, *Liberal Islam: A Sourcebook* (Oxford: Oxford University Press, 1998), 14; al-ʿAwwā, *Fī al-Nithām al-Siyāsī lil Dawla al-Islāmiyya*, 55–56; al-ʿAwwā, "Ahl al-Dhimma fī al-Nithām al-Huqūqī al-Islāmī," 180.

41. Muhammad ʿImāra, interviewed by the author, Cairo, 2007.

42. al-ʿAwwā, "Ahl al-Dhimma fī al-Nithām al-Huqūqī al-Islāmī," 182.

43. al-ʿAwwā, *Fī al-Nithām al-Siyāsī lil Dawla al-Islāmiyya*, 67.

44. Kurzman, *Liberal Islam*, 14–16; al-ʿAwwā, "al-Taʿaddudiyya al-Siyāsiyya min Manthūr Islāmī," 133; al-ʿAwwā, *Fī al-Nithām al-Siyāsī lil Dawla al-Islāmiyya*, 117.

45. Reda Okasha, "Dr Selim Al-Awa in His Special Interview: The Khilafa System Is Not Inspired," *al-Liwāʾ al-Islāmī (Arab-West Report)*, December 16–22, 1999.

46. al-ʿAwwā, "Ahl al-Dhimma fī al-Nithām al-Huqūqī al-Islāmī," 182; al-ʿAwwā, *Lil Dīn wa al-Watan Fusūl fī ʿAlaqat al-Muslimīn bi Ghayr al-Muslimīn*, 22; al-ʿAwwā, *Fī al-Nithām al-Siyāsī Lil Dawla al-Islāmiyya*, 257.

47. *Siyāda*. al-ʿAwwā, "Ahl al-Dhimma fī al-Nithām al-Huqūqī al-Islāmī," 182.

48. Tāriq al-Bishrī, interviewed by the author, 2003; al-Bishrī, *al-Muslimūn wa al-Aqbāt fī Itār al-Jamāʿa al-Wataniyya*, 135–136.

49. However, it is a mistake to argue that the state is peculiar to the region. Ayubi argues that the state "may not be an Arab or an Islamic peculiarity," since there "are indeed potentially both non-individualistic and non-European paths to the state"; Nazih Ayubi, *Over-Stating the Arab State: Politics and Society in the Middle East* (London: I.B. Tauris, 1999), 15, 3.

50. al-ʿAwwā, *Lil Dīn wa al-Watan Fusūl fī ʿAlaqat al-Muslimīn bi Ghayr al-Muslimīn*, 21–22; Muhammad Salīm al-ʿAwwā, interviewed by the author, 2003.

51. al-Bishrī, *Bayn al-Jāmiʿa al-Dīniyya wa al-Jāmiʿa al-Wataniyya fī al-Fikr al-Siyāsī*, 33.

52. Tāriq al-Bishrī, interviewed by the author, 2003.

53. al-Bishrī, *al-Muslimūn wa al-Aqbāt fī Itār al-Jamāʿa al-Wataniyya*, 681.

54. al-Bishrī, *Bayn al-Jāmiʿa al-Dīniyya wa al-Jāmiʿa al-Wataniyya fī al-Fikr al-Siyāsī*, 33.

55. al-Bishrī, *al-Muslimūn wa al-Aqbāt fī Itār al-Jamāʿa al-Wataniyya*, 5.

56. The terms al-Bishrī uses are *al-mawrūth* (indigenous) and *al-wāfid* (introduced); ibid., 681.

57. Ibid., 680.

58. Ibid., 43.

59. Huwaydī, *Muwātinūn lā Dhimmiūn*, 123–124.

60. ʿImāra, *al-Islām wa al-ʾAqaliyāt*, 17–19, 43; Muhammad ʿImāra, *Samāhat al-Islām* (Cairo: al-Falāh, 2002), 32.

61. Muhammad ʿImāra, interviewed by the author, 2003.

62. al-Bishrī, *Bayn al-Jāmiʿa al-Dīniyya wa al-Jāmiʿa al-Wataniyya fī al-Fikr al-Siyāsī*, 681.

63. Rafīq Habīb, *Hadārat al-Wasat: Nahwa Usūliyya Jadīda* (Cairo: Dār al-Shurūq, 2001), 5, 168–169, 219. Rafīq Habīb, *Ihyāʾ al-Taqālīd al-ʿArabiyya* (Cairo: Dār al-Shurūq, 2003), 5; Rafīq Habīb, interviewed by the author, Cairo, 2003.

64. Rafīq Habīb, interviewed by the author, 2003; Habīb, *Ihyāʾ al-Taqālīd al-ʿArabiyya*, 64.

65. a.n.m., "Strongholds of Orthodoxy: Whatever the Copts' Place in Society at Large, the Heart of Their Religious and Community Life Remains Intact," *Cairo Times (Arab-West Report)*, February 4–10, 1999.

66. Yūsuf al-Qaradāwī, *al-Sahwa al-Islāmiyya Min al-Murāhaqa ilā al-Rushd* (Cairo: Dār al-Shurūq, 2002), 225.

67. Rafīq Habīb, interviewed by the author, 2003; a.n.m., "Strongholds of Orthodoxy."

68. Rafīq Habīb, interviewed by the author, Cairo, 2007.

69. Ibid.; Rafīq Habīb, interviewed by the author, 2003.

70. Habīb, *Hadārat al-Wasat*, 233–234.

71. Huwaydī, *Muwātinūn lā Dhimmiūn*, 120.

72. Patricia Crone, "Mawlā," in *Encyclopaedia of Islam²* (Leiden: Brill, 1991).

73. Huwaydī, *Muwātinūn lā Dhimmiūn*, 158.

74. Tāriq al-Bishrī, interviewed by the author, 2003; al-Bishrī, *al-Muslimūn wa al-Aqbāt fī Itār al-Jamāʿa al-Wataniyya*, 135–136.

75. Muhammad ʿImāra, interviewed by the author, 2003.

76. ʿImāra, *al-Islām wa al-ʾAqaliyāt*, 19.

77. Ibid., 17, 19; ʿImāra, *Samāhat al-Islām*, 45.

78. al-ʿAwwā, *Fī al-Nithām al-Siyāsī lil Dawla al-Islāmiyya*, 249.

79. Ibid., 246.

80. al-Qaradāwī, *al-Sahwa al-Islāmiyya min al-Murāhaqa Ilā al-Rushd*, 225–226.

81. Tāriq al-Bishrī, interviewed by the author, 2003.

82. Fahmī Huwaydī, interviewed by the author, Cairo, 2007.

83. Abū al-'Ilā Mādī and Shaykh Fawzi Fadil al-Zefzaf, "Citizenship within the New Religious Address" (paper presented at the Egyptian German Dialogue Forum Evangelical Academy, Hanover, Germany, April 9–13, 2003).

84. The term that is used is *thawābit*. Fahmī Huwaydī, interviewed by the author, 2007; Abū al-'Ilā Mādī, interviewed by the author, Cairo, 2007.

85. Abū al-'Ilā Mādī, *al-Wasat Party Program (2004)* (Cairo: al-Azzazy Press, 2004), 7.

86. Mādī, "Citizenship within the New Religious Address."

87. Abū al-'Ilā Mādī, interviewed by the author, Cairo, 2003.

88. Mādī, *al-Wasat Party Program (2004)*, 3–4.

89. Abū al-'Ilā Mādī, interviewed by the author, 2003.

90. Fahmī Huwaydī, interviewed by the author, 2007.

91. 'Isām al-'Aryān, interviewed by the author, Cairo, 2003; 'Isām al-'Aryān, interviewed by the author, Cairo, 2007.

92. Nabīl 'Abd al-Fattāh, interviewed by the author, Cairo, 2007.

93. 'Abd al-Mun'im Abū al-Futūh, interviewed by the author, Cairo, 2007; 'Abd al-Mun'im Abū al-Futūh, interviewed by the author, Cairo, 2003; 'Abd al-Mun'im Abū al-Futūh, "Makānat al-Muwātana fī al-Mafhūm al-Islāmī Lil islāh" (unpublished paper, Cairo, 2008).

94. Abū al-Futūh, "Makānat al-Muwātana fī al-Mafhūm al-Islāmī lil islāh."

95. Ibid.

96. 'Abd al-Mun'im Abū al-Futūh, interviewed by the author, 2003.

97. Ibid.; Said Shu'eeb, "Dr Abdel Monem Abul Futouh: We Do Not Object to a Christian Being Elected President of Egypt," *al-Sharq al-Awsat (Arab-West Report)*, October 5, 2003, 15.

98. Muhammad Habīb, interviewed by the author, Cairo, 2007.

99. Ibid.

100. Muslim Brotherhood, "The Muslim Brotherhood's Program," http://www.ikhwanweb.com/Article.asp?ID=812&SectionID=70, 7, 34; Muslim Brotherhood, "Barnāmij al-Hizb" (2007), 13.

101. Muslim Brotherhood, "Barnāmij al-Hizb," 16.

102. Ibid., 14, 10; Bahey eldin Hassan, "Muslim Brothers Party's Platform in Egypt from a Human Rights Perspective" (paper presented at the Center for the Study of Islam and Democracy conference "Political Islam and Democracy—What Do Islamists and Islamic Movements Want?" May 2008).

103. Muhammad Mahdī 'Ākif, "Muslim Brotherhood Initiative on the General Principles of Reform in Egypt," (circular, Cairo, 2004), 32.

104. Muhammad Ma'mun el-Hodaiby, "Upholding Islam," *Harvard International*

Review 19, no. 2 (1997): 29; Muhammad Ma'mun al-Hudaibi, *A Quiet Discussion on Heated Issues* (Cairo: al-Falāh, 2000), 56.

105. Ma'mūn al-Hudaybī, interviewed by the author, Cairo, 2003.

106. 'Isām al-'Aryān, interviewed by the author, 2003.

107. Yūsuf al-Qaradāwī, *The Lawful and the Prohibited in Islam*, trans. M. Siddiqi, K. al-Hilbawi, and S. Shukri (Cairo: al-Falah, 2001), 336; Muhammad Tharwat, "Duktūr Yūsuf al-Qaradāwi Yurīd an an Yatakhalas min Kalimat Dhimmī wa Yabdiluhā bi Muwātin," *al-Midān*, July 31, 2003.

108. al-Qaradāwī, *al-Sahwa al-Islāmiyya min al-Murāhaqa ilā al-Rushd*, 225.

109. Muhammad Habīb, interviewed by the author, 2007.

110. Kamāl al-Sa'īd Habīb, *al-Harakat al-Islāmiyya min al-Muwājaha ilā al-Murāja'a* (Cairo: Maktabat Madbūlī, 2002), 205.

111. Ibid.

112. Mamdūh Ismā'īl, interviewed by the author, Cairo, 2003.

113. Saad Eddin Ibrāhīm, interviewed by the author, Cairo, 2003.

114. Abū al-'Ilā Mādī, interviewed by the author, 2003; Husayn 'Abd al-Rāziq, "al-Ikhwān al-Muslimūn . . . Bayn al-Khārij wa al-Dākhil," *al-Ahālī*, March 17, 2004.

115. Samīr Murqus, interviewed by the author, Cairo, 2003.

116. Nabīl 'Abd al-Fattāh, interviewed by the author, Cairo, 2003.

117. Rafīq Habīb, interviewed by the author, 2007.

118. Shayma al-Shami, "Dr. Muhammad Imara Apologizes to Copts, Admits Mistakes in His Controversial Book," *Arab-West Report*, November 1, 2007.

Chapter 6

1. Tāriq al-Bishrī, *Bayn al-Jāmi'a al-Dīniyya wa al-Jāmi'a al-Wataniyya fī al-Fikr al-Siyāsī* (Cairo: Dār al-Shurūq, 1998), 37; Fahmī Huwaydī, *Muwātinūn lā Dhimmiūn: Mawqi' Ghayr al-Muslimīn fī Mujtama'a al-Muslimīn*, 3rd ed. (Cairo: Dār al-Shurūq, 1999), 121; Muhammad 'Imāra, *al-Islām wa al-'Aqaliyāt: al-Mādī, wa al-Hādir, wa al-Mustaqbal* (Cairo: Maktabat al-Shurūq al-Dawliyya, 2003), 51; Muhammad Salīm al-'Awwā, "al-Ta'addudiyya al-Siyāsiyya min Manthūr Islāmī," *Minbar al-Hiwār* 6, no. 20 (1991): 130; 'Abd al-Mun'im Abū al-Futūh, "Makānat al-Muwātana fī al-Mafhūm al-Islāmī lil Islāh" (Cairo, 2008).

2. Ann Lambton, *State and Government in Medieval Islam: An Introduction to the Study of Islamic Political Theory* (Oxford: Oxford University Press, 1981), 310.

3. Ibid.

4. Nadav Safran, *Egypt in Search of Political Community: An Analysis of the Intellectual and Political Evolution of Egypt, 1804–1952* (Cambridge, MA: Harvard University Press, 1961), 23–24.

5. Vivian Fu'ād, interviewed by the author, Cairo, 2007.

6. al-'Awwā, "al-Ta'addudiyya al-Siyāsiyya min Manthūr Islāmī," 129–130; Fahmī

Huwaydī, "Taqdīm Fahmī Huwaydī," in *al-Aqbāt: al-Kanīsa am al-Watan; Qissat al Bābā Shanūda al-Thālith*, ed. Abdul Latīf al-Manāwī, 9 (Dār al-Shabāb al-ʿArabī, 1992); ʿImāra, *al-Islām wa al-ʾAqaliyāt*, 12.

7. Muhammad Salīm al-ʿAwwā, "Ahl al-Dhimma fī al-Nithām al-Huqūqī al-Islāmī," *al-Hayāt al-Tayyiba*, no. 11 (4th year) (2003), 179; al-ʿAwwā, *Fī al-Nithām al-Siyāsī Lil Dawla al-Islāmiyya* (Cairo: Dār al-Shurūq, 1989), 116, 246; al-ʿAwwā, "al-Taʿaddudiyya al-Siyāsiyya min Manthūr Islāmī," 130, 134.

8. al-ʿAwwā, *Fī al-Nithām al-Siyāsī lil Dawla al-Islāmiyya*, 67; al-ʿAwwā, "al-Taʿaddudiyya al-Siyāsiyya min Manthūr Islāmī," 133–135.

9. Fahmī Huwaydī, *Lil Islām Dimuqrātiyya* (Cairo: Markaz al-Ahrām, 1993), 97–98, 150.

10. Ibid., 150.

11. Muhammad Salīm al-ʿAwwā, "Jawāz Tarshīh al-Aqbāt wa al-Nisāʾ li Majlis al-Shaʿab wa Intikhābhum," *al-Shaʿab*, November 21, 1995.

12. Fahmī Huwaydī, interviewed by the author, Cairo, 2003.

13. Huwaydī, *Muwātinūn Lā Dhimmiūn*, 172.

14. al-ʿAwwā, *Fī al-Nithām al-Siyāsī lil Dawla al-Islāmiyya*, 251; al-Bishrī, *Bayn al-Jāmiʿa al-Dīniyya wa al-Jāmiʿa al-Wataniyya fī al-Fikr al-Siyāsī*, 28; Muhammad ʿImāra, interviewed by the author, Cairo, 2003.

15. al-ʿAwwā, "Jawāz Tarshīh al-Aqbāt wa al-Nisāʾ li Majlis al-Shaʿab wa Intikhābhum."

16. Tāriq al-Bishrī, *al-Muslimūn wa al-Aqbāt fī Itār al-Jamāʿa al-Wataniyya*, 2nd ed. (Cairo: Dār al-Shurūq, 1988), 682, 685, 688; Tāriq al-Bishrī, interviewed by the author, Cairo, 2003. This idea is echoed by Huwaydī, who argues that now we have institutional *wilāya* rather than personal *wilāya*; Fahmī Huwaydī, interviewed by the author, Cairo, 2007.

17. The term given for this is *al-wilāya al-ʿāmma* or *al-wilāya al-kubrā*.

18. Muhammad ʿImāra, interviewed by the author, Cairo, 2007.

19. Abū al-ʿIlā Mādī, *al-Wasat Party Program (2004)* (Cairo: al-Azzazy Press, 2004), 7.

20. Rafīq Habīb, interviewed by the author, Cairo, 2007.

21. Muhammad Salīm al-ʿAwwā, interviewed by the author, Cairo, 2003.

22. Tāriq al-Bishrī, interviewed by the author, 2003.

23. Muhammad ʿImāra, interviewed by the author, 2007.

24. Fahmī Huwaydī, interviewed by the author, 2003.

25. Fahmī Huwaydī, interviewed by the author, 2007.

26. Muhammad Mahdī ʿĀkif, "Muslim Brotherhood Initiative on the General Principles of Reform in Egypt" (Cairo: 2004), 31–32; Muslim Brotherhood, "Barnāmij al-Hizb," (2007), 14; Muhammad Habīb, interviewed by the author, Cairo, 2007.

27. Rafīq Habīb, interviewed by the author, 2007.

28. Ibid.

29. Muhammad Habīb, interviewed by the author, 2007.

30. Said Shu'eeb, "Dr Abdel Monem Abul Futouh: We Do Not Object to a Christian Being Elected President of Egypt," *al-Sharq al-Awsat (Arab-West Report)*, October 5, 2003.

31. Amira Howeidy, "Jumping the Gun," *al-Ahram Weekly*, October 25–31, 2007.

32. The term that is used is *thawābit*.

33. I have chosen to use the term "public order" as opposed to "public policy."

34. Gerhart Husserl, "Public Policy and Ordre Public," *Virginia Law Review* 25, no. 1 (1938): 38.

35. Ibid., 42.

36. Maurits Berger, "Apostasy and Public Policy in Contemporary Egypt: An Evaluation of Recent Cases from Egypt's Highest Courts," *Human Rights Quarterly* 25 (2003): 725.

37. Maurits Berger, "Public Policy and Islamic Law: The Modern *Dhimmī* in Contemporary Egyptian Family Law," *Islamic Law and Society* 8, no. 1 (2001), 89.

38. Berger, "Apostasy and Public Policy in Contemporary Egypt," 725.

39. Berger, "Public Policy and Islamic Law," 104.

40. Rafīq Habīb, interviewed by the author, 2007.

41. Muhammad 'Imāra, interviewed by the author, 2007.

42. Fahmī Huwaydī, interviewed by the author, 2003; Muhammad 'Imāra, interviewed by the author, 2003.

43. Muhammad 'Imāra, interviewed by the author, 2007.

44. Huwaydī, *Lil Islām Dimuqrātiyya*, 97, 150, 154.

45. Fahmī Huwaydī, interviewed by the author, 2003.

46. Yūsuf al-Qaradāwī, *State in Islam* (Cairo: al-Falāh, 1998), 45–46.

47. Muhammad Salīm al-'Awwā, interviewed by the author, 2003.

48. 'Isām Sultān, interviewed by the author, Cairo, 2003.

49. Tāriq al-Bishrī, interviewed by the author, 2003.

50. Muhammad 'Imāra, interviewed by the author, 2003.

51. Brotherhood, "Barnāmij al-Hizb," 10–11.

52. 'Isām Sultān, interviewed by the author, Cairo, 2007.

53. Abū al-'Ilā Mādī, interviewed by the author, Cairo, 2007; Mādī, *al-Wasat Party Program (2004)*, 4.

54. Abū al-'Ilā Mādī, interviewed by the author, 2007.

55. Fahmī Huwaydī, interviewed by the author, 2007; Rafīq Habīb, interviewed by the author, 2007.

56. The terms used are *'Ibadāt* and *mu'āmalāt*; Fahmī Huwaydī, interviewed by the author, 2003.

57. ʿĀkif, "Muslim Brotherhood Initiative on the General Principles of Reform in Egypt," 10.

58. Rafīq Habīb, interviewed by the author, 2007.

59. Mustafa Yassin, "Dr. Salim al-ʿAwwā at an Intellectual Meeting in the Saudi Embassy: 'Copts Are Not Ahl al-Dhimma . . . We Are All Citizens on an Equal Level,'" ʿAqīdatī (Arab-West Report), August 3, 2004; Muhammad Salīm al-ʿAwwā, "al-ʿAlaqāt Bayn al-Muslimīn wa Ahl al-Kitāb," al-Muslim al-Muʿāsir 22, no. 85 (199?), 35.

60. Yūsuf al-Qaradāwī, The Lawful and the Prohibited in Islam, trans. M. Siddiqi, K. al-Hilbawi, and S. Shukri (Cairo: al-Falah, 2001), 180.

61. Tāriq al-Bishrī, interviewed by the author, 2003.

62. Muhammad Salīm al-ʿAwwā, interviewed by the author, 2003.

63. al-ʿAwwā, Fī al-Nithām al-Siyāsī lil Dawla al-Islāmiyya, 249.

64. Muhammad ʿImāra, Samāhat al-Islām (Cairo: al-Falāh, 2002), 32; al-ʿAwwā, Fī al-Nithām al-Siyāsī lil Dawla al-Islāmiyya, 249, 252.

65. Muhammad ʿImāra, interviewed by the author, 2007.

66. al-ʿAwwā, "al-ʿAlaqāt Bayn al-Muslimīn wa Ahl al-Kitāb," 27.

67. Huwaydī, Muwātinūn lā Dhimmiūn, 60, 120; Huwaydī, "Taqdīm Fahmī Huwaydī," 8–9.

68. Abū al-ʿIlā Mādī, interviewed by the author, 2007.

69. ʿImāra, al-Islām wa al-ʾAqaliyāt, 20.

70. Fahmī Huwaydī, interviewed by the author, 2003.

71. Fahmī Huwaydī, interviewed by the author, 2007.

72. Rafīq Habīb, interviewed by the author, 2007.

73. Ibid.

74. Muhammad ʿImāra, interviewed by the author, 2007.

75. Muhammad Habīb, interviewed by the author, 2007.

76. ʿĀkif, "Muslim Brotherhood Initiative on the General Principles of Reform in Egypt," 13.

77. Mādī, al-Wasat Party Program (2004), 7.

78. Abū al-ʿIlā Mādī, interviewed by the author, 2007.

79. Muhammad Salīm al-ʿAwwā, Punishment in Islamic Law (Indianapolis: American Trust Publications, 1982), 50–51.

80. Muhammad Salīm al-ʿAwwā, interviewed by the author, 2003; Muhammad ʿImāra, interviewed by the author, 2003.

81. Tāriq al-Bishrī, interviewed by the author, 2003.

82. Fahmī Huwaydī, interviewed by the author, 2003.

83. Muhammad Salīm al-ʿAwwā, interviewed by the author, 2003; al-ʿAwwā, Fī al-Nithām al-Siyāsī lil Dawla al-Islāmiyya, 262.

84. Huwaydī, Muwātinūn lā Dhimmiūn, 173–174; Fahmī Huwaydī, interviewed by the author, 2007.

85. Wilfred Cantwell Smith, *The Meaning and End of Religion: A Revolutionary Approach to the Great Religious Traditions* (San Franciso: Harper and Row, 1978), 84.

86. Muhammad Ibn Khaldun, *The Muqaddimah: An Introduction to History*, trans. Franz Rosenthal, ed. N. J. Dawood (Princeton. NJ: Princeton University Press, 1967), 154–155.

87. L. Gardet, "Dīn," in *Encyclopaedia of Islam²* (Leiden: Brill, 1965).

88. 'Imāra, *al-Islām wa al-'Aqaliyāt*, 47–48.

89. Muhammad Salīm al-'Awwā, interviewed by the author, 2003.

90. Muhammad 'Imāra, interviewed by the author, 2007; Fahmī Huwaydī, interviewed by the author, 2007.

91. al-Qaradāwī, *State in Islam*, 80.

92. al-Bishrī, *Bayn al-Jāmi'a al-Dīniyya wa al-Jāmi'a al-Wataniyya fī al-Fikr al-Siyāsī*, 34.

93. 'Abd al-Mun'im Abū al-Futūh, interviewed by the author, Cairo, 2007.

94. In Arabic, *hizb madanī lahu murja'iyya islāmiyya*. Muhammad Habīb, interviewed by the author, 2007; Muslim Brotherhood, "The Muslim Brotherhood's Program," http://www.ikhwanweb.com/Article.asp?ID=812&SectionID=70; Brotherhood, "Barnāmij al-Hizb," 14; Abū al-'Ilā Mādī, "Religious and Political Pluralism: The Islamic Concept of State and Society in Modernity" (paper presented at the meeting "Islamic Perspectives in Secular Societies—Modern Scholars of Islamic Questions for the West," Berlin, June 21–22, 2002); Abū al-'Ilā Mādī, interviewed by the author, 2007; 'Isām Sultān, interviewed by the author, 2007.

95. Tāriq al-Bishrī, interviewed by the author, 2003.

96. Fahmī Huwaydī, interviewed by the author, 2007; Tāriq al-Bishrī, interviewed by the author, 2003.

97. Rafīq Habīb, interviewed by the author, 2007.

98. Muhammad 'Imāra, interviewed by the author, 2007.

99. Tāriq al-Bishrī, interviewed by the author, 2003; al-Bishrī, *Bayn al-Jāmi'a al-Dīniyya wa al-Jāmi'a al-Wataniyya fī al-Fikr al-Siyāsī*, 688.

Chapter 7

1. Vivian Fu'ād, interviewed by the author, Cairo, 2007.

2. Nushin Atmaca, "Discussion about Art. 2," *Arab-West Report*, n.d.

3. Kamāl Zākhir Musā, "Copts and the Constitutional Amendments," *Ruz al-Yūsuf*, January 12, 2007.

4. Atmaca, "Discussion about Art. 2," 6.

5. Ibid.

6. Michael Munīr, interviewed by the author, Virginia, 2009.

7. E.g., Mamdūh Halīm, a Coptic author and researcher; Atmaca, "Discussion about

Art. 2," 9. Sāmī Harak, the founder of the Misr al-Umm party, argues against the state's adopting a particular religion; Atmaca, "Discussion about Art. 2," 9.

8. Rifat Fikrī, pastor of the Evangelical Church in 'Ard Sharīf, Shubrā in Cairo; Atmaca, "Discussion about Art. 2," 8.

9. Atmaca, "Discussion about Art. 2," 8.

10. Munīr Fakhrī 'Abd al-Nūr, interviewed by the author, Cairo, 2007; Atmaca, "Discussion about Art. 2," 8.

11. Atmaca, "Discussion about Art. 2," 8.

12. Ibid., 11.

13. Ibid.

14. "Freedom of Belief between Shariah [Islamic Jurisprudence] and the Constitution," Fifth Annual Convention for the Egyptian Union of Human Rights Organization, January 11, 2007.

15. Atmaca, "Discussion about Art. 2," 11.

16. Ibid.

17. Ibid., 13.

18. Nabīl Luqā Bibāwī, "Pope Shenouda and the Second Article of the Constitution," *al-Akhbār (Arab-West Report)*, February 28, 2007. Dr. Rasmī 'Abd al-Malik, dean of the Institute of Coptic Studies, takes a similar position; Wafā' Wasfī, "Would a Constitution Based on Citizenship Encourage Copts to Participate in Social and Political Life?" *Ruz al-Yūsuf (Arab-West Report)*, March 2, 2007.

19. Īhāb Hijāzī, "Christian Intellectuals: The Second Article of the Constitution Guarantees Religious Freedom for Non-Muslims," *October (Arab-West Report)*, March 19, 2007.

20. Atmaca, "Discussion about Art. 2," 3.

21. Ibid., 6.

22. Rafīq Habīb, interviewed by the author, Cairo, 2007.

23. Michael Munīr, interviewed by the author, 2009.

24. Yūsuf Sidhum, interviewed by the author, Cairo, 2007; Mīlād Hannā, interviewed by the author, Cairo, 2007.

25. Cornelis Hulsman, interviewed by the author, Cairo, 2007.

26. Cornelis Hulsman, "Interview with Kamāl Zākhir Mūsa about His Conviction in the Need for Church Reform," special for *Arab-West Report*, November 8–14, 2006.

27. Michael Munīr, interviewed by the author, 2009.

28. Yūsuf Sidhum, interviewed by the author, 2007; Samīr Murqus, interviewed by the author, Cairo, 2007.

29. Munīr Fakhrī 'Abd al-Nūr, interviewed by the author, 2007; Cornelis Hulsman, interviewed by the author, 2007.

30. Munīr Fakhrī 'Abd al-Nūr, interviewed by the author, 2007.

31. Mīlād Hannā, *The Seven Pillars of the Egyptian Identity* (Cairo: General Egyptian Book Organisation, 1989), 55.

32. Bishop Murqus, interviewed by the author, Cairo, 2007.

33. Najīb Jabrā'īl, interviewed by the author, Cairo, 2007.

34. Bishop Thomas, interviewed by the author, Anafora, near Cairo, 2007.

35. Samīr Murqus, interviewed by the author, 2007.

36. Cornelis Hulsman, interviewed by the author, 2003; Bishop Thomas, interviewed by the author, Anafora, near Cairo, 2007.

37. Sana al-Sa'id, "Pope Shenouda in an Interview with *al-Wafd*: Wafa' Costantine Was Not Forced to Convert Back to Christianity," *al-Wafd (Arab-West Report)*, January 6, 2005.

38. Adel Guindy, "Family Status Issues among Egypt's Copts: A Brief Overview," *MERIA* 11, no. 3 (2007): 5.

39. Ibid., 7.

40. a.n.m., "Marriage and Divorce between the Church Rules and the Judiciary Rulings [2]," press review for *Arab-West Report*, April 5–11, 2008.

41. Sharif al-Dawakhili, "Anger in Coptic Churches following Dar Al-Ifta's Permission of Polygamy in Christianity," *al-Dustūr (Arab-West Report)*, February 2, 2009.

42. Muna al-Mallakh, "The Church's Restrictions on Copts' Divorce Is the Highest Motive for Changing Religion," *al-Muswwar*, January 7, 2005.

43. Bishop Murqus, interviewed by the author, 2007; Najīb Jabrā'īl, interviewed by the author, 2007.

44. Samīr Murqus, *al-'Ākhar . . . al-Hiwār . . . al-Muwātana* (Cairo: Maktabat al-Shurūq al-Dawliyya, 2005), 177.

45. Yūsuf Sidhum, interviewed by the author, 2007.

46. Samīr Murqus, interviewed by the author, 2007.

47. Munīr Fakhrī 'Abd al-Nūr, interviewed by the author, 2007; Mīlād Hannā, interviewed by the author, 2007; Sa'īd Shu'ayb, "Dr. Mīlād Hannā: Copts in Egypt Are Second-Class Citizens," *al-'Arabī (Arab-West Report)*, May 5, 2004.

48. Mīlād Hannā, interviewed by the author, 2007; Hannā, *The Seven Pillars of the Egyptian Identity*, 10.

49. Vivian Fu'ād, interviewed by the author, 2007.

50. Yūsuf Sidhum, interviewed by the author, 2007.

51. Cornelis Hulsman, interviewed by the author, 2007.

52. Najīb Jabrā'īl, interviewed by the author, 2007.

53. Bishop Murqus, interviewed by the author, 2007.

54. Bishop Thomas, interviewed by the author, 2007.

55. Samīr Murqus, interviewed by the author, Cairo, 2003.

56. Rafīq Habīb, interviewed by the author, Cairo, 2003.

57. Sawsan Hulsman, "Escalations following the Alleged Conversion of a Priest's Wife to Islam," special for *Arab-West Report*, December 15–21, 2004.

58. Hulsman, "Interview with Kamāl Zākhir Mūsa about His Conviction in the Need for Church Reform."

59. Yūsuf Sidhum, interviewed by the author, Cairo, 2003.

60. Michael Munīr, interviewed by the author, 2009.

61. Rafīq Habīb, interviewed by the author, 2007.

62. Ibid.

63. Bishop Thomas, interviewed by the author, 2007.

64. Cornelis Hulsman, interviewed by the author, 2007.

65. Yūsuf Sidhum, interviewed by the author, 2007.

66. Cornelis Hulsman, "Freedom of Religion in Egypt" *Arab-West Report*, September 4, 2003.

67. Hānī Labīb, "The Removal of Religious Affiliation from Identity Cards . . . A Secular Heresy to Conceal the Identity of Egyptians," *Ruz al-Yusuf (Arab-West Report)*, September 3, 2006.

68. Vivian Fu'ād, interviewed by the author, 2007; Rafīq Habīb, interviewed by the author, 2007.

69. 'Ilā Jalāl, "Baheb al-Sima Controversy Continues," Press review for *Arab-West Report*, June 23–29, 2004.

70. Rafīq Habīb, interviewed by the author, 2007.

71. Vivian Fu'ād, interviewed by the author, 2007.

72. Yūsuf Sidhum, interviewed by the author, 2007.

73. Yūsuf Sidhum, "Yes, 'Mosques and Churches Are No Courtyard for Politics' . . . But . . . ," *al-Watanī (Arab-West Report)*, January 20–26, 2000.

74. Yūsuf Sidhum, interviewed by the author, 2007.

75. Ibid.

76. Bishop Thomas, interviewed by the author, 2007.

77. a.n.m., "Marriage and Divorce between the Church Rules and the Judiciary Rulings [2]."

78. Rafīq Habīb, interviewed by the author, 2007.

79. Najīb Jabrā'īl, interviewed by the author, 2007.

80. Bishop Murqus, interviewed by the author, 2007.

81. Rafīq Habīb, interviewed by the author, 2007.

82. Rafīq Habīb, interviewed by the author, 2003.

83. Rafīq Habīb, interviewed by the author, 2007; Ahmed Murad, "Muslim and Coptic Thinkers Uncover the Plan of Rejecting Arabism and Islam," *al-Liwā' al-Islāmī (Arab-West Report)*, February 26, 2004.

84. Vivian Fu'ād, interviewed by the author, 2007.

85. Samīr Murqus, interviewed by the author, 2007.

86. Ibid.

87. Ibid.

88. Hannā, *The Seven Pillars of the Egyptian Identity*, 10, 120.

89. Mīlād Hannā, *Acceptance of the Other* (Cairo: al Ahram Center for Political and Strategic Studies, 2001), 30.

90. Shuʿayb, "Dr. Mīlād Hannā: Copts in Egypt Are Second-Class Citizens."

91. Rafīq Habīb, interviewed by the author, 2007.

92. Yūsuf Sidhum, interviewed by the author, 2003; Munīr Fakhrī ʿAbd al-Nūr, interviewed by the author (Cairo, 2003); Vivian Fuʾād, interviewed by the author, Cairo, 2003.

93. Samīr Murqus and Vivian Fuʾād, "Our Experience: Dialogue Based on Citizenship," in *al-ʾĀkhar . . . al-Hiwār . . . al-Muwātana*, ed. Samīr Murqus, 162 (Cairo: Maktabat al-Shurūq al-Dawliyya, 2005).

94. Cornelis Hulsman, interviewed by the author, 2007.

95. Bishop Murqus, interviewed by the author, 2007.

96. Vivian Fuʾād, interviewed by the author, 2007.

97. Vivian Fuʾād, interviewed by the author, 2003.

98. Samīr Murqus, interviewed by the author, 2007.

99. Murqus and Fuʾād, "Our Experience Dialogue Based on Citizenship," 153.

100. Hannā, *Acceptance of the Other*, 129.

101. Ibid., 13, 32–33, 117, 46, 18.

102. Fahmī Huwaydī, interviewed by the author, Cairo, 2007.

103. Muhammad ʿImāra, interviewed by the author, Cairo, 2007.

104. Muhammad ʿImāra, *al-Islām wa al-ʾAqaliyāt: al-Mādī, wa al-Hādir, wa al-Mustaqbal* (Cairo: Maktabat al-Shurūq al-Dawliyya, 2003), 47.

105. Yūsuf Sidhum, interviewed by the author, 2007.

106. Samīr Murqus, "The Religious Revival/Awakening," (Germany, 2006), 9; Murqus and Fuʾād, "Our Experience Dialogue Based on Citizenship," 156.

107. Samīr Murqus, interviewed by the author, 2007.

108. Murqus and Fuʾād, "Our Experience Dialogue Based on Citizenship," 161.

109. Samīr Murqus, interviewed by the author, 2007.

110. Nabīl ʿAbd al-Fattāh, "The Nation State and Citizenship in Egypt," *al-Dustūr (Arab-West Report)*, October 18, 2006; Sidhum, "Yes, 'Mosques and Churches Are No Courtyard for Politics' . . . But . . . ."

111. Muhammad Shāban, "Nabil Abdel Fattah: There Will Be No Renewal of Religious Discourse without Real Political Reform," *al-Qāhira (Arab-West Report)*, December 16–December 23, 2003.

112. ʿAbd al-Fattāh, "The Nation State and Citizenship in Egypt."

113. Muhammad Salāh, "Marqus: Muslim Brotherhood–Coptic Dialogue of No Avail," *Ruz al-Yūsuf (Arab-West Report)*, January 26, 2006.

114. Murqus, "The Religious Revival/Awakening . . . ," 6, 12.

115. Bishop Murqus, interviewed by the author, 2007; Samīr Murqus, interviewed by the author, 2007.

116. Magdi Khalil, "The Muslim Brotherhood and the Copts," *Watani International (Arab West Report)*, December 3, 2006; Mīlād Hannā, interviewed by the author, 2007; Yūsuf Sidhum, interviewed by the author, 2007.

117. Mīlād Hannā, interviewed by the author, 2007.

118. Mīlād Hannā, interviewed by the author, Cairo, 2003; Cornelis Hulsman, interviewed by the author, Cairo, 2003.

119. Bishop Murqus, interviewed by the author, 2007; Yūsuf Sidhum, interviewed by the author, 2003.

120. Gihan Shahine, "Bad Cards," *al-Ahram Weekly*, December 29–January 4, 2006; Munīr Fakhrī ʿAbd al-Nūr, interviewed by the author, 2003.

121. Ibrahim Abu-Rabiʿ, Introduction to Fouad Zakariyya, *Myth and Reality in the Contemporary Islamist*

Movement, trans. Ibrahim M.Abu-Rabiʿ (London: Pluto Press, 2005), ix.

122. Nabīl ʿAbd al-Fattāḥ, interviewed by the author, Cairo, 2007.

123. Yūsuf Sidhum, interviewed by the author, 2007.

124. Munīr Fakhrī ʿAbd al-Nūr, interviewed by the author, 2007.

125. Cornelis Hulsman, "Interview with Munīr Fakhrī ʿAbd Al-Nūr," *Arab-West Report*, January 21, 2009.

126. Cornelis Hulsman, interviewed by the author, 2007.

127. Bishop Thomas, interviewed by the author, 2007.

128. Yūsuf Sidhum, interviewed by the author, 2007.

129. Rafīq Habīb, interviewed by the author, 2007.

130. Muhammad Salīm al-ʿAwwā, "The Church and Politics," *al-Usbūʿ (Arab-West Report)*, February 21, 2005.

131. al-ʿAwwā, "Aren't the Muslim Brothers Egyptian Citizens?" *al-Usbūʿ (Arab-West Report)*, November 28, 2005.

132. Muhammad ʿImāra, interviewed by the author, 2007.

133. Tāriq al-Bishrī, "Church Entrenches Copts' Isolation from Society," *al-Usbūʿ (Arab-West Report)*, November 16–22, 2005.

134. Ibid.

135. Rafīq Habīb, "The Wafa Issue Was Overt Defiance of the State's Legal and Constitutional Authority," *al-Usbūʿ (Arab-West Report)*, January 17, 2005.

136. Ibid.

137. Rafīq Habīb, interviewed by the author, 2007.

138. Muhammad ʿImāra, interviewed by the author, 2007.

139. Fahmī Huwaydī, interviewed by the author, 2007.

140. Murqus, "The Religious Revival/Awakening . . . ," 7.

141. Ibid., 8.

142. Samīr Murqus, interviewed by the author, 2003.

143. Samīr Murqus, interviewed by the author, 2007.

144. Samīr Murqus, *al-Muwātana wa al-Taghayīr: Dirāsa ʿAwliyya hawl Taʾsīl al-Mafhūm wa Tafʿīl al-Mumārasa* (Cairo: Maktabat al-Shurūq al-Dawliyya, 2006), 59.

145. Samīr Murqus, interviewed by the author, 2007.

146. Ibid.

147. Murqus, *al-Muwātana wa al-Taghayīr*, 62; Hannā, *The Seven Pillars of the Egyptian Identity*, 179.

148. Murqus, *al-ʾĀkhar . . . al-Hiwār . . . al-Muwātana*, 59, 165.

149. Shuʿayb, "Dr. Mīlād Hannā: Copts in Egypt Are Second-Class Citizens."

150. Mīlād Hannā, interviewed by the author, 2007.

151. Ibid.

152. Yūsuf Sidhum, interviewed by the author, 2007.

153. Ibid.

154. Munīr Fakhrī ʿAbd al-Nūr, interviewed by the author, 2007.

BIBLIOGRAPHY

Interviews with the Author
All interviews took place in Cairo unless otherwise stated.
ʿAbd al-Fattāḥ, Nabīl. August 27, 2003.
———. June 5, 2007.
ʿAbd al-Latīf, Umayma. March 26, 2003.
ʿAbd al-Nūr, Munīr Fakhrī. September 4, 2003.
———. May 31, 2007.
Abū al-Futūḥ, ʿAbd al-Munʿim. August 19, 2003.
———. June 14, 2007.
———. May 25, 2008.
al-ʿAryān, ʿIsām. July 9, 2003.
———. June 16, 2007.
———. June 10, 2008.
al-ʿAwwā, Muhammad Salīm. March 9, 2003.
al-Bishrī, Tāriq. February 27, 2003.
al-Ghazālī, ʿAbd al-Hamīd. May 27, 2008.
al-Hamalawy, Hossam. March 20, 2003.
al-Hudaybī, Muhammad Maʾmūn. July 12, 2003.
al-Saʿīd Habīb, Kamāl. September 6, 2003.
al-Zayyāt, Muntasir. July 2, 2003.
Fuʾād, Vivian. September 4, 2003.
———. June 4, 2007.
Habīb, Muhammad. June 21, 2007.
Habīb, Rafīq. July 7, 2003.
———. June 4, 2007.

Hannā, Mīlād. September 5, 2003.

———. May 23, 2007.

Hulsman, Cornelis. August 9, 2003.

———. May 21, 2007.

Huwaydī, Fahmī. February 10, 2003.

———. June 18, 2007.

Ibrāhīm, Saad Eddin. April 1, 2003.

'Imāra, Muhammad. March 13, 2003.

———. June 25, 2007.

Ismā'īl, Mamdūh. August 12, 2003.

Jabrā'īl, Najīb. June 4, 2007.

Mādī, Abū al-'Ilā. July 7, 2003.

———. June 26, 2007.

Munīr, Michael. May 28, 2009 (Virginia, USA)

Murqus, Bishop. August 25, 2003.

———. May 29, 2007.

Murqus, Samīr. September 3, 2003.

———. May 30, 2007.

Ramzī, Mamdūh. August 13, 2003.

Salāh, Muhammad. August 17, 2003.

Shahīn, 'Imād. June 29, 2003.

Sidhum, Yūsuf. August 7, 2003.

———. May 28, 2007.

Stacher, Joshua. June 22, 2008.

Sultān, 'Isām. August 3, 2003.

———. June 3, 2007.

Thomas, Bishop. June 22, 2007 (Anafora, Egypt).

Written Sources

'Abd al-Fattāh, Nabīl. "The Nation State and Citizenship in Egypt." *al-Dustūr (Arab-West Report)*, October 18, 2006, 25.

'Abd al-Malik, Nabīl. "Al-Hiqba al-Qibtiyya . . . wa Kayfa Nuthahhiruhā?" *Ruz al-Yusuf* 34 (2003): 34–35.

'Abd al-Mun'im, 'Abd al-Fattāh. "'Awdat Tanthīm Shukrī Mustafā." *al-'Arabī*, September 14, 2003.

———. "The Cease-Violence Initiative Is a Final Choice for Aboud Al-Zomor." *al-'Arabī (Arab-West Report)*, March 14, 2004.

'Abd al-Nāsir, Gamāl. *Draft of the Charter*. Cairo: United Arab Republic Information Department, 1962.

'Abd al-Qudūs, Muhammad. "Limāthā Nuʻārid Fikr Majmaʻ al-Adyān." *al-Daʻwa*, January 1980, 20–21.

'Abd al-Rahmān, 'Umar. *Kalimat al-Haqq*. Cairo: Dar al-'Itisām, n.d.

'Abd al-Rāziq, Husayn. "Al-Ikhwān al-Muslimūn . . . bayn al-Khārij wa al-Dākhil)." *al-Ahālī*, March 17, 2004.

'Abd al-Salām Faraj, Muhammad. "The Neglected Duty." In *The Neglected Duty*, edited by Johannes Jansen, 159–230. London: Macmillan, 1994.

Abdin, Amira Shamma. "Modernist Interpretations of the Status of Non-Muslims in Muslim Society." Master's thesis, School of Oriental and African Studies (SOAS), 1995.

Abdul Latif, Omayma. "Defending the Faith." *al-Ahram Weekly*, October 24–30, 2002.

Abedin, Syed Z. "Al-Dhimma: The Non-Believers' Identity in Islam." *Islam and Christian-Muslim Relations* 3, no. 1 (1992): 40–57.

Abū al-Futūh, 'Abd al-Munʻim. "Makānat al-Muwātana fī al-Mafhūm al-Islāmī lil Islāh." Cairo, 2008.

Abū Magd, Ahmed Kamāl. *Hiwār al-Muwājaha*. Cairo: Dār al-Shurūq, 1988.

Abu-Rabiʻ, Ibrahim M. *Contemporary Arab Thought: Studies in Post-1967 Arab Intellectual History*. London: Pluto Press, 2004.

———. "Contemporary Islamic Thought: One or Many?" In *The Blackwell Companion to Contemporary Islamic Thought*, edited by Ibrahim M. Abu-Rabiʻ, 1–20. Oxford: Blackwell, 2006.

———. *Intellectual Origins of Islamic Resurgence in the Modern Arab World*. Albany: State University of New York Press, 1996.

———. Introduction to Fouad Zakariyya, *Myth and Reality in the Contemporary Islamist Movement*. Translated by Ibrahim M. Abu-Rabiʻ. London: Pluto Press, 2005.

'Ādil, Shaymā'. "Statistics: 27 Copts in the Parliament in 1942, No Copts in the Parliament in 1957, and Three in 2005." *al-Misrī al-Yawm (Arab-West Report)*, May 20, 2009.

Afsaruddin, Asma. *The First Muslims: History and Memory*. Oxford: Oneworld, 2007.

Ahmed, Leila. *Women and Gender in Islam: Historical Roots of the Modern Debate*. New Haven, CT: Yale University Press, 1992.

Ajami, Fouad. *The Arab Predicament*. Cambridge: Cambridge University Press, 1993.

'Ākif, Muhammad Mahdī. "Muslim Brotherhood Initiative on the General Principles of Reform in Egypt." Circular. Cairo, 2004.

al-'Asīrī, Muhammad. "Murshid al-Ikhwān Yahkum Misr Siran." *Sawt al-Umma*, August 11, 2003, 8–9.

al-'Awwā, Muhammad Salīm. "Ahl al-Dhimma fī al-Nithām al-Huqūqī al-Islāmī." *al-Hayāt al-Tayyiba*, no. 11 (4th year) (2003): 179–185.

———. "al-'Alaqāt bayn al-Muslimīn wa Ahl al-Kitāb." *al-Muslim al-Muʻāsir* 22, no. 85 (199?): 27–38.

———. "al-Taʿaddudiyya al-Siyāsiyya min Manthūr Islāmī." *Minbar al-Hiwār* 6, no. 20 (1991): 129–138.

———. "Aren't the Muslim Brothers Egyptian Citizens?" *al-Usbūʿ (Arab-West Report)*, November 28, 2005, 4.

———. "The Church and Politics." *al-Usbūʿ (Arab-West Report)*, February 21, 2005, 4.

———. *Fī al-Nithām al-Siyāsī lil Dawla al-Islāmiyya.* Cairo: Dār al-Shurūq, 1989.

———. "Jawāz Tarshīh al-Aqbāt wa al-Nisāʾ li Majlis al-Shaʿab wa Intikhābhum." *al-Shaʿab*, November 21, 1995.

———. *Lil Dīn wa al-Watan Fusūl fī ʿAlaqat al-Muslimīn bi Ghayr al-Muslimīn.* Cairo: Nahdat Misr, 2006.

———. *Punishment in Islamic Law.* Indianapolis: American Trust Publications, 1982.

al-Bannā, Hasan. *Majmūʿat Rasāʾil al-Imām al-Shahīd Hasan al-Bannā.* Beirut: Dār al-Andalus, 1965.

———. *Six Tracts of Hasan al-Bannā: A Selection from the Majmūʿat Rasāʾil al-Imām al-Shahīd Hasan al-Bannā.* Accra, Ghana: Africa for Publishing and Distribution, 2006.

al-Bāz, Muhammad. "Abū Al-ʿAlā Mādī: al-Hudaybī Khatr ʿalā al-Ikhwān." *Sawt al-Umma*, September 1, 2003.

———. "al-Hudaybī—Nurīd an Natafāhum maʿa al-Dawla . . . Lakin la Ahad Yurīd an Yasmaʿ Lanā." *Sawt al-Umma*, August 25, 2003, 9.

al-Bishrī, Tāriq. *Al-Muslimūn wa al-Aqbāt fī Itār al-Jamāʿa al-Wataniyya.* 2nd ed. Cairo: Dār al-Shurūq, 1988.

———. *Bayn al-Jāmiʿa al-Dīniyya wa al-Jāmiʿa al-Wataniyya fī al-Fikr al-Siyāsī.* Cairo: Dār al-Shurūq, 1998.

———. "Church Entrenches Copts' Isolation from Society." *al-Usbūʿ (Arab-West Report)*, November 16–22, 2005, 5.

al-Bukhari, Muhammad Ibn Ismail. *Sahih al-Bukhari.* 9 vols. Riyadh: Darussalam, 1997.

al-Dawakhili, Sharif. "Anger in Coptic Churches following Dar al-Ifta's Permission of Polygamy in Christianity." *al-Dustūr (Arab-West Report)*, February 2, 2009.

———. "Coptic Church Made a Plan to Escalate against the Regime after Copts Were Excluded from the Shura Council." *al-Dustūr (Arab-West Report)*, June 22, 2007, 4.

al-Dhaydī, Mashārī. "Ayna Yaqif al-Islāmiyyūn Min Mafhūm al-Wataniyya?" *al-Sharq al-Awsat*, October 14, 2003, 12.

al-Faris, Robier. "The Figure That Brings on a Headache." *Watani International (Arab-West Report)*, May 13, 2007.

al-Fātih, Alī. "Samīr Murqus: Munthu 1952 wa Jamīʿa al-Tayārāt al-Fikriyyat Rahīna al-Sirāʿa bayn al-Dawla wa al-Ikhwān al-Muslimīn." *al-Qāhira*, February 10, 2004, 5.

al-Gawhary, Karim. "Copts in the 'Egyptian Fabric.'" *Middle East Report* (1996):21–22.

al-Ghazālī, Muhammad. *Al-Islām al-Muftarā 'alayhi Bayn al-Shuyū'iyīn wa al-Ra'smāliīn*. 7th ed. Cairo: Nahdat Misr, 2006.

———. *Humūm Dā'iyya*. Cairo: Dār al-Bashīr, n.d.

———. *Jihād al-Da'wa bayn 'Ajz al-Dākhil wa Kayd al-Khārij*. Cairo: Dār al-Nahda, 2001.

———. *Min Hunā Na'lam . . . !* 6th ed. Cairo: Nahdat Misr, 2006.

al-Ghazzali, Abu Hamid. *Imam Gazzali's Ihya Ulum-Id-Din*. Translated by al-Haj. Maulana Fazul-Ul-Karim. 4 vols. Lahore: Sind Sagar Academy, 1978.

al-Hamalawy, Hossam. "Fear of the Beard." *Cairo Times* 7, no. 7 (2003): 14–19.

———. "Stuck in the Middle." *Cairo Times* 6, no. 35 (2002).

———. "Wannabes." *Cairo Times*, January 9–15, 2003, 8.

al-Hudaibi, Muhammad Ma'mun. *The Principles of Politics in Islam*. 2nd ed. Cairo: Islamic, Inc., 2000.

———. *A Quiet Discussion on Heated Issues*. Cairo: al-Falāh, 2000.

Ali, Muhammad. "The Copts Forewarn: Mubarak Deceived Us and Sectarian Sedition Might Be Back." *Sawt al-Umma (Arab-West Report)*, October 17, 2005, 6.

al-Jamā'a al-Islāmiyya. "al-Ab'ād al-Haqīqiyya lil-Fitna al-Tā'ifiyya." *al-Da'wa*, June 1980, 22–23.

———. http://www.egyig.com/.

———. "Safhāt min Mithāq al-'Amal al-Islāmī." In *Al-Nabī al-Musallih-al-Rāfidūn*, edited by Said Ahmed Rif'at, 165–177. London: Riyad al-Rayyes, 1991.

———. Cairo University. "Lessons from Iran." In *Islam in Transition: Muslim Perspectives*, edited by John J. Donohue and John L. Esposito, 246–251. New York: Oxford University Press, 1982.

al-Jamā'at al-Jihād al-Islāmī, "Wathīqat Muhākamat al-Nithām al-Siyāsī al-Misrī—1982." In *Al-Nabī al-Musallih-al-Rāfidūn*, edited by Said Ahmed Rif'at, 273–284. London: Riyad al-Rayyes, 1991.

al-Kharbāwī, Tharwat. "Abānā Alathī fī al-Rūwda." *Sawt al-Umma*, September 1, 2003.

al-Khawaga, Dina. "Le Debat sur les Coptes: Le Dit et le Non-Dit." *CEDEJ: Egypte Monde Arabe* 20, no. 4 (1994): 67–76.

al-Mahallāwī, Ahmad. *Khutub al-Shaykh Ahmad al-Mahallāwī Hawla Kul ma Yuhim al-Muslim fī Dīnihi wa Dunyahi*. 2 vols. Cairo: Dār al-'Itisām, n.d.

al-Mallakh, Muna. "The Church's Restrictions on Copts' Divorce Is the Highest Motive for Changing Religion." *al-Musawwar*, January 7, 2005, 23–25.

al-Masrii, 'Amr. "The Alexandria Demonstrations . . . What's Next?" Press review in *Arab-West Report*, October 17, 2005.

———. "Wafā's Conversion to Islam Was Due to Social Marital Problems." Press review in *Arab-West Report*, January 5–11, 2005.

al-Māwardī, 'Alī Ibn Muhammad. *The Ordinances of Government: A Translation of al-Ahkām al-Sultāniyya w'al-Wilāyat al-Dīniyya*. Translated by Wafaa H. Wahba. Great Books of Islamic Civilization. London: Garnet Publishing, 1996.

al-Misrī, 'Amr. "Wafaa Costantine, 'The Woman Who Set the Coptic Church on Fire.'" Press review in *Arab-West Report*, December 8–14, 2004.

al-Namnam, Hilmī. "Hal la Tazāl Bilād al-Gharb Dār al-Kufr wa 'Anād?" *al-Musaw-war*, November 23, 2001, 52.

al-Qā'ūd, Hilmī. "Istirāha . . . Thumma Mādhā." *al-Da'wa*, July 1978.

al-Qādī, 'Alī. "Tahdīd al-Nasl Bayn Islām wa al-Misīhiyya." *al-Da'wa*, June 1981, 40–41.

al-Qaradāwī, Yūsuf. *al-Sahwa al-Islāmiyya Min al-Murāhaqa ilā al-Rushd*. Cairo: Dār al-Shurūq, 2002.

———. *al-Shaykh al-Ghazālī Kamā 'Ariftuhu Rihlat Nusf Qarn*. Cairo: Dār al-Shurūq, 2000.

———. *The Lawful and the Prohibited in Islam*. Translated by M. Siddiqi, K. al-Hilbawi, and S. Shukri. Cairo: al-Falah, 2001.

———. *Non-Muslims in Islamic Society*. Translated by Khalil Muhammad Hamad and Sayed Mahboob Ali Shah. Indianapolis: American Trust Publications, 1985.

———. *State in Islam*. Cairo: al-Falāh, 1998.

al-Qattan, Najwa. *"Dhimmis in the Muslim Court: Documenting Justice in Ottoman Damascus (1775–1860)."* Ph.D. diss., Harvard University, 1996.

al-Qā'ūd, Hilmī. "Istirāha . . . Thumma Mādhā." *al-Da'wa*, July 1978.

al-Rahhāl, Sālim. "Amrīka wa Misr wa al-Haraka al-Islāmiyya." In *Al-Nabī al-Musallih-al-Rāfidūn*, edited by Said Ahmed Rif'at, 179–184. London: Riyad al-Rayyes, 1991.

al-Rāziq, 'Alī 'Abd. "Message Not Government, Religion Not State." In *Liberal Islam: A Sourcebook*, edited by Charles Kurzman, 29–233. New York: Oxford University Press, 1988.

al-Sa'īd, Rif'at. "Hikayāt al-Irhābī al-Muta'silim fī Misr: Al-Ikhwān al-Muslimīn." *al-Ahālī*, August 20, 2003, 5.

al-Sa'id, Sana. "Pope Shenouda in an Interview with *al-Wafd*: Wafā' Costantine Was Not Forced to Convert Back to Christianity." *al-Wafd (Arab-West Report)*, January 6, 2005, 57.

al-Sa'īd Habīb, Kamāl. *Al-Aqaliyāt wa al-Siyāsa fī al-Khibra al-Islāmiyya*. Cairo: Maktabat Madbūlī, 2003.

———. *Al-Harakat al-Islāmiyya min al-Muwājaha ilā al-Murāja'a*. Cairo: Maktabat Madbūlī, 2002.

———. "Min Manthūr Jamā'at al-Jihād al-Islāmī." In *Al-Nabī al-Musallih-al-Rāfidūn*, edited by Said Ahmed Rif'at, 200–216. London: Riyad al-Rayyes, 1991.

al-Salīmī, Bāhir. "Laysat Qunbulat Mauqūta: al-'Alāqat Bayn Mashākil al-Aqbāt wa Tawāzanāt al-Hukūma." *al-Midān*, July 24, 2003, 7.

al-Shami, Shayma. "Dr. Muhammad Imara Apologizes to Copts, Admits Mistakes in His Controversial Book." *Arab-West Report*, November 1, 2007.

al-Shaʿrāwī, Shaykh Muhammad Mutawallī. *Al-Shaykh al-Imām Muhammad Mutawallī al-Shaʿrāwī fī al-Hukm wa al-Siyāsa*. Egypt: Dār al-Asmā', 1990.

———. *Jamīʿa Fatāwā al-Shaʿrāwī*. 10 vols. Cairo: Dār al-Jalīl, 1999.

———. *Min Fayd al-Rahmān fī Tarabiyyat al-Insān: Min Qawl al-Imām al-Shaykh Muhammad Mutawallī al-Shaʿrāwī*. Cairo: Kitāb al-Dhahabi, 1986.

al-Shatir, Khairat. "No Need to Be Afraid of Us." *Guardian*, November 23, 2005.

al-Tabarī. *History of the Prophets and Kings (Tā'rīkh al-Rusul wa al-Mulūk)*. Translated by Michael Fishbein. Vol. 8, *The Victory of Islam*. Albany: State University of New York Press, 1997.

———. *History of the Prophets and Kings (Tā'rīkh al-Rusul wa al-Mulūk)*. Translated by Ismail Poonawala. Vol. 9, *The Last Years of the Prophet*. Albany: State University of New York Press, 1998.

———. *History of the Prophets and Kings (Tā'rīkh al-Rusul wa al-Mulūk)*. Translated by Khalid Blankinship. Vol. 11, *The Challenge to Empires*. Albany: State University of New York Press, 1993.

al-Tahtāwī, Rifa'a Badawi Rafi. "Fatherland and Patriotism." In *Islam in Transition: Muslim Perspectives*, edited by John J. Donohue and John L. Esposito, 11–15. New York: Oxford University Press, 1982.

al-Tilmisānī, ʿUmar. "Hā'ulā'i al-Jahūd: lā ʿAhd Lahum wa lā Dhimma" *al-Daʿwa*, October 1979, 4–5.

———. "Manhaj Allah . . . aw . . . al-Damār!!" *al-Daʿwa*, January 1979, 4–5.

Altman, Israel Elad. "The Egyptian Muslim Brotherhood after the 2005 Elections." *Current Trends in Islamist Ideology* 4 (2006): 5–21.

al-Zayyat, Montasser. *The Road to al-Qaeda: The Story of Bin Lāden's Right-Hand Man*. London: Pluto Press, 2004.

al-Zumur, ʿAbūd, "Manhaj Jamāʿāt al-Jihād." In *Al-Nabī al-Musallih-al-Rāfidūn*, edited by Said Ahmed Rif'at, 110–126. London: Riyad al-Rayyes, 1991.

a.n.m. [author not mentioned]. "al-Aqbāt fī Murājʿāt Qādat al-Jamāʿāt al-Islāmiyya." *al-Midān*, August 21, 2003, 6.

———. "al-Masīhiūn fī Misr wa al-Hukm Yashra Allah." *al-Daʿwa*, February 1977.

———. "al-Naʿara al-Tā'ifiyya allati Yathiruhā al-Nasārā." *al-Daʿwa*, June 1980, 60–64.

———. "ʿAwdat Thāhira al-Mulsiqāt al-Dīniyya ʿAlā al-Sayyārāt." *Ruz al-Yūsuf*, January 9, 2004, 22–23.

———. "The Baha'i Case as an Ordeal of Citizenship and Freedom of Belief in Egypt." *Cairo Institute for Human Rights Studies*, January 16, 2007.

———. "Haqā'iq Nuqadimuha lil-Mas'ūlīn Hawl Ahdāth al-Zawiya al-Hamra." *al-Daʿwa*, July 1981, 20–21.

———. "Major Jihadi Cleric and Author of Al-Qaeda's Shari'a Guide to Jihad: 9/11 Was a Sin." *Memri*, December 14, 2007.

———. "Marriage and Divorce between the Church Rules and the Judiciary Rulings [2]." Press review in *Arab-West Report*, April 5–11, 2008.

———. "Muhammad Hijāzī, Bahā'īs, and Freedom of Creed in Egypt." Press review in *Arab-West Report*, April 2, 2008.

———. "Muqābalat al-Usbū' fī Dair Anbā Bishoy." *al-Musawwar*, October 10, 2003, 16–36, 64–65.

———. "Muwājaha ma'a al-Rajl alathī 'Azal al-Bābā Munthu Nusf Qarn." *al-Musawwar*, July 4, 2003, 52–54.

———. "Qānūn al-Ahwāl al-Shakhsiyya al-Jadīd." 2000.

———. "Should Copts Have a Quota of Parliamentary Seats?" *al-Jumhurriyya*, October 13, 2005, 7.

———. "Strongholds of Orthodoxy: Whatever the Copts' Place in Society at Large, the Heart of Their Religious and Community Life Remains Intact." *Cairo Times (Arab-West Report)*, February 4–10, 1999.

———. "The Supreme Administrative Court Ruled in Favor of Reverted Converts." Press review in *Arab-West Report*, February 17, 2008.

———. "Tharwat al-Kharabawy Broke from the Muslim Brotherhood and Reveals Secrets: Al-Hudaiby Dreams of Ruling Egypt." *al-Ahrām al-'Arabī (Arab-West Report)*, June 12–18, 2003, 24, 25.

An-Na'im, Abdullahi Ahmed. *Islam and the Secular State: Negotiating the Future of Shari'a*. Cambridge, MA: Harvard University Press, 2008.

Ansari, Hamied. "Sectarian Conflict and the Political Expediency of Religion." *Middle East Journal* 38 (Summer 1984): 397–417.

Armanios, Febe. "'The Virtuous Woman': Images of Gender in Modern Coptic Society." *Middle Eastern Studies* 38, no. 1 (2002): 110–130.

As'ad, Gamāl. "Mahākamat Aqbāt al-Mahjar." *Sawt al-Umma*, February 23, 2004, 7.

Asad, Talal. *Formations of the Secular: Christianity, Islam, Modernity*. Stanford, CA: Stanford University Press, 2003.

———. "The Idea of an Anthropology of Islam." Occasional Papers. Washington, DC: Center for Contemporary Arab Studies, Georgetown University, 1986.

———. "Q & A AsiaSource Interview with Talal Asad." *AsiaSource* (2002).

———. "Reflections on Laïcité and the Public Sphere." *Social Science Research Council Items and Issues* 5, no. 3 (2005): 1–5.

Atiya, A. S. "Kibt." In *The Encyclopædia of Islam²*, 90–95. Leiden: Brill, 1986.

Atmaca, Nushin. "Discussion about Art. 2." *Arab-West Report*, n.d., 1–18.

'Auwīs, 'Abd al-Halīm. "Masīrat al-Ta'rīkh bayna al-Islām wa al-Misīhiyya." *al-Da'wa*, September 1978, 12–14.

'Awād, 'Ātif. "Al-Huriyyāt wa al-Sharī'a 'inda al-Ikhwān." *Sawt al-Umma*, September 1, 2003, 7.

———. *Samāhat al-Islām*. Cairo: al-Falāh, 2002.

Ayalon, Ami. "Egypt's Coptic Pandora's Box." In *Minorities and the State in the Arab World*, edited by Ofra Bengio and Gabriel Ben-Dor. Boulder, CO: Lynne Rienner Publishers, 1999, 33–72.

Ayubi, Nazih. *Over-Stating the Arab State: Politics and Society in the Middle East*. London: I.B. Tauris, 1999.

———. *Political Islam: Religion and Politics in the Arab World*. London and New York: Routledge, 1991.

———. "Islamic State." In *The Oxford Encyclopædia of the Modern Islamic World*, edited by John Esposito, 318–325. New York: Oxford University Press, 1995.

Azuri, L. "As Part of Its Struggle against the Muslim Brotherhood, the Egyptian Regime Comes Out against the Concept of a Cleric-Led State." http://www.memri .org/bin/opener_latest.cgi?ID=IA34107.

Baker, Raymond. *Islam without Fear: Egypt and the New Islamists*. Cambridge, MA: Harvard University Press, 2003.

Bayat, Asef. *Making Islam Democratic*. Stanford, CA: Stanford University Press, 2007.

Behrens-Abouseif, Doris. *The Political Situation of the Copts, 1798–1923*. 2 vols. Edited by Benjamin Braude and Bernard Lewis. Vol. 2, *Christians and Jews in the Ottoman Empire: The Functioning of a Plural Society*. New York: Holmes and Meier Publishers, 1982.

Berger, Maurits. "Apostasy and Public Policy in Contemporary Egypt: An Evaluation of Recent Cases from Egypt's Highest Courts." *Human Rights Quarterly* 25 (2003): 720–740.

———. "Public Policy and Islamic Law: The Modern *Dhimmī* in Contemporary Egyptian Family Law." *Islamic Law and Society* 8, no. 1 (2001): 88–136.

Betts, Robert Brenton. *Christians in the Arab East: A Political Study*. Atlanta: John Knox, 1978.

Bibāwī, Nabīl Luqā. "Pope Shenouda and the Second Article of the Constitution." *al-Akhbār (Arab-West Report)*, February 28, 2007.

Bosworth, C. E. "The Concept of *Dhimma* in Early Islam." In *Christians and Jews in the Ottoman Empire: The Functioning of a Plural Society*, edited by Benjamin Braude and Bernard Lewis. New York: Holmes and Meir Publishers, 1982, 37–51.

Boyle, Kevin, and Adel Omar Sherif, eds. *Human Rights and Democracy: The Role of the Supreme Constitutional Court of Egypt*. Vol. 3. Cimel Book Series. London: Kluwer Law International, 1996.

Boyle, Kevin, and Juliet Sheen. *Freedom of Religion and Belief: A World Report*. London: Routledge, 1997.

Braude, Benjamin. "Foundation Myths of the *Millet* System." In *Christians and Jews in the Ottoman Empire: The Functioning of a Plural Society*, edited by Benjamin Braude and Bernard Lewis, 69–88. New York: Holmes and Meier Publishers, 1982.

Braude, Benjamin, and Bernard Lewis. Introduction to *Christians and Jews in the Ottoman Empire: The Functioning of a Plural Society*, edited by Benjamin Braude and Lewis Bernard. New York: Holmes and Meier Publishers, 1982.

Brown, Carl. *Religion and State: The Muslim Approach to Politics*. New York: Columbia University Press, 2000.

Bulliet, Richard. *The Case for Islamo-Christian Civilization*. New York: Columbia University Press, 2004.

Burgat, Francois. *Face to Face with Political Islam*. London: I.B. Tauris, 2002.

Cahen, C. "*Dhimma*." In *The Encyclopædia of Islam²*, 227–31. Leiden: Brill, 1965.

Carter, B. L. *The Copts in Egyptian Politics*. London: Croom Helm, 1986.

Coulson, Noel. *A History of Islamic Law*. Edinburgh: Edinburgh University Press, 1964.

Courbage, Youssef, and Philippe Fargues. *Christians and Jews under Islam*. London: I.B. Tauris, 1998.

Crone, Patricia. *God's Rule: Government and Islam*. New York: Columbia University Press, 2004.

———. "Mawlā." In *The Encyclopædia of Islam²*, 874–882. Leiden: Brill, 1991.

Crone, Patricia, and Martin Hinds. *God's Caliph: Religious Authority in the First Centuries of Islam*. Cambridge: Cambridge University Press, 2003.

Davison, Roderic. "The *Millets* as Agents of Change in the Nineteenth-Century Ottoman Empire." In *Christians and Jews in the Ottoman Empire: The Functioning of a Plural Society*, edited by Benjamin Braude and Bernard Lewis, 319–338. New York: Holmes and Meier Publishers, 1982.

Desai, Meghnad. *Rethinking Islamism: The Ideology of the New Terror*. London: I.B. Tauris, 2007.

Dupret, Badouin. *A Return to the Shariah: Egyptian Judges and Referring to Islam*. Edited by John Esposito and Francois Burgat. London: Hurst, 2003.

Dūs, Sharīf. "'Āshat Misr." *al-Ahkbār*, December 16–23, 2003, 23.

Eickelman, Dale, and James Piscatori. *Muslim Politics*. Princeton, NJ: Princeton University Press, 1996.

el-Affendi, Abdelwahab. "Muslim or Citizen?" *Centre for the Study of Democracy Bulletin* 8, no. 1 (2000–2001).

el-Dubaa, Mohammed. "Essam Sultan the Leader of the Wast Party Talks about Mamoun El-Houdeibi Though This Causes Family Embarrassment. He Says, 'If the Muslim Brotherhood Had a Martial Court, They Would Have Sentenced Us to Death by Hanging.'" *Arab-West Report*, December 5, 1997.

el-Hodaiby, Muhammad Ma'mun. "Upholding Islam." *Harvard International Review* 19, no. 2 (1997).

Elshoubaki, Amr. "Old Jihad, New Jihad." *al-Ahram Weekly*, February 28–March 5, 2008.

Fahmī, Viola. "The Truth behind the Coptic Wrath against Church Leadership." *al-Ahālī (Arab-West Report)*, April 9, 2008.

Fattal, Antoine. *Le Statut Légal des Non-Musulmans en Pays d'islam*. Vol. 10 of *Recherches Publiées sous la Direction de L'institute de Lettres Orientales de Beyrouth*. Beyrouth: Imprimerie Catholique, 1958.

Fāyid, al-Shaykh Mahmūd. "Samāhat al-Islām ma'a Ghayr al-Muslimīn." *al-Da'wa*, October 1980.

"Freedom of Belief between Shariah [Islamic Jurisprudence] and the Constitution." Fifth Annual Convention for the Egyptian Union of Human Rights Organization, January 11, 2007

Friedmann, Yohanan. *Tolerance and Coercion in Islam: Interfaith Relations in Muslim Tradition*. Cambridge: Cambridge University Press, 2003.

Gaffney, Patrick D. *The Prophet's Pulpit: Islamic Preaching in Contemporary Egypt*. Berkeley: University of California Press, 1994.

Gardet, L. "Dīn." In *The Encyclopædia of Islam²*, 293–296. Leiden: Brill, 1965.

Guindy, Adel. "Family Status Issues among Egypt's Copts: A Brief Overview." *MERIA* 11, no. 3 (2007): 1–10.

Guirguis, Magdi. "The Organization of the Coptic Community in the Ottoman Period." In *Society and Economy in Egypt and the Eastern Mediterranean, 1600–1900: Essays in Honor of André Raymond*, edited by Nelly Hanna and Raouf Abbas, 201–216. Cairo: Cairo University Press, 2005.

Habashi, Fadi. "Resorting to Religious Names in Times of Crises!" *Sawt al-Umma*, January 10, 2005.

Habīb, Rafīq. *Hadārat al-Wasat: Nahwa Usūliyya Jadīda*. Cairo: Dār al-Shurūq, 2001.

———. *Ihyā' al-Taqālīd al-'Arabiyya*. Cairo: Dār al-Shurūq, 2003.

———. "The Wafa Issue Was Overt Defiance of the State's Legal and Constitutional Authority." *al-Usbū' (Arab-West Report)*, January 17, 2005.

Haddad, Yvonne. "Christians in a Muslim State: The Recent Egyptian Debate." In *Christian-Muslim Encounters*, edited by Yvonne Yazbeck Haddad and Wadi Zaidan Haddad, 381–398. Gainesville: University Press of Florida, 1995.

———. "Islamist Depictions of Christianity in the Twentieth Century: The Pluralism Debate and the Depiction of the Other." *Islam and Christian-Muslim Relations 7*, no. 1 (1996): 75–93.

———. "Islamists and the Challenge of Pluralism," 3–24. Occasional Papers. Washington, DC: Center for Contemporary Arab Studies, Georgetown University, 1995.

Halliday, Fred. "'Orientalism' and Its Critics." *British Journal of Middle Eastern Studies* 20, no. 2 (1993): 145–163.

Hamzawy, Amr. "The Muslim Brotherhood's Party Platform." *Carnegie Endowment*

for International Peace (2007). http://carnegieendowment.org/events/?fa=eventDe
tail&id=1076&prog=zgp&proj=zted.

Hannā, Mīlād. *Acceptance of the Other.* Cairo: al-Ahram Center for Political and Strategic Studies, 2001.

———. *The Seven Pillars of the Egyptian Identity.* Cairo: General Egyptian Book Organisation, 1989.

Hasan, S. S. *Christians versus Muslims in Modern Egypt.* Oxford: Oxford University
Press, 2003.

Hassab, Bisan. "Tariq al-Bishri: The Application of Shar'iah in Egypt Will Not Affect
the Rights of Copts because the Principle of Citizenship Is Fundamentally Rooted
Therein." *al-Dustūr (Arab-West Report)*, May 14, 2007, 5.

Hassan, Bahey Eldin. "Muslim Brothers Party's Platform in Egypt from a Human
Rights Perspective." Paper presented at the Center for the Study of Islam and Democracy conference "Political Islam and Democracy—What Do Islamists and Islamic Movements Want?" May 2008.

Hawting, Gerald. *The Idea of Idolatry and the Emergence of Islam: From Polemic to
History.* Cambridge: Cambridge University Press, 1999.

Heikal, Muhammad. *Autumn of Fury.* London: Andre Deutsch, 1983.

Hijāzī, Īhāb. "Christian Intellectuals: The Second Article of the Constitution Guarantees Religious Freedom for Non-Muslims." *October (Arab-West Report)*, March 19,
2007.

Hirschkind, Charles. *The Ethical Soundscape: Cassette Sermons and Islamic Counterpublics.* New York: Columbia University Press, 2006.

Hodgson, Marshall. *The Venture of Islam: Conscience and History in a World Civilization.* Vol. 1, *The Classical Age of Islam.* Chicago: University of Chicago Press, 1974.

———. *The Venture of Islam: Conscience and History in a World Civilization.* Vol. 3, *The
Gunpowder Empires and Modern Times.* Chicago: University of Chicago Press, 1974.

Hourani, Albert. *Arabic Thought in the Liberal Age, 1978–1939.* Cambridge: Cambridge
University Press, 1984.

———. *A History of the Arab Peoples.* Cambridge, MA: Harvard University Press, 1991.

———. *Minorities in the Arab World.* Oxford: Oxford University Press, 1947.

Howeidy, Amira. "Jumping the Gun." *al-Ahram Weekly*, October 25–31, 2007.

Hulsman, Cornelis. "Dangerous Developments." *Arab-West Report*, September 6, 2003.

———. "Different Middle Eastern Christian Responses to Living in a Muslim Environment." Special for *Arab-West Report*, December 5, 2006.

———. "Do Not Claim Something That Cannot Be Proven: The Origin of Some Christian Persecution Stories." *Arab-West Report*, November 17–23, 2004.

———. Editorial, *Arab-West Report*, August 12, 2003.

———. Editorial, *Arab-West Report*, July 10, 2008.

———. "Egyptian Villagers Resist Monastery's Growth." *Free Copts*, July 25, 2008.

——. "Freedom of Religion in Egypt." *Arab-West Report*, September 4, 2003.

——. "Interview with Dr. Philippe Fargues about Coptic Statistics." *Arab-West Report*, December 20, 2008.

——. "Interview with Kamāl Zākhir Mūsa about His Conviction in the Need for Church Reform." Special for *Arab-West Report*, November 8–14, 2006.

——. "Interview with Munīr Fakhrī 'Abd Al-Nūr." *Arab-West Report*, January 21, 2009.

——. "Special for Arab-West Report." *Arab-West Report*, August 9, 2003.

Hulsman, Sawsan. "Escalations following the Alleged Conversion of a Priest's Wife to Islam." Special for *Arab-West Report*, December 15–21, 2004.

Huntington, Samuel. "The Clash of Civilisations." *Foreign Affairs* 72, no. 3 (1993): 22–49.

Hussein, Taha. *The Future of Culture in Egypt*. Translated by Sidney Glazer. Ann Arbor, MI: American Council of Learned Societies, 1954.

Husserl, Gerhart. "Public Policy and Ordre Public." *Virginia Law Review* 25, no. 1 (1938): 37–67.

Huwaydī, Fahmī. *Lil Islām Dimuqrātiyya*. Cairo: Markaz al-Ahrām, 1993.

——. *Muwātinūn lā Dhimmiūn: Mawqi' Ghayr al-Muslimīn fī Mujtama'a al-Muslimīn*. 3rd ed. Cairo: Dār al-Shurūq, 1999.

——. "Taqdīm Fahmī Huwaydī." In *Al-Aqbāt: Al-Kanīsa am al-Watan; Qissat al Bābā Shanūda al-Thālith*, edited by Abdul Latīf al-Manāwī, 8–14. Cairo: Dār al-Shabāb al-'Arabī, 1992.

Ibn Ishaq. *The Life of Muhammad: A Translation of Ishaq's Sirat Rasul Allah*. Translated by A. Guillaume. Edited by Ibn Hisham. Lahore: Oxford University Press, 1968.

Ibn Kathir, Ismail Ibn Umar. *Tafsir Ibn Kathir*. Translated by Shaykh Safiur-Rahman al-Mubarakpuri. 10 vols. Riyadh: Darussalam, 2000.

Ibn Khaldun, Muhammad. *The Muqaddimah: An Introduction to History*. Translated by Franz Rosenthal. Edited by N. J. Dawood. Princeton, NJ: Princeton University Press, 1967.

Ibn Naqqash. "The Jizya's Meaning: Edict of Caliph Al-Amir Bi-Ahkam Illah (1101–1130)." In *The Dhimmi: Jews and Christians under Islam*, edited by Bat Ye'or, 188–189. Rutherford. NJ: Fairleigh Dickinson University Press, 1985.

Ibn Qayyim al-Jawziyya. "Places of Worship, Clothes and Behavior of Dhimmis." In *The Dhimmi: Jews and Christians under Islam*, edited by Bat Ye'or, 196–198. Rutherford, NJ: Fairleigh Dickinson University Press, 1985.

Ibn Rushd. *The Distinguished Jurist's Primer (Bidāyat al-Mujtahid wa Nihāyat al-Muqtasid)*. Translated by Imran Ahsan Khany Nyazee. Vol. 1, *Great Books of Islamic Civilization*. London: Garnet Publishing, 1994.

——. "The Legal Doctrine of Jihad: The Chapter on Jihad from Averroes' Legal Handbook *Al-Bidāya*." In *Jihad in Classical and Modern Islam*, edited by Rudolph Peters, 27–42. Princeton, NJ: Princeton University Press, 1996.

Ibn Taghribirdi. "Dismissal of Christian Officials in Egypt (1410)." In *The Dhimmi: Jews and Christians under Islam*, edited by Bat Ye'or, 198–199. Rutherford, NJ: Fairleigh Dickinson University Press, 1985.

Ibn Taymiyya. *Answering Those Who Altered the Religion of Jesus Christ*. Translated by Bayan Translation Services. al-Mansura, Egypt: Umm al-Qura, 2003.

'Ibrāhīm, Muhammad 'Alī. "About Their New Program." *al-Gumhūrriyya*, September 15, 2007.

Ibrahim, Saad Eddin. *The Copts of Egypt: Freedom to Worship*. London: Minority Rights Group International, 1996.

'Imāra, Muhammad. *Al-Islām wa al-'Aqaliyāt: al-Mādī, wa al-Hādir, wa al-Mustaqbal*. Cairo: Maktabat al-Shurūq al-Dawliyya, 2003.

Issawi, Charles. "The Transformation of the Economic Position of the *Millets* in the Nineteenth Century." In *Christians and Jews in the Ottoman Empire: The Functioning of a Plural Society*, edited by Benjamin Braude and Bernard Lewis, 261–286. New York: Holmes and Meier Publishers, 1982.

Jad al-Haqq, Sami, and Hani Ahmed Rizq. "Sectarian Tension in Shubra." *Sawt al-Umma (Arab-West Report)*, April 21, 2007, 11.

Jalāl, 'Ilā. "Baheb al-Sima Controversy Continues." Press review in *Arab-West Report*, June 23–29, 2004.

Kamāl, Yusuf. "Al-Jizya: Qā'idat al-Takāful Lighayr al-Muslimīn. "*al-Da'wa*, January 1980, 11–14.

Kamali, Mohammad H. "Fundamental Rights of the Individual: An Analysis of *Haqq* (Right) in Islamic Law." *American Journal of Islamic Social Sciences* 10, no. 3 (1993): 340–366.

Karpat, Kemal. "*Millets* and Nationality: The Roots of the Incongruity of Nation and State in the Post-Ottoman Era." In *Christians and Jews in the Ottoman Empire: The Functioning of a Plural Society*, edited by Benjamin Braude and Bernard Lewis, 141–170. New York: Holmes and Meier Publishers, 1982.

Kepel, Gilles. "Islamism Reconsidered: A Running Dialogue with Modernity." *Harvard International Review* 22, no. 2 (2002): 22–27.

———. *The Prophet and Pharaoh: Muslim Extremism in Egypt*. Translated by Jon Rothschild. London: al-Saqi, 1985.

———. *The Trail of Political Islam*. London: I.B. Tauris, 2002.

Khālid, Usāma. "Haqīqat Ightisāb al-Fatayyāt fī Mahalāt al-Tawhīd wa al-Nūr wa Awlād Rajab." *Sawt al-Umma*, March 22, 2004, 7.

Khalil, Magdi. "The Muslim Brotherhood and the Copts." *Watani International (Arab West Report)*, December 3, 2006.

Kishk, Shaykh. *Al-Munāthara*. Cairo: Nur lil Intāg wa al-Tawzi'a al-Islāmī, n.d.

Kraemer, Joel L. *Humanism in the Renaissance of Islam: The Cultural Revival during the Buyid Age*. Leiden: Brill, 1992.

Kramer, Gudrun. *"Dhimmi* or Citizen? Muslim-Christian Relations in Egypt." In *The Christian-Muslim Frontier: Chaos, Clash, or Dialogue?* edited by N. J. Nielsen. London: I.B. Tauris, 1998, 33–49.

Kurzman, Charles. *Liberal Islam: A Sourcebook.* Oxford: Oxford University Press, 1998.

Kymlicka, Will. *Contemporary Political Philosophy: An Introduction.* 2nd ed. Oxford: Oxford University Press, 2002.

Labīb, Hānī. "Amrīka . . . wa Muhawalāt al-Saytara 'Alā Misīhī Misr munthu al-Qarn 19." *al-Midān*, August 21, 2003, 5.

———. "The Removal of Religious Affiliation from Identity Cards . . . A Secular Heresy to Conceal the Identity of Egyptians." *Ruz al-Yūsuf (Arab-West Report)*, September 3, 2006, 6.

Lamb, Christina. "Egyptian Police 'Crucify' and Rape Christians." *Sunday Telegraph*, October 25, 1998.

Lambton, Ann. *State and Government in Medieval Islam: An Introduction to the Study of Islamic Political Theory.* Oxford: Oxford University Press, 1981.

Lane, Edward. *An Arabic-English Lexicon.* 8 vols. Beirut: Librairie du Liban, 1874.

———. *Manners and Customs of Modern Egyptians.* New York: Cosimo, 2005.

Lapidus, Ira. "The Conversion of Egypt to Islam." *Israel Oriental Studies* 2 (1972): 248–262.

———. "The Separation of State and Religion in the Development of Early Islamic Society." *International Journal of Middle East Studies* 6, no. 4 (1975): 363–385.

Lewis, Bernard. *The Political Language of Islam.* Chicago: University of Chicago Press, 1988.

Little, Donald. "Coptic Conversion to Islam under the Bahri Mamluks 692–755/1293–1354." *British Society for Oriental and African Studies* 39, no. 3 (1976): 552–569.

Lombardi, Clark. *State Law as Islamic Law in Modern Egypt: The Incorporation of the Sharī'a into Egyptian Constitutional Law.* Studies in Islamic Law and Society. Leiden: Brill, 2006.

Lynch, Marc. "The Muslim Brotherhood's Party Platform." *Carnegie Endowment for International Peace* (2007), http://carnegieendowment.org/events/?fa=eventDetail&id=1076&prog=zgp&proj=zted.

Maalouf, Amin. *The Crusades through Arab Eyes.* London: al-Saqi, 1984.

Mādī, Abū al-'Ilā. *Al-Wasat Party Program (2004).* Cairo: al-Azzazy Press, 2004.

———. "Religious and Political Pluralism: The Islamic Concept of State and Society in Modernity." Paper presented at the conference "Islamic Perspectives in Secular Societies—Modern Scholars of Islamic Questions for the West," Berlin, June 21–22, 2002.

Mādī, Abū al-'Ilā and Shaykh Fawzi Fadil al-Zefzaf. "Citizenship within the New Religious Address." Paper presented at the Egyptian German Dialogue Forum Evangelical Academy, Hanover, Germany, April 9–13, 2003.

Makari, Peter E. *Conflict and Cooperation: Christian-Muslim Relations in Contemporary Egypt.* Syracuse, NY: Syracuse University Press, 2007.

Makari, Victor E. *Ibn Taymiyya's Ethics: The Social Factor.* American Academy of Religion Series 34. Chico, CA: Scholars Press, 1983.

Malak, Magdy. "Converts in Court." *Watani International,* May 13, 2007.

Mashhour, Mustafa. *Provisions of the Soul.* Cairo: al-Falāh, 2000.

Masters, Bruce. *Christians and Jews in the Ottoman Arab World: The Roots of Sectarianism.* Cambridge: Cambridge University Press, 2001.

Maudūdī, Abul A'lā. *Rights of Non-Muslims in Islamic State.* Translated by Khurshid Ahmad. Lahore, Pakistan: Islamic Publications, 1982.

Moussalli, Ahmed. *The Islamic Quest for Democracy, Pluralism, and Human Rights.* Gainesville: University Press of Florida, 2001.

Mubārak, Hishām. *Al-Irhābiūn Qādimūn: Dirāsat Muqārana bayn Mawqif al-Ikhwān al-Muslimīn wa Jamā'āt al-Jihād min Qadiyyat al-'Unf (1929–1994).* Cairo: Kitāb al-Mahrūsa, 1995.

Munīb, 'Abd al-Mun'im. "If the People Want It, Why Not Apply Shari'ah in Egypt." *al-Dustūr (Arab-West Report),* October 22, 2008.

Murad, Ahmed. "Muslim and Coptic Thinkers Uncover the Plan of Rejecting Arabism and Islam." *al-Liwā' al-Islāmī (Arab-West Report),* February 26, 2004.

Murqus, Samīr. *Al-Muwātana wa al-Taghayīr: Dirāsa 'Awliyya Hawl Ta'sīl al-Mafhūm wa Taf'īl al-Mumārasa.* Cairo: Maktabat al-Shurūq al-Dawliyya, 2006.

———. "Humūm al-Shabāb al-Qibtī." *al-Qāhira* 121 (1992): 64–72.

———. "Our Experience: Dialogue Based on Citizenship," *al-'Ākhar . . . al-Hiwār . . . al-Muwātana.* Cairo: Maktabat al-Shurūq al-Dawliyya, 2005.

———. "The Religious Revival/Awakening . . ." Paper presented at a conference in Germany, 2006.

Murqus, Samīr, and Vivian Fu'ād. "Our Experience: Dialogue Based on Citizenship." In *al-'Ākhar . . . al-Hiwār . . . al-Muwātana,* edited by Samīr Murqus, 151–164. Cairo: Maktabat al-Shurūq al-Dawliyya, 2005.

Musā, Kamāl Zākhir. "Copts and the Constitutional Amendments." *Ruz al-Yūsuf,* January 12, 2007, 6.

Muslim, Ibn Hajjaj al-Qushayri. *Sahīh Muslim: Being Traditions of the Sayings and Doings of the Prophet Muhammad as Narrated by His Companions and Compiled under the Title al-Jāmi'-us-sahīh.* Trans. 'Abdul Hamīd Siddīqī. 4 vols. Lahore: Kashmiri Bazar, 1971.

Muslim Brotherhood. "Barnāmij al-Hizb." 2007.

———. "Mb Parliamentary Bloc Wishes Christians Merry Christmas." http://www.ikwanweb.com/article.php?id=668.

———. "The Muslim Brotherhood's Program." http://www.ikhwanweb.com/Article.asp?ID=812&SectionID=70.

Mustāfa, Shukrī. "Al-Nas al-Kāmil Li Aqwāl wa I'tirāfāt." In *Al-Nabī al-Musallih-al-Thā'irūn*, edited by Said Ahmed Rif'at, 53–109. London: Riyad al-Rayyes, 1991.

Najjar, Fauzi. "Book Banning in Contemporary Egypt." *Muslim World* 91 (Fall 2001): 399–424.

Nāsif, 'Umād. *Duktūr 'Umar 'Abd al-Kāfī . . . .* Cairo: Dār al-Hadaf lil Nashr, 1993.

Nelson, Cynthia. "Religious Experience, Sacred Symbols, and Social Reality: An Illustration from Egypt." *Humaniora Islamica* 2 (1974): 253–266.

Nūr, Muhammad. "The Electoral Card . . . A Basic Condition for Coptic Marriage." *Ākhir Sā'a*, January 28, 2009.

Okasha, Reda. "Dr Selim Al-Awa in His Special Interview: The Khilafa System Is Not Inspired." *al-Liwā' al-Islāmī (Arab-West Report)*, December 16–22, 1999.

Philipp, Thomas. "Copts and Other Minorities in the Development of the Egyptian Nation State." In *Egypt from Monarchy to Republic: A Reassessment of Revolution and Change*, edited by Shimon Shamir. Boulder, CO: Westview, 1995, 131–150.

Qamaruddin, Khan. *The Political Thought of Ibn Taymiyya*. Islamabad, Pakistan: Islamic Research Institute, 1973.

Qasim, Tal'at Fu'ad. "What Does the Gama'a Islamiyya Want? An Interview with Tal'at Fu'ad Qasim." *Middle East Report* 198 (January–March 1996): 40–46.

Qutb, Sayyid. *Al-Islām wa Muskilat al-Hadāra*. Cairo: Dār al-Shurūq, 1983.

———. *Fī Zilāl al-Qur'ān*. 6 vols. Beirut: Dār al-Shurūq, 1982.

———. *Hādhā al-Dīn*. Kuwait: Maktabat al-Faysal, 1989.

———. *Milestones*. Delhi: Millat Book Center, n.d.

———. *Social Justice in Islam*. Translated by John Hardie. New York: Octagon Books, 1970.

Rabī', Shirīn. "Exclusive: The First Interview with Nāhid Mitwallī Who Has the Highest Voice among All the Converts to Christianity." *Sawt al-Umma (Arab-West Report)*, September 10, 2007, 9.

Rajab, Mustafa. "The End of the Jamā'at al-Islāmiyah." *Rose al-Yūsuf (Arab-West Report)*, September 18, 2006, 26.

Reiss, Wolfram. Abridged by Cornelis Hulsman. "Renewal in the Coptic Orthodox Church: Notes of the Ph.D. Thesis of Revd. Dr. Wolfram Reiss," 1–32. Cairo, *Arab-West Report*, 2001.

Richards, Donald. "Dhimmi Problems in Fifteenth-Century Cairo: Reconsideration of a Court Document." *Studies in Muslim-Jewish Relations* 1 (1993): 127–163.

Rizq, Hamdī. "15 Million Copts." *al-Misrī al-Yawm (Arab-West Report)*, July 7, 2007.

Robinson, Chase F. *Islamic Historiography*. Cambridge: Cambridge University Press, 2003.

Saeed, Abdullah, and Hassan Saeed. *Freedom of Religion, Apostasy, and Islam*. Burlington, VT: Ashgate, 2004.

Safran, Nadav. *Egypt in Search of Political Community: An Analysis of the Intellectual and Political Evolution of Egypt, 1804–1952.* Cambridge, MA: Harvard University Press, 1961.

Sa'īd, 'Abd al-Hāfiz. "Applying Islamic [Rules] in All Affairs of Life Is Something Impossible Now." *Sawt al-Umma (Arab-West Report)*, August 30, 2004.

———. "Will the Jihad Organization Announce from Tura Prison That It Has Abandoned Violence?!" *Sawt al-Umma (Arab-West Report)*, March 15, 2004.

Salāh, Muhammad. "Brotherhood Leader Resigns and Attacks the Guidance Bureau (Misr: Qiyādī Yastaqil min al-Ikhwān wa Yahmīl 'Alā Matkab al-Irshād)." *al-Hayāt*, September 14, 2003, 7.

———. "Marqus: Muslim Brotherhood–Coptic Dialogue of No Avail." *Ruz al-Yūsuf (Arab-West Report)*, January 26, 2006, 3.

Salāma, Usāma. "Egypt Torn Apart by Extremist Muslim Brotherhood Members and Copts." *Ruz al-Yūsuf (Arab-West Report)*, January 27, 2007.

———. "Waiting for a Law That Will Criminalize Discrimination between Muslims and Christians." *Ruz al-Yūsuf (Arab-West Report)*, February 10–16, 2007.

Sālih, Majdī. "What Does the Prime Minister Mean by Saying 'Egypt Is Secular'?" *al-Usbū' (Arab-West Report)*, May 29, 2006.

Salim, Arskal. *Challenging the Secular State: The Islamization of Law in Modern Indonesia.* Honolulu: University of Hawai'i Press, 2008.

Samaan, Makram, and Soheir Sukkary. "The Copts and Muslims of Egypt." In *Muslim-Christian Conflicts: Economic, Political, and Social Origins,* edited by Suad Joseph and Barbara L. K. Pillsbury, 127–155. Boulder, CO: Westview, 1978.

Saqqā, Katia. "Constitutional Amendments according to Nawāl al-Sa'dāwī." *Arab-West Report*, February 15, 2007.

Schulze, Reinhard. "Mass Culture and Islamic Cultural Production in 19th Century Middle East." In *Mass Culture, Popular Culture, and Social Life in the Middle East,* edited by Georg Stauth and Sami Zubaida, 189–207. Boulder, CO: Westview, 1987.

Sedra, Paul. "Class Cleavages and Ethnic Conflict: Coptic-Christian Communities in Modern Egyptian Politics." *Islam and Christian-Muslim Relations* 10, no. 2 (1999): 219–235.

Shāban, Muhammad. "Nabil Abdel Fattah: There Will Be No Renewal of Religious Discourse without Real Political Reform." *al-Qāhira (Arab-West Report)*, December 16–23, 2003, 21.

Shahine, Gihan. "Bad Cards." *al-Ahram Weekly*, December 29, 2005–January 4, 2006.

———. "Jumbled Reactions." *al-Ahram Weekly*, August 18–24, 2005.

Shaltut, Mahmud. "A Modernist Interpretation of Jihad: Mahmud Shaltut's Treatise *Koran and Fighting.*" In *Jihad in Classical and Modern Islam,* edited by Rudolph Peters, 59–102. Princeton, NJ: Princeton University Press, 1996.

Shepard, William. "Sayyid Qutb's Doctrine of Jahiliyya." *International Journal of Middle East Studies* 35, no. 4 (2003): 521–545.

Shibl, Muhammad. "Islam and the Kitabis." *October (Arab-West Report)*, November 30–December 5, 2000.

———. "Who Says That You Represent the True Religion (Man Alathī Qāl Innakum Tumaththilūn Sahīh al-Dīn)." *al-Qāhira*, July 22, 2003, 22.

Shu'ayb, Sa'īd. "Dr. Mīlād Hannā: Copts in Egypt Are Second-Class Citizens." *al-'Arabī (Arab-West Report)*, May 5, 2004.

Shu'eeb, Said. "Dr Abdel Monem Abul Futouh: We Do Not Object to a Christian Being Elected President of Egypt." *al-Sharq al-Awsat (Arab-West Report)*, October 5, 2003, 15.

Shukri, Tamir. "The Administrative Court: Moving from One Religion to Another Abuses Islam." *Arab-West Report*, May 2–8, 2007.

Sidhum, Yūsuf. "Ahdāth Qariya Jirzā Fasl Jadīd fī Musalsal Karīh." *al-Watanī*, November 23, 2003, 1.

———. "Civil Register Victims." *Watani International (Arab-West Report)*, June 5, 2007, 1.

———. "On the Shura Elections." *Watani International (Arab-West Report)*, June 17, 2007, 1.

———. "Yes, 'Mosques and Churches Are No Courtyard for Politics' . . . But . . . ," *al-Watanī (Arab-West Report)*, January 20–26, 2000.

Singerman, Diane. "The Muslim Brotherhood's Party Platform." *Carnegie Endowment for International Peace* (2007), http://carnegieendowment.org/events/?fa=eventDetail&id=1076&prog=zgp&proj=zted.

Sirri, Odai. "Improving Trend." *Cairo Times* 6, no. 32 (2002): 8.

Sirriyeh, Elizabeth. "Wahhabis, Unbelievers, and the Problems of Exclusivism." *British Society for Middle East Studies* 16, no. 2 (1989): 123–132.

Sivan, Emmanuel. "Eavesdropping on Radical Islam." *Middle East Quarterly* (March 1995): 1–19.

———. *Interpretations of Islam, Past and Present*. Princeton, NJ: Darwin Press, 1985.

———. *Radical Islam: Medieval Theology and Modern Politics*. New Haven, CT: Yale University Press, 1985.

Smith, C. D. "The Crisis of Orientation: The Shift of Intellectuals to Islamic Subjects in the 1930's." *International Journal of Middle East Studies* 4 (1973): 382–410.

Smith, Wilfred Cantwell. *The Meaning and End of Religion: A Revolutionary Approach to the Great Religious Traditions*. San Francisco: Harper and Row, 1978.

Spencer, Robert, ed. *The Myth of Islamic Tolerance: How Islamic Law Treats Non-Muslims*. Amherst, NY: Prometheus Books, 2005.

Stacher, Joshua. "The Brothers and the Wars." *Middle East Report* 250 (Spring 2009).

———. "Post-Islamist Rumblings in Egypt: The Emergence of the Wasat Party." *Middle East Journal* 56 (Summer 2002): 415–432.

Stillman, Norman A. "Dhimma." In *Medieval Islamic Civilization: An Encyclopedia*, edited by Josef W. Meri, 205–207. New York: Routledge, 2006.

Tammam, Hossam. "Mb Goes Rural." *al-Ahram Weekly*, October 23–29, 2008.

———. "Too Old School to Strike." *al-Ahram Weekly*, April 2–8, 2009.

Tharwat, Muhammad. "Duktūr Yūsuf al-Qaradāwi Yurīd an Yatakhalas min Kalimat Dhimmī wa Yabdiluhā Bi Muwātun." *al-Midān*, July 31, 2003, 10.

Thomas, Bishop. "The Experience of the Middle East's Largest Christian Community during a Time of Rising Islamization." Paper presented at the Hudson Institute, July 18, 2008.

Tritton, A. S. *The Caliphs and Their Non-Muslim Subjects: A Critical Study of the Covenant of 'Umar*. London: Frank Cass, 1970.

Trofimov, Yaroslav. "Muslim Brotherhood Falters as Egypt Outflanks Islamists." *Wall Street Journal*, May 15, 2009.

Van Nispen Tot Sevenaer, Christian. "Changes in Relations between Copts and Muslims (1952–1991) in the Light of Historical Experience." In *Between Desert and City: The Coptic Orthodox Church Today*, edited by Nelly Van Doorn-Harder and Kari Vogt, 22–34. Oslo: Novis forlag, 1997.

Vikør, Knut S. "The Sharī'a and the Nation State: Who Can Codify the Divine Law?" In *The Middle East in a Globalized World: Papers from the Fourth Nordic Conference on Middle Eastern Studies, Oslo, 1998*, edited by Bjørn Olav Utvik and Knut S. Vikør, 220–250. Bergen, Norway: Nordic Society for Middle Eastern Studies, 2000.

Ward, Seth. "A Fragment from an Unknown Work by al-Tabari on the Tradition 'Expel the Jews and Christians from the Arabian Peninsula (and the Lands of Islam).'" *Bulletin of the School of Oriental and African Studies* 53, no. 3 (1990): 407–420.

Wasfī, Wafā'. "Would a Constitution Based on Citizenship Encourage Copts to Participate in Social and Political Life?" *Ruz al-Yūsuf (Arab-West Report)*, March 2, 2007.

Watt, Montgomery. "Al-Hudaybiyya." In *The Encyclopædia of Islam²*, 539. Leiden: Brill, 1965.

Wehr, Hans. *A Dictionary of Modern Written Arabic*. Edited by Milton Cowan. Beirut: Librairie du Liban, 1980.

Wood, Leonard. "Shari'ah Revivalist Thought in the First Years of the Shari'ah Lawyers' Bar Association Journal, 1929–1931." *Maghreb Review* 32, nos. 2–3 (2007): 196–217.

Yassin, Mustafa. "Dr. Salim al-'Awwa at an Intellectual Meeting in the Saudi Embassy: 'Copts Are Not Ahl al-Dhimma . . . We Are All Citizens on an Equal Level.'" *'Aqīdatī (Arab-West Report)*, August 3, 2004.

Ye'or, Bat, ed. *The Dhimmi: Jews and Christians under Islam*. Rutherford, NJ: Fairleigh Dickinson University Press, 1985.

Zakariyya, Fouad. *Myth and Reality in the Contemporary Islamist Movement*. Translated and with an introduction and bibliography by Ibrahim M.Abu-Rabi'. London: Pluto Press, 2005.

Zebiri, Kate. *Muslims and Christians Face to Face*. Oxford: Oneworld, 1997.

Zollner, Barbara. *The Muslim Brotherhood: Hasan al-Hudaybi and Ideology*. London: Routledge, 2009.

Zubaida, Sami. *Islam, the People and the State: Political Ideas and Movements in the Middle East*. London: I.B. Tauris, 1993.

———. *Law and Power in the Islamic World*. London: I.B. Tauris, 2005.

Zuhdī, Karam. *Hurmat al-Ghulwūw fī al-Dīn*. Cairo: Maktabat al-Turāth al-Islāmī, 2002.

———. "The Leader of al-Jamāʿa al-Islāmiyya Speaks inside the High-Security Prison." *al-Sharq al-Awsat*, July 16, 2003.

———. *Mubādarat Waqf al-ʿUnf Ruʾya Wāqiʿiyya wa Nathara Sharʿiyya*. Cairo: Maktabat al-Turāth al-Islāmī, 2002.

———. *Taslīt al-Adwā' ʿAlā mā Waqaʾ fī al-Jihād min Ikhtā'*. Cairo: Maktabat al-Turāth al-Islāmī, 2002.

Zuhdī, Karam, ʿAlī Muhammad ʿAlī al-Shārif, Muhammad ʿIsām al-Dīn Darabāla, Hamdī ʿAbd al-Rahmān ʿAbd al-ʿAthīm, Fuʾād Mahmūd al-Dawālibī, and Nājih Ibrāhīm ʿAbd Allah. *Al-Nash wa al-Tabyīn fī Tashīh Mafāhīm al-Muhtabasīn*. Cairo: Maktabat al-Turāth al-Islāmī, 2002.

INDEX

Abbasid Empire, 15, 20, 22, 123
'Abd al-Fattāh, Nabīl, 182, 183
'Abd al-Kāfī, 'Umar, 54, 105, 113
'Abd al-Karīm, 57
'Abd al-Nūr, Fakhrī, 215n34
'Abd al-Nūr, Munīr Fakhrī, 69–70, 71,
   83–84, 108, 114, 167, 169, 170, 183, 188,
   215n34
'Abd al-Rahmān, 'Umar, 115–17, 227n152
Abrahamic faiths. *See* People of the Book
Abū al-Futūh, 'Abd al-Mun'im, 50, 53, 57,
   59, 140–41, 152, 162
Abū Bakr, 19
Abū Fānā monastery, 76
Abū 'Ubayda, 21
Abū Zayd, Nasr, 59, 88
Abu Hanifa, 94
Abu-Rabi', Ibrahim M., 55
Administrative Judiciary, 85
Adoption, 87
Afsaruddin, Asma, 14
Ahrām, al- (newspaper), 84, 125
Ahram Weekly, al- (newspaper), 51
Ajami, Fouad, 43
'Ākif, Muhammad Mahdī, 49, 52, 60–61
'Alī, Muhammad, 30, 36, 187
American Coptic Union, 76

Anticolonialism, 40, 132, 133, 138
Apostasy, 23–24, 87–89, 97, 159–60
Arabia, 27
Arab-Islamic civilization, 135–37, 180
Arab nationalism, 41–42
Arabs: early Christian, 19; in Egypt, 29–
   30; *jizya* payments of, 20; stranger-
   protection tradition of, 18
Article 2, of Egyptian Constitution, 7, 46,
   58–61, 63, 64, 68, 86, 166–68, 187
'Aryān, 'Isām al-, 50, 53, 98, 140, 143
'As, 'Amr Ibn al-, 29
Asad, Gamāl, 126
Asad, Talal, 3, 5, 35
Asyut, Egypt, 72–73
'Awwā, Muhammad Salīm al-, 56, 125–33,
   138, 148, 150–51, 154–59, 184, 229n10
Ayalon, Ami, 80
Ayubi, Nazih, 27, 208n35
Azhar, al-, 40, 45, 52, 55–56, 81, 83, 152, 172,
   184–85; Islamic Research Academy,
   58, 93, 125; University of, 14, 42

Badawī, 'Abd al-Hamīd, 170
Badi', Muhammad, 52–3
Bahā'īs, 9, 89–90, 97, 158–59, 175, 188, 194,
   195, 199n31